THE ORIGIN OF THE GRAIL LEGEND

THE ORIGIN OF THE
GRAIL LEGEND

BY

ARTHUR C. L. BROWN

NEW YORK / RUSSELL & RUSSELL

1966

PN
686
.G7
B7
1966

PREFACE

THIS BOOK owes much to the kindness of scholars in Dublin who, while I was planning it, welcomed and assisted me. First among these are: Professors R. I. Best, Eóin Mac Neill, Douglas Hyde, Osborn Bergin, the late E. J. Gwynn, T. F. O'Rahilly, R. A. S. Macalister, and Séamus Ó Duilearga.

To no one does the book owe more than to George Lyman Kittredge, the great teacher at Harvard University. To him and to Professor Fred Norris Robinson I am indebted not only for much of the training that enabled me to undertake the work but also for countless acts of encouragement and assistance during many years. None of these scholars is accountable for any errors or hazardous views set forth in this book, for which I alone am responsible.

To Professor William A. Nitze of the University of Chicago I have various obligations which I wish to acknowledge. My thanks are due also to Professor T. H. Parry-Williams of Aberystwyth, and Professor Henry Lewis of Swansea. Among many others who have helped me I wish to mention Professors Vernam Hull, T. P. Cross, the late K. G. T. Webster, my colleague J. W. Spargo, J. J. Parry of the University of Illinois, and Myles Dillon of the University of Wisconsin.

At various libraries I have received numerous courtesies, notably at the Newberry Library, the National Library of Ireland, and the Harvard College Library, and I am indebted to the kindness of Mr. Dumas Malone, Director of the Harvard University Press. I wish to thank the American Council of Learned Societies for a grant from the Carnegie Fund which made possible the printing of this book.

For bibliography see the notes. Nearly every book here mentioned is in the Newberry Library.

A. C. L. B.

January 1, 1943

CONTENTS

THE ORIGIN OF THE GRAIL LEGEND

ABBREVIATIONS

BB   Book of Ballymote   ⎫   Irish MSS which, except for
LL   Book of Leinster   ⎪   *LU,* are quoted by page
LU   Book of the Dun [Cow]   ⎬   from the facsimiles pub-
                                   ⎪   lished by the Royal Irish
YBL   Yellow Book of Lecan   ⎭   Academy

CMT   *Cath Maige Tured* (Battle of Moytura)

ITS   Irish Texts Society

LG   *Lebor Gabála Érenn* (Book of the Taking of Ireland)

Mab.   *Mabinogion* (ed. Ellis and Lloyd)

MLN   *Modern Language Notes*

OCT   *Oided Chloinne Tuirenn* (Fate of the Children of Tuirenn)

PMLA   *Publications of the Modern Language Association*

RIA   Royal Irish Academy

ZCP   *Zeitschrift für celtische Philologie*

ZFS   *Zeitschrift für französische Sprache und Literatur*

ZRP   *Zeitschrift für romanische Philologie*

Introduction

AMONG stories that the world will not willingly let die, the quest of the Grail takes a high place. Although as a whole this story has never been told in the grand manner, it manifestly belongs to great literature. The Grail is often sought but seldom or never found. This baffling search for an unattainable good is something that every human being can understand and appreciate. Perceval, burdened with his great quest that can never be accomplished, appeals to frustrated human nature somewhat as Hamlet does with his impossible task of a world to set right.

People who read or retell the Grail story often inquire eagerly where it came from. So far the answer has been that the first Grail quest was told by Chrétien de Troyes, a clever and adroit Frenchman, about the year 1175. Among Chrétien's romances there is one, *Cligès*, which has little connection with any flamboyantly marvelous world. His other romances, however, *Erec*, *Lancelot*, and *Yvain*, progressively contain more and more strange, fairylike episodes, until finally his Grail story or the *Perceval* is chiefly made up of marvelous adventures. The object of the following pages is to unravel the origin of these episodes, especially in the unfinished *Perceval*, which is the oldest known Grail story.

Some readers of Chrétien's romances, following the analogy of what happens today, have thought it possible that Chrétien invented these marvelous episodes himself and adorned them with a few Celtic names to give an exotic appeal. This theory can scarcely hold ground against the evidence of the following pages. Limits to this theory have always existed, because those who read widely in mediaeval literature rather often conclude that Chrétien's marvelous episodes were not solely his own contrivance but were based on partly rationalized fragments of some mythology.

The mythology that Chrétien used could not have been Germanic mythology, the ruins of which were unheeded and were known only to backwoodsmen. Chrétien's mythology must have given notable place to love-making, which receives no emphasis in Germanic mythology.

Some have supposed that Chrétien might have derived his marvelous episodes from classical mythology.[1] They have failed to realize that, previous to the Renaissance, classical mythology lacked vitality. Only when quickened by a large admixture of living beliefs did it influence new forms, as in the English *Sir Orfeo* and, as will appear in these pages, in the romances of Chrétien. In the important matter of courtly love Chrétien could have found nearly all his ideas in Ovid, but a change has been made that transforms these ideas into a new system. Chrétien's work is more than a mere modification of the *Metamorphoses*. In Ovid the man controls the affairs of love. In Chrétien the lady is supreme and manages everything to suit herself. This turning of Ovid's rules upside down implies the presence of new material.

---

[1] Charles B. Lewis, *Classical Mythology and Arthurian Romance* (London: Milford, 1932), is beset by this idea. See a review by F. E. Guyer, *Modern Philology*, XXX (1932), 223–224. See also G. Paris's review of Foerster's edition of *Cligès* (*Journal des savants* [1902], pp. 57–69, 289–

The present study of the marvelous episodes in Chrétien's romances does not necessitate a discussion of the beginnings of courtly love. It is enough to remark that, although the literary expression of courtly love among the troubadours before the time of Chrétien may possibly have owed its start to an impetus from Arabic love songs,[2] this origin, even if true, has little bearing on the developed doctrine as it appears in his romances. The important thing is that courtly love corresponded to a need felt by the aristocratic classes. By gradual changes in society, women had attained a higher position, and the new romances were written for them to hear and read as well as for the men.

Courtly love is not derived from Christian theology or from any doctrine about the Virgin Mary. Like democracy, however, it is an ideal that could have arisen only among people dominated by Christian teaching. Both democracy and courtly love are ideals, I think, that have their basis in the doctrine taught by the Church with fiery enthusiasm, that all men and women are the children of God. Holding this marvelous idea of the dignity of human nature, retainers who had devoted themselves body and

---

309, 345–357, 438–458, 641–655), especially his remarks on Chrétien's relations to Ovid, pp. 289 f.

[2] See A. R. Nykl, "L'Influence arabe-andalouse sur les troubadours," *Bulletin hispanique*, XLI (Bordeaux, 1939), 303–315. Dr. Nykl thinks that the first troubadour, Guillaume de Potiers, while in Syria, 1101–1102, could have listened to Arabic songs, have remembered the melodies, and have acquired "des idées plus raffinées sur l'amour" (p. 313). The usual view is set forth by F. Gennrich, *Zur Ursprungsfrage des Minnesangs*, Deutsche Vierteljahrsschrift für Literaturwissenschaft und Geistesgeschichte, VII (Halle, 1929), 187–228. Additional references are in G. Ehrismann, *Geschichte der deutschen Literatur bis zum Ausgang des Mittelalters*, Teil II (Munich, 1927), Abschnitt 2, pp. 2 f.; and Sidney Painter, *French Chivalry* (Baltimore: Johns Hopkins Press, 1940).

spirit to the service of a feudal lord found it possible to develop a similar transcendent devotion toward a feudal mistress; this is the essence of courtly love. It is no objection to this theory that the code drawn up by Andreas Capellanus is anticlerical and indeed opposed to ordinary ethics, for that is not the only development of courtly love. Courtly love as elaborated by Dante is in accordance with Christian doctrine.[3] Some have suggested that sources for Chrétien's marvelous episodes might perhaps be found in oriental folklore. This is a vast field to explore, but so far nobody has discovered convincing parallels. A Land of Women found in some oriental mythologies is described with a grossness not characteristic of the Arthurian romances. Whoever sets out on a quest for oriental parallels will probably have an experience like that of Professor Hodges, who searched through the ten volumes of R. F. Burton's translation of the *Arabian Nights*[4] for parallels to Chrétien's marvelous episodes. He found two parallels, which he prints, and then decides that they are without significance.

Christian ritual and legend have been urged as a source for some of the marvelous material in *Perceval*. Everyone

---

[3] Courtly love and the cult of the Virgin doubtless arose out of the same background, but courtly love came first. Karl Vossler, *Die philosophischen Grundlagen zum "süssen neuen Stil"* (Heidelberg, 1904); E. Wechssler, *Das Kulturproblem des Minnesangs*, I (Halle, 1909). Cf. Urban T. Holmes, *History of Old French Literature* (New York: Crofts, 1937), p. 172; and R. L. Kilgour, *The Decline of Chivalry* (Harvard University Press, 1937), p. xxi.

[4] Printed by the Burton Club for private subscribers only (n. d., c. 1907). See J. C. Hodges, "Two Otherworld Stories," *MLN*, XXXII (1917), 280-284. Another eastern parallel that has been suggested is in N. M. Penzer's edition of C. H. Tawney, *The Ocean of Story* (London, 1925), III, 183-196.

today knows that the Grail story is connected with the chief service of the Christian church. Most later mediaeval Grail stories show the influence of Chritian ritual, but in *Perceval*, the oldest Grail story, traces of this influence appear at two or three points only. Love-making and sensual delight are too prominent in the rest of *Perceval* to make it reasonable to explain the book as in the beginning a Christian legend. It is not for nothing that the Roman Catholic Church has ever regarded the Grail story as somewhat heterodox.[5] The Grail story must have its roots in some pagan mythology where love-making was no sin.

Only the Celts knew a Happy Other World (Mag Mell, "Honey Plain") peopled with ladies who were on the one hand stately and imperious and on the other astoundingly beautiful and devoted to love-making. The Irish early effected a compromise by which pagan joy in love-making and Christian asceticism were combined into one narrative. By various adjustments to churchly requirements the Irish kept their pagan mythology alive down almost even to our day. The Bretons and the Welsh doubtless made similar adjustments, although few examples of their early story-telling have survived.

All men delight in drawing pictures of a perfect world. In the Middle Ages men were locating their Utopias beyond the grave. For western Europe, Irish stories about Mag Mell supplied a longing men felt for such a Utopia. In the sixth, seventh, and eighth centuries Ireland was the most learned and in some respects the most artistic country in western Europe; music and letters flourished there. Even

[5] R. Heinzel, *Über die französischen Gralromane*, Denkschriften der Wiener Akademie der Wissenschaften, philos.-hist. Klasse, XL (1891), 179.

in the tenth and eleventh centuries Irish singers and story-tellers had nothing to learn from French artists. It was natural for Frenchmen to turn to Ireland and to Irish intermediaries, Welshmen and Bretons, for good stories.

The earliest known borrowing of this kind is the St. Brendan story. The Latin *Navigatio Sancti Brendani*, which arose before the year 950, was popular in Europe for two hundred years. Its source was an Irish life of St. Brendan which has not survived in its original form. The *Navigatio* calls the big fish, upon which the saint and his companions landed, Iasconius, a name evidently coined from Irish *iasc*, meaning "fish." In the year 1121 an Anglo-Norman version of the Brendan story called the big fish Jacoine.[6] In this form the Irish word *iasc* in the early twelfth century entered French. The passage of this word from Irish into French proves that before the time of Chrétien Irish words and Irish ideas might have reached the French.

It is well-nigh certain that before the time of Chrétien stories of Welsh or Breton origin describing the delights of the Celtic Elysium were popular in France. About 1174 Queen Eleanor and her daughter Marie de Champagne were employing Andreas Capellanus [7] to set forth their doctrine of courtly love. It seems probable that they found in the haughty *fée* of the Celtic Elysium a fitting heroine for their code, which demanded a lady far superior to her lover in splendor and power. The Irish *fée* was independent, capricious, mistress of herself and her fancies, and not unlike

---

[6] E. G. R. Waters, *The Anglo-Norman Voyage of St. Brendan* (Oxford University Press, 1928), p. 45, vs. 839; see also p. xxii.

[7] Edition E. Trojel, *Andreae capellani regii Francorum de amore libri tres* (Copenhagen, 1892). Cf. Amy Kelly, "Eleanore of Aquitaine and Her Courts of Love," *Speculum*, XII (1937), 1-19.

the great ladies who ruled over the French courts of love.[8]

Chrétien, the most skillful French writer of his day, working, as he tells us, at the command of Marie and re-telling stories that were known before, centers them round the figure of Arthur, ancient king of Britain. His romances, which are preserved in expensive manuscripts, have supplanted all others and are the oldest French Arthurian tales that have come down to us. Doubtless he told the Arthurian stories better than they had ever been told before, but perhaps his chief accomplishment was to establish their vogue among the nobility.

About a generation earlier Geoffrey of Monmouth had lifted the figure of Arthur into aristocratic notice. Geof-frey was called an impostor. By this was meant not so much that he invented tales about Arthur as that he brazenly inserted a fairy monarch[9] into serious history. Chrétien owes but little to Geoffrey, or to Wace, who rewrote and expanded Geoffrey's *Historia*. It is even difficult to fit the Arthurian adventures related by Chrétien into the time-scheme of Geoffrey's *Historia Regum Britanniae*. Geof-frey, to be sure, gives Arthur twelve years of peace (bk. ix, chap. 10), but this is at the beginning of his reign when Gawain and Ivain are children. No other period of peace is mentioned before the last battle. Arthur's adventures, as related by Chrétien, must take place after the battle of Camlan and after he has gone to Avalon, and indeed, as we shall see, this is evidently the case.

Since the beginning of the thirteenth century, when Jean

[8] See Alfred Nutt, *Studies in the Legend of the Holy Grail* (London, 1888), p. 232. On the word *fée* see J. Bolte and L. Mackensen, *Hand-wörterbuch des deutschen Märchens*, II (Berlin, 1934), 74.

[9] See A. C. L. Brown, *Speculum*, II (1927), 449–455.

Bodel,[10] in some now famous verses, called the Arthurian romances "contes de Bretaigne" (Bretaigne means either Wales or Brittany), it has been a widely held opinion that Chrétien's marvelous episodes have at least some basis in Celtic fairy lore.

It is well known, however, that the resemblance between ancient Irish stories and episodes in Chrétien's romances is not close enough to impress a casual reader. The atmosphere of the Irish stories is quite different from that of Chrétien's Arthurian romances. In the Irish there may be omissions, but whatever is said is put distinctly and with great vividness. In Chrétien's romances the connection of events is often purely decorative, and things are told in a sophisticated and indirect way. It is possible to print an outline of the *Serglige ConCulaind*, which is the most comprehensive ancient Irish Journey to Fairyland story, side by side with an outline of Chrétien's *Yvain* and say, as Bruce did, "Except that in each the lover runs mad, on losing his mistress, the two stories have virtually nothing in common." [11]

[10] E. Stengel and F. Menzel, editors, *Jean Bodels Saxenlied*, Ausgaben und Abhandlungen, XCIX–C (Marburg, 1906–1909), 29:

> "N'en sont que trois materes à nul home entendant:
> De France et de Bretaigne et de Romme la grant;
> Ne de ces trois materes n'i à nule samblant.
> Li conte de Bretaigne s'il sont vain et plaisant
> Et cil de Romme sage et de sens aprendant,
> Cil de France sont voir chascun jour aparant."
> (vss. 6–11)

In calling *chansons de geste* "true," Troy stories "informing," and Arthurian romances "trifling," Jean Bodel assuredly does not imply that the latter were fabricated by contemporaries, but that they are fairy stories and unhistorical.

[11] J. D. Bruce, *The Evolution of Arthurian Romance*, Hesperia, Ergän-.

Anybody who thought the matter out could predict that a mere mechanical juxtaposition of an ancient Irish tale and a French romance would probably be unimpressive. Let us consider a moment what the relationship of Irish stories to the marvelous episodes in Chrétien's romances can conceivably be. It is not anything very close. Nobody supposes that Chrétien borrowed from any Irish story that now exists, nor even that he borrowed from any Irish story at all; the utmost that can be imagined is that his sources were Welsh or Breton adaptations of Irish originals, and in all probability his immediate sources were French retellings of these Welsh or Breton adaptations. Chrétien's romances are, therefore, at least three steps removed from the Irish tales. The Irish stories have, moreover, been completely rewritten. They have been ennobled into the realm of chivalry and adorned with the elegancies of courtly love. This transformation had probably been effected before the stories came to Chrétien, and, according to any theory, he did his best to intensify the metamorphosis. The scenario of a journey to a mysterious land where a hero fights a giant and wins the hand of a beautiful lady had, we may suppose, become a stock incident with Breton and Welsh harpers. The formula had been borrowed by French trouvères and had developed with additions and changes into something that resembled the tone of Chrétien's romances.

Under these circumstances a likeness in plot between an Irish story and a marvelous incident in Chrétien's romances could not be expected to be striking enough to impress the casual reader. No solid proof, therefore, that Chrétien used plots drawn from Irish stories can be built up, except

zungsreihe, VIII and IX (Göttingen and Baltimore, 1923; reissued, 1928), I, 99.

by analyzing both Irish and French motive by motive. The task before us is to analyze first the Irish tales and then the marvelous episodes of Chrétien's romances in this way. This detailed analysis is something like trying to interpret an inscription written in a difficult language. Whoever is unwilling to give it close attention can make nothing of it. I understand the position of an observer who declares the hieroglyphics undecipherable and laughs at a man who toils for years trying to interpret them.

There are, indeed, several monsters of the dark which may frighten anyone who would follow the present argument. One such monster is the perception that Chrétien was a novelist perhaps of Rudyard Kipling's type. Since Kipling is assumed to have invented all his plots, it is supposed that Chrétien did the same. Another monster is a belief that nearly all folk tales are international and that it is precarious business to attempt to determine by little earmarks whether a particular story comes from Ireland or from India. Finally, there is the three-headed monster of the Celtic languages, Breton, Welsh, and Irish, and a fear that one must learn all three in order to test the argument.

Despite these difficulties, the present discussion, it is hoped, may be listened to, because, if proof that the marvelous episodes in Chrétien's romances have their roots in Celtic mythology can be established, it will be an important contribution to literary history. The theory is that the Celts have enriched general European culture, that their ancient religion has, through the Arthurian romances, contributed a slender but undying thread of the marvelous to our conception of romance, and that the Irishmen, undominated by pure reason, contrived to combine two warring principles — the one of pagan delight in sensual pleasure, the other of Christian renunciation of such pleasure — into one narrative. It is believed that by doing this they flooded Europe with intriguing pictures of love-making. These pictures, doubtless because they represented knights as doing penance and hearing Mass, escaped the absolute condemnation of monks and clergy, and the Arthurian legend with its mixture of hedonism and ascetism is alive even today.

CHAPTER I

The Scenario of the Journey
to Fairyland

WHOEVER attempts a detailed analysis by motive
will discover, I think, both in the Irish tales and
in Chrétien, a pattern or scenario of a Journey to Fairyland that recurs again and again. A reasonable explanation of the facts is that this scenario must have existed
somewhere before Chrétien, that it went through a long
course of development during which it assumed several
varying forms, and that Chrétien was captivated by this
scenario and borrowed five or six different forms of it which
he chose at different stages of its development. The contrary hypothesis, that of invention by Chrétien, will not
explain the varying forms he used. This hypothesis supposes that Chrétien once, by pure chance, hit upon the
scenario. Accordingly, all Chrétien's later uses of the
scenario must be explained as derived, somehow, from his
first accidental invention. To be specific, this hypothesis
asserts that the occurrence of the scenario in the Joy of
the Court episode, U,[1] in *Erec*, was an accident and supposes
that Chrétien, finding that the formula pleased his readers,
tried it again in V, W, X, Y, Z, and AA. If this hypothesis
were true, the later stories ought to show traces of having
been derived from U, but this is not the case; Chrétien's

[1] These letters U, V, etc., designate portions of Chrétien's romances;
see pp. 92, 99, etc.

marvelous episodes V, W, etc., are not borrowed from U. The hypothesis cannot be right, because it would compel us to believe that Chrétien hit upon the scenario five or six times by pure chance.

It is a piece of bad luck that the present argument must rest upon a detailed study of a large number of ancient Irish and Welsh Journeys to Fairyland. A hurried reader may skip the details which are contained in the next chapter and may use Chapter II for reference only. This is possible because it is not necessary to summarize a large number of stories in order to compile from them a composite scenario. A sufficiently complete scenario for the present argument can be extracted from a single ancient Irish story, the *Serglige ConCulainn*, "Cuchulinn's Sickbed," and, to follow the argument, only the following analysis of this story need be read.

The *Serglige* has been retold by somebody who barely lets us see that Cuchulinn visited fairyland, and who either did not understand or sought to suppress the marvelous journey thither. He regarded fairyland as an adjacent province of Ireland. He has kept nearly all the incidents of the Journey to Fairyland, but some in a form difficult to recognize until they are compared, as is done in the next chapter, with other Irish and Welsh stories of the type.

The main features of Celtic fairyland, perhaps, did not differ greatly from those of the land of the dead as pictured by many heathen European peoples. For the sake of clearness, it is well to set forth here what those features were. The beautiful passage in the sixth book of the *Aeneid*, which must have been known in ancient Ireland, is as good a starting point as any. Here Virgil tells us of the *navita* (vs. 385), Charon, who demands payment; the watchful

Cerberus; and the two castles under the rule of Pluto with mention of Orcus (vs. 273), Palinurus (vs. 337), and of the sedge (*ulva*, vs. 416) on the gloomy shore. The first castle (*moenia*, vs. 548) is on a rock surrounded by a three-fold wall and a river of flame; it is an iron tower and beside it sits Tesiphone in a bloody robe (*palla succinta cruenta*, vs. 555). The second castle (*moenia*, vs. 631) has music and feasting, and widens out into Elysian Fields.

Germanic stories often substitute for the boatman a perilous bridge of iron or gold. At the first castle the iron tower may revolve, and may be decorated with human heads.[2] Sometimes a river separates the two castles; in the *Odyssey* (bk. xi), for example, are several rivers. Sometimes the second castle is square, facing the four winds, and this cosmic palace may be a borrowing from oriental and Biblical tradition. Sometimes there is a feast within beside a fire, or without in a garden dominated by the first castle.

The first castle is in Irish the *dún* of the giants or Fomorians, and in French the Dolorous Tower. The second castle is in Irish Mag Mell, and in French the Castle of the Maidens.

The *Serglige*[3] was put together before the time of Chrétien. Its age is in no way doubtful, for it exists in a manuscript of 1106, and, although it has been in part retraced and even expanded by an early thirteenth-century scribe, nobody thinks that he added anything except ancient material.[4] Like many other ancient sagas, it is compilatory in

[2] Elard Hugo Meyer, *Germanische Mythologie* (Berlin, 1891), p. 134; and on the two castles see p. 352.

[3] The *Serglige* is marked C in the list of twenty stories, p. 44.

[4] R. Thurneysen, *Die irische Helden und Königsage* (Halle, 1921), pp. 29–31. R. I. Best and O. Bergin, *Lebor na Huidre* (Dublin, 1929), pp. xvi–xxi, 104–126.

character but goes back in the main to the eighth century. It was pieced together in the early twelfth century out of two older versions: *a*, eighth-century, and *b*, which, though reworked in the eleventh century, rests upon eighth-century materials. A rather full outline [5] is as follows:

The country of the *fées* is ruled by two kings: Labraid, "swift hand-on-sword," and Failbe, "the fair" (l. 3679). Each has one hundred and fifty warriors, but all the other inhabitants of the land are women (l. 3622). The protagonists of the story are two daughters of Aed Abrat, "fire of the eyebrow," and their names are Fann, "teardrop," and LíBan, "splendor of women." Fann has either deserted her husband, Manannán mac Lir (version *a*), or has been deserted by him (version *b*). Fann and LíBan first appear in bird form; their song puts the warriors to sleep. Later, after Cuchulinn has hurled his dart and injured one of them, they come as women dressed one in green and the other in purple. They strike Cuchulinn and throw him into an illness for a year. Still later they cure him on condition that he fight for Labraid against his foes. Aengus, their brother, appears to Cuchulinn and tells him that Fann is in love with him and that her love will be his reward. LíBan comes to invite Cuchulinn.

Instead of going with LíBan, Cuchulinn sends Laeg his charioteer; LíBan takes Laeg by the shoulder and remarks that he cannot return alive unless a woman protects him (l. 3351). She ferries him in a bronze boat to the island Mag Mell, where he talks with the fairy folk, and then they both return

[5] My summary is from the text of *Lebor na Huidre* (*LU*) as printed by Best and Bergin. References are to ll. 3221–4039 in this edition. The text is also in E. Windisch, *Irische Texte* [I] (Leipzig, 1880), 205–227. On the compilatory character of this saga, see Thurneysen, *Heldensage*, pp. 413–415, 667. The first part he calls version *b*; the latter, version *a*. An English translation is in A. H. Leahy, *Heroic Romances of Ireland* (London, 1905), I, 57 f.

to Cuchulinn. [Version *b* ends here and version *a* begins l. 3540.] Laeg sets out again with LíBan to visit fairyland. Together they go past two double-headed serpents, over Mag Lúada (l. 3655, cf. l. 3745) [6] and past Bile Buada, "Bile the Victorious." They go on together over Oenach Emna to Oenach Fidga, where Aed Abrat and his daughters dwell. After talking with the fairy folk, they return again to Cuchulinn.

Laeg gives Cuchulinn a favorable account, tells him that a battle is arranged for that day and persuades him to go with LíBan. The enemies have three kings: Senach Siaborthe, Eochaid Iúil, and Eogan Inbir. Eogan Inbir has summoned the troops of Manannán to his aid, and they are a host clad in red.[7] Cuchulinn, after slaying Senach Siaborthe and Eochaid Iúil, delivers Mag Mell and enjoys Fann's love.

The fairy palace is a place of abundance, and contains one hundred and fifty couches for one hundred and fifty ladies (l. 3370) who wear "gay colored garments." [8] LíBan says

[6] The story also mentions Mag Cruaich, Mag Fidga, Mag Denna, and Mag Mell. Probably all stand for Mag Mór, or Plain of the Dead. Bile is probably the same as Balar, king of the Fomorians; see Sir John Rhŷs, *Lectures on Celtic Heathendom* (London, 1888), p. 678.

[7] The text is: "Slog find forderg formnib ech domroipnitar forom leth, munter Manandan meic Lir cotagart Eogan Inbir" (ll. 3866–3867); "A fair host, very red, with splendid horses, pursued me to where I stood, the people of Manannán son of Ler, whom Eogan Inbir had summoned." Nothing in the *Serglige* gives a reason why the hostile folk should be red; consequently Professor Myles Dillon, the latest commentator, hesitates to translate *forderg*, "very red," although he remarks: "Some such notion as 'with red banners' or 'with red cloaks,' may be present" ("On Three Passages in Lebor na Huidre," *Speculum*, XV [1940], 282). It is the people of Manannán who are "very red," not the Fomorian troops. Since, however, they are led by Eogan Inbir and fight on the Fomorian side, they are perhaps clad in red Fomorian uniform. Hostile warriors that we call Fomorians appear in red in a number of Irish and Welsh stories analyzed below.

[8] Line 3763. This palace corresponds to the Castle of Maidens in French.

that Labraid has golden hair, and that pillars of silver and of glass stand in the palace where he dwells (l. 3651). Laeg says that there are fifty couches at the right and fifty at the left. The posts of the couches are gilded. The light they have is a glittering precious stone. Fann's beauty stuns the beholder (l. 3755). The music in the palace takes away the strength of the listeners (l. 3770). Outside graze horses with parti-colored manes, some dun color, some purple-brown. Trees with wonderful fruit grow there, and a never-failing cask of joyous mead is poured out.

At the end Fann returns to her fairy husband, Manannán. For a time Cuchulinn goes insane at losing her, but is finally cured by a "drink of forgetfulness."

When Laeg reaches Mag Mell he is recognized by Labraid on account of his purple cloak (l. 3675). This was probably a fairy gift, because Emer says (ll. 3541 f.) that Laeg has often visited fairyland. According to the Irish story F,[9] Laeg's father, Riangabar, is a king in fairyland.

Fairyland here, although it is called Mag Mell and is inhabited by the friendly Tuatha Dé, is dominated by a castle named Dún Inbir (l. 3968) which is ruled by three hateful kings. These three tyrants, who must be conquered or slain before the fairies can enjoy freedom, are Senach Siaborthe (*síabrac*, "demon"), Eochaid Iúil, and Eogan Inbir (*inber*, "estuary" or "river-mouth"). The last is doubtless identical with Eogan Inbir who is mentioned in *Lebor Gabála Érenn* (*LG*) [10] and elsewhere, as fighting

---

[9] Page 56. Laeg is a fairy helper, like Humbaut in the romance of that name (ed. J. Stürzinger and H. Breuer, *Gesellschaft für romanische Literatur*, vol. XXXV [Dresden, 1914]); like Gyfre in *Sir Launfal* (ed. W. H. French and C. B. Hale, *Middle English Metrical Romances* [New York, 1930], p. 356, vs. 327); like Cass Corach in R (p. 81) and the guide in T (p. 85).

[10] "Book of the Taking of Ireland," ed. R. A. S. Macalister, pt. IV,

against the Tuatha Dé. It will therefore be safe to identify these three hostile rulers with traditional enemies of the Tuatha Dé and call them Fomorians. Labraid fights a *conchend*, "Doghead" (l. 3629), and the Dogheads were Fomorians. The Fomorians here may have been at first, as suggested, sham enemies and under the control of the *fée*, but they have been turned into rulers of her land.

In version *b* of the *Serglige*, Dún Inbir appears to be the *dún* of the giants, for Cuchulinn tells LíBan that he cast his spear into the *dúnad* of Eogan Inbir and heard a groan from Eochaid Iúil.[11] In version *a*, however, Dún Inbir is a name for Mag Mell. Manannán comes from the "plains of Eogan Inbir," and Fann once lived with Manannán "in the *griana* (sun-chamber) of Dún Inbir" (l. 3968). Here then Mag Mell is named after Eogan Inbir. It appears therefore, that in this very ancient Irish story the supremacy of the *fée* is enough obscured so that her land is named after a Fomorian. This is also shown by one of the names for fairyland, *in domon Duind*, "the world of Donn" (l. 3546). Donn, as Meyer has shown, was king of the dead. Additional evidence may be found in A and D. In A the *fées* are the "people of Tethra" (a Fomorian), and in D, Mag Mell is "the Kingdom of Goll" (a Fomorian).[12]

The *Serglige* retains a hint that in an earlier form the *fée* was supreme and that the fairy folk were not really slain. If Fann were truly in danger from the giants, she

---

ITS, XLI (Dublin, 1941), 124, redaction "R¹." On the Dogheads see pp. 84, 246.

[11] This *dún* corresponds to the French Dolorous Tower. *Dúnad* (l. 3859), the verbal noun of *dúnaim*, "to shut," probably means the same as *dún*. Thurneysen assigns this statement of Cuchulinn to version *b* (*Heldensage*, p. 424).

[12] Pages 41 and 45.

would at once upon her first appearing have asked Cuchulinn for help instead of making him ill and then after a year's delay appearing again to ask his aid. This long introduction appears to be a survival from an earlier form of the story in which Fann could afford to wait a year because Senach Siaborthe and his fellow giants were merely employed by her to test Cuchulinn. She was in no actual danger from the giants, although according to the laws of her fairy nature she was obliged to keep up the custom of a yearly combat with them.

Another hint of the original supremacy of the *fée* may be noticed in the description of a dangerous passage on the way to Mag Mell, at the place, no doubt, where Laeg sees "two double-headed serpents" (l. 3748). Here LíBan takes Laeg by the shoulder [13] and tells him that he cannot come out alive unless a woman (i.e., a *fée*) protects him. It is noteworthy that protection comes from a *fée* and not from a Fomorian, which indicates that at first the *fée* was more powerful than the Fomorian.

Some scholars think that Irish and Welsh fairy belief was invented by pre-Celtic tribes that lived under matriarchy.[14] Certainly Celtic *fées* were not at first subject to husbands. In an earlier form of the *Serglige*, we may conjecture, Manannán was only one among several suitors. Fann sends him away when she wants Cuchulinn and recalls him when she pleases. The *Serglige* has been worked over by somebody who did not comprehend the supremacy of Fann. He fancied that Manannán would be angry at being dis-

[13] "Ocus geibthi ar gúalaind" (l. 3351), which could be translated, "she takes him upon her shoulder."

[14] Otto Löhmann, *Die Sage von Gawain und dem Grünen Ritter,* Schriften der Albertus-Universität, XVII (Königsberg, 1938), 69 f.

missed by her, and so invented the absurd notion that Manannán's forces fought on the side of the Fomorians. This could have been no part of the primitive story.

The *Serglige* is manifestly of pagan origin, but the redactor of our text has included two or more Christian passages, as follows: Laeg calls fairyland Tenmag Trogaigi, "fiery plain of Trogaige" (l. 3521), which may signify that the Irish redactor identifies it with the Christian hell. Later (l. 3758), Laeg refers to the "race of Adam before he sinned." In some lines at the end of the *Serglige* the redactor tells us that, before Christianity came, demons had power to take bodily shape and to fight with men; ignorant people regarded these spirits as immortal beings "and named them *síde*."

The *Serglige* represents three giants as tyrannizing over Mag Mell. It is possible that they were exalted to this position by Christian influences which, as has been noticed, tried to explain LíBan and Fann as inhabiting the country of the fiends. *Thomas of Erceldoune* relates that fairies owe tribute to the fiends of hell.[15]

On the other hand, it is possible that the three giants transformed themselves from servants to rulers of the *fée* without much influence from Christianity. Such a change is natural enough. The giants were called Fomorians and were connected with everything evil: with darkness, with winter, and with the land of the dead.

The Irishman was ever very close to the invisible world. For him a fairy or a giant lurked behind every bush. His vision of Mag Mell was singularly vivid. It was probably

[15] Edition A. Brandl (Berlin, 1880), p. 91. See F. J. Child, *English and Scottish Popular Ballads* (Boston, 1883), I, 318. On tribute paid by fairies see p. 115.

connected with the "boldness of the Celt"[16] of which we read in Greek and Latin writers. Both the continental and the insular Celts, in accordance, no doubt, with the doctrine of their druids, expected to meet their friends in the other world. Of course fairyland and the land of the dead were not identical, but the Irish located both regions either on islands or beneath lakes or hills, and confusion was inevitable.[17] The Irish were renowned for their knowledge of Latin classics, and it would seem that they made a synthesis of ideas about the land of the dead, which they found in the classics and elsewhere,[18] with their own brilliant vision of Mag Mell.

Traces of this syncretism appear in our oldest Irish stories. Thus in the *Serglige* the double-headed serpents (l. 3748) are a modification of the Cerberus motive, and the bronze boat (l. 3357) a variation of Charon's skiff.[19] It is also

[16] See "fortissimi Celtae" in J. Zwicker, *Fontes historiae religionis Celticae* (Berlin and Bonn, 1934–1936), III, 337, and especially Aelianus, quoted in I, 87, ll. 24–31.

[17] J. Baudiš, "Mabinogion," *Folk-Lore*, XXVII (1916), 38 f.; J. T. Honti, "Celtic Studies and Folk Tale Research," *Béaloideas*, VI (Dublin, 1936), 38; S. Singer, *Ehrismann-Festschrift*, ed. P. Merker and W. Stammler (Berlin, 1925), pp. 63 f., and *Die Artussage* (Bern and Leipzig, 1926).

[18] Stefania Strassberg calls the material that Chrétien used in *Lancelot* a combination of Irish and Latin elements (*Die Entführung und Befreiung der Königin Ginevra: ein Beitrag zur Erläuterung des Lancelot von Crestien de Troyes* [Berlin, 1937], pp. 12–13). Probably the Irish wrought the synthesis, but the Welsh, or even the French predecessors of Chrétien, may have had a hand in the changes. "From whatever quarter the Celtic material reached French writers, much of it had undergone extensive modification before they received it" (G. L. Kittredge, *A Study of Sir Gawain and the Green Knight* [Cambridge: Harvard University Press, 1916], p. 241).

[19] Not to mention that the adjective "very red" applied to the enemies may imply the color of blood, which in the *Aeneid* is associated with the tower of the dead.

tolerably clear that not only were the Irish and Welsh *fées* sometimes associated with the land of the dead, but that from the earliest times they could be either beautiful or hideous, and their land could be either a beautiful and blessed country, or a dangerous and dreadful region. Nor was it the Celtic *fée* alone that combined the beautiful and the terrible; Circe and even Calypso in the *Odyssey* did the same.[20]

On page 25, twenty motives that occur in the *Serglige* are disentangled from their context and printed in tabular form. In the first column are the motives; in the second the Irish and Welsh stories in which the motives appear; and in the third the French romances.

In the table, motive *q*, which tells of a wounded Hospitable Host, is important for the discussion in the following pages which tends to show that the Fisher King in Chrétien's *Perceval* is such a host. In the *Serglige*, the presence of motive *q* depends upon the meaning of the first word in the phrase *créchtach a thóeb*, "wounded his side." Líban thus characterizes the fairy king, Labraid: "ready in counsel, munificent to everyone, eager for battle, wounded his side." [21] *Créchtach* might imply a wound that disabled Labraid for war, but, on the other hand, it might signify nothing more than that he is a veteran warrior.[22] The first

[20] Cornelia C. Coulter, "The Happy Otherworld and Fairy Mistress Themes in the Odyssey," *Transactions of the American Philological Association*, LVI (1925), 47.

[21]   Urlam do rath
             rurtech do chách
             saigthech do cath
             créchtach a thóeb (ll. 3398–3401).

[22] Examples of the first sense are: "they escaped though wounded," *créchtaig* (*Togail Bruidne Da Derga*, ed. Eleanor Knott, Mediaeval and Modern Irish Series, vol. VIII [Dublin, 1936], l. 704; *Tochmarc Ferbe*,

MOTIVES	IRISH AND WELSH STORIES	FRENCH ROMANCES
a. The hero is summoned to fairyland and sets out.	A, C, D, E, F, G, P, S	W, X, Y
b. He crosses a water by a boat or a bridge.	A, C, D, E, F, H, S, T	U, V, X, Y, Z, AA
c. He meets a serpent or other beast.	C, E, G, H, S	V, W, AA
d. He is protected by a woman.	A, C, E, F	V, W, X, AA
e. He comes to a great plain.	C, D, E, F, G, T	W, AA
f. [Dolorous Tower.] A tower is inhabited by tyrants or giants. This tower may take the form of a red castle or red island. Beside the tower may be a garden with food and damsels.	C, E, G, H, Q, S, T	U, V, W, X, Y, AA
g. The hero is feasted by a Hospitable Host who may be a fisherman or herdsman, or by several hosts.	C, D, E, F, R, S	U, V, W, X, Y, Z, AA
h. [Castle of Maidens.] The feast is in a palace which may be square, facing the four winds, and where are many women.	C, D, E, F, L, R, S, T	U, V, W, X, Y, Z, AA
i. The feast is abundant and talismans are mentioned.	C, D, E, F, G, I, L, O, R, S, T	V, W, Y, Z, AA
j. The beauty of the heroine is astonishing.	C, K, T,	U, W, X, Y
k. The palace has silver or copper pillars.	C, F, L, T	Z
l. It is illuminated by precious stones.	G, L, T	Z, AA
m. The Hospitable Host and the heroine need to be delivered from the tyrant or tyrants of the tower.	C, D, F, J, K, O, R, S, T	V, X, Y, AA
n. A battle against the tyrant has been arranged.	C, D, F, J, K, M, O, R	U, V, W, X, Y, AA
o. The tyrant is dressed in red or black.	E, Q	U, V, W, X, AA
p. The hero conquers and slays the tyrant.	C, D, E, F, G, H, J, M, R, S, T	U, V, W, X, Y
q. The Hospitable Host, after the tyrant's death, becomes vigorous. The tyrant's blood heals him of a wound.	F	Manessier's *Perceval* vs. 44615 (see p. 28).
r. The hero marries the heroine.	A, B, C, D, E, F, G, H, K, L, P, S, T	W, Y
s. She brings him the sovereignty of the land.	C, H	W, Y, AA
t. Return of the hero to his own country is dangerous or impossible.	A, C, D	U, V, W, X, Y, AA

meaning is supported by the context, which, to explain
Labraid's need for Cuchulinn's help, implies a disabling
wound. I am not certain, however, that the redactor of our
text of the *Serglige* understood that Labraid was disabled.
According to him, LíBan urges Cuchulinn to come to the
aid of the fairy folk "because Labraid is the best of the warriors in the world."[23] This may be, of course, an assertion
of his general reputation and not a statement that he is ready
to enter battle now. It does not deny that he is wounded,
but it leaves doubtful the existence of a disabling wound.
Motive *q* must rest upon the testimony of other ancient
Irish stories.

Three such stories exist, of which two are invasions 4 and
7 in *Lebor Gabála Érenn*[24] (*LG*). In invasion 4 Partholon
fights Cichol: "Partholon received a mortal wound. Also
it was of the gory darts of those wounds that he died after
a long time following the battle." After mentioning events
which prove that he survived for twenty years, *LG* adds:
"In the plain of Elta of Edar, Partholon died of the venom[25]
of the wounds inflicted on him in the battle of Cichol."
Later we shall see that Partholon and Cichol are merely

---

ed. W. Stokes and E. Windisch, *Irische Texte*, III, ii [Leipzig, 1897],
p. 514, l. 727). Of the second sense: Conall Cernach is "battle-scarred
and battle-victorious," *créchtaig, cathbúadaig* (*Scéla Mucce Meic Dathó*,
ed. R. Thurneysen, Med. and Mod. Irish Ser., VI [1935], § 15, l. 10).
Thurneysen and other translators of the *Serglige* have taken *créchtach*
in the second sense. On the etymology of *crécht*, see G. S. Lane, *Language*, XIII (1937), 23, who connects it with a root meaning "to wither";
cf. Anglo-Saxon *scrincan*.

[23] "Ar is e láech as lech di ocaib domain" (l. 3346).

[24] Edition Macalister, pt. III, *ITS*, XXXIX (1940), 14, 20, redactions
"R²," and "R³."

[25] The Fisher King was wounded by a poisoned spear, according to
Wolfram's *Parzival* (ed. E. Martin [Halle, 1900–1903], vs. 479, 8).

other names for Nuadu and Balar. Partholon's survival as ruler for twenty-seven years after his wound is, as Macalister notes, rather unrealistic.[26] The long interval proves, I think, that the wound is like that of Nuadu [27] and implies that he lived in retirement in bondage to Fomorian enemies.

In invasion 7, in the first battle of Moytura, Nuadu, king of the Tuatha Dé, loses an arm. In consequence of this wound, he yields the kingship to Bres, who enforces Fomorian tyranny for seven years. Then, a silver arm having been made for Nuadu, he reigns for twenty years. It is implied that Fomorian tyranny continues till Lug arrives and, at the second battle of Moytura, slays Balar and liberates the Tuatha Dé. Since two of the invasions in LG make the king of the fairy folk suffer for many years from a wound, motive q must surely have been a part of the mythical story out of which the invasions were constructed.

A third unmistakable instance of a fairy king wounded by a giant, and, in this case, healed by the slain giant's blood, occurs in the tenth-century Irish story of Dael Dermait,[28] F. In this story Coirpre Cundail is one of several fairy kings who have been wounded by a giant named Eochu Glas. After Cuchulinn has cut off the giant's head, the fairies, including, of course, their kings, bathe in the giant's blood and are cured of the wounds inflicted by the giant.

These ancient stories establish motive q and render it probable that créchtach in the Serglige originally meant

---

[26] Lebor Gabála, III, 92.

[27] Another trace of the wound is a statement that the Dagda, an earlier king of the Tuatha Dé, "died eighty years afterward" of a javelin wound received "in the great battle of Mag Tuired" (Lebor Gabála, IV, 184, redaction "R³"). The Dagda, I suppose, borrowed the story of Nuadu's wound.

[28] Page 58.

that Labraid was disabled. To heal a wound by the blood of the giver of the wound is a savage idea that would be blurred over by later writers. The barbaric flavor of this incident probably caused it to be suppressed in most of even the Irish stories. It is noteworthy evidence, therefore, and a proof for the Irish origin of the wounded king of the Grail castle, that Manessier, the second continuator of Chrétien's unfinished *Perceval*, has kept something very like this motive. According to Manessier, the Grail King's enemy, who has wounded him and made him helpless, is named Partinal of the Red Tower. Manessier says that Perceval cures the king of his wound by cutting off Partinal's head and bringing it to the Grail castle. When the king hears that the head is being brought, he leaps to his feet strong and well.[29]

The following pages tend to show that the Fisher King and Arthur are parallel figures, and both are hypostases of Nuadu. Modred, who wounds Arthur, is like the Irish Fomorian, Morc, grandson of Lot.[30] Geoffrey calls Modred son of Loth, and he calls Loth king of Lothain and of Norway.[31] The romances make him king of the Orkneys. All three regions were regarded as Fomorian land, or the land of the dead. Although Geoffrey probably did not know it, Modred and Lot were evil kings of the dead, and Gawain, Modred's brother, a good king of the land of the dead (Galloway).[32]

[29] Manessier's continuation (C. Potvin, *Perceval le Gallois* [Mons, 1866–1871], VI, 130, vss. 44615–44662).

[30] *Lebor Gabála*, ed. Macalister, III, 122, 192.

[31] *Historia regum Britanniae*, ed. A. Griscom (London and New York, 1929), bk. viii, chap. 21, p. 428; bk. ix, chap. 11, p. 446.

[32] See p. 142, and cf. A. C. L. Brown, "Arthur's Loss of Queen and Kingdom," *Speculum*, XV (1940), 1–11.

Arthur was wounded by Modred at Camlan and went to Avalon. Nuadu was wounded by a Fomorian named Sreng [33] in the first battle of Moytura (Mag Tuired) and withdrew to a fairy hill or *síd*. Mag Tuired means "plain of the towers," one of which was doubtless the tower of the dead. The two battles of Moytura were in origin one battle. Both were magical and were fought partly in the clouds. The recurrent battle in which a *fée* who is virtually the sovereignty loses a friendly husband and gains a hostile one, or vice versa, is always mythologically speaking the same battle of good and evil. [34]

The battle of Camlan in which Medraut (Modred) wounded Arthur is not one of the twelve battles told by Nennius. [35] It was added by the tenth-century *Annales Cambriae*, [36] doubtless after Arthur had inherited in popular tradition the exploits of the god Nuadu. Arthur, I think, borrowed Camlan and the entire story of the wound from Nuadu. [37] Camlan was a copy of Moytura and like it an Armageddon or battle of good and evil. This is proved by the angels and devils who, according to *Kulhwch and Olwen*, aided the contestants: "Mofran the son of Tegid [escaped] because of his hideousness. . . . Everybody thought he was a devil aiding. . . . And Sande of the Angel Face. No one speared him in the Battle of Camlan because of his beauty. Everyone thought he was an angel aiding." [38]

[33] *LG*, ed. Macalister, IV, 63.

[34] Page 267.

[35] *Historia Britonum*, ed. T. Mommsen, *Monumenta Germaniae historica*, Auctorum antiquissimorum XIII, Chronica minora III (Berlin, 1894), 111.

[36] Edition J. Loth, *Les Mabinogion* (Paris, 1913), II, 372.

[37] Page 310.

[38] *Mabinogion*, translated by T. P. Ellis and J. Lloyd (Oxford Uni-

The wounding of the god Nuadu, his yielding of wife and country to a giant, and his retirement to an underground fairy palace where he lived in weakness till the coming of the youthful god Lug, must have been one of the chief stories in ancient Irish mythology. It is not strange to find it the basis of *LG*, the mythical history of Ireland, and to believe that it may be the source of the Grail story, the greatest of Arthurian romances. A parallel seems to exist between the wounded Nuadu and a wounded god in other mythologies, as, for example, the annual wound of Adonis and of Thammuz: the wounded Nuadu is apparently an example of an older god displaced by a younger, as Uranus was by Cronus, and Cronus by Zeus.

In Chapter II all important ancient Irish and Welsh Journeys to Fairyland are studied. The stories there outlined are related to five different types of folk tales which must be rather carefully defined. The first three types have been discussed by George Lyman Kittredge,[39] and, as a basis for further study, I quote in a condensed form his definitions:

I. The Fairy Mistress. — An immortal woman, a *fée*, resident in the land of youth is enamored of a mortal hero, and summons him to her presence.

II. The Giant's Daughter. — A hero makes his way into the Other World and desires to marry the daughter of its

---

versity Press, 1929), I, 182; henceforth referred to as *Mab*. Six hundred and sixty-six is the number of the beast (Revelation 13:18). Modred at Camlan divided his forces into six bodies of six thousand six hundred and sixty-six each (Geoffrey, *Historia,* bk. xi, chap. 2, p. 499). Geoffrey did not understand an allusion to Armageddon (if there is one), for he made Arthur choose a company of six thousand six hundred and sixty-six, but this statement about Arthur lacks in the Welsh *Brut*.

[39] *Gawain*, pp. 231–237.

ruler. The god is angry and wishes to destroy the intruder.

III. The Enchanted Princess. — The land of the *fée* is under a spell that has made it generally invisible and inaccessible and filled it with hideous defenders. This evil has been wrought by a wicked enchanter.

To these types I venture for the sake of the present discussion to add more two more:

IV. The Land of the Dead. — This is like III except that the enchanter has become a king of the dead[40] and the heroine is his prisoner.

V. The Recurrent Battle. — A god and a giant fight for possession of a lady who is virtually the country personified. The god is conquered; but later the lady's son grows to manhood, slays the giant, and wins the lady.

In type I the *fée* is a powerful goddess, and the giants whom the hero must fight are nothing but phantoms conjured up by her in order to prove the hero's courage. The *fée* is bound by the laws of her divine nature to test the hero in this way.

In type II the giants have become actual monsters of evil who have ruined fairyland. The *fée*, no longer supreme, summons the hero because she wishes him to fight the giants and to free her country. The idea of the ruin of fairyland by giants is new in the discussion of Arthurian romances and of primary importance to the present argument.[41]

---

[40] On the land of the dead see W. Hertz, *Spielmannsbuch* (5th ed., Stuttgart, 1931), p. 365, and "Totenreich" in H. Bächtold-Staübli, *Handwörterbuch des deutschen Aberglaubens*, VIII (Berlin, 1936–1937), 1087.

[41] The importance of this idea was first suggested to me by Dr. Douglas Hyde, who, in explaining "The Lad of the Ferule," writes: "[The hero] Murough was enticed down into Tír na n-Óg [fairyland] in order to set free the country which had been ruined by a giant. I feel quite

In type III the giants have become enchanters. The hero must fight the giants in order to free the country from enchantment. The change from type II is a species of rationalization or adaptation to more sophisticated hearers.[42] People who did not believe in heathen gods believed in magicians and in the possibility of enchantment. The stories developed in this way when retold, as we may suppose, in France. Progressive rationalization in type III sometimes almost obliterates the battle. Stories of the "open sesame" type introduce an idea that the spell may be broken if the hero will ask the right question. This, I believe, has happened in Chrétien's Grail romance, where the battle with Clamadeu has been sidetracked [43] and where to ask the right question has become Perceval's great exploit. He must not be prompted, but if he of his own accord asks the right question it will heal the Fisher King's wound and break the enchantment that rests upon the kingdom.

In type IV the giants are transformed into kings of the dead, and the enchantment which they have fastened upon the land is a deathlike sleep. The hero must conquer death and deliver captives from his prison. The development of type IV may or may not be due to the influence of Christian teaching. Traces of type IV are found in some of the oldest Irish stories, and later stories like Q and T belong entirely to this type.

In type V an immortal *fée* has a son, whom she brings up to fight a battle with a tyrannical giant who is her mas-

---

certain that this is the way the story would be understood, and was meant to be understood, by all native Irish readers" (*ITS*, I [1899], viii–x).

[42] See Kittredge's discussion of progressive rationalization in *Gawain*, p. 239.

[43] See below, p. 237.

ter, to conquer the giant, and to marry her himself. Presently another giant wounds and conquers the hero and seizes upon the lady. It is a recurrent battle.

Long before the time of Chrétien, these five types were firmly established, and it is not possible to settle the order of their appearance.[44]

The recurring battle of type V is explained by some as a winter and summer combat. They believe that type V is based upon games that were performed in countries round the Mediterranean Sea in order to secure, according to popular belief, the fertility of the land. In these annual games were three or more actors: one dressed in white represented the friendly gods; another in black or red, the evil giants; and the third, a lady, was a *fée* or earth goddess. The games pictured the annual battle of summer and winter.

Some think that the Celts adopted these games, and bring forward the Glas Ghabhleann story as proof that seasonal games existed in Ireland, but, despite the interest of this story,[45] its basis in ritual games is not established. In short, evidence for the performance of summer and winter

[44] See Kittredge, *Gawain*, p. 242.

[45] Page 160. See W. Mannhardt, *Wald- und Feldkulte* (Berlin, 1904–1905), II, 274 f.; J. G. Frazer, *Golden Bough*, 3d ed., IV (London, 1911), 254–259; "Sommer und Winter," *Handwörterbuch d.·deutsch. Aberglaubens*, VIII, 30; A. H. Krappe, *Balor with the Evil Eye*, Institute of French Studies (New York: Columbia Univ., 1927), pp. 21, 29, 71; *Science of Folk-Lore* (London, 1930), pp. 273, 309; *Mythologie universelle* (Paris, 1930), pp. 363 f. Krappe connects with seasonal games an Egyptian myth of a combat between Set and Osiris for Isis and the later triumph of Horus. Macalister discusses seasonal games in *Lebor Gabála*, pt. II, pp. 263 f. Recent speculative books are: Lord F. R. S. Raglan, *The Hero* (London, 1936), pp. 281 f., and S. H. Hooke, *The Labyrinth* (New York, 1935).

games in ancient Wales or Ireland is unsatisfactory. Eóin Mac Neill writes: "In the sixteenth century it was still the custom for mummers at the great traditional festivals to wear various, strange disguises, including paper masks representing animals' heads," [46] but apparently he does not believe that these mummers presented a summer and winter combat.

It is possible that the Irish battle of Moytura began by being a battle between good and evil; that is, between good fairies, or Tuatha Dé, and bad fairies, or Fomorians; and that this idea may be older than the notion of summer battling winter. In these stories good fairies are mostly women and evil fairies mostly men. In *BéBind daughter of Trén*, Q,[47] are described both a "land of women" and a "land of men," and the last seems to be a Fomorian land. It has often been noticed that in fairy stories a lovely and a friendly *fée* has for father or husband an evil giant. That the battle was between a friendly and a harmful fairy may have been the primary idea.

That our stories of type V have been touched by the notion of a seasonal or periodic combat is probable,[48] but the following pages begin from what we know. We know that stories M and R,[49] which belong to type V, existed in Ireland before the time of Chrétien. In M a battle recurs every Hallowe'en. In R a battle recurs every third or seventh year. The formula of type V, in which the heroine

[46] *Celtic Ireland* (Dublin, 1921), p. 62.

[47] Page 80.

[73] Page 73. On the recurrent battle see *Béaloideas*, IV (1934), 342. Such a battle is in *Kulhwch and Olwen* (*Mab.*, I, 189): "Gwythyr the son of Greidaw, and Gwynn the son of Nudd fight every May Day until the Day of Judgment" for Creiddylad, daughter of Lludd.

[49] Pages 77, 81.

is wife alternately to a god and a giant, can be traced in D, where the heroine is wife first to Fiachna, then to Goll, and finally to Fiachna again; in J, where Pwyll and Arawn are successively husbands to the heroine; and in T,[50] where the heroine is wife to Teigue, is carried off by Cathmann, and is finally restored to Teigue. The Irish *fée* Medb had a succession of husbands who were alternately friendly and hostile.[51]

In this chapter it has been pointed out that the marvelous episodes in Chrétien's romances are built round a formula, and that this formula appears in a number of early Irish and Welsh stories. The Irish story, C, in which the formula is best seen, has been carefully summarized, and from this story a scenario containing all important motives that make up the formula has been constructed. Several types of popular tales employ various motives that belong to the formula. Five such types of fairy tales have been defined. In the next chapter all important ancient Irish and Welsh stories that exemplify the formula are studied.

[50] Page 44.
[51] Page 326.

CHAPTER II

Twenty Ancient Irish and Welsh Journeys to Fairyland

THE OBJECT of this chapter is to study how far the twenty stories here summarized corroborate the scenario which, in the last pages, has been deduced from the Irish *Serglige*. Several of these twenty stories are well known, and their testimony to the Celtic origin of fairy material in French Arthurian romances has not escaped attention; but no study of the whole set of stories considered together has appeared.[1] The list includes eight Irish stories and three Welsh stories that were written down before the time of Chrétien; seven stories which, though not recorded till the late twelfth century, are bona fide Irish; and two other Irish stories which, though recorded later, are included here because they show no traces of influence coming from French romances, and because they probably illustrate the stage of development reached by Celtic stories at the time when they could have operated upon French romances. No conclusion is based solely upon these last two stories.

Several of these stories belong to Kittredge's three types.[2]

---

[1] See K. Meyer and A. Nutt, *The Voyage of Bran* (London, 1895–1897), I, 144–288; A. C. L. Brown, "Iwain," *Studies and Notes*, VIII (Harvard University Press, 1903), 28 f.; T. P. Cross, *Modern Philology*, XII (1915), 623 f.

[2] Page 30.

To type I belong A and B, stories in which there is no fighting and where the supremacy of the *fée* is unmistakable. This supremacy may perhaps be discovered also in C and D. In both these stories the warriors, whom the hero must slay before he can win the hand of the *fée*, were probably at first phantoms sent by her in order to test the hero's valor. In neither of these stories does the *fée* seem to be in any fear of these adversaries. Possibly she was merely obliged by the laws of her fairy nature to cause her lover to fight with these warriors, who were all the time under her control. As these stories stand, however, they have been influenced by type II, in which the supremacy of the *fée* is obscured.[3] To type I, in which a *fée* is supreme over the action, belong L, N, P, and perhaps O.

To type II, The Giant's Daughter, belong E, F, G, and H. Since the giant's home is in fairyland, these stories contain incidents of the Journey to Fairyland, just as if they belonged to type I. These stories have been confused with type I, and in what follows an attempt is made to restore E, F, and G, so as to make them conform to type I. For the present argument, however, it makes no difference whether these reconstructions are accepted or not, since in any case these stories contain incidents of a Journey to Fairyland.[4]

To type III, The Enchanted Princess, belong, on the whole, M and R, although in M it is a city, not a princess, that is enchanted or injured, and in R the princess is not

---

[3] Compare Kittredge, *Gawain*, p. 232, n. 4: "Some of the tests applied to mortal lovers by fairy mistresses are certainly borrowed from other types of *märchen*."

[4] Cf. Kittredge, *Gawain*, p. 234: "In both [types I and II] the hero must go to the Other World."

said to be enchanted but merely in danger from periodical attacks by Fomorians.

Not one of the following stories is a folk tale. The ancient Irish did not record a folk tale unless it happened to enshrine some vivid bit of topographical or genealogical lore, or unless it was made over into saga. Of the following stories A makes the freshest impression. It was preserved, no doubt, because it explains King Art's name, Óenfer. In the same way B escaped oblivion because it accounts for the periodic weakness (*ces noiden*) of the Ulstermen. C, E, and H have been wrought into the Cuchulinn saga and doubtless much altered in the process. Of the rest, perhaps D[5] is the nearest to an ancient Irish fairy tale, but it, too, has been completely remade into saga. Every one of these stories is the work of an artist who has a long tradition behind him, and who believes himself to be a scholar and historian as well as entertainer.

In all of the twenty stories outlined below the hero is a mortal. A favorite Irish hero is Cuchulinn, who in C, E, F, and H, rescues a semi-divine princess from giant Fomorians. Parallels may be found in other mythologies as in the story of how Hercules helped the gods to conquer the giants.[6]

[5] Compare also N.

[6] Otto Gruppe, *Griechische Mythologie und Religionsgeschichte* (Munich, 1906), I, 436. On the war of gods and giants see G. Dumézil, *Le Festin d'immortalité* (Paris, 1924), p. 112, and Krappe, *Mythologie universelle*, p. 281.

A. ECHTRA CONLI: ADVENTURES OF CONLE
(abdrt) [7]

This first story is a splendid example of the original sovereignty of a *fée*, who here appears as a goddess supreme over events. According to the evidence of language, this story is very old, even older than *Imram Brain*.[8] Both *Echtra Conli* and *Imram Brain* were in *Cín Droma Snechta*, a lost manuscript which was written about 920. *Echtra Conli* runs in brief as follows: [9]

One day on the hill of Uisnech, Conle, the son of King Conn, the hundred-fighter, sees a woman in wonderful garments. "I come from the lands of the living," she says, "where there is no death nor fault nor sin. We partake of perpetual feasts without preparation. Peace rules with us without strife. It is a great *síd* [elf mound], in which we dwell; therefore it is that we are called *síd*-folk." [10] She loves Conle and has come to invite him to Mag Mell (*a*). Before she departs she gives him an apple. On this apple he lives for a month; for it is not diminished, however much he eats of it, but remains whole. No other food seems to him worthy to be eaten except his

---

[7] In these summaries the occurrence of any of the twenty motives from the scenario is indicated by a parenthesized small letter.

[8] Page 271.

[9] Edition J. Pokorny, ZCP, XVII (1928), 193–205. My summary follows Pokorny's translation. On the date he remarks, "Die sprachformen in unserem Texte weisen deutlich auf dessen Entstehung in der Mitte der ersten Hälfte des 8. Jahrhunderts hin." On *Cín Droma Snechta* see Thurneysen, *Heldensage*, pp. 15 f., and compare his statement in ZCP, XX (1935), 218.

[10] "Síd már itáam, conid desuidiu nonnainmnigther áes síde." It may be that the author of these words meant to suggest also a possible meaning: "Great is the peace in which we are; therefore it is that we are called 'peaceful folk.'"

apple. He is, moreover, seized with longing for the woman he has seen.

At the end of a month at the same place the mysterious woman appears again and sings the following verses:

> A woeful seat it is upon which Conle sits
> Between short-lived mortals
> In expectation of terrible death.
> The living ones, the ever-living ones, invite thee.
> They will call thee to the people of Tethra
> Who behold thee every day
> In the assemblies of thy fatherland
> Among thy dear relatives.[11] . . .
> We must enter my ship of glass (*b*) (*d*),
> If we are to reach Síd Bóadach, "Hill of Victory."
> There is another land.[12]
> I see the sun is setting.
> However far it is, we shall arrive before night.
> It is a land that
> Pleases the thought of every visitor.
> No one dwells in it
> Except women and maidens.

Conle springs into her ship of glass (*b*), goes away with her (*r*), and has never been seen since. After Conle has departed, King Conn remarks to his other son, Art: "Art, you

[11] ZCP, XVII, 198, § 4.

> N(ó)allsuide saidess Conle
> iter marbu duthaini
> oc indnaidiu éco óathmair.
> To-t-chuiretar bíi bithbí.
> At-gérat do dóinib Tethrach
> ar-dot-chíat cach díe
> i n-dálaib t'athardai
> iter du gnáthu inmaini.

[12] "Fíl tír n-aill," "there is another world." The *fée* also calls it Mag Mell, "Plain of Happiness," Tír Subathar, "Land that pleases," Tíre Béo,

are all alone today" (*t*). From this remark Art is called Art Óenfer, "Art, the lone man."

The supremacy of the *fée* is here absolute. Is her Mag Mell, however, subject to the control of Fomorians or kings of the dead? J. A. MacCulloch thought not.[13] She could not, he wrote, be inviting Conle to the Land of Death, because in the verses she urges him to flee from the fear of dying. Perhaps, however, she means: "In my land Conle will be forever freed from the fear of death." MacCulloch thought that the reference to Tethra merely meant that Conle was "a mighty warrior, one of those whom Tethra would have approved." In support of this explanation he translated the words, *atgérat do dóinib Tethrach*, "thou art a champion to Tethra's people." This translation must be rejected. Pokorny's translation, "they will call thee to the people of Tethra," is correct.[14] The fairies are Tethra's people.

Tethra is a Fomorian,[15] and, like Eogain Inbir in C and

"Lands of the Living." It corresponds, I think, to the French Castle of Maidens.

[13] *The Religion of the Ancient Celts* (Edinburgh, 1911), pp. 374 f. See also his article, "Blest, Abode of the," in J. Hastings, *Encyclopaedia of Religion and Ethics* (New York, 1908–1922), II, 692.

[14] Kuno Meyer hesitated to translate *dóini Tethrach*, "Tethra's people" (*Sitzungsberichte der Preuss. Akademie der Wissenschaften*, XXXII [Berlin, 1919], 545), but Pokorny has shown that this is an archaic use of *dóini* for the later *muinter* (ZCP, XVII, 203, n. 3).

[15] Pokorny connects the name Tethra with that of an Old Norse giant, Thiasi. Both come from the stem that appears in Latin *tetrax*, "pheasant." According to a gloss in *LU*, fol. 50 r (ed. Best and Bergin, p. 124), Tethra's wife, too, had a bird-name, *Badb*, "crow." Cormac's *Glossary*, § 1207, *Anecdota from Irish Manuscripts* (ed. O. Bergin and others, IV [Halle and Dublin, 1912], 104), calls Tethra a king of the Fomorians, and quotes from *Immacaldam in Dá Thuarad*, the phrase *etir triuna Tetrach*, "among Tethra's mighty men." The *Immacaldam*,

Goll in D, he is the guardian of a fairy realm. In these three stories fairyland is named after a giant guardian. This seems to mean that the Irish had already adopted the picture of Hades given in the *Aeneid*, where Pluto (here Tethra) is ruler both of the Tower of the Dead and the Elysian Fields. The framework of A implies that Conle will never come back. Art would not have been named "the lone man" unless Conle's return was impossible. Impossibility of return suggests that he went to the land of the dead, to which his eating the fairy apple probably pledged him.[16] Early Irish writers thought that he became a king there. The prose *Dinnshenchas*[17] mentions "Connla's well of wisdom" undersea in Tír Tairngire. Connla Cael Corrbacc of F may possibly not be the same man, but Conla of T is. This proves that by the time *Echtra Thaidg* was written (fourteenth century or earlier) it was believed that the *fée* had taken Conle to the land of the dead.

B. CES ULAD: WEAKNESS OF THE ULSTERMEN

(*ir*)

In this story the power of the *fée* is almost as apparent as in *Echtra Conli*. This story contains no account of the

---

which has been edited by W. Stokes (*Revue celtique*, XXVI [1905], 27), seems to picture Tethra as a lord of the grave. A bard says: "I go into the mountain of youth, into the plain of age . . . into an abode of clay . . . among Tethra's mighty men." In *Cath Maige Tured*, § 25, Tethra is a king of the Fomorians; and, § 162, Tethra's sword speaks and tells what it has done (p. 230, 233).

[16] Persephone, having eaten, could not return from Hades (*Hesiod, the Homeric Hymns and Homerica*, ed. H. G. Evelyn-White [Loeb Classical Lib., London, 1914], hymn ii, vss. 372 f.) Cf. A. Le Braz, *La Légende de la Mort* (Paris, 1922–1923), II, 121, n. 1.

[17] Edition W. Stokes, "Rennes Dinnshenchas," *Rev. 'celt.*, XV (1894), 457.

Journey to Fairyland and belongs to what Kittredge calls "antitype two"[18] in which a *fée* comes from fairyland to stay with a mortal. It gives a reason for the weakness (*ces*) from which the Ulstermen suffered in the *Táin Bó*, and was probably written down in the eighth century.[19]

Crunnchu is a prosperous widower living in a lonely Ulster house. One day a handsome woman enters and takes charge of things as if she has been there before. Her name is Macha, as the learned say. She does not speak till after she has milked the cows in the evening.[20] She dwells with him for some time as his wife (*r*), and he prospers through her. "Thanks to her they lack nothing — neither food, clothing, nor property."[21] When the next *oenach* (yearly feast) comes round she says: "Do not go, for our union will continue only if you do not speak of us at the feast." Crunnchu goes nevertheless and boasts that his wife can run swifter than the king's horses. The king of Ulster thereupon compels her to run in the games against his horses. After winning the race she gives birth to twins, named Fír and Fial, and dies.[22] Therefore the place

[18] *Gawain*, p. 231. On the swan-maiden form of this type, see H. Holmström, *Studier över Svanjungfrumotivet i Völundarkvida* (Malmö, 1919).

[19] E. Windisch (*Berichte der K. Sächs. Gesellschaft der Wissenschaften, phil.-hist. Klasse*, XXXVI [Leipzig, 1884], 342 f.), under the title "Noinden Ulad," prints and translates this story from *LL*, and from Harleian 5280, a fifteenth-century manuscript. The latter contains the older version, which I summarize; see Thurneysen, *Heldensage*, pp. 360 and 667.

[20] On the motive of silence, see p. 128.

[21] "Ni búi ni ba terc dóib lee-si di cach thorud eter biad ocus etach ocus indbass" (Windisch, *Berichte*, p. 338). This is undoubtedly motive *i*, "the abundant feasting in fairyland."

[22] That Macha dies is implied in all versions, but is not explicitly stated except in a version printed by Thurneysen (*ZCP*, XII [1918], 253). By a process of rationalization the return of a fairy mistress to her land is often attributed to death: see Kittredge *Gawain*, p. 213, n. 3; T. P. Cross, *Mod. Phil.*, XII, 625, n. 2; A. Nutt in D. MacInnes, *Folk and Hero Tales*, Waifs and Strays of Celtic Tradition, II (London, 1890), 485.

where the annual games are held is called Emain Macha, "Twins of Macha." Macha prophesied that the Ulstermen would be punished by an annual weakness (*ces*), and the prophecy was fulfilled.[23]

C. SERGLIGE CONCULAINN: SICKBED OF CUCHULINN

This unusually comprehensive story has been outlined above.[24] In it characters who once were gods and giants fight to win a lady. A mortal hero finally brings victory to the gods and rescues the lady. This type of plot recurs often in other stories outlined below.

D. ECHTRA LAEGAIRE: ADVENTURES OF LAEGAIRE [25]

(abcghimnprt)

In this story the *fée* is Fiachna's wife. She has been carried off by Eochaid mac Sail and is living with Goll mac Duilb. No woman messenger, but Fiachna, one of the kings of fairy-

---

[23] According to the text in *LL*, Macha was daughter of Sainreth mac Imbaith, "Strangeness son of Ocean." She is most likely the same as Macha wife of Nuadu (see p. 233 and Thurneysen, *Heldensage*, p. 245), who, like Queen Medb, is virtually the country personified; but see Meyer, *Rev. celt.*, XXXIII (1912), 95. In the *Táin Bó Cualgne* (ed. E. Windisch [*Ir. Texte*, Extraband, Leipzig, 1905], l. 5799), and the metrical *Dinnshenchas* (ed. E. Gwynn, I–V [Royal Irish Academy, Todd Lecture Series, VIII–XII, Dublin], IV [1903], 407), Macha is Badb, Tethra's wife. This means, I think, that she is wife alternately to a Hospitable Host (Nuadu) and to a giant (Tethra). By a similar alternation in D, the heroine is wife to Fiachna and then to Goll. In J, the heroine lives as wife with Pwyll and then with Arawn. In T, LíBan is wife to Teigue and is carried off by Cathmann.

[24] Page 17.

[25] Summarized from the edition and translation by T. P. Cross, *Mod. Phil.*, XIII (1916), 731–739, from *LL*. This story is somewhat older at least than the date of the manuscript (1156–1166). K. Meyer thought the poetic speeches might be compositions of the tenth century (*The Voyage of Bran*, I, 183). See K. Jackson, *Speculum*, XVII (1942), 377.

land, comes himself to ask the aid of a mortal hero (*am*). A battle, he says, is set for that day (*n*). Laegaire volunteers to help Fiachna and reaches fairyland, which is called Plain of Two Mists (*e*), by diving after Fiachna into a lake (*b*). Fairyland, the kingdom of the *fées*, is ruled by two kings, Fiachna mac Retach and Aed mac Finn. Bands of women are mentioned, and fifty women appear to entertain Laegaire's fifty warriors. The enemies of fairyland are three kings, Eochaid mac Sail; Goll ("blind" or "one-eyed") mac Duilb; and Donn ("dark") mac Nera.[26] When Laegaire arrives, Eochaid has already been slain, and, in the battle which Laegaire enters, Goll is slain and Fiachna's wife is restored to him. After Goll is slain, however, Fiachna's wife (*p*) remarks, "I loved Goll mac Duilb."

The abundance at the fairy palace is clearly pictured[27] (*ghi*). Fiachna says: "Good are my steeds, delightful are my women. . . . (My people) have blue swords . . . golden hair . . . and are skilled at playing *fidchell* (chess)." Laegaire speaks of "ale coming in (abundance) . . . drinking mead from crystal cups . . . chess boards of *findruine* (white-bronze) . . . the noble wistful music of the *síd* . . . thirty cauldrons, thirty drinking horns. . . . I was master of a blue sword." The general name for fairyland is again Mag Mell. Goll is *rí dúin Maige Mell*. Fiachna's wife was in the *dún Maige Mill*. Laegaire captured this fort, and was given the daughter, Dergreine, as a wife (*r*).

After a year in Mag Mell, Laegaire wishes to get tidings of his own land (*t*). "If you would come back," says Fiachna, "take horses with you and do not get down from them." Laegaire goes to Ireland, finds the men of Connaught in *penach*,

---

[26] Galam and his son, Donn, who led the Milesian invasion in *LG* are, I think, the same as Goll and Donn here (see p. 265).

[27] This corresponds to the feast at the Castle of Maidens in French romances.

"assembly," bids them farewell, and returns to stay with Fiachna as joint ruler of *in dún Maige Mell.*

The remark by Fiachna's wife, "I loved Goll mac Duilb," shows, I think, that she was originally a *fée* and in control of the whole action. It was not against her will that the Fomorian Goll detained her. The narrator, however, did not understand the situation, and did not give the *fée* to Laegaire as his reward, which is the expected outcome of this type of story. For him, she was Fiachna's wife; so he restores her to Fiachna and gives to Laegaire Fiachna's daughter Dergreine, "Tear of the Sun."

It is possible that this story pictures an older form of the Irish other world in which no Dolorous Tower existed, but solely a Castle of Maidens, or dwelling of friendly fairies, which had fallen under the yoke of Fomorians. It would seem, however, that these hostile Fomorians, Eochaid mac Sail, Goll mac Duilb, and Donn mac Nera, must have been thought of in the story as having some home, and if so this would be a Dolorous Tower.

E. Tochmarc Emire: Wooing of Emer [28]

(bcdefghijopr)

Cuchulinn goes to Luglochta Loga to woo Emer, daughter of Forgall Monach (§ 9) [who according to § 48 is nephew

---

[28] An older version — of which the first part as far as the mention of the plain of Tethra is in *LU* (a MS of 1106), and the rest is supplied from Oxford, Raw. B, 512 (fifteenth-century MS), a rewriting done before 1064 of a late eighth-century text (Thurneysen, *Heldensage,* pp. 378 and 667) — has been edited and translated by Kuno Meyer in *Rev. celt.,* XI (1890), 433 f. A later version made about 1150 (*Heldensage,* p. 382) has been edited by A. G. Van Hamel from *RIA,* D., iv, 2 (fourteenth-century and other MSS), *Compert ConCulainn and Other Stories,* Med. and Mod. Irish Ser., III (Dublin, 1933). An edition by Meyer is in

to Tethra, King of the Fomorians].[29] Cuchulinn finds Emer on the green before Forgall's *dún*[30] with many maidens about her engaged in needlework (§ 10).[31] "Where did you sleep last night?" she asks. Cuchulinn replies, "We slept, and food was cooked for us in the house of the man who calls the cattle of the plain of Tethra (§ 17).[32] (The fragment in *LU* ends

---

ZCP, III (1900), 229 f., and a translation by him in *Archaeological Review*, I (1888), 70 f., 299 f. See H. Hessen and G. O'Nolan, ZCP, VIII (1910), 498 f., and Thurneysen, *Heldensage*, pp. 382–395. My summary follows Van Hamel's text and section numbers, and in general agrees with Meyer's translation of the later and fuller version. Since this version took shape before the rise of French Arthurian romance, everything in it is of importance to the present argument. Sections 1 to 17 below are in the ancient manuscript *LU*; nevertheless, for the sake of those who wish to trace the growth of the story, I have enclosed in square brackets whatever is unsupported by the older and shorter version.

[29] Van Hamel's vocabulary says, "Luglochta Loga is a district in the east of Ireland south of the Boyne," but his text reads (§ 17), "do Luglochtaib Logha .i. do gortaib" (i.e., to gardens of Lug), which is very likely a hint that it is fairyland.

[30] Monach means "shape-shifter"; see *Cóir Anmann*, § 205, in W. Stokes and E. Windisch, *Ir. Texte*, III, ii, 372. Forgall is a giant because Emer says he "excels all men in strength" (ed. Ván Hamel, p. 28, § 19). He is doubtless a shape-shifting Fomorian.

[31] This *dún* was once, I think, a Dolorous Tower, and Emer not the giant's daughter but his wife, a captive *fée*. The picture has been rationalized here to that of a daughter on a lawn outside her father's castle. Emer's needlework, however, may be original, because *fées*, whether captive or not, are often found at needlework. In the next story a *fée* and her daughters are at embroidery (p. 57). In the *Odyssey* (v, 60; x, 225), at the coming of the hero, Calypso and Circe are weaving. See Hertz, *Spielmannsbuch* (1931), p. 353; and Chrétien, *Yvain*, where three hundred maidens are captive in a garden and at work at embroidery (p. 113).

[32] This man who "calls the cattle" is a Hospitable Host. Later Cuchulinn tells his charioteer, "The man in whose house we slept is the fisherman of Conchobar. Roncu is his name. It is he that catches the fish on his line under the sea; for the fish are the cattle of the sea, and the

here.) [Emer then imposes on Cuchulinn a number of riddling conditions, three of which are thus interpreted by him. He is to slay one hundred men at every ford from Ailbine to the Boyne, together with Scennmenn *monach*, "shape shifter," her father's sister, who will change herself into every shape there to destroy him and his chariot (§ 53). He is to kill three companies of nine men, but spare her three brothers. He is to carry away her and her sister (Fial), with their weight of gold and silver, out of Forgall's *dún* (§ 54).]

Forgall goes to King Conchobar to urge that Cuchulinn be sent to Domnall [and to Scathach] to learn feats of war. Cuchulinn consents to go [and Forgall promises rewards, provided Cuchulinn goes]. Cuchulinn speaks with Emer "before he sets out in his ship" (*b*). [Emer warns Cuchulinn that Forgall is sending him to Scathach out of malice, and advises him "to be on his guard wherever he goes lest he shall destroy him" (§ 59).]

Cuchulinn sets out with Conchobar [Conall] and Laegaire, and comes to Domnall (§ 60). The latter's daughter Dornoll ("Big-Fist"), who is not beautiful, falls in love with Cuchulinn, and when refused grows angry. After the [four] three heroes depart to find Scathach, Dornoll raises a supernatural vision that causes Cuchulinn's companions to turn back (§ 61). According to another version Forgall raises this vision.

After Cuchulinn parts from all his companions, he encounters a "dreadful beast like a lion which fought with him but did him no harm" (*c*). Cuchulinn rides on the beast and is laughed at by some youths who saw him (§ 63). He rides

---

sea is the plain of Tethra, a king of the kings of the Fomorians" (§ 31). In Broccán's Hymn (W. Stokes and J. Strachan, *Thesaurus Palaeohibernicus* [Cambridge Univ. Press, 1901–1903], II, 347), Ronchenn had the *criol*-of-plenty. It is a reasonable conjecture that Ronchenn, "seal head," is an old name for Brión, the lord of the talismans. According to the mythological story in *CMT*, the Hospitable Host is Nuadu, but Nuadu is, I think, only another name for Brión.

on this beast [33] for four days [till "they came to the boundary of the region where men dwelt and to an island where lads were playing *lochán*. They laughed at the sight unusual to them of a hurtful beast doing service to a man. Cuchulinn then leaped off and the beast parted from him and he said good-bye to it."] He is then greeted in a large house in a glen by a maiden of beautiful form [34] who remembers when they studied together at the house of Ulbecca the Saxon. She gives him drink and food (*dgj*). Later a youth named Eochu Bairche gives him a similar greeting, and teaches him the way across *Mag n-Dobail*, "the Plain of Ill-Luck" (§ 65) (*e*). "The youth gave him a wheel and told him to follow its track thence across one half the plain. He also gave him an apple that he might follow the ground as that apple would follow it" (*i*). He says that there is "a large glen before him and one narrow rope across it, yet that is the way to the house of Scathach" [35] (*b*). [Cuchulinn goes over the Plain of Ill-Luck and over the *Glend Gaibthech*, "Glen Perilous," which is full of spectres and monsters sent by Forgall to destroy him. Scathach dwells on an island to be reached only by the *Droichet na n-Daltae*, "Bridge of the Fosterlings" (§ 67). The middle of this bridge is higher than the two ends, so that if one springs upon one end, the other flies up and throws him off. Cuchulinn tries three times unsuccessfully, and the men lament him. . . . He makes his salmon-leap to the middle of the bridge,[36] reaches

---

[33] This lion was probably at first a variant of Cerberus, who has taken over Charon's task of transporting a visitor to the land of the dead.

[34] This helpful maiden is like Lunete in *Yvain*, and like the damsels with cups in the *Elucidation* (p. 423).

[35] "Bui glend mar arachind. Oentet coel tairiss, noch ba si a chonair do thig Scathchai" (the older text, edited by K. Meyer, *Rev. celt.*, XI, 446). Later Aife met Cuchulinn, *forsan tét*, "upon the rope" (p. 450), and Ess Enchenn, *forsintét* (p. 452). In all these places Meyer, doubt-less wrongly, emended to *sét*, "path." See his note, p. 456.

[36] *Foglaim ConCulainn*, a fifteenth-century version of *Tochmarc Emire* (ed. Stokes, *Rev. celt.*, XXIX [1908], 118), says that the bridge

the island], and strikes the door of Scathach's fort (*h*). "He struck the door of the *dún* with the hinder end of his spear so that it went through it" (§ 68). Uathach, "the dreadful," the daughter of Scathach, "the shadow," comes to the door, and is so pleased with Cuchulinn that she willingly complies with her mother's suggestion that she sleep with him. Cuchulinn breaks her little finger, and she screams aloud. A warrior who comes, Cochor Crufe [Cochair Cruibne],[37] is slain by Cuchulinn (*p*). "Sorrowful was the woman Scathach at this (§ 69), so that he said to her that he would take upon himself the services of the man who had fallen" [so that he became the leader of her host and her champion in his stead].

On the third day Uathach tells Cuchulinn how he can gain his wishes from her mother, Scathach (§ 71). Following instructions, he overpowers Scathach with his sword, and gains from her his three wishes, namely: to teach him without neglect, to marry him with payment of dowry (by herself), to tell him what should befall him, for she was a prophetess.

---

became as thin as a hair, as sharp as the edge of an *orrladh*, and as slippery as an eel. Stokes thinks that this story throws light on *Tochmarc Emire*, but Thurneysen (*Heldensage*, p. 396, n. 4) demurs. One of Cuchulinn's numerous feats was the *faeburchles*, "sword-edge-feat." For references, see *cless* in E. Windisch, *Wörterbuch* (*Ir. Texte*, I). *Foglaim ConCulainn* describes Scathach's *dún* as follows (§ 17): "From the bower where Scáthach was, Cuchulinn was seen . . . and thus was her bower: with seven huge doors to it, and seven windows between every two of the doors, and seven rooms between every two windows, and thrice fifty girls in each 'of those rooms with purple mantles and blue." These people watched Cuchulinn cross the Bridge of the Fosterlings; as in V, *Lancelot* (p. 102), Bademagu watched from *une tor* the hero cross a sword-bridge; and as in AA, *Perceval*, many ladies from windows in Chastel Merveilleus watched Gawain in a boat crossing a terrible river (p. 138). Scathach's *dún*, Bademagu's tower, and Chastel Merveilleus are, I think, different forms of the Castle of Maidens.

[37] *Cocuir*, in the St. Gall *Priscian*, glosses *murex* (*Thesaurus Palaeohibernicus*, II, 124). To this compare Welsh, *coch*, "red." The warrior is evidently a red Fomorian (*o*).

[According to some versions Cuchulinn carried her to the seashore and there slept with her. "Uathach was then mate to Cuchulinn, and Scathach taught him skill in arms."]

Scathach is at war with Queen Aífe (§ 74). On the day of battle, to save Cuchulinn from danger, she gives him a sleeping potion, but the potion that would have held another twenty-four hours holds him but one, and he enters the battle.[38] Fighting in aid of Scathach's two sons, he slays three warriors of Aífe: Cuar, Cat, and Crufe, sons of Ilsúanaig, "great sleeper" (§ 75). The next day he slays the three sons of Ess Enchenn, "bird-head," Ciri, Biri, and Blaicne (§ 77). Scathach tells Cuchulinn that Aífe loves nothing so much as her chariot and horses. So, when he fights Aífe upon the rope of tricks (§ 76), and she breaks his weapons, he calls out that her chariot is falling into the glen. When she turns her head he conquers her. To save her life she gives him three wishes: to be subject to Scathach, to let him spend a night with her, and to bear him a ·son (Conlui). Cuchulinn next meets upon the rope of tricks an old blind woman who tries to kill him. She is Ess Enchenn, who wishes to revenge the death of her sons. [The next incident, that of Ruad King of Isles, has been influenced by Viking stories and may be omitted.]

Cuchulinn returns to Ireland [by ship] (§ 80), goes to Luglochta Loga, and attacks Forgall's *dún* [which is encircled by three ramparts] (*f*). He slays three groups of eight or nine men but spares Emer's three brothers: Scibur, Ibur, and Cat [Forgall, in fleeing from Cuchulinn, falls over one of the ramparts and dies]. Cuchulinn carries off Emer and her foster-sister, with their weight of gold and silver [At the ford he kills Scenmenn, Forgall's sister (here Scenmenn seems to be a man) with her company of one hundred men] and escapes with Emer (§ 86) (*r*).

---

[38] Aífe and Ess Enchenn are hostile in this scenario· and play the rôle usually taken by Fomorians.

Irish story tellers often split the Hospitable Host into several personages who successively entertain or help the hero. The Hosts here are five: Roncu, Domnall, a "maiden of beautiful form," Eochu Bairche, and Scathach.

Objection has been made that *Tochmarc Emire* does not conform to the type of Journey to Fairyland that we are studying.[39] Everybody will grant that the story has been changed, and most people will agree that Forgall was originally a giant, and that Emer was his captive and probably at first his wife. Later refinement of manners called Emer his daughter, rationalized Forgall into a neighboring king, and made him ruler of a *bruiden* (hostel) in Ireland.[40] Notwithstanding this change, Cuchulinn is at the end the cause of Forgall's death, although the last narrator has not understood and tries to represent the death as accidental. Cuchulinn's original hostility to Forgall appears, however, because the next thing he does is to kill Forgall's sister Scenmenn "at the ford."

The giant Forgall is in control of the action. He arranged, we are told, the bridge, and the *urthracht* (spectres) of the glen, on the way to Scathach's house, which shows that he is like the king of the dead in *Visio Tnugdali*,[41] who exercises control over the monsters which swim in the river beneath the Bridge of Dread. Forgall sent Cuchulinn

[39] Professor M. B. Ogle in the *American Journal of Philology*, XXXVII (1916), 405, wrote: "Scathach differs from all other fairy mistresses in this type of story in that she is sought by the hero instead of seeking him without his knowledge, and sought too not to be his paramour but his teacher in the art of war."

[40] The eighth-century *Scéla Mucce Meic Dathó* (ed. Thurneysen, p. 1) mentions Bruden Forgaill Manaich as one of six hostels or "feasting halls" in Ireland. Pokorny unimaginatively makes Manach refer to the Fir Manach, a tribe living near Lusk (ZCP, XI [1917], 170, 182).

[41] Edition A. Wagner (Erlangen, 1882), p. 19.

to Scathach hoping that he might be slain. The name Uathach, "dreadful," must not mislead us into thinking that
Scathach, Uathach, and Aífe are Fomorians or hostile
witches. They are *fées* who can be lovely if they choose;
that Cuchulinn loses no time in taking every one of the
three for a mistress proves this. They are *fées* who are controlled in some way by the giant or demon Forgall, who,
like Tethra in A, seems to be the ruler of the land. Those
who fail to see this are simply stumbling over the double
aspect of both *fées* and fairyland; they may be either
charming or horrible.[42]

The story implies that Cuchulinn is a youth, and there
is nothing improbable in a *fée* like Scathach giving him in-
struction in warlike deeds. So Bodbmall trained Finn, the
merfeine showed Lanzelet how to shoot arrows, and the
witches of Gloucester taught Peredur the use of arms.[43]
Scathach and Uathach are not truly hostile to Cuchulinn.
Uathach has fallen in love with him before Cuchulinn
fights and slays her mother's champion Cochair Cruibne.
Cochair Cruibne is their tool anyhow so that battle with
him is merely one of those tests that *fées* require. The plot
ought to lead up next to a great battle with Forgall the
giant; but that battle has been obliterated, and for it have
been substituted trifling combats against Queen Aífe and
three warriors, and Ess Enchenn and three sons.

Forgall, since he is a nephew of the Fomorian king Tethra,
is a Fomorian, and his *dún* in Luglochta Loga, surrounded
by three ramparts that Cuchulinn must leap (§ 86), is, I

[42] See H. Güntert, *Kundry*, Germanische Bibliothek (Heidelberg,
1928), pp. 28 f.

[43] K. Meyer, "The Boyish Exploits of Finn," *Eriu*, I (1904), 181;
Lanzelet, ed. K. A. Hahn (Frankfurt a. M., 1845), vss. 275–300; *Mab.*,
II, 98.

think, a Dolorous Tower.[44] No matter how one explains Forgall's *dún*, analogy from the other stories here assembled indicates that Scathach's *dún* is a Castle of Maidens (Mag Mell); and, even if one refuses to regard Scathach as a *fée* who has adopted a terrifying disguise, one can scarcely deny that her abode is in the Land of the Dead (*scath*, "shadow"). To be sure, our versions say that her land is "beyond the Alps," and in one place it is called Alba, "Scotland." Editors interpret these locations literally, but they may both refer to the Land of the Dead. The ancient Irish sometimes located the Land of the Dead in Scotland.[45]

On his way to Scathach's land, Cuchulinn experiences a number of adventures. A damsel of great beauty supplies him with drink and food (*gh*); he finds a lionlike beast, a rolling apple, a wheel, a rope-bridge at the farther end of which is Scathach's castle, from the windows of which women watch his perilous crossing, and finally Cochor Crufe, a red champion who must be slain. *Tochmarc Emire* proves that these adventures were known in Ireland before the rise of French Arthurian romances. That Chrétien had some sort of connection with Irish literary tradition, as represented by *Tochmarc Emire*, seems indicated by his echoing certain of the Irish descriptive names. *Glend Gáibthech*, "glen perilous," and *Mag n-Dobail*, "plain of ill luck" (§ 67), seem echoed in "Fontainne Perilleuse" (*Yvain*, vs. 810), and "Chastel de Pesme Avanture" (*Yvain*, vs. 5109).

---

[44] In the *Aeneid* the tower has three walls (p. 16). The *dún* of Scath has seven walls (p. 67). In the Babylonish epic, hell has seven walls (M. Landau, *Hölle und Fegefeuer in Volksglaube* [Heidelberg, 1909], p. 79).

[45] Page 344.

F. Fled Bricrenn ocus Longes mac n-Duil Dermait:
The Feast of Bricriu and the Exile of the Sons of Dael
Dermait

(abdghkimnpqr) [46]

At a feast given to King Conchobar by Bricriu in Emain
Macha, the latter declares that his food ought not to be en-
joyed without a brave deed of the Ulstermen.[47] Conchobar's
twelve champions at once depart into different "fifths" (provinces) of Ireland to seek adventure.

Cuchulinn, one of the twelve champions, accompanied by
his charioteer, Laeg, son of Riangabar, and his foster son,
Lugaid Red Stripe, meets Maine with a company of three
hundred, and Finnchaem the daughter of Eochu Ronn the king
of the Ui Maine. When Laeg and Lugaid attempt to assail
Finnchaem, she declares that she has fallen in love with Cuchulinn because of stories about him. Cuchulinn leaps to her
side, and she embraces and kisses him. As the company goes on
to Cruachan, Cuchulinn cuts off the heads of three robbers
that they meet in the woods. Ailill, king of Cruachan, wishes
to stick their heads upon his palisade, but Cuchulinn insists on
retaining them.

Next morning Eochu Ronn comes with a band of men. There
is an *indell* ("charm" or perhaps "contrivance") upon the javelin that he carries. As soon as he sees Cuchulinn he hurls the
javelin at him. Cuchulinn sets an *indell* against the javelin. It
turns back toward Eochu and pierces the neck of his horse.
The horse makes a spring and throws Eochu off. Cuchulinn
then seizes Eochu in his arms and carries him into the fort.

[46] Summarized from Stokes and Windisch, *Ir. Texte*, II, i, 173 f. This
story, which arose in the tenth century (Thurneysen, *Heldensage*, p.
668), is in the Yellow Book of Lecan, a fourteenth-century manuscript.

[47] Arthur's refusal to eat till he has heard an adventure (*Perceval*,
ed. A. Hilka [Halle, 1932], vs. 2824) has often been compared.

Eochu says to Cuchulinn, "May you have no rest either sitting or lying until you know what drove the sons of Dael Dermait from their land."

When Cuchulinn returns to the feast in Emain Macha he feels as if his clothing and the earth were burning under him [48] (*a*). He sees that he must die unless he finds out the answer to Eochu's question. Accompanied by Laeg and Lugaid, he sets out and meets nine poets and afterwards nine smiths. Both companies ask for food and drink. With the words, "Do you make a servant of me!" Cuchulinn slays them all. At the seashore he meets the son of the King of Alba in a ship bringing silk and drinking horns to King Conchobar. He puts the question he is henceforth to put to everybody, "What drove the sons of Dael Dermait out of their land?" "I do not know," replies the King of Alba, "but here is my ship (*b*) and a *muir indell* (sea-charm) to help you." Cuchulinn carves an *ogam* (secret writing) on a javelin and bids the king's son take it and occupy his seat at the feast which is still going on in Emain Macha.[49]

After a day and a night in the ship, Cuchulinn, Laeg, and Lugaid come to a large island that is surrounded by a silver wall and a copper palisade. The king of this island is Riangabar, the father of Laeg, Cuchulinn's charioteer, who welcomes them for his son's sake. Riangabar's palace has roof poles and pillars of white bronze (*k*). It has one hundred and fifty couches each provided with a chess board, a checker board, and a harp. A bath is made ready for the visitors and mead is poured out. Presently horns are heard outside and fifty warriors enter, every two of whom carry between them a pig or an ox, and a beaker of mead (*g*). Fifty more come bearing firewood. At

[48] Page 60, n. 57.
[49] Evidently the sea-charm directed the ship to the destined place. Rhŷs suggests that the *ogam* gave the king's son Cuchulinn's shape, so that the latter's absence from the feast was unnoticed (*Celtic Heathendom*, p. 346).

their head is a man in a purple mantle who enters the house before his people and bids the guests welcome. A meal for one hundred (*h*) is prepared; roast pig and roast ox are made ready [First Host]. To Cuchulinn's question, "What drove the sons of Dael Dermait out of their land?" Riangabar replies, "I will find out. Their sister and her husband are on an island to the southward." The visitors see, in the palace, Riangabar's queen and three daughters engaged in embroidery.[50] That night Etan the Fair, one of Riangabar's three daughters, is given to Cuchulinn.

Cuchulinn and his companions go to the island to which Riangabar directs them. This island (called "Dael's land" in the verses) belongs to Connla Cael Corrbacc ("thin crooked hook"), who is of giant size [Second Host]. His wife is Achtlann, daughter of Dael Dermait. Her three brothers have evidently been carried off by Eochaid Glas.[51] In reply to Cuchulinn's question, "What drove the children of Dael Dermait out of their land?" Achtlann says, "I know, and I will go with you till you find out, and it is prophesied that by you they will be healed."

A third island is reached by Cuchulinn and Achtlann, his guide, in a boat. This island is surrounded by a white wall, near which they meet two women cutting rushes. Cuchulinn inquires the name of the land. One of the women sings some verses in reply, in which she says that seven kings rule in the island who are rich in troops ready for war. Cuchulinn, thinking apparently that she means to frighten him, slays her with his fist. He then asks the other woman to tell him the names of the kings, and she replies: Dian mac Lugdach, Leo mac Iachtain, Eogan *Findeach* ("white horse"), Fiachnai *Fuath* ("spectre"), Coirpre Cundail, Cond *Sidi* ("elf"), Senach Sal-

[50] On the needlework motive, see p. 47.

[51] This was Thurneysen's conjecture (*Heldensage*, p. 473), which now seems established by analogy from G. In G (p. 62) a hospitable host's twenty-three sons have been slain by the giant Yspaddaden.

dercc. Laeg takes this woman's mantle on his back till they come to the *aurla* (lawn) of the *dún* (*d*). Coirpre Cundail comes out of the fortress and fights with Cuchulinn. After Coirpre Cundail is conquered he becomes hospitable, carries Cuchulinn into his fortress, gives him a bath, and makes his daughter sleep with him [Third Host]. He also answers Cuchulinn's question as to what drove the sons of Dael Dermait out of their land, but we are not told what the answer is.

Next morning the giant named Eochu Glas who is holding the sons of Dael Dermait captive (*m*), challenges Coirpre to battle (*n*). Cuchulinn and Coirpre go to meet him at *in glend ar cend in trenfir*, "the glen of the strong man." [52] Cuchulinn fights in Coirpre's stead. Eochu is so enormous that Cuchulinn perches on the rim of his shield like a fly, and is twice blown off into the sea by his breath. Cuchulinn at last slays him with the *gae bulgae* (*p*), and cuts off his head. The *sidhaighi* (*fées*) come from the east and the west to bathe in the giant's blood, and are thus healed from wounds that he has inflicted upon them (*q*). The sons of Dael Dermait are set free. Cuchulinn spends a night at Coirpre's *dún* and receives wonderful gifts. He spends the next night with Connla. The third night he is with Riangabar, and he sleeps again with Etan. Then Cuchulinn returns to the feast in Emain Macha, where he finds his share of food and drink is awaiting him and where he tells his adventures. Then he goes back to Ailill and Medb, where Eochu Ronn makes peace with him and gives him his daughter Finnchaem (*r*).

If this story had any original unity, the giant at the end, Eochu *glas*, "green," was once identical with the giant at the beginning, Eochu *ronn*, "chain." The identity of the two Eochu's is required by this type of plot which demands that the giant shall be slain before the hero marries his

---

[52] *Ir. Texte*, II, i, 183. This glen of the giant corresponds to a Dolorous Tower.

daughter; so in the next story the giant Yspaddaden must be slain before Kulhwch marries Olwen.[53] Eochu *ronn's* horse is called *brec-glas*, "speckled-green," which, since a green horse ought to belong to a green rider, is doubtless a surviving hint that Eochu *ronn* is the same as Eochu *glas*. The original identity of the giants, however (although probable), is not important for the present argument. In any case this story contains various incidents of the Journey to Fairyland. The *sidhaighi* (of 1. 264, *Ir. Texte*) are doubtless the seven *flaithi*, "princes" (of ll. 221 f.): Dian Mac Lugdach, Leo mac Iachtain, Eogan Findeach, Fiachnai Fuath, Coirpre Cundail, Cond Sidi, and Senach Saldercc. These people, and their followers perhaps, have been wounded by the giant, and only his blood can heal them. That is to say, Coirpre Cundail, who is the chief Hospitable Host of this story (earlier Hosts are Riangabar and Connla Cael), has been wounded by Eochu and needs the help of a youthful hero.[54]

Eochu *glas* in this story has probably borrowed traits from the king of the dead. His epithet *glas*, "green," may be a sign that he belongs to the Land of Death. His blowing Cuchulinn from the edge of his shield reminds a reader of the monster, Lucifer, who in *Visio Tnugdali*[55] blew away wicked souls, and afterwards drew them back by his breath. Dael *Dermait* could mean Dael "the forgotten," and may be a way of saying that he has been killed by the giant. The *dún* of Coirpre Cundail is the Castle of Maidens, and where Eochu *glas* lives in the glen of the giant is the equivalent of a Dolorous Tower.

[53] Page 63.
[54] This resembles *CMT*, where Nuadu is wounded and needs to be rescued by Lug (p. 231).
[55] Edition A. Wagner, p. 37.

G. Kulhwch and Olwen
(acefimpr)

This next story is Welsh. It is the oldest extant Arthurian romance, and took shape as early as 1125.[56]

A stepmother puts a destiny [57] upon Prince Kulhwch (a) not to marry till he can win Olwen, daughter of Yspaddaden Benkawr, "head giant." Kulhwch goes to the court of his cousin, King Arthur, to ask aid. At first the porter refuses Kulhwch admission but offers him lodgings outside the castle, "a woman to sleep with you, and pleasing songs." Arthur, however, orders the porter to admit Kulhwch. His palace contains talismans, a mantle, a sword called Caledfwlch, etc. Arthur does not go with Kulhwch on the quest for Olwen, but sends some of his warriors, namely: Cai as leader, Bedwyr the swift, Cynddelig the guide, Gwrhyr the interpreter, Gwalchmai who always obtains what he seeks, and Menw, the enchanter.

They set forth and "came to a great open plain (e) until they saw a great fort (f), the greatest of forts in the world."

[56] Summarized and quoted from the translation of Ellis and Lloyd, *Mab.*, I, 170 f. References on the date have been collected by A. C. L. Brown, *Speculum*, XV (1940), 4, n. 2; and by R. S. Loomis, "The Arthurian Legend before 1139," *Romanic Review*, XXXIII (1941), 15. The Red Book text has been printed by John Rhŷs and J. G. Evans, *The Text of the Mabinogion from the Red Book of Hergest* (Oxford University Press, 1887), I, 100–143, and the White Book text by J. G. Evans, *The White Book Mabinogion* (Pwllheli, 1907), pp. 226–254.

[57] *Tynged* is here perhaps equivalent to *geis*. Similar to this *tynged* are the longing felt by Connle in A, the year's illness of Cuchulinn in C, the conditions put by Emer and her father upon Cuchulinn in E, the quest imposed by Eochu *ronn* upon Cuchulinn in F, and the *geis* put by a stepmother upon Art to go on a quest in S. On *geis*, see J. R. Reinhard, *The Survival of Geis in Mediaeval Romance* (Halle, 1933), pp. 24, 232, 301.

Before the fort is "a huge flock of sheep without end or beginning to it." On top of a mound is a shepherd keeping the sheep, "and near him is a shaggy mastiff larger than a stallion, whose breath burnt down bushes and trees" (c). Menw puts an enchantment upon the dog so that he can harm no one. "Who own yonder castle?" they ask. "Idiots of men are you," replies Custennin, the shepherd.[58] "Throughout the world is it known that it is the fort of Yspaddaden, the chief giant. . . . He is my brother who despoiled my wife." "We are come to seek Olwen," they say. "No one ever returned alive from that quest," says the shepherd. When the shepherd goes away, Kulhwch gives him a ring of gold which he carries home to his wife. Custennin's wife asks him how he got the ring; in reply he says, "Behold a corpse did I see coming in on the waves;[59] and never saw I a more beautiful corpse than it. And on its finger did I find this ring." "Show me that corpse," she says. "O woman, him who owns the corpse you shall see here at evensong." "Who is that?" she asks. Custennin replies, "It is Kulhwch son of Kilydd."

When the visitors arrive at Custennin's house, his wife greets them with joy. Cai, the leader of Arthur's knights, seizes a piece of wood, and, when Custennin's wife attempts to throw her arms around him, he places the log of wood between her

[58] *Mab.*, I, 193.
[59] Yspaddaden, with his "greatest of forts" beyond "a great open plain," shows traces of having been regarded as a king of the dead. Custennin is a Charon who carries dead people or corpses across the river of death to the all-receiving castle. His words, "Behold a corpse," etc., are, I think, a reference to this mythological background. My friend Professor J. J. Parry tells me he is unconvinced. He thinks the words, "a corpse did I see," are mere bluster on the part of Custennin, and he calls my attention to the White Book, which at this point reads, "A corpse did I see coming in on the ebb tide" (*Mab.*, I, 194; "Yn dyvot gan yr ertrei," instead of "gan y tonneu," "on the waves," ed. J. G. Evans, p. 473 [also numbered 237]). To "come in" on "the ebb" does seem nonsense.

arms and she squeezes it out of shape.[60] She brings her one remaining son, Goreu ("best"), out of concealment, and says her other twenty-three sons have been slain by the giant Yspaddaden, father of Olwen (*m*). Kulhwch and his companions are entertained and, at Cai's request, Olwen comes to Custennin's house. She tells Kulhwch that her father's life will last only till she takes a husband, and that he can never win her unless he procures everything that her father shall require.

When she returns to her home, Kulhwch and his companions follow, and, after slaying nine porters that are at the nine gates, they enter Yspaddaden's fort (*f*). They ask him to give Olwen as wife to Kulhwch. He refuses and, as they arise to go, hurls a stone spear. Bedwyr catches it and hurls it back so that it pierces the giant's thigh.[61] The next day they go again, with a similar experience, only this time Menw catches the stone spear and hurls it back, piercing the giant's eye.[62] Finally the giant promises his daughter to Kulhwch if he will procure certain objects which are then enumerated in a list of thirty-eight quests. The last of the quests, namely that for the sword of Gwrnach the giant, they undertake first. Arthur does not accompany them on this quest any more than he did against Yspaddaden.

Gwrnach's castle resembles Yspaddaden's. Kulhwch and his companions see "a great castle built of stone and mortar, the largest of forts in the world," and outside of it they meet a black man. "Who owns the fort?" say they. "Fools of men

---

[60] Custennin is a Hospitable Host. This dangerous embrace is, perhaps, merely the storyteller's way of emphasizing the size and strength of Custennin and of his wife.

[61] This is explained by Eochu's javelin, which had a charm. Cuchulinn, however, set a counter-charm which made it turn back against its owner (p. 55). Eochu and Yspaddaden are parallel figures.

[62] Like Balar and other Fomorians, he perhaps had originally but one eye.

that you are," he replies. "There is no one in the world who does not know who own this fort. Gwrnach, the giant, owns it." Cai, Bedwyr, and Goreu in one way or another gain admittance. They cut off Gwrnach's head and return, bringing his sword, to King Arthur's court.

After this Arthur accompanies Kulhwch and helps in the remaining quests. When all the objects have been obtained, Kulhwch, Caw, Goreu, and others, but not Arthur, go to the castle of Yspaddaden. Caw shaves the giant, Goreu cuts off his head, "fixes it on the castle stake," [63] and Kulhwch obtains Olwen (pr).

This story is of the Giant's Daughter type and has certainly been rewritten. The interminable lists of quests may be disregarded as not belonging to the original thread of the narrative. No one has before pointed out that here, as in the other genuine Welsh Arthurian tale, *The Dream of Rhonabwy*, and in more than one of Chrétien's romances, Arthur is enchanted and is actually in the outskirts of the Land of the Dead. This certainly is his situation in *The Dream of Rhonabwy*, where the battle of Camlan is in the past, and where Arthur is one of those men of huge stature of old time who, like Ossian and Cailte in the Irish *Acallam*,[64] laugh at the puny folk whom they see alive.

It is my theory that here in *Kulhwch and Olwen* Arthur is a revenant, like Cuchulinn in the *Siaburcharpat*, H, and

---

[63] "Ae dodi ar bawl y gatlys" (Red Book text, p. 143).

[64] In *The Dream of Rhonabwy* a horseman says, "I was a messenger at the Battle of Camlan between Arthur and Medrawd" (*Mab.*, II, 8); and later Arthur laughs at the little men who guard Britain (*Mab.*, II, 10). Compare the *Acallam* (ed. W. Stokes and E. Windisch, *Ir. Texte*, IV, i, ll. 61–62 [my translation]): "Fear fell upon the clerics before those big men (Ossian and Caeilte), for they were not people of the same epoch or time as the clerics."

like Ossian in Micheál Coimín's *Laoi Oisín ar Tír na n-Og*.[65] Like other Hospitable Hosts in fairyland – like Labraid in C, Fiachna in D, and Coirpre Cundail in F – Arthur is oppressed by giants and needs the help of a mortal hero, Kulhwch, to deliver him. The last narrator of *Kulhwch and Olwen* has not understood that Arthur is in fairyland, but the evidence is in the text. The porter says that two-thirds of Arthur's life is past. This makes Arthur an old man; and, since he was not old at the battle of Camlan, this puts the action of *Kulhwch and Olwen* after that. That Camlan is in the past is proved by mention of three men who escaped from that battle.[66] Arthur is therefore dwelling in Avalon or fairyland.

Gwrnach and Yspaddaden in this story are giants who correspond to Irish Fomorians. Not till Yspaddaden has been rendered helpless and Gwrnach has been slain, does Arthur attempt anything. Yspaddaden explains the situation to Kulhwch by saying, "You cannot force him [Arthur] and this is the reason; he is under my hand." [67] This remark in which the giant asserts control over Arthur is lacking in the Red Book text, and consequently has escaped the notice of commentators. It implies that Arthur has been enchanted by the giants and, as I think, the enchantment has been interpreted by some redactor as death. Arthur here is in the same situation as Arthur in *Sir Perceval*, who was "sick and sore" [68] and unable to move until the

[65] Page 66. The *Laoi Oisín* has been edited by T. Flannery (Dublin, 1910); see his p. 67.

[66] *Mab.*, I, 176, 182.

[67] "Dan uŷ llaw i ŷ mae ef" (J. G. Evans, *White Book*, p. 243, col. 485, l. 8; *Mab.*, I, 209).

[68] Edition F. Holthausen (Heidelberg, 1913), vs. 1078. See A. C. L. Brown, *Mod. Phil.*, XXII (1924), 93 f.

Red Knight was slain. Here, as in *Sir Perceval*, Arthur can be rescued solely by a destined hero. Kulhwch is such a hero. Neither Chrétien nor the author of *Kulhwch and Olwen*, seems to have understood that Arthur was enchanted, but enchantment is, in my opinion, a key that unlocks the puzzle of Arthur's inactivity both here and in other romances.

In *Kulhwch and Olwen* the Dolorous Tower is divided into two castles: Yspaddaden's castle and Gwrnach's castle. Both are "the largest in the world," which means, as I believe, that they both are pictures of the all-receiving (πολυδέκτης) mansion of the dead. Like Charon in classic myth, the shepherd, Custennin, collects payment for what he does. His dog, larger than a stallion, that "burnt down bushes and trees with his fiery breath" is like Cerberus. The nine gates of Yspaddaden's castle are like the seven walls of hell in the Babylonish epic. The "castle-stake" upon which Yspaddaden's head is fixed is a token of the castle of the dead.

The Castle of Maidens also appears twice, once as King Arthur's castle and again as Custennin's house. Hospitable Hosts often assist the hero in battling the giants. Thus in C, Aed and Labraid help Cuchulinn; in D, Fiachna helps Laegaire; and in E, Coirpre accompanies Cuchulinn to meet the giant. So here Arthur, Goreu, and the latter's father, Custennin, help Kulhwch, and it is Goreu that finally cuts off Yspaddaden's head.

H. Siaburcharpat ConCulainn: The Spectral Chariot
of Cuchulinn

(*bcfiprs*) [69]

Cuchulinn appears long after his death to King Laegaire
and tells a story in verse:

5

A journey I went —
O Laegaire, but that was an hour!
That I might give great battles
Against Lochlann [70] on the north.

6

A certain hero in it met me
After I had come on the journey: —
Thirty cubits in height —
That was his size!

7

After that I attacked him,
After we had fought three times:

[69] The translation of J. O'Beirne Crowe (*Royal Hist. and Archaeol.
Assoc. of Ireland, Journal*, 4th series, I [1871], 371 f.), slightly altered
after comparison with the Irish text in *Anecdota* (III, 49–56) and with that
in Best and Bergin (*Lebor na Huidre*, pp. 278–287). According to Thurneysen (*Heldensage*, p. 668), this saga was written in the tenth century.

[70] Lochlann here means Fomorian land or the Land of Death, as in
R (p. 81). In later times it came to mean Norway. The change of
meaning is pointed out by J. Rhŷs in *Celtic Heathendom*, p. 355, and in
Arthurian Legend (Oxford University Press, 1891), p. 11; and by Nutt
in MacInnes, *Folk and Hero Tales*, pp. 411, 420. Lochlann seems to be
fairyland in *Aided Lugdach*, where Forgaill, daughter of the King of
Lochlann, appears in bird form (ed. C. Marstrander, *Ériu*, V [1911],
208). See A. Bugge, *On the Fomorians and the Norsemen* (Christiania,
1905), p. vii; and G. Murphy, *Béaloideas*, III (1931), 97.

I flung off his head in the battle,
So that the king fell (*p*).

8

After that there fell
A great defect of them: —
Seven fifties of every single battle,
When their number was taken.

9

It was after that that I bound
On them, for their share,
Seven hundred talents of white-silver,
With seven hundred talents of gold —
That was the tribute.

10

A journey I went, O Laegaire (*b*),
For plunder to the Land of Scath [shadow]:
Dún Scaith in it with its locks of irons —
I laid hand upon it.

11

Seven walls about that city —
Hateful was its color [71] (*f*):
A rampart of irons on each wall,
On that were nine heads.

12

Doors of iron on each side —
Against me not great defences:
I struck them with my leg,
So that I made them into fragments.

[71] *LU* reads "ba etig a dend" (ed. Best and Bergin, p. 282). *Anecdota* (III, 54) reads "ba heitigh a dend." *Dend* means "color"; see Kuno Meyer, *Contributions to Irish Lexicography* (Halle, 1906), p. 611. The color was "hateful," I suppose, because it was bloody red.

13

There was a pit in the *dún*,
Belonging to the king, it is related: —
Ten serpents burst (*c*)
Over its border — it was a deed!

14

After that I attacked them,
Though very vast the throng,
Until I made bits of them,
Between my two fists.

15

A house full of toads,
They were let fly at us:
Sharp, beaked monsters,
They stuck in my snout.

16

Terrible, dragonlike monsters
To us they used to fall:
Strong, glittering, sharp, horse-shaped [72]
Many of them fell upon us.

17

After that I attacked them,
When a rush was made on me:
I ground them till they were particles
Between my two palms (*p*).

18

There was a caldron in that *dún*,
The Calf of the Three Cows:
Thirty joints in its stomach —
It was not a charge for it (*i*).

[72] See Thurneysen, ZCP, XII (1918), 284.

19

They [the cows] used to frequent that caldron
Delightful was the contest:
They used not to go from it on any side,
Until they left it full.

20

There was much gold and silver in it —
Wonderful was the find:
I took away that caldron
And the daughter of the king (rs).

21

The three cows we carried off —
They swam boldly over the sea:
There was a load of gold for two men
To each of them on her neck.

22

After we had come upon the ocean,
Which was vast by the north,
My curach's crew were drowned
By the hard storm.

23

After that I floated them,
Though it was a great danger: —
Nine men upon each of my two hands,
Thirty on my head.

24

Eight upon my two thighs —
They clung to my body:
Thus I swam the ocean
Until I was in the harbor.

I have omitted a number of verses that follow, in which Cuchulinn declares that his sufferings in the Land of Scath, though great, were nothing compared to what he endured in the Christian Purgatory where he encountered the devil. He seems to contrast the heathen Land of Giants (Scath) with Purgatory. It is probable that in the above verses Lochlann and Scath are identical, and that Cuchulinn is describing a single expedition in which he slew the King of Giantland and carried off the daughter and the caldron.

The plausible reconstruction of this story would explain the heroine as at first a *fée* who, with her cows and her celebrated caldron called the "Calf of the Three Cows" (a symbol of plenty corresponding probably to the Grail), fell into the power of a Fomorian giant [73] and needed to be rescued. As in preceding stories, however, this reconstruction is by no means necessary. It is sufficient to regard the story as belonging to the Giant's Daughter type.

That the giant's land, Scath, has here been at least partially identified with the land of the dead can scarcely be doubted. The seven walls, the "hateful color" [doubtless of blood], the locks on the doors of iron [iron is a mark of the underworld], the toads and serpents, and, finally, the heads on pikes, are signs of the castle of the dead.

Later Irish narrators, probably wrongly, identified this castle in the land of Scath with Cathair ConRoi and the heroine of the story with Bláthine. A ninth-century Irish saga, *Aided ConRoi* (Death of Cu Roi),[74] about Cu Roi runs as follows:

[73] Thurneysen thinks that the cows and caldron have been transferred into this story from *Aided ConRoi* (*Heldensage*, p. 570). They may, I conjecture, have been inserted here in place of a cup of plenty such as is usually found in fairyland or in the Castle of Maidens.

[74] Summarized from Thurneysen, *Heldensage*, pp. 432 f.

Cuchulinn persuades Bláthine ("Floweret") to betray her giant husband, Cu Roi, who lives in Cathair ConRoi. Cuchulinn slays him and carries off his wife, his three cows that give "every day sixty sextarii of milk" in a copper kettle which was called the "Calf," and the kettle.

In *Fled Bricrend* [75] is another version of the story which ascribes to Cu Roi a revolving fortress, but neither this nor the preceding story relates any incidents of a Journey to Fairyland.

A ninth-century Irish story about a *síd*, in this case Brug na Boinne, a fairy hill, near the Boyne River, runs as follows:

I. De Gabáil int Sída: The Seizure of the Fairy Hill
(*i*) [76]

Dagán [which seems to be a name for the Dagda] is king of the Tuatha Dé. Even after the Sons of Míl conquer Ireland, his power is great, for the Tuatha Dé destroy the corn and milk of the Sons of Míl, till they make the friendship of the Dagda.

The Dagda divides the fairy mounds of Ireland among the princes of the Tuatha Dé. By a trick, Aengus Mac Oc obtains Síd in Broga, the Dagda's own dwelling, so that the Dagda departs from it and Mac Oc dwells there. "Wonderful truly is that land. Three trees with fruit are there always, and a pig eternally alive, and a roasted swine, and a tankard with marvelous liquor, and never do they all decrease" (*i*).

The cows, tankard, trees, pigs, and ale are a peasant's notion of plenty; and probably have been substituted by

[75] G. Henderson, *ITS*, II (1899), 102, § 80.
[76] Summarized from an edition and translation by Dr. Vernam Hull, *ZCP*, XIX (1931), 55-58; on the date see p. 54, n. 1. Thurneysen believes that the last paragraph relating the marvels of the *síd* is part of the ninth-century story.

some narrator for the magic dish-of-plenty which one expects to find in Mag Mell or Castle of Maidens.

In the first branch of the Welsh *Mabinogi* occur two fairy mistress stories that may be considered next. These stories probably arose in the early twelfth century, and they reflect a considerably more developed form of society than those previously summarized.

J. PWYLL AND ARAWN

(*mnp*) [77]

Pwyll, while hunting, encounters a pack of dogs that are of a color he has never seen before. They are "glittering brilliant white and their ears red." The master of these fairy dogs is Arawn, king of Annwn.[78] He proposes to Pwyll an exchange of kingdoms, his object being to have Pwyll take his place in a single combat that has been appointed for one year from that time. The antagonist is Hafgan, a king with whom Arawn is continually at war (*m*).

Arawn declares to Pwyll, "I will put you in Annwn in my place, and I will give you the fairest lady you ever saw to sleep with you each night, and my form and semblance shall be upon you, so that there shall not be a page of the chamber, nor an officer, nor any other person who has ever followed me who shall know that I am not you. . . . One year from tonight there is an appointment between me (*n*) and Hafgan at the ford. Be you there in my likeness and one stroke that

[77] Summarized from *Pwyll Prince of Dyved*, *Mab.*, I, 4–16.

[78] These are the famous *cwn Annwn*, "dogs of hell," which have red ears or red spots (J. Rhŷs, *Celtic Folklore, Welsh and Manx* [Oxford University Press, 1901], I, 215–216). The red is, I think, a sign that they belong to the red tower of the dead. Gringuljete, Gawain's horse that belonged to the Grail castle, and was doubtless an otherworld beast, had red ears (p. 185). In the ninth-century *Táin Bó Fráich*, the *fée* BéFind gave her son cows that were white with red ears (ed. Mary E. Byrne and Myles Dillon, *Med. and Mod. Irish Ser.*, V [Dublin, 1933], l. 6).

you shall give him he shall not survive, and, though he ask
you to give him a second stroke, give it not. I gave him one.
Nevertheless he fought with me next day as well as before." [79]
Pwyll agrees to this and goes to Annwn in Arawn's shape,
where he takes his place beside a queen of wonderful beauty.
At night, however, he always turns from her and lets her
alone. "Of all the courts of the earth that he had seen, this
was the best supplied with food and drink and vessels of gold."
When the day appointed for the combat is at hand the fairy
hosts assemble. A horseman makes this announcement: "It is
between two kings that this appointment is, and that between
their two bodies. And both are claimants against the other,
and that for land and soil. And you can all stand aside, and
leave it between those two alone." The two kings fight in a
ford and Pwyll gives to Hafgan one deadly stroke and no
more (*p*). Afterwards he reexchanges with Arawn, "who
gives to Pwyll his own form and semblance, and he also takes
his own form and semblance." Then Pwyll returns to Dyfed.

K. PWYLL AND RHIANNON

(*jmnpr*) [80]

Pwyll visits the top of a mound called Gorsedd Arberth, concerning which the tradition is that if a nobleman sits there he
will either receive blows or see a prodigy. He has no sooner
sat down than he sees a lady riding past on a white horse
with a garment of shining gold silk upon her. As no one can
tell who she is, he despatches one of his followers to pursue
her. After a chase on foot the man returns, saying that he
cannot overtake her. Pwyll gives him the swiftest horse he
has, but the man is even then unsuccessful. "There must be
some kind of illusion there."

[79] The yearly battle here suggested might have something to do with
the ritual games mentioned above (p. 33). It is plain that Arawn needs
the help of a mortal hero.

[80] Summarized from *Mab.*, I, 16–29.

The next day Pwyll returns to the mound. Again he sees the lady. Again he despatches a mounted servant, and again pursuit is unsuccessful. The third day Pwyll himself mounts on a swift steed and pursues the lady. Finding himself unable to gain on her, he exclaims, "For the sake of the man you love best, stay for me." At this she stops and waits for him to come up. She is the most beautiful lady Pwyll has ever seen (*j*). She tells him she came solely for love of him. She is Rhiannon, who, at the end of a year, is to be married to Gwawl, a suitor whom she detests (*m*). She will marry no one unless it be Pwyll. At her suggestion, Pwyll promises to come at the end of a year to fight Gwawl and rescue her for himself.

At the appointed day (*n*) Pwyll comes and is received by Rhiannon at a feast. But an unknown petitioner comes in to ask a boon. Pwyll rashly promises him whatever he shall desire. He asks for Rhiannon. It is Gwawl, who has disguised himself in rags in order to trick Pwyll. Pwyll's princely honor keeps him from breaking his word once given, and he hands Rhiannon over to Gwawl. However, she persuades Gwawl to depart for a year's time, and before sending Pwyll away she gives him a magic bag and instructs him how to entrap his hated rival.

At the end of a year the two suitors return to Rhiannon and Pwyll entraps Gwawl in the bag. His enemy once in the bag, Pwyll blows his horn. His warriors, who are in ambush without, enter and seize all who attempt to resist. Each warrior as he passes deals a blow at the bag (*p*). At length, to escape the punishment of the bag, Gwawl agrees to leave Pwyll in possession of Rhiannon (*r*).

The next stories are from the *Acallam na Senórach*, which did not take shape till toward 1200,[81] but which nobody supposes to be influenced in any way by French romance.

[81] Thurneysen, *Heldensage*, p. 48, and E. Gwynn, *Ériu*, X (1926), 74–75.

A sign of its later origin is that the differentiation between Tuatha Dé and Fomorians is breaking down. This distinction between hostile Fomorians and friendly Tuatha Dé has been so far everywhere observed, unless Manannán's troops fighting on the hostile side in the *Serglige* be an exception.[82] In the *Acallam*, however, the Tuatha Dé are commonly hostile to Finn, and act like Fomorians. Both Aillén in M and Bodb Derg in O behave as if they had taken over the rôles of Fomorians. The probable explanation is that by the time the *Acallam* was composed Ireland had been for centuries Christian. The Tuatha Dé, it was said, had retired beneath hills or lakes. They were, therefore, easily confused with Fomorians.[83] According to *CMT*, Tuatha Dé and Fomorians intermarried, and could not therefore have been thought of as very different from each other.

The next story is primitive in putting the *fée* in control of the action; and perhaps the test proposed by her to a wooer, namely, that he compose a poem descriptive of her palace, may also be old.[84]

L. CRÉDE, DAUGHTER OF CAIRBRE
(*gikl*) [85]

Cael ua Nemnainn, the hundred-slayer, is warned that of all Ireland's women Créde is the arch-deceiver, and is told of the

[82] Page 22.

[83] See A. H. Krappe, "Lancelot et Guenièvre," *Rev. celt.*, XLVIII (1931), 109 f.

[84] Compare in Cormac's *Glossary* (*Anecdota*, IV, 90, s.v. *prúll*), where an old woman, who is evidently a *fée*, tests visitors by requiring them to match a half-quatrain. The *prúll* story is outlined and discussed by Kittredge in *Gawain*, p. 276.

[85] Summarized from the *Acallam* (ed. Stokes and Windisch, *Ir. Texte*,

test which she proposes.[86] He has been brought up, however, in the Brug *Braenach*, "Fort Perilous" [which is probably the same as Brug mac ind Oc], by a fairy foster-mother who has supplied him with the poem needed for this adventure. Cael and his followers reach Créde's palace at Loch Cuire near the hills called the Paps of Ana, and they make the *dórd fiansa* (a song) before the door. Golden-haired girls appear at balconies, and Créde, accompanied by one hundred and fifty women, comes forth.[87] Cael passes the required test by reciting his poem. He and his company are entertained, and Créde grants him her love.

Cael's poem runs in substance as follows: Yellow-haired Créde has a bower of silver and yellow gold with a roof of birds' wings. Her couch is of gold made by Tuile [88] in the east, and has curtains running upon copper rods (*k*). Fairy birds on the eaves furnish sleep-giving music. Her house is a hundred feet from corner to corner. Each couch has four posts with a precious stone (*l*) at the head of every post. There is a *dabach*, "vat," of bronze containing mead (*g*), and an apple tree from which four apples fall at once into a horn.[89] Four retainers serve every four guests with mead from the horn and with an apple apiece (*i*).

IV, i, ll. 744–868). A translation is in S. H. O'Grady, *Silva Gadelica* (London, 1892), II, 119 f.

[86] Gawain was warned in this way about Orguelleuse (*Perceval*, vss. 6752 f.).

[87] This is a Castle of Maidens like Blancheflor's in *Perceval* (p. 127).

[88] Tuile is probably the same as the smith Trebuchet in *Perceval*, vs. 3679 (see p. 132).

[89] This horn is probably square, so that an apple may fall into each corner of it. Créde's palace is square, like the Grail castle. Her service of four guests by four retainers is exactly like the Grail feast in Wolfram, *Parzival*, vss. 237, 1 f. (see p. 182).

M. Aillén mac Midhna
(np) [90]

For twenty-three years on every Hallowe'en, Aillén of the Tuatha Dé, with fire from his mouth, burns up Tara, the royal city (n). At last Finn by the aid of a talismanic spear and mantle overcomes, slays him, and puts his head on a stake outside the city (p).

Aillén's mother comes and calls for a physician, apparently to restore Aillén to life: "Come hither, O she-physician of Amairtha. By Fiacha mac Congha's spear, by the fatal mantle, and by the pointed javelin, Aillén is slain."

In this story Finn, a youth brought up in the wilderness by a foster-mother and equipped with a magic spear with which he slays Aillén is a remarkable parallel to Perceval.[91] This story, by locating fairyland (Castle of Maidens) at Tara invites the question, Where is fairyland? The Irish believed that it was Ireland of long ago. When the sons of Míl, who were hostile, and who took over the rôle of Fomorians, invaded the island, the fairies withdrew under ground or under water. The early history of Ireland (LG) is invented out of battles fought between fairies (Tuatha Dé) and Fomorians. Both LG and CMT picture the fairy king Nuadu as reigning at Tara. The Welsh too believed that Britain long ago in the golden age of King Arthur was fairyland. They called it Lloegr (Logres). In G, inasmuch as Kulhwch visits Arthur, fairyland is doubtless Britain. In the Irish stories I, L, O, and P, fairyland, although underground in hollow hills, is Ireland. In R, fairyland, as here, seems to be Ireland. The upshot of the matter is that fairy-

---

[90] Summarized from the *Acallam*, ll. 1654–1771; *Silva Gadelica*, II, 142.   [91] See A. C. L. Brown, *Mod. Phil.*, XVIII (1920), 205 f.

land is either Ireland or Britain of long ago. It is a part of this belief that fairies are not seen today because they have hidden themselves under lakes or in hollow hills.

It is probable that Aillén's true name was Aed, "fire"; that he is said to be of the Tuatha Dé by some mistake; and that he was in origin a red Fomorian. I infer this because *Macgnímartha Finn* calls him Aed,[92] because he fights with fire, which marks him as a red warrior, and because, like the Red Knight in the English *Sir Perceval*, he has a witch-mother. The mother here seeks for a *banliaigh*, "woman-physician," apparently, like the mother in *Sir Perceval*, with the hope of restoring her son to life.

N.   Dáirenn, Daughter of Bodb Derg [93]

Dressed in a green mantle, sitting on a rock by a ford, Dáirenn seeks the love of Finn. When refused, she gives him mead out of a white silver cup which intoxicates him for the rest of the day and makes him fight against his own companions, who scatter in terror. Cailte finally calms them, saying that Finn's behavior is due "to a cozening fairy woman's mischief."

This malicious *fée* called Dáirenn is a striking parallel to the hateful Orguelleuse of AA.[94]

O.   Sliab na mBan: Hill of the Women
(imn) [95]

In a snowstorm in a forest on Sliab na mBan, Finn and six of his warriors lose track of a fawn which they are hunting. Having lost their way, they find shelter in a palace with a crystal floor, where they are feasted by twenty-eight war-

[92] *Ériu*, I (1904), 188.
[93] Summarized from the *Acallam*, ll. 4940–4979; *Silva Gadelica*, II, 221.   [94] Page 136.
[95] Summarized from the *Acallam*, ll. 5005–5370; *Silva Gadelica*, II, 222 f.

riors, each with a lovely damsel at his side. Six damsels entertain the visitors with food and with drink from many goblets,
horns, and cups (*i*), while another damsel plays the harp
[Castle of Maidens]. In reply to Finn's question as to who
they are, the warriors tell him that they are sons to Midir
the yellow-haired, and to Findchaem, the daughter of the
King of Síd Monad. Donn the eldest warrior says, "We have
had three battles against the forces of Bodb Derg (*m*) and
tomorrow another battle is appointed (*n*). We sent yonder
bare-headed woman in the shape of a fawn to lead you here
because we need your help."

Finn and his companions spend a year in this palace and
fight three battles against Bodb Derg and his followers of the
Tuatha Dé. They are helped by a fairy physician who can
cure dreadfully wounded men. King Cormac, having noticed
Finn's long absence from Tara, arises one day at a feast and
inquires whether any have tidings of the lost warriors. However, after more than a year spent at Sliab na mBan, Finn returns to Tara.[96]

In this story Bodb *Derg*, "red," acts like a Fomorian.
Perhaps his epithet "red" led to his being transformed into a
Fomorian just as the name *Aed*, "fire," in the preceding
story probably led to Aillén's becoming a Fomorian. Here
Bodb Derg's dwelling would be a Dolorous Tower.

P. Étáin Fairhair
(*agr*) [97]

Étáin Fairhair, daughter of Aed Whitebreast, King of the
Elfmound of Ben Etair (Howth) falls in love with Oscar and
sends Bé-mannair, daughter of Aingcél, a *banechlach*, "woman-

---

[96] In *Perceval* (ed. Hilka, vs. 4136), Arthur under similar circumstances
asks for news about Perceval.

[97] Summarized from the *Acallam*, ll. 5638–5724; a translation is on
p. 227 of the same volume.

messenger," and a shape-shifter, to lure Oscar and his followers to Ben Etair (*a*). Bé-mannair appears to Oscar and his followers and proposes a footrace. In this way she entices twenty hundred of them to Étáin's elf mound at Ben Etair [Castle of Maidens]. Here they are entertained, bathed, and feasted by King Aed (*g*). Oscar marries Étáin (*r*), and she bears him three sons: Luath, Indell, and Oscar.

The supremacy of the *fée* is here plainly marked. As in A and I there is no adversary who must be conquered.

Q. BéBind, Daughter of Trén

(*fho*) [98]

Fairyland consists of two separate kingdoms. The kingdom of the *fées* is Tír na n-Ingen, "Land of Maidens" [Castle of Maidens] and the nearest country to it is Tír na Fer, "land of men" [Dolorous Tower]. The two kingdoms are so named because Trén, king of the Land of Maidens (*h*), has one hundred and forty-nine daughters, of whom BéBind is one, and only three sons; whereas Cétach Crobderg, the king of the Land of Men (*f*), has one hundred and sixty sons and but one daughter.[99] BéBind has been given three times in marriage to Aed Alaind, one of the sons of Cétach, and is running away to escape him. As she is crossing the sea, she meets three fishermen [100] who suggest that she go to Ireland and ask for Finn's protection. BéBind reaches the shore of Ireland in safety and puts herself under Finn's protection. A giant, however, arrives from the sea, slays BéBind, and departs before anyone can stop him. The giant is BéBind's detested suitor Aed Alaind.

[98] Summarized from the *Acallam*, ll. 5916–6082; *Silva Gadelica*, II, 238.

[99] Perhaps this separation of men and women is a hint that it is the land of death that is meant (see p. 139).

[100] Certain manuscripts of *LG* tell of three fishermen coming from Spain to Ireland (p. 249). Spain is a name for the land of the dead. The three fishermen both in *LG* and here are, I conjecture, the triform god Brión.

In this story BéBind, "white woman," is a *fée*, and Cétach *Crobderg*, "hundred-fighter, red-handed" (*o*), a Fomorian. Cétach's son is *Aed*, "fire," a name perhaps referring to the red color of the Fomorians. The picture of Aed arriving suddenly and slaying BéBind is a picture, I think, of Death coming suddenly and seizing his victim.

R. BéBind, Daughter of Elcmar
(*ghimnp*) [101]

Aed Minbrecc of the Tuatha Dé is king of the *síd*, "elf mound," at Assaroe, and his queen is BéBind, "white woman," daughter of Elcmar of the Brug.[102] Their enemies are Garb *mac Tairb*, "rough son of bull," of Lochlann, his brother Eolas, "knowledge," and a *bangaisccedach*, "woman-warrior," named BéDreccain, "she-dragon," [103] daughter of Iruaith, who come every third year (l. 6857), or every seventh year (l. 7267), with an army across the sea to attack the Tuatha Dé (*m*).

Cailte, who has been wounded by Mane, son of the King of Lochlann, has learned that only BéBind can cure him, and sets out with his friend Cass Corach to find her. They arrive first at Síd Duma, where they are welcomed by Fer-Maisse, "man-of-beauty," who comes out in a green mantle and is found to be Cass Corach's own brother.[104] Then they enter the *síd*,

[101] Summarized from the *Acallam*, ll. 6802–7283 and pp. 254–258; *Silva Gadelica*, II, 247–254.

[102] Since the Brug is the immemorial home of the Dagda and his caldron, we are not surprised to learn that BéBind has "the remnant of the Tuatha Dé Danann's drink of healing, and of Goibniu's ale," and that "it was she that distributed the drink to the Tuatha Dé." Clearly this is a way of saying that she has the unfailing caldron. The enemies of the Tuatha Dé are evidently Fomorians, and Lochlann is not Norway but the land of the dead (p. 66).

[103] A "knight of the dragon" plays a similar rôle in Gerbert's continuation of *Perceval* (ed. Mary Williams [Paris, 1922–1925], vss. 8979 f.).

[104] Cass Corach is a fairy helper like Laeg in C (p. 19).

where they are greeted by its ruler Fergus *Foltfind*, "fair hair," a son of the Dagda. Fergus brings to Cailte the broken weapons of the Tuatha Dé: a sword named *Crocosccur*, "blood of mangling," a spear named *Ben Bodbda*, "warlike woman," and a javelin named *Deoghbais*, "drink of death." Cailte repairs the sword, adjusts the spear to its spearhead, and, after breaking seven shafts, fits the barbed javelin-head to a shaft. Fergus now tells Cailte that it is in the prophecies that BéDreccain shall die by the sword, one of two attacking kings by the javelin, and Garb by the spear. "It was my fate," says Cailte, "to do some deed for which the men of Erin, and Alba, and the Tuatha Dé would be thankful. Who knows but my fate is that I should do it today?" [105]

Cailte and Cass Corach, after a stay of three days, tell their host Fergus of their wish to find BéBind; Fer Maisse offers to accompany them to BéBind's home, the *síd* of Assaroe (*h*). When they arrive they find, in front of the *síd*, Aed and Ilbrecc, who welcome them. "Dear to us is this welcome," says Cailte. Presently BéBind comes to them out of the *síd*, surrounded by her one hundred and fifty fair ladies. To Cass Corach and to Fer Maisse she gives three loving kisses, and sits down on the turfed mound. Cailte and his companions are then entertained at a feast in the *síd* (*gi*) [Castle of Maidens].

On the third day the enemies, Garb, Eolus, and BéDreccain, come across the sea in ships and attack the *síd* (*n*). In the ensuing battle Cailte slays Garb with the spear; Cass Corach kills BéDreccain with the sword; and Fer Maisse pierces Eolus with the javelin (*p*). Cailte, Fer Maisse, and Cass Corach, after having thus delivered the Tuatha Dé from their enemies, free them also from three evil birds that are set upon them

---

[105] So Gawain and Perceval do not know that there is any test till they have been given the broken sword to mend. Like Cailte, Perceval is a destined hero. On the parallel to Chrétien's *Perceval* see Dr. Walter Pennington, "An Irish Parallel to the Broken Sword of the Grail Castle," *MLN*, XLIII (1928), 534–536.

from Benn Boirche. As a reward for his efforts, Cailte is cured
of his wound by BéBind. At parting she gives him a *léne*,
"shirt," which has magic power to prevent his ever being
opposed; a fringed crimson *brat*, "mantle," from Tír Tairngire
"Land of Promise"; and a *duban*, "fishhook," that always
catches a fish.

This is the only Irish or Welsh story that resembles the
Grail legend in introducing a broken sword. It agrees with
M and with *LG* in identifying fairyland with Ireland. Perhaps it resembles French romances a little more than the
other Irish stories because it is later, and exhibits a stage of
development that Irish stories had reached just at the time
when they most influenced Welsh and French romances.
It seems, however, to be free from influences coming from
French romances. The Dolorous Tower, which is not mentioned in this story, would be in Lochlann, the country
from which Garb, Eolas, and BéDreccain come.

S. Echtra Airt ocus Tochmarc Delbchaime: Adventures of Art and the Wooing of Delbchaem

(*abcfghimpr*) [106]

Art, son of the King of Ireland, is visited by a fairy woman
named Bécuma, who puts a *geis*, "magic injunction," upon him
to search for Delbchaem, "fair form," daughter of Morgan
(*a*). Art sets out on his expedition; at Inber Colptha, "Boyne
mouth," he finds a ship (*b*) and travels in it from island to
island till he comes to a beautiful land full of apples, birds, and
flowers. Here is a hospitable house thatched with bird-wings

[106] Summarized from the edition and translation by R. I. Best from
the Book of Fermoy, a fifteenth-century manuscript (*Ériu*, III (1907),
150–173). *Echtra Airt* is in list B, and is therefore substantially as old
as the twelfth century. On list B of Irish "prime tales" see Thurneysen,
Heldensage, pp. 23–24.

in which is a company of women with Creide *Firalaind,* "truly beautiful," daughter of Fidech Long-Haired at their head (*hj*). When he has declared that he is Art, son of the King of Ireland, Creide puts on him a variegated mantle adorned with gold and tells him that his coming has long been decreed (*g*). She welcomes him to her palace, which has doors of crystal and inexhaustible vats (*i*) [Castle of Maidens]. She tells him how to find Delbchaem, daughter of Morgan, and about the dangers of the journey. Creide's two sisters, Finscoth and Aeb, are at Morgan's *dún* (*m*).

Art sails over sea and traverses a forest where there are seven hags and a bath of melted lead prepared for him. He passes a forked glen full of toads, encounters lions lying in wait (*c*), crosses a narrow bridge over an icy river, and slays by a pillar-stone a giant named Curnan Cliabsalach, who is son to Duscad, "wakeful," Morgan's doorkeeper. Next he overcomes Ailill Black Teeth and cuts off his head. He forces Ailill's wife to tell him the way to Morgan's *dún* which is in the land of wonders. In the land of wonders he encounters Coinchend *Cendfada,* "long head," Morgan's wife, who is daughter of Concruth, King of the *Coinchind,* "dogheads." She has arranged all these dangers: the hags, the bath of lead, the toads, the mountain full of lions, the icy bridge, Curnan, and Ailill, in order to slay Art. Morgan's *dún* has a palisade of bronze adorned with heads (*f*). Delbchaem is in a "bright shining bower set on a pillar." Art slays Coinchend, puts her head on the one stake which is vacant in the palisade, and possesses himself of her daughter Delbchaem. Later he slays Morgan and brings away Delbchaem with much gold and silver to Tara (*pr*).

Coinchend belongs to the Dogheads who were, in Irish fabulous history (*LG*) evil giants, and who were identical or were confused with Fomorians.[107] The heroine, Delbchaem,

[107] Page 20.

could not have been at first a daughter of the Doghead, Coinchend, and the giant, Morgan. She is a *fée* whom the giants have imprisoned and she is glad to have Art carry her away. She and Creide are evidently companion-*fées*, like Fann and Líban in C. Creide helps Art in his rescue of Delbchaem. Her two sisters, Finscoth and Aeb, are in Morgan's *dún*, probably as prisoners. In this story types I and II are confused, but in any case it contains successive incidents of the Journey to Fairyland. The toads signify the land of the grave. The lions near a bridge are, I think, a trace of Cerberus and the Bridge of Dread. The palisade of human heads on pikes here, as in H, marks a Dolorous Tower or Castle of Death.

T. Echtra Thaidg mheic Chéin:
Adventures of Teigue son of Cian
(*befghijklmpr*) [108]

Cathmann, son of Tabarn and king of the Allmarach, "oversea folk," who lives in the beautiful land of Fresen to the southeast near Spain [evidently the island of the dead for which Spain is a common term], makes a raid upon Munster and carries off Teigue's wife Líban, daughter of Conor Redbrows, and his two brothers, Airnelach and Eoghan. Teigue fights with the Allmarach and manages not only to save himself and forty of his men, but to capture one man of the Allmarach. With the captive as a guide, they pursue Cathmann. They build a ship and sail upon the western ocean (*b*).

The first island to which they come contains monstrous sheep, and the second, strange birds. After a six weeks' voyage, they land at a beautiful island where there are trees bearing

[108] My summary is based on an edition from the Book of Lismore, a fifteenth-century manuscript, and a translation by O'Grady, *Silva Gadelica*, text, I, 342–359; translation, II, 385–401.

wonderful fruits upon which feed birds that sing marvelous melodies. They march over a wide smooth plain (e) till they see three hills, each crowned with a fortress.

In the first fortress, which is of marble, they find the fairest of the world's women, Gothnia's daughter, wife of Sláinghe (j). She tells Teigue that in this fort dwell all Ireland's kings, from Heremon, son of Milesius, to Conn of the hundred battles. The country's name is Inis Locha, "lake island." Two kings, Ruadrach and Dergcroiche, sons of Bodhb, reign over it.

In the second fortress, which is golden in color, they find Cessair, daughter of Bethra son of Noah. She informs Teigue that his coming has been foretold. She is the first woman who came to Ireland before the Flood, with three men, Bith, Fintan, and Ladra. They are all here in eternal life. The country's name is Inis Derglocha, "red lake island," because of a red lake in it containing an island which is enclosed by a palisade of gold and is called the Isle of Patmos, in which are all the saints and righteous. This is the earth's fourth paradise, the other three being Inis Daleb in the south of the world, Inis Escandra in the north, and Adam's Paradise. Adam's seed that are righteous dwell in this fourth paradise.

In the third fortress, which has a silver rampart, they find Veniusa, and with her a youth feasting on a golden apple (h). The youth is Connla, son of Conn, and she is the damsel of many charms that brought him hither. They two spend their time admiring each other but are guilty of no impurity.[109] Nearby is a vast house with a silver floor and four doors [110] of bright gold (k). It is illuminated by gems of crystal and carbuncle (l), and it is the destined abode of the Christian kings of Ireland. Beside it is an apple tree having both blossoms and ripe fruit. Here they meet Clídna Cheinnfionn, "fair head," daughter of Gennan mac Treon of the Tuatha Dé, who

[109] This is perhaps a hint that it is the land of the dead, where the sexes are separated.
[110] This is a cosmic palace with four doors facing the four winds.

is the sweetheart of Ciabhan.[111] She bestows on Teigue three birds that accompany him and furnish marvelous music.[112] She also gives him a cup that will turn water into wine, and talismanic armor (gi). She foretells to Teigue that, whenever he shall lose the cup, he will die and come thither to dwell with her. On the departure of Teigue and his troop she asks how long it seems that they have stayed. "One day," they answer. She tells them it has been a whole year.

Teigue and his followers continue their voyage in search of the island of Fresen. Clídna's birds sing for them on the way, and, as they look back, the land is hidden by a magic veil. After a day and a half on the sea, they come to the land of Fresen. Here Teigue, exploring, encounters his brother Eogan employed in ferrying visitors across an arm of the sea to a dún in which are the king of Fresen, and Cathmann.[113] Eogan tells him that their brother Airneluch is here as a slave and gathers firewood, and that Teigue's wife is Cathmann's prisoner (m). She has demanded a respite of one year from Cathmann, which expires that night. Two sons of Cathmann, Eochaid Airmderg, "red arm," and Tuire Tortbhuilleach, "of ponderous blows," will take sides with Teigue and attack Cathmann's dún (f).[114] The king has with him in his dún

---

[111] Clídna is sweetheart of Ciabhan in the Acallam, ll. 3833 f. (translated in Silva Gadelica, II, 201). Her story in the Dinnshenchas of Tonn Clídna (edited by Stokes from LL, in Rev. celt., XV [1894], 437) runs as follows: "Clídna, daughter of Genann son of Trén, went out of Tulach dá Roth, 'Hill of Two Wheels,' out of Mag Mell in Tir Tairngire with Iuchna Curly Locks to get to the Mac ind Óc. Iuchna practiced guile upon her. He played music to her in the nai creduma, 'boat of bronze,' wherein she lay, so that she slept thereat, and then he turned her back to Clídna where she was drowned by the Wave of Clídna."

[112] These birds, like the three birds in Branwen (Mab., I, 67), are doubtless a manifestation of Brión. So are three fishermen met on the sea by BéBind (p. 80).

[113] Eogan, who is here a Hospitable Host, plays the rôle of Charon.

[114] So, in G, Custennin helped against his brother the giant. The king here does nothing. The action is managed by his "brother," Cath-

Illann *Aithesach*, "exultant," his only son, and Conan *Codait-chenn*, "hardheaded," chief of his household.

Teigue now brings his troop from the ship and together they storm the *dún*. Eogan and Conan slay each other, likewise Tuire and Illann. Nothing is said about the king. Teigue finally slays Cathmann and cuts off his head (*p*). He establishes Eochaid *Airmderg* son of Cathmann as king of Fresen, and returns to Ireland bringing home in triumph his two brothers and Líban, "splendor of women," his wife (*r*).

The author of this story was influenced by vision-literature and doubtless from such sources derived his Biblical and classical names: Noah, Adam, Patmos, Venusia. He appears, however, to be untouched by influences coming from French romance, and the general plan of his story at least is Irish. Fairyland is explicitly identified with the land of the dead. Teigue is told by Clídna that, after his death, he shall come to dwell with her. Teigue's brother plays the part of Charon conveying visitors in a boat to Cathmann's *dún*, which is surely a Dolorous Tower.

Echtra Thaidg is too recent to be substantial evidence for the existence of any particular motive in Ireland before the time of Chrétien. It is outlined here merely as an illustration of a scenario which has been based upon older Irish stories.

The twenty stories summarized above, no two of which conform to quite the same pattern, corroborate the motives of our scenario.[115] In the summaries each motive is

---

mann, and at the end the king is forgotten. Cathmann is slain. Why is not the king also slain? Possibly because the king is Death in person. The king and Cathmann make a pair that resembles Conaing and his seneschal Morc, Donn and his seneschal Amargen (see p. 386).

[115] Page 25.

marked at every occurrence by a parenthesized letter, so that anyone who has traced a letter through this chapter has obtained a conspectus of the evidence on that motive. It remains to sum up the evidence upon two controversial motives.

Confusion between Fairyland and the Land of the Dead

In E (p. 48) "the beast like a lion," and the "rope bridge" and in G (p. 61) the giant porter, Custennin, who collects payment and his huge dog, are pretty surely modifications of Cerberus, the Bridge of Dread, and Charon. In G are "corpses coming in" (p. 61). In H "toads and serpents" (p. 68), and in J the dogs of Annwn (p. 72) indicate the Land of Death. In S (p. 84) the lion and the bridge occur again, and in T (p. 87) we are told that the dead come to this land.

Since confusion with the land of the dead is apparent in E,[116] and many later stories, it probably existed already in A. In A the fairies are "Tethra's people" (p. 41). Tethra is a Fomorian, a hostile giant, and seems to be a ruler of the unhappy dead. By calling the *fées* "Tethra's people" the text suggests that in this, our oldest Journey to Fairyland story, confusion with the land of the dead was already present. In any case this confusion arose long before Chrétien.

Red and the Tower of the Dead

In E (p. 50) the adversary is named Cochor, "red." In H (p. 67) the fort of "shadow land," which, because defended by toads and serpents, is surely a castle of the dead,

[116] Written before 1050 (Thurneysen, *Heldensage*, pp. 382, 667).

is said to be "of a hateful color." This "hateful color" must be red, which as we know, for example, from the *Aeneid* (p. 16) was the traditional color of those belonging to the tower of the dead. In J (p. 72) the dogs of Annwn have red ears, doubtless as a sign that they come from the tower of the dead. In M (p. 77) the giant who fights with fire has for one of his names *Aed*, "fire"; in O the adversary is Bodb the red; and in Q the adversary is Cétach *Crobderg*, "red hand" (pp. 79, 80). It is possible, though by no means certain, that *forderg*, "very red" in C (p. 18), is a reference to the red color of those who hail from the land of the dead.

Having established our scenario upon a solid basis of ancient Irish and Welsh documents, our next concern is with the French romances. Since Chrétien is the author of the oldest French romances about King Arthur that have come down to us, any attempt to explain the origin of Arthurian romance must center round these. All others are later and may be influenced by his. The task before us is to search for the scenario of a Journey to Fairyland in Chrétien's romances.

CHAPTER III

Four Marvelous Episodes in Chrétien's Early Romances

BY a study of the *Serglige ConCulainn* a rather full scenario of an ancient Irish Journey to Fairyland has been established.[1] From the twenty stories summaried above it appears that the topography of fairyland includes two castles, a Dolorous Tower or castle of giants and a Castle of Maidens or *fées*. Reserving *Perceval* for a later chapter, let us examine the marvelous incidents in Chrétien's earlier romances to find out whether they conform to the Celtic scenario. In particular, in every story which is summarized from Chrétien, a Dolorous Tower and a Castle of Maidens will be sought for.

No startling resemblances between Chrétien's romances and Irish stories are to be anticipated. Chrétien, no doubt, has changed nearly all his stories into type III (Enchanted Princess)[2] and has explained all marvels as a result of enchantment; his aim was to adapt his stories to the sophisticated taste of twelfth-century France. Under these conditions parallels between Irish stories and Chrétien's romances are not obvious but must be arrived at by study.

In the following summaries the occurrence of any of the twenty motives from the scenario[3] is indicated by a parenthesized small letter, so that the reader may easily examine

[1] Page 24.　　　　[2] Page 31.　　　　[3] Page 25.

the evidence. The four marvelous incidents are as follows: U, La Joie de la cort, *Erec*, vss. 5367–6410 [4] (*c.* 1168); V, *Lancelot*, the main plot (*c.* 1172); W, *Yvain*, the main plot (*c.* 1173); X, Pesme Avanture, *Yvain*, vss. 5107–5770 (*c.* 1173).

U. LA JOIE DE LA CORT
(*bghjnopt*)

The adventure called the Joy of the Court is the most dangerous in the world, and, for seven years, none has returned from it. The scene of the adventure is Brandigan, an island city surrounded by a deep, swiftly rushing river (*b*).

As Erec rides along the street, the people of Brandigan deride him. Evrain, king of Brandigan, entertains him and his company at supper (*b*).[5] (No heroine is mentioned.) They have in abundance all that heart desires: birds, venison, fruit, and wines of different kinds (*g*). (Talismans are not mentioned.)

Whoever undertakes the Joy of the Court adventure must fight an unknown antagonist. The battle takes place the next day in a garden which through enchantment (*nigromance*, vs. 5742) is enclosed by a wall of air that prevents anything from entering, just as if it were a wall of iron; here birds sing; here flowers and ripe fruits are found in winter time; whoever attempts to carry away any of the fruit can find no exit.[6]

---

[4] References are to editions by W. Foerster. The dates are those usually given, but see U. T. Holmes, *Old French Literature*, p. 167.

[5] Brandigan here represents the Castle of Maidens. In Wolfram's *Parzival* (vs. 220, 9) Brandigan is the chief city of Iserterre (isles de terre), the land of Clâmide, who is cousin to Mabonagrain. Clâmide is, I think, the Irish Fomorian giant, Galam (see p. oo).

[6] The garden here represents a Dolorous Tower and perhaps the reference to "a wall of iron" is a trace of a former iron tower. The danger of a theft from fairyland is in *Imram Maeile Dúin*, § 11 (p. 273).

Through a narrow entrance King Evrain, his people, and all Erec's company enter the garden. They see a row of pikes upon which are impaled heads with helmets on them. Upon the one stake which is vacant hangs a horn (*n*).

Erec goes on alone down a path without companion of any sort till he comes to a girl of marvelous beauty (*j*) reclining on a silver couch beneath the shade of a sycamore tree. As Erec approaches he is attacked by a red giant of a man (*o*), a foot taller than any knight Erec has ever seen. They fight, first on horseback, then on foot; the red knight is conquered. He then tells Erec that the beautiful girl on the couch had made him promise never to leave the garden till some knight should come and conquer him at arms (*p*). "She intended to keep me absolutely shut up with her all the days of my life (*t*). These helmets belong to those that I have put to death. I am called Mabonagrain. Now blow that horn, for then you will release me and the joy will begin." The girl is unhappy at Mabonagrain's defeat, but is soon cheered by Enide, Erec's wife, whom she learns is her cousin.

Brandigan, the seat of Evrain's castle, is an island surrounded by a deep, rushing river. This is no ordinary stream. In V the corresponding river is:

> Roide et bruiant, noire et espesse,
> Si leide et si espoantable
> Con se fust li fluns au deable.
> (*Lancelot*, vss. 3024-3026)

In Z the river outside the Grail castle is called:

> L'eve roide et parfonde.
> (*Perceval*, vs. 2988)

In the eight-century *Echtra Nerai* (ed. K. Meyer, *Rev. celt.*, X [1889], 221 f.) summer fruits are brought out of a *sid*.

In AA the river before Chastel Merveilleus is:

> une riviere parfonde
> Et si lee que nule fonde
> De mangonel ne de perriere
> Ne gitast outre la riviere,
> Ne arbaleste n'i treisist.
>
> (*Perceval*, vss. 7227–7231)

Many Irish stories mention no river,[7] but picture fairyland as an island in the ocean. H. R. Patch has argued that this river and the bridge that often accompanies it are oriental material that has been worked over by the Irish.[8] He is probably right. The important point is that both river and bridge, whatever their origin, came to Chrétien from Celtic sources; they existed in Irish story before his time.

The oldest or eleventh-century version of *Tochmarc Emire*, E, by its mention of a ship, and of a rope bridge that must be crossed to reach Scathach's house, implies that the place is cut off by some sort of river.[9] To prove that this river was in Irish before the time of Chrétien we do not need, therefore, the testimony of the twelfth-century version which explains that Scathach's house was on an island and could be reached only by the Bridge of the Fosterlings.[10]

[7] Pages 39, 17, 56, 69, 80, 83, 85.

[8] "Some Elements in Mediaeval Descriptions of the Otherworld," *PMLA*, XXXIII (1918), 631 f.

[9] *Tochmarc Emire*, ed. Kuno Meyer, *Rev. celt.*, XI (1890), 446: "Asbert fris bui glend mar ar a chind. Oentet cael tairiss, noch ba si a chonair do thig Scathchai." "There was a great glen before him. One narrow rope across it, yet that was the way to Scathach's house."

[10] *Tochmarc Emire*, ed. A. G. Van Hamel, *Compert ConCulainn and Other Stories*, Med. and Mod. Irish Ser., III (Dublin, 1933), 49, § 67. M. B. Ogle ("The Perilous Bridge and Human Automata," *MLN*, XXXV [1920], 136) tried to argue that the twelfth-century version, which is

It is justifiable to regard this river in *Erec* as the boundary of fairyland. It is in origin, no doubt, the boundary of the land of the dead. In *Lancelot*, V, the corresponding stream is called, "li fluns au deable." [11] In Gerbert's *Continuation of Perceval* the Pui de Montesclaire, which the context proves to be fairyland, is "beyond the river Gordane." [12] This name shows that a contemporary knew the boundary of fairyland was the same as the river of death (Jordan).

Feeble bridges over a terrible stream in E, S, U, V, and Y [13] are clearly forms of the Bridge of Dread, well known in visions of hell and paradise. The lion or lions near this bridge in E, S, and V, and other hostile beasts in otherworld journeys go back, I suppose, to Cerberus for their origin. [14]

In V the lions that Lancelot imagined that he saw at the end of the sword bridge are, as Gaston Paris long ago observed, [15] the same beasts as those that in *Visio Tnugdali* [16] waited in the water below the Bridge of Dread to devour unfortunate souls that fell off. Lancelot found that these beasts were only phantoms, just as Hercules, when he visited Hades, drew his sword against Medusa but was told by Hermes that she was only a phantom. [17] The boatman

---

unique in mentioning the Bridge of the Fosterlings, might be later than Chrétien. This is impossible; Thurneysen (*Heldensage*, p. 382) puts the date of this version, which he calls "III," about 1150.

[11] Verse 3026.

[12] Edition Mary Williams, vs. 9306.

[13] Pages 49, 84, 92, 101, 127.

[14] In Roman times the middle head of Cerberus was that of a lion (M. Landau, *Hölle und Fegefeuer*, p. 71; see also his chap. iv).

[15] *Romania*, XII (1883), 509 f.

[16] Edition A. Wagner, pp. 17-19. See now J. A. MacCulloch, *Mediaeval Faith and Fable* (London, 1932), pp. 186 f.

[17] J. G. Frazer, *Apollodorus*, Loeb Classical Library (London, 1921), I, 235.

in T and especially the *notonier* in AA, who demands payment for crossing the river, have taken the place of Charon.

Evrain is a Hospitable Host. His castle with "les puceles qui carolent" and with "quanque cuers desirre" [18] is a Castle of Maidens. Mabonagrain is a giant or tyrant and his red color is a trace of a Red Fomorian tower. We read that the heroine keeps Mabonagrain a prisoner in the garden. This could be interpreted as a trace of type I (Fairy Mistress), according to which both host and tyrant were mere tools of the *fée*, conjured up by her to test the hero's valor and subject at all times to her control. More likely this statement is due to the influence of some tale like that of Merlin imprisoned in walls of air by the *fée* Viviane.[19] Our story of Mabonagrain and the lady has almost certainly passed through the stage of type II (Giant's Daughter), in which the hospitable host is a deserted husband and the tyrant is an interloper who ought to be slain. The lady at this stage is Evrain's wife and has been abducted by Mabonagrain, just as, in D, Fiachna's wife has been abducted by Goll. A trace of this stage is that Evrain has no wife.

Chrétien has developed the story into type III (Enchanted Princess or Garden), and does not suggest that the lady is Evrain's wife. By ascribing the entire action to an enchantment or spell, fastened upon the people concerned, that compels them to behave as they do, Chrétien reconciles the story to Christian dogma and to the beliefs of the day. Magic was an admitted possibility. Since there is joy at the ending of the enchantment, the garden must be a prison. It

---

[18] *Erec,* vss. 5504 and 5584.

[19] "Merlin," ed. H. O. Sommer, *The Vulgate Version of the Arthurian Romances* (Washington, 1908–1916), II, 451 f.

is the garden beside a Dolorous Tower. What the "joy" is Chrétien does not tell. Perhaps those are right who explain the name "Joy of the Court" as a misunderstanding of *inis subai*, "isle of joy," one of the names for Mag Mell.[20]

The motive of a Dolorous Tower may include, in or adjacent to the tower, a garden in which is a feast and a number of *fées* who are captives to the king of the dead. In German mediaeval legend a Dolorous Tower has developed into a *Rosengarten* with a giant defender.[21] In the second story from Andreas Cappelanus, quoted below,[22] is a Dolorous Tower, a meadow with food, and a duel with a giant. In *Tochmarc Emire*, E, Emer is encountered at needlework with her maidens on a playing field or meadow in front of Forgall's castle. It is somewhere near here that Forgall dies when pursued by Cuchulinn. In an earlier form of the story a duel probably took place.

Every one of the marvelous incidents in Chrétien's romances, except perhaps *Lancelot*, V, shows traces of this garden. In *Erec*, U, is a garden with fruit and a duel. In *Lancelot*, V, is a garden containing what seems to be a world tree. Here a duel takes place while Queen Guenevere looks on from a tower.[23] But Godefroi de Leigni, who wrote these concluding verses in which this is told, fails to indicate that this is a Dolorous Tower. In the main story of *Yvain* the Dolorous Tower is the castle of Esclados with its terrible portcullis. The Fountain Perilous beside a world tree, where birds sing a service of song and where

[20] E. Philipot, "Un Épisode d'Erec et Enide," *Romania*, XXV (1896), 261 f.

[21] G. Ehrismann, *Geschichte der deutschen Literatur*, Teil II, Absch. 2, p. 135.

[22] Page 346. The fruit of fairyland is mentioned in stories A, I, and L.

[23] Verses 6994–7022.

the duel is fought, is doubtless a trace of the garden. In the *Chastel de pesme avanture*, X, three hundred captive maidens or *fées* working at needlework are in a meadow enclosed by stakes. Yvain fights two "kobolds," although it is not said that the battle is in this meadow. In the first part of *Perceval*, Y, a Dolorous Tower has become a red and green tent. Beside the tent is a meadow. In the tent are food and a damsel who is evidently a *fée*. In the Chastel Merveilleus part of *Perceval*, a Dolorous Tower apparently revolves. Within are a garden and many *fées*.[24]

Probably a row of pikes crowned with human heads signified a castle of the dead and was a recognized decoration of a Dolorous Tower.[25] In *Erec*, U, is such a row of iron pikes, and a single vacant pike awaits the head of the next adventurer. In *Pesme Avanture*, X, the "large, round stakes"[26] that enclose the meadow were probably once crowned with heads. In *Perceval*, Y, Orguelleus, the giant, vows to cut off the Welsh lad's head at once.[27] Why is he desirous of Perceval's head unless to put on a stake in his garden? In the account of the garden of *Perceval*, AA, we are told that Orguelleuse has caused the heads of many brave men to be cut off.[28] The heads were probably mounted on stakes at the garden.

The oldest known occurrence of a row of iron stakes, each crowned with a human head, is at the castle of Scath, "shadow," in the tenth-century Irish saga, *Siaburcharpat ConCulainn*, H.[29] No vacant stake awaiting the next adventurer appears here, but this piquant detail is not lacking in *Echtra Airt*, S,[30] in the row of stakes at the court of the

[24] Page 137.
[25] Page 107.
[26] *Yvain*, vs. 5192.
[27] *Perceval*, vs. 831.
[28] Verse 6756.
[29] Page 67.
[30] Page 84.

giant Morgan. In the Welsh *Kulhwch and Olwen*, G, although no row of stakes is mentioned, the head of the giant Yspaddaden is cut off and "fixed on the castle stake." [31]

Because the Irish handle the motive very skillfully, and because examples in recently collected Irish tales are numerous, Archer Taylor has argued that the motive of the vacant stake is Irish.[32] It evidently passed from Ireland by Welsh or Breton intermediaries to the romances of Chrétien. This palisade of heads signifies that the garden in *Erec* was once a Dolorous Tower.

V. LANCELOT

(bcdfghmnopt)

Meleagant, coming to Camelot, announces to King Arthur that he holds in prison many of Arthur's people and will release them if he is conquered in a neighboring wood by one of Arthur's knights accompanied by Guenevere. Kay, by a threat to leave Arthur's court, extorts from him and from Guenevere the promise of an unspecified boon.[33] Too late Arthur learns that Kay's boon is that he may be Guenevere's champion in the wood. All foresee that Meleagant will conquer Kay; nevertheless Meleagant and Kay go off with the Queen. "All bewail her as if she lay dead upon a bier." [34] Lancelot,

[31] Page 63.

[32] "The Motif of the Vacant Stake in Folklore and Romance," *Romanic Review*, IX (1918), 21–28. A. H. Krappe has suggested an ultimate origin for the motive in India but has not denied that it reached Chrétien from Celtic sources (*Göttingische gelehrte Anzeigen* [1928], p. 382). On the general idea see G. Huet, *Revue d'ethnographie et de sociologie*, IV (1913), 373–380; G. Ehrismann, [*Paul und Braune*] *Beiträge zur Geschichte d. deutschen Sp. u. Lit.*, XXX (1905), 39; and Kittredge, *Gawain*, p. 246.

[33] On the savage custom of the boon, see p. 313.

[34] This is the first of many hints that Meleagant is Death personified.

who is one of a crowd of knights that sets out in pursuit, overtaxes his steed. He and Gawain become separated from the rest of the knights and meet a dwarf of low origin, driving a cart and carrying a long switch. The dwarf bids Lancelot to climb up into the cart, promising that he will help him get news of the Queen. After some hesitation Lancelot mounts the cart and Gawain follows on horseback.

The first lodging to which the dwarf leads them is at "une tor sor une roche bise." Here Lancelot, Gawain, and the dwarf are derided by the townspeople but are handsomely received by a damsel and her two maidens, who bring green mantles for the two knights. In the hall are three beds, one of which, the Perilous Couch,[35] is chosen by Lancelot. This is the first test. At midnight a lance having a pennon all ablaze descends and just misses him. The next morning Lancelot and Gawain learn that Meleagant has defeated Kay and taken the Queen to Gorre, a land from which no stranger returns (t). It must be reached either by a water passage or by a sword bridge (b). Gawain chooses the former; so he and Lancelot separate.

The second lodging is large and sumptuous. Here a damsel offers Lancelot entertainment provided he will share her couch. A sumptuous repast is spread at her castle, although no servants are visible; he is forced to fight men-at-arms whom she conjures up.[36] The formal test outside this castle is a tomb. He who can raise its lid will liberate the prisoners from the kingdom from which no one escapes. Lancelot raises it.

At the third lodging place Lancelot meets a vavasor [first Hospitable Host] and his son returning from a hunt (g). He asks Lancelot to stay at his house and sends his son ahead to

[35] A perilous couch is also in AA (p. 140). G. Paris remarks that the threatening lance will kill everyone except the best knight in the world (*Romania*, XII [1883], 466). J. Vendryes compares a blazing lance in early Welsh poetry (*Rev. celt.*, XLVII [1930], 419).

[36] She is clearly a *fée* testing Lancelot (see Kittredge, *Gawain*, p. 264).

make preparation. His wife with five sons and two fair daughters comes up. One of the daughters gives her mantle to Lancelot (*d*). They entertain him and tell him that they are from the land of Logres and are prisoners here (*m*). They warn him of the dangers before him. Two of the vavasor's sons accompany Lancelot from this point to the sword bridge. The next test is a "stony passage" guarded by a knight on horseback and by two men with axes. After Lancelot has forced this obstacle he comes to a castle gate. A portcullis descends behind him and another in front, leaving him imprisoned. He tries to dispel what he supposes to be enchantment by having recourse to a ring that has been given him by his foster mother, who is a *fée*.[37] Finding that his prison is not imaginary but real, he cuts his way out.

At the fourth lodging place [second Hospitable Host], Lancelot is received by a lady and her children. The master and two of his sons presently return from a hunt bringing game,[38] and a rich repast is prepared, of which all partake. A challenger, proud as a bull, interrupts them, with whom Lancelot fights. After Lancelot has subdued this aggressor, a maiden who rides on a tawny mule, and who, as we learn later, is Bademagu's daughter, approaches and demands the vanquished warrior's head. Lancelot restores the vanquished warrior's sword, conquers him over again, and then cuts off his head. The damsel promises to repay Lancelot's service and rides off with the head. The next day comes the test of the sword bridge.

After crossing this bridge over a swift and terrible stream (*b*), Lancelot finds by consulting his fairy ring that two lions (*c*) that he thinks he sees at the end of the bridge are illusions

[37] In a more primitive form of this story this *fée* was probably Guenevere, or Guenevere's companion, namely Bademagu's daughter (see A. C. L. Brown, *Mod. Phil.*, XVII [1919], 364).

[38] This is a close parallel to a Hospitable Host bringing game in F (p. 56).

produced by enchantment. At the window of a strong tower sits Bademagu [third Hospitable Host], watching him (*h*). Bademagu offers him aid and entertains him for a night.[39]

The next morning on a tourney field in front of the tower Lancelot fights a combat with Meleagant for the release of Guenevere (*n*). Many ladies, including Guenevere, are spectators. A "wise maiden," who is probably Bademagu's daughter, by questioning Guenevere finds out Lancelot's name and, by calling to him, encourages him to defeat Meleagant. Bademagu, fearing that Meleagant will be slain, interrupts the combat. It is agreed that the fight shall be renewed at Arthur's court within a year from the time when Meleagant shall choose to challenge Lancelot.

When Guenevere meets Lancelot after the battle, she reproaches him for having hesitated to mount the cart in order to reach her. She later keeps a love tryst with him, but the arrival of a false letter persuades her to return to Arthur's court. Lancelot is then lured, by a dwarf with a deceitful letter, to the house of Meleagant's seneschal, where he is held prisoner. During her husband's absence, the seneschal's wife supplies Lancelot with red armor belonging to her husband and lets him go to take part in a tournament at Arthur's court (*o*). On his return to the seneschal's house Lancelot is seized by Meleagant, who imprisons him in a stone tower [Dolorous Tower] that he has built on an island near Gorre (*f*). From this prison he is rescued by Bademagu's daughter (*d*) who seeks him, helps him to escape, and takes him to her beautiful house [Castle of Maidens]. Here she provides him with a bath, fresh clothes, and a wonderful horse. Lancelot tells her she may "command his heart and body," but he leaves her and sets

[39] Bademagu here plays the part of a Hospitable Host, and his daughter that of a *fée* who directs the action. Since he is friendly, he ought not to be father to the tyrant or giant Meleagant. Chrétien has probably changed something in his original (see p. 436).

out for Arthur's court. He arrives just as Gawain and Meleagant are about to fight (n). In this final battle Lancelot, who
fights in Gawain's place, conquers Meleagant and cuts off
his head (p).

The incoherences of this story have been rather generally
explained [40] by the theory that Guenevere was originally
a *fée* who controlled the entire action and that she arranged
the various ordeals and battles in order to test her lovers,
Lancelot and Gawain, and to lead them to her. In accepting
this theory, I would add that the dwarf must have been in
her service, for only through him could she have heard of
Lancelot's hesitation to mount the cart (vs. 4502). It is
also clear to me that the cart belongs to the land of the dead.
It is the "grisly cart" in which, according to Chaucer,
"Pluto fetched Proserpina." [41] Nothing else will explain
why it was such a feat of courage for Lancelot to mount it.

As the story stands, it is probable that Bademagu's daughter is identical with Lancelot's fairy foster-mother, mentioned at the house of the first Host as having given him a
ring. It is she who, at the house of the second Host, incites
Lancelot to kill the proud challenger. It is probably she
who, at the house of Bademagu, the third Host, encourages
Lancelot to defeat Meleagant. It is she who rescues Lancelot from Meleagant's stone tower, entertains him at her own
palace, and gives him a wonderful horse. In thankfulness
Lancelot says to her:

[40] G. Paris, *Romania*, X (1881), 465 f., and XII (1883), 459 f.; K. G. T.
Webster, *Englische Studien*, XXXVI (1906), 337 f., and [Harvard]
Studies and Notes, XVI (1934), 207 f.; T. P. Cross and W. A. Nitze,
Lancelot and Guenevere (University of Chicago Press, 1930), pp. 57 f.

[41] Edition W. W. Skeat, *Complete Works of Chaucer* (Oxford University Press, 1899–1904), IV, 454, E2233. See also p. 349.

Par vos sui de prison estors,
Por ce poez mon cuer, mon cors,
Et mon servise et mon avoir,
Quant vos pleira, prandre et avoir.

(vss. 6705–6708)

Chrétien does not tell who this helpful damsel is. Godefroi de Leigni, who completed Chrétien's unfinished romance, reveals that she is Bademagu's daughter (vs. 6262). It is all but certain that the damsel of the blazing lance at the first lodging and the temptress of the second are likewise Bademagu's daughter in disguise.

In Journeys to Fairyland, the different lodging places are different pictures of fairyland. In E, F, and G, a Journey to Fairyland is lengthened by introducing a number of Hosts.[42] Often these various Hosts and damsels are different manifestations of one Host and one damsel whose business it is to lure the hero onward. Here Guenevere, as has been said, was at first a *fée* who managed the entire action. She corresponds to Fann in C, Finnchaem in F, and Laudine in W. Bademagu's daughter was the companion-*fée* who helped to guide the hero. She corresponds to LíBan in C, Achtlann in F, and Lunete in W.

The parallelism extends to such minute points as that Laeg in F, on entering the stronghold of the Hospitable Host wears a mantle given him by a woman of the place,[43] while here, at both the first and the third lodging, Lancelot wears a mantle brought him by damsels of the house. In Wolfram's *Parzival* the hero on entering the Grail castle is

---

[42] Pages 49, 57, 62. On the splitting of a Hospitable Host into two or more figures, see Cross and Nitze, *Lancelot*, pp. 9 and 54.

[43] Page 58.

given a mantle [44] belonging to the Grail maiden to wear. This seems to be something more than the familiar custom of supplying a visiting knight with a cloak.

The incoherences of our story are due to rationalization. In Welsh and Breton before the time of Chrétien, Guenevere, because she was King Arthur's queen, was deprived of her fairy power (just as Emer, Cuchulinn's queen, was in E),[45] and was regarded as a mortal. If Guenevere and Bademagu's daughter be considered mortals, their knowledge of events is miraculous, and the daughter's actions most unreasonable.

Stories telling of the abduction of a queen by a foreign marauder were popular in ancient Ireland and were called *aitheda*.[46] Whether we regard Guenevere as originally a *fée* or not, it is clear that *Lancelot* belongs to this type of story, and that as in many *aitheda* the marauder has been identified with death. In T, for example,[47] Teigue's wife LíBan is carried off by marauders to what is plainly a land of the dead, and is finally rescued, much as Guenevere is here carried off and rescued.

Pagan Irish Mag Mell was devoted to love-making. Every one of the lodging places in a story of this type is a picture of Mag Mell and its amorousness. In F the reader will notice that Cuchulinn is presented with a lady-love

[44] Page 181.

[45] Page 46.

[46] Dr. J. J. Parry calls my attention to a remark in T. M. Chotzen, *Recherches sur la poésie de Dafydd ab Gwilym* (Amsterdam, 1927), p. 295: "Les histoires d'enlèvements étaient parmi les plus goûtées dans les pays celtiques: l'Irlande avait ses *Aitheda*, le Pays de Galles ses contes sur Gronw Pebyr et Blodeuwedd, sur Melwas et Gwenhywfar, sur Trystan et Essylt." Almost the same thing was said by Thurneysen, *Heldensage* (1921), p. 429.

[47] Page 85.

both by the first Host and by the third. A Celtic custom of offering one of the daughters of the house, or at least one of the servants, to pass the night with a guest [48] may be in the background. Chrétien, in adapting these stories to twelfth-century France, weakened most of these love episodes, as for example in W, into mere mention of beautiful maidens.

Here at the first lodging Lancelot and Gawain meet "a damsel elegantly attired, than whom there was none fairer in the land, and with her two lovely and beautiful maidens. . . . They received Gawain joyously" (vss. 435–441). "The damsel sat by Sir Gawain. They would not have changed their lodging place to seek any other, for all that evening the damsel showed them great honor" (vss. 456–462). At the second lodging there is more, for Lancelot meets a forthputting damsel who has evidently been employed by the *fée* that originally managed affairs to tempt him (vss. 954–1290). At the third lodging place (first Host) are "two fair and charming daughters who are still unmarried" (vss. 2061–2062). After his release from the stone tower in the passage partly quoted above (vss. 6705–6706), Bademagu's daughter when she entertains him at her palace is charmed with Lancelot.[49] Lancelot in truth had as many love affairs as Laegaire or Cuchulinn.

In *Kulhwch and Olwen*, as has been said,[50] Arthur, like other Hospitable Hosts in stories of this type, is in the power of giants. That Arthur is leading an enchanted life somewhere on the borders of the land of the dead is the situ-

---

[48] These are pictures of *Mag Mell* and not necessarily transcripts from life in ancient Wales or Ireland. On the custom, see Kittredge, *Gawain*, p. 267; Krappe, *Mythologie*, p. 293.

[49] On the general idea, see Cross and Nitze, *Lancelot*, p. 18, n. 2.

[50] Page 63.

ation, I think, in all of Chrétien's romances. It is apparent in *Lancelot* and in *Perceval*, and I think it can be shown in *Erec*, *Cligès*, and *Yvain*.

In *Erec*, among princes who held land in fief from Arthur, according to the remarkable lists of names, were the following: "Maheloas. . . . li sire de l'Isle de Voirre" (vss. 1946–1947); "Guigomar. . . . de l'Isle d'Avalon fu sire" (vss. 1954–1955); "Bilis, li rois d'Antipodés" (vs. 1994). Here the *Isle de Voirre* is the Fomorian tower of the dead. Maheloas is the Welsh Melwas and the Meleagant of our story. Avalon is where Arthur went after the battle of Camlan; and l'Antipodés, no doubt by some confusion, is evidently a name for the lower world. Since these kings of the lower world hold land from Arthur, he must already be located somewhere in the land of the dead.

Other names in *Erec* corroborate this inference. A few verses later a visitor at Arthur's tournament is: "Le roi de la Roge Cité" (vs. 2192). The "Red City" is the tower of the dead. The following are, I think, all princes of the land of the dead: "Li Vaslez de Quintareus" (vs. 1723); "Yders del Mont Dolereus" (vs. 1724); "Amauguins" (vs. 1726); "Loz li rois," and "Keu" (vss. 1737–1739).

Cligès is so superficially Arthurian that it need hardly be considered. The episode of Angrés in it, however, seems to be a feeble imitation of Arthur's battle with Modred, and this would imply that the part of Arthur's life referred to was mostly after the battle of Camlan.

In *Yvain*, Arthur, by a short journey, arrives at the [Fomorian] castle of Esclados, which could hardly be possible unless he were already residing in the land of the dead.

My hypothesis that Camlan is in the past and that Arthur is leading an enchanted life in some castle belonging to the land of the dead explains his inactivity in all of Chrétien's romances, as for example at the beginning of *Erec* and of *Yvain*. In two of the romances, *Lancelot* and *Perceval*, this inactivity becomes inability.

Did Chrétien understand this? In the lists of names in *Erec* referred to above, which must be of Irish origin although, no doubt, they reached Chrétien in another language, are many Fomorians who have been conquered and, according to Arthur's custom, have been received as members of the Round Table. The Welsh who transmitted these stories probably knew that Arthur had taken the place of Nuadu as king of the Tuatha Dé in their wars against Fomorians. The Welsh doubtless understood that the action of *Lancelot* and of *Perceval* takes place after the battle of Camlan, and after Arthur has removed to the land of the dead, but while he is still subject to depredations from the kings of the dead whom he has not yet reduced to vassalage.

Chrétien, who from the time that he wrote *Erec* was familiar with the names of Fomorians, probably did not understand the importance of the war between them and Arthur. Anyhow in *Lancelot* and in *Perceval* he leaves Arthur's helplessness unexplained. Perhaps just as Shakespeare, who knowing that his skill in depicting human character would make a play live, was content in *King Lear*, *Cymbeline*, and in *Winter's Tale* to adopt improbable plots, so Chrétien by the time he began his unfinished *Perceval* had gained such confidence in his ability to command attention by making his characters behave like real men and women that he did not take pains to make his plots comprehensible.

The helplessness of Arthur in *Lancelot* is manifest. We are told over and over again that Arthur's people are prison-

ers in a foreign land. It is nowhere said that he is prisoner
in a Dolorous Tower; but if we suppose that he is not truly
at Camelot [51] but is lying wounded in an enchanted palace
at the outskirts of the land of the dead and is subject to
attacks by giants from a Dolorous Tower, it will explain
the puzzles of the romance. This is why Arthur does
nothing when Meleagant comes to insult him by telling
him that he has many of Arthur's people prisoners and will
not let them go.[52] This is why the rescuers of Queen
Guenevere find themselves in the land of the dead from the
very outset of their quest.

In *Perceval* this enchantment explains why, near the beginning, Arthur allows the Red Knight [53] to insult him and
to spill wine upon Guenevere. In *Perceval*, Arthur is not a
prisoner, of course, but he is exposed to raids by giants
from a Dolorous Tower. His castle is not truly at Carduel
but in Orcanie,[54] i.e., Orcus or Hades. The Red Knight
comes like Meleagant to insult Arthur and to carry off some
of his possessions. Arthur can be rescued only by the
destined hero, Perceval. The Red Knight is a Fomorian
and a king of the dead like Meleagant.

In *Lancelot*, Bademagu's castle, from which he watches
Lancelot cross the sword bridge, is a Castle of Maidens. It
is the same castle, I suppose, as Scathach's *dún* at the far end
of the Bridge of the Fosterlings in E.[55] Since it is Guenevere's prison, it is perhaps adjoining or attached to a
Dolorous Tower. The warrior "plus orguelleus que n'est
uns tors," [56] whose head Lancelot cut off, is one of the

---

[51] Verse 34.
[52] Verses 53–62.
[53] Verses 945–961. See pp. 126, 250, 393.
[54] Verses 839 and 8889.

[55] Page 49.
[56] Verse 2582.

giants. He is like Orguelleus "de la lande" in Y and Orguelleus "de la roche" in AA.[57] Meleagant is another giant.
Like Mabonagrain in U and like the Red Knight in Y, he
probably dresses in red. We are told that Meleagant's
seneschal had a suit of red armor which his wife lent to
Lancelot to wear at a tournament at King Arthur's court.
If the seneschal wore red armor,[58] it is safe to infer that his
master, Meleagant, did the same. Red armor goes with a
red tower, and the Dolorous Tower in other stories is often
red. The prison built by Meleagant for Lancelot is, doubtless, another picture of a Dolorous Tower.

W. YVAIN

(acdefghijnoprst)

Before Yvain's journey a knight named Calogrenant attempts the adventure of the Fountain Perilous. Calogrenant
after riding all day crosses a plain (e) and approaches a castle.
A Hospitable Host strikes a gong of copper outside, and he
and his lovely daughter welcome and entertain the visitor
[Castle of Maidens]. The daughter brings him a mantle spotted
with peacock plumes.[59] Calogrenant, the next day, is defeated
in battle at the Fountain Perilous and returns to Arthur's
court.

Yvain next sets out and visits first this Hospitable Host,
whose beautiful daughter entertains him. He comes next to a
giant herdsman. Then he comes to the Fountain Perilous, a

[57] *Perceval*, vss. 3817, 8646.

[58] "Et la dame tantost li baille
      Les armes son seignor vermoilles." (*Lancelot*, vss. 5519–5520)

See also vss. 5663, 5734, 5882, 6046, 6083. In the prose *Lancelot*, Meleagant
has red hair (Sommer, *Vulgate Romances*, IV, 41).

[59] Variegated attire is characteristic of Celtic fairies in K, M, and elsewhere. On peacock feathers, see p. 195.

rain-making fountain, to disturb which amounts to a challenge
(*n*). He fights an adversary named Esclados the Red (*op*),
who flees and escapes under the portcullis of his castle (*f*),
which falls and cuts Yvain's horse in two [*Dolorous Tower*].
Lunete, the messenger of the heroine Laudine (*a*), protects
Yvain (*d*) [*second Castle of Maidens*], feasts him (*gh*), and
gives him a ring that makes him invisible (*i*). Esclados dies
of his wounds, and Yvain marries Laudine, his widow (*jr*).
When Yvain wishes to visit Arthur's court, Lunete gives him
another ring, which, it must be inferred, would enable him to
find his way back whenever he wished to return to Laudine.
Yvain stays at Arthur's court longer than he promised, loses
the ring,[60] and goes mad (*t*). After having been cured by
magic remedies he finds a lion and a serpent fighting (*c*). He
slays the serpent and is helped by the thankful lion. Returning by a journey of wonders he comes again to the Fountain
Perilous. Here he slays a seneschal, who, with two brothers
(vs. 4413), seems to have seized upon the position, formerly
held by Esclados the Red, as lord of the lady. In this way
Yvain finally regains his position as lord of Laudine and of
her land (*s*).

This story contains two developments that have not been
noticed before. None of the twenty Irish and Welsh tales
outlined in the preceding chapter contains the idea of an
adventurer like Calogrenant who failed. Such an incident,
however, as the Bridge of the Fosterlings in E, where
Cuchulinn failed twice before he finally succeeded, might
give rise to the notion of an adventurer who failed altogether. Chrétien liked the idea of an adventurer who
failed, for he used it again in his *Perceval*. None of the
previous stories tells of the hero's losing the heroine and

[60] See Hertz, *Spielmannsbuch* (1931), p. 373; A. Hertel, *Verzauberte
Ortlichkeiten und Gegenstände* (Hanover, 1908), p. 64.

having to regain her, as Yvain did by a long search and by another combat fought near her castle. To disobey a *fée*'s instructions involves losing her, as is seen in B and is well-known in *Lanval* and *Graelent*.[61] Most of the incidents in *Yvain* have been already studied [62] and only a few points need be touched upon here.

The giant herdsman who points out the road to the Fountain Perilous is apparently a traditional figure belonging to the tangled forest at the edge of the land of the dead. He is like Roncu who "called the cattle" of Conchobar in E, and like Custennin the shepherd in G.[63] Perhaps here, he is the Host of the night before in disguise. In the thirteenth island of *Imram Maeile Dúin* the voyagers see a huge herdsman guarding oxen. Krappe has noted [64] that the first person encountered by Hercules in giantland is the shepherd Menoites who controls the herds of Geryon.

A Castle of Maidens occurs twice. First, it is the castle where the Host's daughter entertains the adventurers, which is particularly described on the occasion of Calogrenant's visit. Calogrenant spent the afternoon tête-à-tête with the daughter in a walled garden, and was annoyed when the Host finally came to conduct them to supper.[65] This is an interrupted love affair and is to be understood as an attenuation of some incident like that of Cuchulinn and Rianga-

[61] See T. P. Cross, *Mod. Phil.*, XII (1915), 641.

[62] A. C. L. Brown, *Iwain*, pp. 27 f., and *PMLA*, XX (1905), 677 f.

[63] Pages 47, 61.

[64] *Mythologie*, p. 294, and *Göttingische gelehrte Anzeigen* (1928), p. 378. C. A. Williams, "Oriental Affinities of the Hairy Anchorite," *University of Illinois Studies*, X (Urbana, 1925–1926), ii; Pokorny, *Deutsche Literaturzeitung*, LI (1930), 2007.

[65] Verses 235 f. Hilka has noted what he calls "a lack of realism" here (*Yvain* [1926], xxxix).

bar's daughter in F.[66] It is a part of the love-making of Mag Mell. A second glimpse of the Castle of Maidens occurs where Lunete rescues Yvain, takes him to her own apartment, provides him with food, and gives him a talismanic ring (vs. 1026). Here Lunete's apartments [Castle of Maidens] appear to be built into the castle of Esclados [Dolorous Tower], just as in C and D where Mag Mell seems to belong, first to giants, and then to fairies.

The Dolorous Tower in this story is plainly the castle of Esclados the Red, which has, "de fer esmolue et tranchant" (vs. 924), a terrible, falling gate. It is easy to recognize in this contrivance a part of the machinery of a Tower of the Dead.

X. Le Chastel de Pesme Avanture
(*Yvain*, vss. 5107–5770)
(*dfghjmopt*)

Yvain, accompanied by a damsel who is leading him on another quest, comes by accident to the "Castle of Pesme Avanture." As they ride along the people deride him. A lady tells him about the Castle of Ill Adventure, but advises him against entering it. He goes on, however, and a surly porter admits him to the castle. He sees a *prael* (meadow or playground) enclosed with pointed stakes [*Dolorous Tower*] in which three hundred maidens are imprisoned and made to work at embroidery (*f*). In reply to his questions they tell him that the "rois de l'isle as puceles," while on a journey, has been taken prisoner here by "deus fiz de deable" (vs. 5271), and forced to pay a tribute of thirty of his damsels every year (*m*), and add: "We often see excellent knights come to fight the two devils and lose their lives on our account." Yvain comes to a garden where he finds a gentleman, his wife, and

[66] Page 57.

a very beautiful daughter (*j*). The daughter gives him a spotted mantle (*d*) [*Castle of Maidens*], and they entertain him for the night (*g*). At the table there were "almost too many kinds of food" (*h*) (vs. 5439). Next morning the gentleman tells Yvain that there is a terrible custom (*une mout fiere deablie*, vs. 5468) to be observed. Every visiting knight is obliged to fight two hideous, black (*o*) sons of the devil, and if he can slay them he will receive the daughter and the lordship of the town (*mn*). The devils are armed with crooked wooden clubs that are covered with copper and wound with brass. Yvain slays them both (*p*), and has some trouble to leave the castle without marrying the daughter (*t*).

The meadow here is enclosed by pikes which, although not crowned with human heads, undoubtedly connect it with the gardens in U, Y, and AA. All four gardens are Fomorian towers.[67] The "Isle as puceles" here is a Castle of Maidens. The king of the "Isle as puceles," we are told, was taken prisoner while on a journey. It might be supposed that this locates the "Isle" at a considerable distance from the "Chastel de Pesme Avanture." The maidens seem to be all here, however, so that it is probable that in Chrétien's original the Castle of Maidens and the Fomorian tower were adjacent. The tyrant has here been rationalized into two black kobolds (*netuns*, vs. 5513) called "fiz de deable." Chrétien represents the whole situation as due to enchantment (*deablie*, vs. 5468). The enforced combat is called a "custome et rante assise" (vs. 5502). The tribute of thirty damsels yearly exacted by these kobolds may be an invention of the Irish from their stories about Fomorian tribute. According to a poem by Eochaid Ua Flainn,[68]

[67] Pages 92, 125.
[68] He died in 1004; Macalister, *Lebor Gabála*, III, 172.

Fomorians took two-thirds of the children each year as tribute. There may also be influence from some other type of story,[69] but *Thomas of Erceldoune* contains the idea of a tribute paid by fairies to the fiends. Here in X the "rois de l'isle as puceles" is a Hospitable Host and entertains splendidly, but his palace is dominated by two tyrants who doubtless inhabit a Dolorous Tower somewhere in the neighborhood.

Every one of the marvelous episodes in Chrétien's romances that has been reviewed in this chapter contains at least eight of the motives in our scenario. In every one of these episodes is a Castle of Maidens and a Dolorous Tower, although in several passages they would seem to be adjoining structures. With the exception of W, where but one maiden is definitely pictured (*Yvain*, 227 f.), the description of the Castle of Maidens preserves a trace of the *sluagh sidhe*, "fairy host," of Celtic belief by mentioning a multitude of maidens: (U) *Erec*, vs. 5504, "Nes les puceles qui carolent"; (V) *Lancelot*, vs. 3542, "Totes les puceles"; (X) *Yvain*, vs. 5194, "Vit puceles jusqu'a trois cainz."

Considering the various stages that must have intervened between Chrétien's romances and his no longer extant Irish originals, the number of resemblances between the marvelous episodes in his romances and our scenario derived chiefly from Irish sources is remarkable.

The evidence set forth in the preceding pages establishes almost beyond a doubt that the marvelous episodes in Chrétien's romances discussed in this chapter rest upon materials that, whatever may have been their ultimate origin, were developed by the Celts in the Celtic manner.

[69] Cf. Gertrude Schoepperle-Loomis, *Tristan and Isolt*, II (Frankfort and London, 1913), 326–337. An *Thomas of Erceldoune*, see p. 22.

CHAPTER IV

Chrétien's *Perceval*

UNLIKE *Erec* and *Cligès*, *Perceval* consists almost altogether of marvelous material. Its construction is like that of an Irish *imram* built up of visits to various wonderful islands, which upon analysis turn out to be forms or fragments of a Happy Other World. *Imram Maeile Dúin*,[1] the best-known of these stories, tells of visits to many islands, most of which are plainly forms of Mag Mell. Chrétien's *Perceval*, in accordance with knightly custom, is not thought of as a voyage but as a journey on horseback. It is like an *imram*, however, in that every castle which the hero visits is a variant of the Happy Other World.

The oldest *imram* was probably a voyage of the god Brión to the Isle of Women and told of but one island. By various processes of repetition and conflation the number of islands was increased until in the *Imram Maeile Dúin* no less than thirty-four separate islands are described. All of these islands are supernatural, and about twenty of them are varying pictures of Mag Mell or the Castle of Maidens. This reduplication of the happy isle has already been pointed out [2] and is no doubt an instinctive way of developing a wonder-voyage. Similar reduplication occurs in Homer's *Odyssey*, where the islands of Circe, Calypso, and Alcinous are different forms of the blessed isle. Chrétien's

[1] Page 272.
[2] A. C. L. Brown, *Iwain*, pp. 66 f.

Perceval is constructed upon the plan of an *imram*, only Perceval journeys on horseback and the islands have become castles. The Castle of Maidens occurs five times: (1) Arthur's hall; (2) Gornemant's castle; (3) Blancheflor's castle; (4) Grail castle; (5) Chastel Merveilleus. Every one of these castles is more or less in the power of a giant Fomorian.[3] Every one of these five castles is beside a river or the sea.

Some evidence remains that in an earlier form of the story these castles were located on islands. In the *Bliocadrans Prologue*, Perceval's mother says that she is going to pray to St. Brendan of Ireland;[4] in *Perceval* she remarks that Perceval's father "was feared among all the islands of the sea" (vs. 419); Arthur's chief enemy is "Rion, king of the isles" (vs. 852); and Blancheflor's enemy is "Clamadeus des isles" (vs. 2776).

Anyone coming to the reading of *Perceval* fresh from a study of Irish *imrama* and the Greek *Odyssey* will, I think, easily understand that these five castles are different glimpses of the castle of bliss. Some of the distinguishing marks of a wonder-voyage are still apparent in *Perceval*.[5]

The multiplicity of Hospitable Hosts encountered by Perceval is best explained not only by the device of repetition but by an hypothesis that two or more Journeys to Fairyland have been attached together. In mediaeval manuscripts, and especially in Irish manuscripts,[6] it is not unusual

---

[3] Gornemant's brother has been killed by Anguingeron (vs. 2309); the sword and spear at the Grail castle may be interpreted as a plea for help.

[4] "A saint Brandain d'Escoce orer" (Hilka, *Perceval*, p. 447, vs. 554).

[5] See R. S. Loomis, "Irish Imrama in the Conte del Graal," *Romania*, LIX (1933), 557-564.

[6] See H. Zimmer, "Über den compilatorischen Charakter der irischen Sagentexte im sogennanten *Lebor na hUidre*," *Zeitschrift f. vgl. Sprach-*

to find several versions of the same theme told one after another, tandem-wise. Sometimes these different versions have been conflated or run together into a single narrative. My hypothesis is that this has happened in *Perceval* where three different variants of our scenario appear. These variants are: (Y) Perceval's Story except for the Grail Castle, (vss. 1–2984; 3690–4602); (Z) Perceval and the Grail Castle, (vss. 2985–3689; 6217–6518); (AA) Gawain and the Chastel Merveilleus, (vss. 4603–6216; 6519–9234).

These three stories may be disentangled from each other as follows. The first, Y, has evidently been retold and reworked most, and from it everything marvelous has been carefully expunged. So thoroughly has this rationalization been accomplished that Chrétien has no notion that King Arthur's castle (vss. 907 f.) is in fairyland. He calls Arthur's residence "Carduel" (vs. 336). He very likely did not realize even that Blancheflor's dwelling, Belrepeire (vs. 1707), is a fairy castle.[7] The next story, Z, consists of two portions: The Grail castle portion (vss. 2985–3689), which has been pretty thoroughly incorporated into Y; and another portion, Perceval's Good Friday visit to his hermit uncle (vss. 6217–6518), which, although it is inserted into AA, stands apart from it like an isolated episode.[8] This

---

forschung, XXVIII (1887), 417–689; and compare p. 244. Many Irish stories (including *Serglige ConCulainn*, summarized, p. 17) show conflation.

[7] The elimination of the marvelous from Y has been noticed by R. H. Griffith (*Sir Perceval of Galles* [University of Chicago Press, 1911], p. 67, n. 2, and p. 127). An idea of what Y was like when it existed separately may be obtained from the English *Sir Perceval*. Compare also *Peredur* Ia (*Mab.*, II, 88 f.) and p. 204.

[8] Wolfram, *Parzival*, bk. ix, makes the Good Friday episode a separate book, formally set off.

second story, Z, is different from Y because it retains plenty of marvels and because it suggests a Christian interpretation for the Grail which is unlike anything in Y. Finally, the absence of fighting in this story suggests that it has had a different development from Y, in which at every stopping place Perceval hears of an adversary who must be fought, except at the Grail castle, which by hypothesis belongs rather to Z. The castles in Z are: the Grail castle, the castle of Trebuchet the smith, and the abode of the hermit. According to the principle of iteration these three must all be forms of the Happy Other World, and yet at none of them is an adversary mentioned. The third story, AA, like Z, contains marvels. Since its hero is not Perceval, it is obviously a different story beginning at verse 4603.

In Count Philip's book, which Chrétien, in verses 66–67 declares was his source, the stories which we call Y, Z, and AA were evidently told one after another. It is impossible to know whether the unknown redactor of this book conflated these three stories into one narrative, or whether some or all of the present rearrangement is due to Chrétien. Chrétien appears to have been a canon of the abbey of Saint-Loup,[9] and consequently he might have introduced the moralizing tone apparent in *Perceval*. He, however, did not moralize in this way in his other romances. For simplicity's sake, therefore, let us attribute all changes to the redactor. He must have introduced the notion that Perceval's leaving his mother was a sin which caused his failure at the Grail castle. No story at all close to folklore would regard Perceval's leaving his mother to become a

[9] L. A. Vigneras, "Chrétien de Troyes Rediscovered," *Mod. Phil.*, XXXII (1935), 341.

warrior as a sin,[10] nor would it represent him as failing in his chief adventure.[11]

Before the redactor worked over the stories, Z may have had a string of introductory adventures that resembled those of Y. If so, the redactor combined the introductory adventures of the two stories into one set. In Y the castle of the Hospitable Host had no doubt been split into three: Gornemant's castle, a second Host's castle, and Belrepeire. For the second Host, who doubtless had talismans, the redactor substituted the Fisherman with sword, spear, Grail, and platter from Z, and he transposed Belrepeire, which in Y had doubtless stood last, to a penultimate place, so that he could represent Perceval as succeeding at Belrepeire but afterwards failing at the Grail adventure. He invented the notion that Perceval failed because of his sin in leaving his mother. He probably inserted into the Good Friday episode monkish advice, like that to hear Mass daily. Most probably Chrétien suggested at this point some connection between the Grail and the cup of the Eucharist.

An examination of the romances shows that the connection with the Mass was at first timidly hinted at, and an identification was perhaps not explicitly made till after Chrétien's time. Be it remembered that, except at one point, Chrétien's *Perceval* is very slightly ecclesiasticized. The procession of the talismans at the Grail castle (vss. 3075–3314) does not suggest a religious ceremony to Perceval or indeed to anybody. It is three thousand verses later in the

[10] R. H. Griffith (*Sir Perceval*, p. 37) made this point.

[11] Before the redactor altered it, Y probably resembled *Peredur* Ia (*Mab.*, II, 88), where, to be sure, Peredur's foster-sister (cousin in *Perceval*, vs. 3600) tells him that he is excommunicate (*ysgymunedic*) for having caused his mother's death, but where there is no other reference to his desertion of his mother or to its preventing his success.

Good Friday episode, and then only by one word *oiste*, twice repeated (vss. 6423, 6425) — generally believed to represent the Latin *hostiam* — that the secret is revealed. The hermit tells Perceval that the Fisherman's father is so spiritual that he eats no food except a single *oiste* brought to him daily in the Grail:

> Et del riche Pescheor croi
> Que il est filz a celui roi
> Qui del graal servir se fet.
> Mes ne cuidiez pas que il et
> Luz ne lamproies ne saumon:
> D'une sole oiste li sainz hon,
> Que l'an an cest graal li porte,
> Sa vie sostient et conforte;
> Tant sainte chose est li graaus,
> Et il est si esperitaus
> Qu'a sa vie plus ne covient
> Que l'oiste qui el graal vient.

> (vss. 6417–6428)

This word *oiste* could hardly have stood in Count Philip's book. Had it been there, the identification of Grail and cup would have been already explicit, and there would have been no hesitation in later romances about declaring the secret. The word *oiste* can hardly be a first step [12] in the ecclesiasticization of the Grail. It is likely that the redactor made some veiled suggestion of identity between the Grail and the cup of the Mass, which Chrétien and his followers developed.

[12] The word *oiste* was not, I believe, written by Chrétien, but I no longer deny that he knew a Christian interpretation of the Grail. See my paper "Did Chrétien Identify the Grail with the Mass?" *MLN*, XLI (1926), 226.

The redactor attached Z to AA by the simple device of identifying a damsel messenger who came at the end of Z with an ugly damsel at the beginning of AA. The damsel messenger came, we may suppose, at the end of Z to summon Perceval to return to defend Blancheflor; and an ugly damsel, at the beginning of AA, came to invite the knights to the adventure of Chastel Merveilleus. The redactor who made this identification regarded Belrepeire as only another aspect of Chastel Merveilleus. He doubtless knew or felt that Belrepeire, the Grail castle, and Chastel Merveilleus were different aspects of the Castle of Fairyland. Very likely he found the three stories in one manuscript, and this suggested to him to string them together into one narrative.

If the original plot of Y could be reconstructed it would probably be parallel to that of Chrétien's *Yvain*. In this original plot Perceval probably did not fail, but in response to the invitation of the sword he delivered Blancheflor's castle (which he must have visited after the Grail castle) from hostile giants, and then left Blancheflor, as Yvain did Laudine, to return to Arthur's court. Like Yvain, and like other heroes who returned from fairyland, he overstayed his time and suffered a mental derangement, a trace of which is preserved in the incident of the blood drops in the snow (vs. 4172). In an earlier form of Y a messenger no doubt came from Blancheflor at this point to reproach Perceval, just as Lunete came in *Yvain*. This messenger, I suppose, reported to Perceval that Blancheflor (like other *fées* when deserted by the hero — like Laudine in *Yvain*) had fallen into the power of a second giant (in *Yvain* called a seneschal) and needed to be delivered a second time.[13] The

[13] For example, in the prose *Lancelot*, Hector rescues a *fée* named

story ought to end by Perceval's rewinning Blancheflor in battle against a seneschal, just as Yvain rewon Laudine. Such a second battle fought to deliver Blancheflor is told in Manessier's continuation.[14] At the end of the story Perceval no doubt stayed with Blancheflor as lord of her castle.[15]

If the Grail castle and Blancheflor's castle are interchanged, it will make the plot of the first part of *Perceval*, Y, Z, closely resemble that of *Yvain*, W.[16] The chief points of resemblance are: both Perceval and Yvain come first to a friendly castle; the Fisherman in Z is a Hospitable Host like the *vavasor* in *Yvain* (v́s. 211); both Perceval and Yvain fight a terrible antagonist; [17] Blancheflor, the heroine of Y, corresponds to Laudine in W; the Grail messenger, who in Wauchier's continuation of *Perceval* is named Rosette, corresponds to the messenger, Lunete, in W. If this hypothesis is right, the action of Y and Z originally ended by the overthrow of a seneschal (just as in W, Yvain overthrows the seneschal of Esclados) and by the reinstatement of Perceval in fairyland. It is a plausible hypothesis, therefore, that in an earlier version of *Perceval* the

Perse at the *Castel lestroite marche*, and slays a tyrant or giant named Morganor (Sommer, *Vulgate Romances*, III, 334–351). At a later point Hector has to rescue Perse again. A new giant named Zelotes has seized her and must be conquered (*ibid.*, V, 412–452).

[14] The giant here is named "Aridès of Cavalon" (ed. Potvin, vs. 41434) or "Caridès" (vs. 41475).

[15] Wolfram finishes his *Parzival* in about this way. He has no seneschal but by some alteration introduces a heathen Feirefîz for Parzival to conquer. Also in *Sir Perceval* the hero returns finally to the heroine.

[16] This is the order of incidents in *Peredur* (see p. 205).

[17] In Y, Perceval fights Clamadeu, who wishes to seize Blancheflor; in W, Yvain fights Esclados li ros, the husband of Laudine. Clamadeu and Esclados are both probably distortions of Galam, the name of the Irish giant.

Grail castle came before Blancheflor's castle, or perhaps that the two castles were originally one, and have been split into two castles as at present.

In the following outline the *Perceval* story is divided into three parts.

Y. PERCEVAL'S STORY EXCEPT FOR THE GRAIL CASTLE
(*Perceval*, vss. 1–2984, 3690–4602) [18]
(*abfhijmnprst*)

The youth Perceval has been brought up by his mother in a forest in ignorance of chivalry. One day he meets five knights in the forest; and the chief knight inquires whether he has seen five other knights and three maidens. Perceval, instead of replying at once, asks the names of the pieces of armor that the knights wear. At last, however, he answers, "Here are *li destroit Valdone* [vs. 298], and the laborers harrowing the land can tell you." Perceval, overwhelmed by the splendor of the knights, wishes to become one. He learns from the chief knight that King Arthur, who knights men, is at Carduel, and, going home, tells his mother that he wishes to seek King Arthur. His mother gives him advice, "Your father, who was feared in all the islands of the sea, was wounded in the time of Uterpandragon and fled to this house in the *gaste forest soutainne* [vs. 75].[19] Your eldest brother went to the King of Escavalon [vs. 463], your second brother to King Ban of Gomeret [vs. 467], and both were slain. Your father died of grief." She consents to his going, however, provides him with a Welsh costume; and, calling him "Biaus filz," starts

---

[18] References are to Hilka's edition (1932).

[19] The Waste Forest *soutainne* or *souterrain*, "under the earth," is probably the forest at the edge of the land of death, and Valdone and Escavalon are pretty surely corruptions of Avalon. In *LG* Tailtiu (Ireland) brings up Lug in a forest (p. 231).

him off; before he has gone a stone's throw, she swoons with grief (*a*).

Perceval comes to a tent of green and red which stands in a meadow by a spring surrounded by rustic booths (vs. 638). He mistakes it for a church. In the tent he finds a damsel whom he forcibly kisses and whose ring he seizes and keeps. He eats one of three pasties that he finds, and, after trying to persuade the lady to eat, leaves the other two pasties. He drinks a cup of wine and leaves the lady weeping.[20] Before long the lady's *ami*, "Orguilleus de la lande," returns from the woods, accuses her of falseness, and says her horse shall not be fed nor her clothes changed till he has cut off the Welsh lad's head.

Perceval next meets a charcoal-burner [21] leading an ass, and inquires the way to Carduel to King Arthur. The charcoal-burner says, "Arthur has fought King Rion, and the king of the isles has been conquered," and adds, "Yonder in a castle by the sea is King Arthur."

Outside the castle gate Perceval meets a knight in red armor

[20] Here, as in E, U, X, and AA, a garden is beside, or has taken the place of, a Dolorous Tower (pp. 47, 92, 113, 137). The red and green tent is a trace of a red Fomorian tower. Orguelleus is a giant and holds the damsel prisoner. She is virtually the country personified. She may have been at first Eriu, then Logres, and then, as here, "de la lande." Since she is a *fée*, she is not surprised. She gives her ring to Perceval because it is a talisman. In *Sir Perceval* it preserves the hero from injury. Both *Sir Perceval* and *Peredur* are more original because they represent the lady as eager to welcome the lad and to give him her ring. *Sir Perceval* is more original in calling the tent a hall. Griffith (*Sir Perceval*, p. 109) has pointed out that Perceval's not eating all of the food in the tent hints that originally the food was never-failing. This damsel, like most *fées*, has a magic cup-of-plenty.

[21] Verse 835. In place of the charcoal-burner, Wolfram (p. 177 below) has a fisherman. This figure was in origin, I suppose, a Charon who for money ferried Perceval over the river of death to Arthur's fairy castle (*g*). Nevertheless, the man with an ass may be a variant, not a corruption. In Apuleius, *Metamorphoses*, VI, 18 (ed. R. Helm [Leipzig: Teub-

holding a gold cup, who says: "Tell the wicked King Arthur to send somebody to defy me, or else to hold his land in fief for me, for it is mine." Perceval rides so dashingly into the hall that he knocks Arthur's hat off (*h*).[22] Arthur welcomes Perceval, who asks that he be made a knight at once. Arthur tells Perceval that his worst enemy, the Vermaus Chevaliers de la forest de Quinqueroi (vs. 951), has just put in a claim to Arthur's land, and after spilling wine on the queen, has carried off a gold cup (*i*). Perceval says, "Give me the arms of the Red Knight who has stolen your cup." Kay shouts to Perceval to go and win the arms, and Perceval departs.

As Perceval goes toward the door, a girl calls out to him, "In all the world there will not be two knights better than thou" (vs. 1043). She smiles, although she has not smiled for "six" (five manuscripts read "ten") years. Kay kicks into the fire a fool (*un sot*, vs. 1054) who is wont to say that the girl will not smile until she has seen the best knight in the world.[23] He then slaps the girl in the face, knocking her down.

Perceval, when he rides outside the castle gates, encounters the Red Knight and strikes him through the eye with a javelot,

---

ner, 1907], p. 141), Psyche going to the underworld meets a lame man driving an ass loaded with wood.

[22] In *Sir Perceval* the hero sits down at Arthur's table, which must be an original feature, since Arthur is here a Hospitable Host. At first, the Red Knight probably carried off the queen (see pp. 250, 393).

[23] In the "Knight of the Red Shield" (J. F. Campbell, *Popular Tales of the West Highlands* [London, 1890–1893], II, 468) is a parallel. In this recently collected Gaelic tale, "Little Treasure," the heroine, who has not smiled for a year, laughs at the arrival of a destined hero. Likewise in *Perceval* the girl who laughs is, I conjecture, the original heroine; that is, she is identical with Blancheflor, with the Grail damsel and (of course not here but in a pristine form of the story) with Guenevere, Arthur's fairy queen. In Wolfram's *Parzival* this laughing girl is called Cunnewâre (p. 178). Arthur's castle, Gornemant's castle, and the Grail castle are different aspects of a fairy castle, and the heroine or *fée* who controls the plot may have been the same throughout. Kay, I suppose, was at first a Fomorian tax-collector (see p. 384).

killing him. Yonet, who has followed, first shows Perceval how to put on the Red Knight's armor and then carries the gold cup back to Arthur. The·fool says to Arthur, "Now your adventures begin" (vs. 1257) and adds that within forty days Perceval will avenge the blow that Kay gave.

Perceval goes on his way and comes to the castle of Gornemant de Goort which is on a river by the sea. Here he is trained in arms, dubbed a knight, and advised to be sparing of speech.

Perceval after being knighted sets out to return to his mother. He happens upon the castle of Belrepeire (vs. 1707), which is also on the sea. The neighboring country is a wilderness of land and water. He crosses a bridge so feeble that it does not look as if it can sustain him (*b*) and beats on the door of the castle till a girl calls down from a window. He asks for lodging. Her reply is:

> " 'Sire' fet el 'vos l'avroiz
> Mes ja gré ne nos an savroiz.' "
> (vss. 1731–1732) [24]

Perceval knocks vigorously again till four axe-men open the door (vs. 1775). Two men, old but not decrepit, and a girl of indescribable beauty named Blancheflor (*j*) receive Perceval. Knights in groups of four, five, and six come in and seat themselves (vs. 1852). (The prose of 1530 says, "two and two, four and four, six and six.") Blancheflor and the two old men do not speak. Perceval remembers the advice of Gornemant and keeps silent.[25] Some at the table whisper

[24] This is doubtless the usual warning at the entrance to fairyland (Castle of Maidens). The knocking, followed by maidens appearing at windows and the coming of a lady, is strikingly like Cael's arrival at Créde's fairy palace in L (p. 76). Compare the Castle of Maidens in Wauchier, *Perceval* (ed. Potvin, vss. 26502 f.).

[25] Perceval's silence is not primarily caused by Gornemant's advice, but is that speechlessness that enshrouds a meeting between a mortal and the fairies, or the dead. At the castle of the Hospitable Host in *Owein*,

that Perceval and Blancheflor would be a fine pair if they weren't so silent (vs. 1868). At last Blancheflor asks Perceval from what place he has ridden that day. "From Gornemant's castle," he answers. "He is my uncle," says she. "I have another uncle, a prior and a holy man, and all the food I have in this castle is six loaves and a bottle of wine that he has sent me." [26]

In the middle of the night Blancheflor comes to Perceval's couch and beseeches him to save her from King Clamadeu des isles (vs. 2005), who wishes to carry her off (*m*). Anguingueron, the seneschal of King Clamadeu, is besieging her castle and has slain most of her warriors (*n*). She says that she is just as sorry over her knights who are in prison as she is over those who are slain:

> "De çaus qui sont an prison mis (*f*)
> Me poise autant con des ocis;
> Car je sai bien qu'il i morront,
> Que ja mes issir n'an porront."
>
> (vss. 2007–2010) [27]

---

the Welsh version of W, the meal was half over before anybody spoke (*Mab.*, II, 33). On silence at a fairy castle see *Romanic Review*, III (1912), 159; J. R. Reinhard, *The Survival of Geis in Medieval Romance* (1933), pp. 158, 237; Hertz, *Spielmannsbuch* (1931), pp. 366–367. In B (p. 43) Macha, when she came to Crunnchu, did not speak till evening. Wild Edric's fairy wife did not speak for one day (Walter Map, *De Nugis Curialium*, dist. II, chap. xii, ed. M. R. James, [Oxford, 1914]). The warriors restored to life in Bran's cauldron were as good as ever, "except that they were not able to speak" (*Mab.*, I, 66). The men on the glass tower in Nennius (p. 253) did not speak. Ovid calls Pluto "rex silentum" (*Metam.*, V, 356).

[26] Verse 1911. It is a plausible conjecture that this "holy man" is the hermit whom Perceval meets (vs. 6341), that the hermit is the Fisherman disguised, and that this food comes from the Grail. In *Peredur* (*Mab.*, II, 92) nuns bring six loaves of bread and a flask of wine. These nuns may be a rationalization of fairy damsels such as we find in the *Elucidation*. Perhaps they originally served food from the Grail. That food

The next day Perceval conquers Anguingueron (*p*) and sends him to King Arthur to say that Perceval intends to come and punish Kay for the blow given the girl. King Clamadeu then besieges Blancheflor's castle and attempts to starve it out, but a ship laden with grain arrives. Perceval finally conquers Clamadeu and sends him to King Arthur to convey another threat to Kay. Arthur is holding court at Dinasdaron (vs. 2732), in Wales, and will not begin his feast until something new is announced. Presently King Clamadeu arrives, bringing Perceval's threat to Kay.

Perceval departs from Belrepeire but promises to return and stay with Blancheflor:

> "Einsi a la voie se met
> Que le revenir lor promet. . . .
> > (vss. 2933–2934)
> 'Je revandrai, se Deus m'amant.' " (*rst*)
> > (vs. 2954)

Z. Perceval and the Grail Castle

(Vss. 2985–3689)

(*bghijkl*)

Continuing his journey, Perceval descends from an *angarde* (vs. 2987), and comes to a river in which is a boat containing two men (*b*). One is managing the oar and the other is fishing with a hook. They tell him there is no bridge. He inquires for lodging. The man who is fishing tells him to ascend the river bank by a narrow passage in the rock. Perceval does as directed, but, since at first he can see nothing, he grows angry at the

---

might be brought from the Grail castle is proved by Sigune's being fed by food brought from the Grail (in Wolfram's *Parzival*, vs. 439, 1).

[27] The prisoners will never leave Clamadeu's prison because it is, as I conjecture, another Dolorous Tower, a prison of the dead. Later we are told that Anguingueron "in this war" has killed Blancheflor's father (vs. 2280), and Gornemant's brother (vs. 2309).

fisherman. Suddenly he catches a glimpse of a tower. It is square (vs. 3054), built of gray stone with two turrets upon it (*h*). As soon as he passes the drawbridge, two squires disarm him, a third takes his horse and a fourth wraps him in a mantle of scarlet. He is conducted into a hall which is just as long as broad. In the midst of the hall on a couch reclines a nobleman who turns out to be the man who was fishing in the boat (vs. 3086). He wears a black sable cap, a purple robe, and before him burns a great fire that is between four brass columns [28] (*k*). While Perceval is talking with the Fisher King, a squire enters carrying a sword "which shall break in one peril" (vs. 3141) (*i*).[29] The squire gives it to the Fisher King, saying, "The golden girl [*sore pucele*, vs. 3145] your niece who is so beautiful, sends this to you." The Fisher King girds Perceval with the sword saying, "It is fated and destined for you." After Perceval and the Fisher King have talked for a time, a squire enters carrying a white lance from the point of which runs a drop of blood. He passes between them and the fire. Perceval remembers Gornemant's advice and refrains from question. Then two squires enter bearing candelabra with lighted candles; next enters a damsel "bele et jante et bien acesmee" (vs. 3223) (*j*), holding in her two hands "un graal" which shines so brightly that it extinguishes the candlelight (*l*). The Grail is of gold adorned with precious stones. Afterward comes a damsel with a platter of silver ("un tailleor d'arjant," vs. 3231).

---

[28] These columns are like the bronze columns in the palace of the *fées* in F (p. 56). The Grail hall is a Castle of Maidens, and this is generally spacious. For instance, in the hall in C are 150 couches for 150 ladies; in F, "a meal for 100 was prepared"; in L, Créde is accompanied by 150 women; in R, BéBind comes with 150 women.

[29] The gift of the sword I conjecture to be a plea for Perceval to defend the Grail folk. Sword, lance, Grail, and platter doubtless originally belonged together and were the talismans upon which the prosperity of the fairy folk depended.

Two squires next bring a table top which they place upon two trestles brought by two other men. Dinner is now served (g). Venison is carved on the platter ("atot le tailleor d'arjant," vs. 3287), and at every course [30] the Grail passes before them. Perceval does not ask concerning the Grail ("cui l'an an servoit," vs. 3293). When it is bedtime, four serving men take by the four corners the bed on which the Fisher King is lying and carry it out. Perceval sleeps in the hall.[31]

Next morning Perceval can find no one. At the bottom of the steps he comes upon his horse saddled, with lance and shield at hand. He rides out across the drawbridge, which ascends behind him instantly. He calls and shouts but no one answers (vs. 3413).[32] Following a forest path, he comes presently to a girl (vs. 3431), holding in her arms her dead lover, who has been slain that morning. She tells Perceval that the castle which he has just left belongs to the Fisher King, who has been wounded by a javelin through his thighs so that his only recreation is fishing. She asks Perceval's name, and he, although he does not know his name, guesses that it is Perceval (vs. 3575).[33] She tells him that, had he spoken and asked concerning the Grail, he would have healed the Fisher King. Per-

---

[30] Wolfram explains why the Grail appeared at every course. "The Grail itself fed the company and whoever stretched out his hand could receive whatever dish he desired" (*Parzival*, vs. 238, 9).

[31] In Irish palaces the *imda*, "couch," upon which the guest sat served as his bed at night.

[32] It is not likely that in the Celtic original Perceval failed. Therefore Krappe (*Balor*, p. 113), is well advised in saying that it is dangerous to use the rising drawbridge here as proof of Celtic origin. Chrétien, he says, used tales that had already been ennobled into the realm of chivalry, and the above passage has no doubt been influenced and altered by the motive of "frustrated redemption." The bridge at Belrepeire, however, I think, may be Celtic and may go back to something like the Bridge of the Fosterlings in E.

[33] A destined hero like Perceval ought to be told his name at the time of his first adventure (see p. 235). Chrétien did not understand this.

ceval was destined to heal the Fisher King; because, however, of his sin in leaving his mother, he failed. The girl, who is his cousin, tells him that his mother died of grief. She points out to him a road and asks him to follow it and overtake the knight who slew her lover; she informs him about the sword that the Fisher King has given him, warning him that it will break, and that only Trebuchet, the smith, can repair it (vs. 3679).

Y AGAIN.   PERCEVAL'S STORY EXCEPT FOR THE GRAIL CASTLE
(Vss. 3690–4602)

Perceval next meets the damsel whom he has kissed in the tent, who is now being ill-treated by her lover. This lover, Orguilleus de la lande, presently arrives and attacks Perceval (vs. 3832). Perceval conquers him and sends him to King Arthur to bear still another threatening message to Kay.

Perceval, while musing one day over some blood drops in the snow (vs. 4187), is assailed by Kay. In the encounter Kay is worsted and his arm broken. Gawain goes in search of Perceval, finds him, and brings him to Arthur's court at Carleon (vs. 4602). [The text here contains some incoherences which appear to have resulted from a combination of Y and Z into one narrative.]

AA.   GAWAIN AND THE CHASTEL MERVEILLEUS [34]
(Vss. 4603–6216)
(bcdefghilmt)

A hideous damsel upon a yellow mule, having a whip in her hand, comes to Arthur's court and rebukes Perceval for

---

[34] "Chastel Merveilleus" is a title not found in Chrétien. He calls this castle "Roche de Sanguin":

> "Li chastiaus, se vos nel savez,
> A non la Roche de Chanpguin. [variant "Sanguin"]
> Maint buen drap et vert et sanguin

not having asked the question which would have healed the Fisher King (vs. 4646):

"You entered the house of the Fisher King, you saw the lance that bleeds, and it was too much trouble for you to open your mouth and speak [vs. 4655]. Why did you not inquire why the drop of blood runs down the point of the white iron, and, of the Grail that you saw, why did you not ask what great man was served out of it. . . . If you had asked, the rich king who suffers so much would have been healed of his wounds and would have held his land in peace, which he cannot govern at all now [vs. 4674]. You know what will happen to the subjects of a king who cannot govern his land and is not healed of his wounds; the ladies will lose their husbands, their lands will be wasted [vs. 4679], the maidens will be unasked in marriage and will remain forlorn,[35] and many knights will die. All this evil will happen by your fault."

After this rebuke, the messenger addresses King Arthur, "I do not know whether you have heard speak of the Chastel Orguelleus. I must be there tonight":

> "Rois, je m'an vois, ne vos enuit;
> Qu'il me covient ancore anuit
> Mon ostel prandre loing de ci.

> I taint an et mainte escarlate,
> S'an i vant an mout et achate." (vss. 8816–8820)

Five MSS read Roche de Sanguin, and the Dutch version reads Roche van Sangwijn (Hilka, *Perceval*, p. liv). Chrétien evidently understood the name of the place to be Roche de Sanguin, and, as he could see no reason for calling it the "Red Castle," he introduced verses 8818–8820. These verses lose their point if one adopts Hilka's reading, Chanpguin. I do not know why Hilka chooses the reading Chanpguin unless it be to avoid almost identical rhyme. He keeps almost identical rhyme elsewhere, however, e.g. *morz, morz* (vss. 6289, 6290, grammatically not identical). On identical rhyme see R. Grosse, *Der Stil des Crestien von Troies* (Heilbronn, 1881).

[35] The prose of 1530 reads "pucelles viollees" (Hilka, *Perceval*, p. 563, l. 41), which agrees with the "Elucidation" (*ibid.*, p. 419).

Ne sai se vos avez oï
Del Chastel Orguelleus parler;
Mes anuit m'i covient aler.[36]
El chastel chevaliers de pris
A cinc çanz et sissante et sis;
Et sachiez qu'il n'i a celui
Qui n'et s'amie avueques lui."

(vss. 4685-4694)

No one can fail of knightly combat who goes to the Chastel
Orguelleus. He who wishes the prize of all the world must
free the damsel seated "au pui qui est soz Montescleire," and
gain the sword "as Estranges Ranges" (vs. 4712).

After the damsel has finished her speech, the knights make
vows: Gawain vows to free the damsel of Montescleire,[37]

---

[36] A fairy ship speeds to never-never land in a few moments. Some
other examples of this motive may be given. In the famous fragment
preserved by Tzetzès of Plutarch's commentary on Hesiod, a fairy boat
laden with the souls of the dead reaches its destination with one stroke
of the oar, Εἰς ταῦτα οὖν εἰσελθόντες μιᾷ ῥοπῇ πρὸς τὴν Βρεταννίαν νῆσον
κατάιρουσι (Didot-Dübner, Œuvres de Plutarque [Paris, 1800], IV, 20).
In a longer account in Procopius the sailors row to their destination in
one hour, whereas with their own ships if they do not sail but depend
on rowing they can hardly cross in a night and a day, ἀλλὰ καὶ μίαν
ἐρέσαντες ὥραν ἐς τὴν Βριττίαν κατάιρουσι (De Bello Gothico, ed. J. Haury
[Leipzig: Teubner, 1800], II, 598). In Echtra Conli, § 5 (p. 40), the fée
declares: "Cid cén ricfem re n-adaig," "although it be far, we shall arrive
before night." In Imram Brain, § 60 (p. 271), Manannán says to Bran,
"Emne co n-ildath féle ricfe ré fuiniud gréne," "Emne with many hues of
hospitality thou wilt reach before the setting of the sun." In Wolfram's
Parzival, the ugly damsel says:

"al hab ich der reise pîn
ich wil doch hînte drûffe sîn." (vss. 318, 23-24)

On this swift ship consult "Seelenüberfahrt" in Handwörterbuch des
deutschen Aberglaubens, VII, 1567.

[37] Verse 4720. Chrétien's text seems defective because Gawain makes
no effort to carry out this vow. The prose of 1530 (ed. cit., p. 564, l. 25)
omits Kahedin. According to it Gawain vowed to free the damsel seated

Girflet *li filz Do* to go to Chastel Orguelleus, Kahedin to ascend Mount Dolereus, and Perceval not to sleep two nights in
the same place till he finds out about the Grail and the lance.
Some fifty knights make similar vows. After the vows, a
knight named Guiganbresil enters and summons Gawain to
fight before the king of Escavalon (vs. 4791). Gawain, on
arriving at Escavalon, is excused from the fight to go seek the
lance that bleeds, and is told: "It is written that the hour will
come when all the land of Logres shall be destroyed by this
lance." [38]

Z AGAIN. PERCEVAL AND THE GRAIL CASTLE
(Vss. 6217–6518)

Perceval wanders for five years until at last on Good Friday
he encounters in a chapel a hermit [39] who turns out to be his
uncle and who tells him about the Grail. His main statement
is, "On a single wafer (*oiste*) which one brings in the Grail, he
(the Grail King who is the Fisher King's father) sustains and
comforts his life. Such a holy thing is the Grail and he is so
spiritual that he does not desire more than the wafer that
comes in the Grail" (vs. 6428).

AA AGAIN. GAWAIN AND THE CHASTEL MERVEILLEUS [40]
(Vss. 6519–9234)

Gawain comes to an *angarde* (vs. 6523), where he finds a
weeping damsel holding a wounded knight named Greoreas

---

at Montescleire, and Girflet to go to Chastel Orguelleus and to ascend
Mont Perilleus or Dolereus.

[38] Verse 6169. The prose of 1530 (p. 581, l. 22) says: "Logres . . . a
jadis par ceste lance esté conquis." This statement may be a reminiscence
of Lug's victory-bringing spear by which the Tuatha Dé conquered Ireland (see p. 228).

[39] In an older form of the story this hermit uncle, it may be conjectured, was the Fisher King in another disguise.

[40] Despite the intervention of other episodes, the deliverance of Chastel

(vs. 6541). This knight tells him that here is the boundary of Galvoie, a dangerous land. Except for his own escape, wounded, no knight has come out of that land alive. Gawain nevertheless goes on till he reaches an island city. Within this city in a meadow beneath an elm he finds a solitary damsel named Orguelleuse mirroring her face.[41] Gawain falls in love with her beauty. She will go with him if he will cross a plank into a garden [42] which she points out, and fetch her palfrey.

Merveilleus must be the adventure called by the ugly damsel "Chastel Orguelleus." W. Golther has noticed that Orguelleuse ought to be queen of Chastel Orguelleus (*Parzival und der Gral* [Leipzig, 1925], p. 187). The explanation that I offer is that as usual there are both a Dolorous Tower and a Castle of Maidens. The Dolorous Tower is Orquelenes (in *Parzival*, vs. 610,26, "Rosche Sabbîns") which was ruled over by Orguelleus de la Roche and Orguelleuse, under Guiromelant who is either Death's deputy or Death in person. Orquelenes is separated by a "gué perilleus" from the Castle of Maidens, which I have called "Chastel Merveilleus" (in *Parzival*, vs. 318,19, "Schastel Marveile"). This is the square, many-chambered castle of the *fées* which is built on the far side of the river of death, like the castle of Bademagu in V (p. 102), and like Scathach's *dún* in E (p. 50). It has fallen into the power of Guiromelant and, until it is delivered, is like a castle of the dead; Chrétien by some blunder names it Roche de Sanguin, "Bloody Rock," which, as in *Parzival*, ought to be the name of Orquelenes.

[41] Probably in the water of a spring as in *Parzival*, vs. 508,17 (on the motive see Hertz, *Spielmannsbuch* [1931], p. 354). The tent-damsel in *Perceval* was by a spring (vs. 638). Galloway is the land of the dead. Orguelleuse is virtually the sovereignty personified. The story goes on to tell how Gawain, by marrying her, becomes a friendly ruler of the land of the dead, thereby displacing Guiromelant, a hostile ruler (see Hilka's note, *Perceval*, p. 745).

[42] This garden from which Gawain fetches the palfrey is, doubtless, adjacent to a Dolorous Tower, like the gardens in E, U, X, and the tent in the meadow in Y (pp. 47, 92, 113, 125). The plank across which Gawain fetched Orguelleuse's palfrey (vs. 6727) evidently leads over the *gué perilleus* to Guiromelant's castle. Guiromelant's words later imply that at his castle some means of crossing the *gué* exist (vs. 8903, eight manuscripts read "bridge"). This garden, therefore, is at the Castle of Orquelenes, a deformation, I think, of Orcus, i.e. Hades, and the tall knight

Gawain crosses the plank into the garden. There he finds a group of people who warn him and say that this evil damsel has caused the heads of many knights to be cut off. It seems to Gawain that the people are in great anguish and distress. He comes to a tall knight sitting under an olive tree who allows him to take the palfrey (f). Gawain makes the palfrey, the head of which is black on one side and white on the other [43] (vs. 6822), go ahead of him across the plank out of the garden to Orguelleuse. She agrees to follow Gawain until he meets shame and death.

Gawain now gathers a healing herb and returns to cure Greoreas. A miserable dwarf mounted on a *roncin* appears. Gawain, after having bound up Greoreas's wounds, is politely helping the tearful damsel, who had been comforting Greoreas, to her palfrey, when he is astounded to see Greoreas spring on Gawain's own horse, Gringalet, and ride off beside the damsel. Orguelleuse bursts into laughter at Gawain's plight. He has no choice but to mount the dwarf's miserable *roncin*, which has a thin neck, a thick head, long hanging ears, and old weak

---

seated under an olive tree (vs. 6782), is Guiromelant. The people in the garden seem to Gawain to be in great sorrow and anguish:

> "Einz s'an va saluant les rotes,
> Et il li randent tuit et totes
> Ses saluz einsi que il sanble
> Que il an aient tuit ansanble
> Mout grant angoisse et grant destresce." (vss. 6773–6777)

The place must be a Dolorous Tower. Wolfram's description of the castle, which he calls Lôgroys, in which this garden is situated, seems to make it a revolving tower (see p. 357).

[43] Since, reasoning from analogy, this palfrey is in a tower of the dead, it is possible to suppose that the motley-color proves that it belongs to a red tower. If the horse had red spots as it does in the Norwegian version (A. Hilka, *Perceval*, p. 747, note to vs. 6822), this would be solid evidence. In the absence of red it is prudent to remember that, as Hilka shows, particolored animals are not confined to Arthurian romances (see p. 72).

stirrups into which he cannot put his feet (vs. 7177).[44] Gawain mounts this wretched nag and, accompanied by Orguelleuse on her palfrey, travels till they come to a plain (e) and a broad river (b), beyond which is a magnificent palace, Ygerne's castle, Roche de Sanguin, built of gray marble on a rock (h). At the windows are five hundred ladies (vs. 7244).[45] Orguelleuse puts her palfrey into a boat that is at the edge of the river and pushes off toward the castle. Gawain is left behind to fight li niés Greoreas, who rides up seated on Gawain's horse, Gringalet, and attacks him (vs. 7302). Gawain overthrows this assailant and regains Gringalet.

A notonier (ferryman) now appears with the boat and declares that he brings greetings from the ladies of the castle (vs. 7373).[46] After he has ferried the two men and Gringalet across the river, the ferryman expects to receive, as customary passage-payment, the horse of the vanquished knight. Gawain, declaring that he does not wish to walk, refuses to part with Gringalet but gives over instead, as prisoner, the conquered knight. The ferryman takes both Gawain and the prisoner to his house, "which is pleasant and joyous enough for a count to lodge in." Gawain has plover, partridge, pheasants, and venison to eat, and wines strong, clear, white and red, to

[44] This dwarf and nag correspond to the dwarf and cart in Lancelot (p. 100). They belong, as did the dwarf there, to the land of the dead. Cf. the dwarf in Lanzelet, ed. K. A. Hahn (Frankfurt, 1845), vss. 420 f., 5416 f., 5641, and 6229 f.

[45] Chastel Orguelleus, which, according to the ugly messenger, had 566 knights, each with his lady, must be the same as this, and both, as has been said, are in origin the square, many-chambered, cosmic castle of the fées.

[46] Heinrich von dem Türlîn in Diu Crône (vs. 16726; ed. G. H. F. Scholl, Stuttgart Verein, XXVII [1852]) calls the notonier Karadas, which probably indicates that he is Charon. He is evidently the same as Caradoc of the Dolorous Tower in the prose Lancelot (Sommer, Vulgate Romances, IV, 90). See "Fährmann" in Handwörterbuch des deutschen Märchen, II, 4.

drink. He is lodged as well as he could wish (vs. 7491) (*g*). The next morning Gawain and his host look out at a window. "Who is lord of yonder castle?" (*h*) Gawain asks. "I do not know," answers the ferryman. "You are a vassal of the castle and do not know?" interrogates Gawain. "I never knew," continues the ferryman, "*Uns clers sages d'astrenomie* (vs. 7548) placed marvelous contrivances in the castle [47] here, which was built for a rich queen named Ygerne. It is defended by five hundred poised arrows. The hall of this castle is enchanted [48] in such a way that no coward or perjurer can live there for an hour. Within are five hundred men, some young and some old, and many ladies. They await the coming of a hero who can defend the palace, end the enchantments, give the ladies in marriage, and dub the youths knights" [49] (vs. 7589) (*m*).

After the ferryman has vainly tried to frighten Gawain [50] from the adventure, he accompanies him on horseback to the castle gate. At the foot of the castle steps, on a bundle of flags, sits alone a man with an *eschace d'arjant*, "silver leg" (vs. 7652), that is banded with gold and jewels.[51] He is smooth-

[47] This Castle of Maidens is ruled by a Fomorian. The ferryman's ignorance of his name probably means that he is Death, the nameless one. Compare the "cité sans non," *Méraugis*, vs. 2815, and the "castiel sans non," *Raguidel*, vs. 5056 (ed. M. Friedwagner, Raoul von Houdenc, *Sämtliche Werke* [Halle, 1897–1909]). This Fomorian is an enchanter (vs. 7545). Wolfram calls him "Clinschor" (p. 196). He is probably Death and his deputy is Guiromelant.

[48] As usual, Chrétien explains the marvels as due to enchantment and regards Death as an enchanter.

[49] In the castle of death there is no marrying nor giving in marriage till the inhabitants are rescued (pp. 80, 86).

[50] This is the usual warning at the entrance to fairyland or to a Castle of Maidens (see p. 76).

[51] In *Humbaut*, a romance of the first half of the thirteenth century, Gawain on a journey to fairyland, which is confused with the land of death, has to fight upon a narrow bridge a man with an *eschace*, "wooden leg" (vs. 1374), but his leg is not of silver as here. Here the man is, I think, the Irish god, Nuadu of the Silver Arm, king of fairyland.

ing with a knife a small rod of ash-wood and says nothing when they pass. "What do you think of his false leg?" inquires the ferryman. "It is not of aspen wood but is very beautiful," replies Gawain. "He is rich in income," answers the ferryman, "and, were I not with you, you would hear something that would astonish you" (vs. 7675).

The doors of the castle are richly adorned. "Li gon et les verveles Furent d'or fin tesmoing l'estoire." The first door is ivory, the second ebony, and the hall within is decorated in bright colors. In the middle stands a golden bed with silver cords, and on every cord hangs a bell. On each bedpost shines a carbuncle with more light than four candles (l). The bed runs on four wheels and moves at a touch. The ferryman calls it "li liz de la mervoille" (vs. 7805). The hall is pierced by four hundred closed windows and one hundred open windows. The ladies can see Gawain through the glass windows from the rooms where they are, but he cannot see them.[52] When the ferryman cannot dissuade Gawain from sitting on the bed, he flees (vs. 7817). The bells ring, the hall trembles, the windows open, the marvels show themselves, and the enchantment begins. From the windows fly arrows so that more than five hundred lodge in Gawain's shield. The windows thereupon close and Gawain pulls the arrows out of his shield[53] (vs. 7845). Presently a serving-man admits a lion that attacks Ga-

[52] I.e., they are ghosts or fées (cf. Hertz, Spielmannsbuch [1931], p. 384).

[53] The boys at Emain Macha threw their 150 toy spears at the youthful Cuchulinn, and they all remained standing in his lath shield (L. W. Faraday, The Cattle-Raid of Cualgne [London, 1904], p. 18). This was perhaps a recognized otherworld test, because Foglaim ConCulainn, a fifteenth-century version of Tochmarc Emire (Rev. celt., XXIX, 124), relates that after a hero has passed the Bridge of the Fosterlings he must be tossed up on the roof and made the target of twenty-seven spears. Because Ireland was regarded as fairyland, the games and wonders of Tara are here transferred to the land of the dead. The lion must be a trace of Cerberus.

wain (*c*). After Gawain slays the lion, its head and claws re-main fixed in his shield.

The ferryman now returns joyously (vs. 7873) and cries out that the wonders are ended. Numerous youths offer their services and take care of Gawain's horse which is outside. A maiden with a circlet of gold, followed by many other maidens, salutes him as lord (*h*). Her page brings him a robe, a coat, a mantle, and a cloak. After some talk about the robe, which Gawain puts on, he and the ferryman ascend the tower to view the country. Gawain suggests going hunting, but the ferryman tells him that he who conquers the wonders of this castle must remain in it forever as its lord (vs. 8024) (*t*). At this news Gawain comes down from the tower very angry. A damsel reports to the queen Gawain's displeasure. The queen says, "He will be joyous when he sees me." She comes to the hall accompanied by one hundred and fifty maidens and as many youths. She talks with Gawain about the Round Table (vs. 8125) and remarks that Arthur is more than one hundred years old [54] (vs. 8170). The youths and maidens remain and serve Gawain and the ferryman a splendid dinner (*i*). Ga-wain spends the night in the magic bed (vs. 8259).

At daybreak the ferryman and Clarissant, Gawain's sister (vs. 8269) are at his bedside (*d*). The queen [55] and the older queen, Ygerne, arrive and beg Gawain not to sally out to attack a knight who, with Orguelleuse, is visible across the river. "She is a harmful lady," they say. The ferryman takes

---

[54] In vs. 8737 he is "over sixty years old." In his *Faula*, Guillen de Torrella finds Arthur in Avalon "over ninety years old" (V. M. O. Denk, *Einführung in die Geschichte der altcatalanischen Litteratur* [Munich, 1893], p. 226). When Kulhwch finds Arthur, two-thirds of Arthur's life have been spent (p. oo).

[55] This unnamed queen, Gawain's mother, is in *Parzival* called Sangîve, and in *Diu Crône*, Morcades (a name which has been probably manufac-tured out of Orcades, "the Orkneys," of which she is queen). The other queen, "Ygerne, la reïne as blanches tresces" (vs. 8207), is in *Parzival*, "Arníve," and in *Diu Crône*, "Igern diu Bluome."

Gawain across the river, where Gawain fights and overthrows the knight, whose name is "Orguelleus de la roche a l'estroite voie, qui garde les porz de Galvoie" (vs. 8648). Orguelleus says he fights Gawain for having passed the forbidden gates of Galvoie. Orguelleuse then leads Gawain to the *gué perilleus* and says, "Orguelleus my lover used to cross this ford and gather flowers from those trees yonder." [56]

Gawain, thinking that he has heard that whoever crosses the *gué perilleus* will gain the prize of all the world, spurs his horse forward. Gringalet misses the leap but swims to the further shore. Here a very handsome knight named Guiromelant greets Gawain and asks what has become of the knight with the four-divided shield (Orguelleus de la roche). "After I conquered him, the ferryman claimed him," replies Gawain (vs. 8559). "No knight ever before crossed this ford," says Guiromelant. "The lady deceived you when she told you that her lover did" (vs. 8600).

Gawain and Guiromelant pledge themselves to speak truth to each other. "What is the name of the city that I see there?" inquires Gawain. "Orquelenes" (vs. 8626) (*m*), answers Guiromelant. "It belongs to me and I hold it in fief from no one.[57]

---

[56] These flowers prove the place to be a garden. Doubtless it is the same garden (Orquelenes) from which Gawain fetched Orguelleuse's palfrey (vs. 6727). It is the garden beside a Dolorous Tower which we have recognized in E, U, X, Y, and at Orquelenes (pp. 47, 92, 113, 125, 136).

[57] Death is subject to no feudal lord. That Gawain, who represents Lug or someone of the Tuatha Dé, should be son of Lot, an evil giant, seems wrong, but in *CMT* Lug is grandson to such a giant, named Balar (p. 229). Mythologically speaking, I suppose that Guiromelant is brother to Lot, Gawain's father, king of the Orkneys. Lot, which in Irish means "destruction," is a suitable name for Death personified. This explains why Gawain finds his dead sister and mother in this palace which is near the Orkneys [Orcus]. If it has any basis outside of Wolfram's fancy, Guiromelant's wish to marry Clarissant (although he has never seen her) in mythology, where wife and sister are often confused, may be explained as follows. She was at first, perhaps, not Gawain's sister but his wife, a

The lady who led you here is Orguelleuse de Logres; Logres is the country where she was born and from which she was brought when small" (vs. 8640). "What is the name of the castle from which I have come, and where I ate and drank last evening?" asks Gawain. At this question, Guiromelant walks away because he thinks Gawain is deceiving him, but when Gawain refers to the *Lit de la mervoille* he returns, kneels down and begs Gawain's pardon. He tells Gawain that the older queen in the castle is Arthur's mother, Ygerne (vs. 8742), and that the other queen is Lot's wife and Gawain's mother. Gawain remarks that Arthur is over sixty, Arthur's mother has been dead for many years, and his own mother for twenty years (vs. 8756).

Guiromelant now says, "I love Clarissant, Gawain's sister, but I hate Gawain because his father, Lot, slew my father, and Gawain slew one of my cousins. Here is a ring to take to Clarissant. The name of this city is *la Roche de Sanguin*[58] [vs. 8817], because scarlet cloth is manufactured here" (*o*).

When Gawain tells his name, it is agreed that he and Guiromelant must fight. Guiromelant, however, says that King Arthur will soon hold court at Pentecost at Orcanie, which is distant but two days' journey.[59] "Send to him to bring his

---

fée, and Guiromelant is Death carrying her off. Gawain and Guiromelant alternate as Tuatha Dé and Fomorian husbands.

[58] In *Parzival*, Guiromelant is called Gramoflanz, and his castle Rosche Sabbins, "Bloody Rock." This is right because it is the Tower of the Dead, and is identical with the Irish "red-cornered rock on the sea" (p. 168). Chrétien's error in transferring the name "Bloody Rock" to Ygerne's castle has been mentioned above (p. 136).

[59] My hypothesis is that both in *Lancelot*, and here in *Perceval*, King Arthur is dwelling in fairyland, and needs to be delivered from the oppression of the king of the dead. Orcanie is a deformation of Orcus (Hades). It cannot be the Orkneys. Arthur never held court in the Orkney Islands. Compare Hilka's note to vs. 8889, in his edition p. 767, "Orcanie als Residenzstadt des Artus ist ein geographisches Unding." (See p. 344.)

people to see our fight. I will lead you to the best harbor in the world because no living man can leap this ford." Nevertheless Gawain makes Gringalet leap the ford and returns to Orguelleuse. She now apologizes for her conduct (vs. 8924), and explains that Guiromelant has slain her lover[60] and has tried to win her. She has forsaken Guiromelant for Orguelleus de la roche, and because she wishes to die has insulted all knights who came to try the adventure. She now asks Gawain to punish her so that no *pucele* shall ever again treat a knight scornfully. "Your will I shall do altogether, sir," she says.

Orguelleuse and Gawain are ferried back across the river by the ferryman. The two queens and the company at the palace welcome her for Gawain's sake. Nothing more is told of Orguelleuse. Gawain learns that his sister Clarissant has never seen Guiromelant nor he her except across the river. Gawain, however, gives Clarissant the ring that has been intrusted to him. All the time she does not recognize her brother.

Gawain sends a squire to invite Arthur to the court to see his combat with Guiromelant (*n*). In the castle the queen prepares five hundred tubs of warm water for five hundred youths to bathe, and also provides equipment for them. The youths sit up all night in the church and the next morning Gawain dubs them knights. He does not tell the company his name, nor does he marry Orguelleuse. At vs. 9234 Chrétien's part of the poem ends. [The next verses tell of the combat, how Clarissant finally stops the combatants, and how she marries Guiromelant.]

The above summary of Chrétien's *Perceval* is divided into three parts on an hypothesis that Z, the middle part, which contains motives *bghijkl*, is a fragment. The hypothesis is that other motives at the beginning and the end of Z were shorn off or obliterated when it was fitted into its present

[60] In *Parzival* (vs. 606,6) this unnamed lover is Cidegast.

position between Y and AA. The presence of motives *bghijkl* shows that Z conforms to the same scenario as Y and AA. All three parts seem to be versions of the same theme and must have a similar origin.

A tripartite division, however, is not necessary to the present argument. Everyone can see a Perceval section and a Gawain section. This bipartite division will suffice, as follows: The Perceval section by reason of Celtic fondness for a triad may have had from the beginning three castles. The present four castles of Y may be explained on the very reasonable supposition that Blancheflor's castle, which of course contained talismans,[61] has been divided into two castles. Some redactor took the talismans away from Blancheflor, glorified them, and located them at another castle, namely our Grail castle, which he invented for Perceval to visit. In this way four castles may have developed in Y without any need to assume another source Z. Either a tripartite or a bipartite division suits the present argument, although in what follows a tripartite division is adopted.

It is next in order to examine any evidence that may exist to prove that Y and AA, whatever their ultimate origin, have been elaborated by the Irish.

Of the two, AA conforms most fully to the scenario, and several other considerations help to establish for it a more or less remote basis in Irish story.

The Hospitable Host in AA is divided into two figures: a "ferryman" and a man with a silver leg. The man with a silver leg reminds one of Nuadu Argetlám, "silver arm," a king who according to Irish pseudo-history in *CMT, LG,*

---

[61] A Castle of Maidens contains talismans in the following Irish or Welsh stories in Chapter II: C, D, F, G, H, L, O, R, S, T.

and other stories, after having been wounded in battle against the Fomorians, wore a silver arm and ruled at Tara over the Tuatha Dé.

Nuadu, who belongs to Irish mythology, demands some consideration. Irish Nuadu (genitive Nuadat) is the Old Welsh god Nodons. As J. Vendryes has shown,[62] Nodons is from a root that attaches itself to the Gothic *nuta* (plural *nutans*), which Ulfilas[63] employs to translate the Greek ἁλιεύς, "fisherman." The ending is *–nt–*. Several inscriptions at Lydney read "D(eo) m(agno) Nodonti (Nudonti, or Nodenti)."

At a rather late period for pagan edifices, namely after the year 364, at Lydney on the Welsh bank of the Severn, and therefore not too far from Irish influences, elaborate buildings were erected in honor of the god Nodons.[64] Mosaics in this Lydney temple represent fish, oars, a triton carrying an anchor, and a fisherman in the act of hooking a fine salmon. Nodons was evidently both a navigator and a

[62] *Rev. celt.*, XXXIX (1922), 384. Nobody doubts that by derivation Nodens means "fisher": W. Stokes, *Urkeltischer Sprachschatz* (Göttingen, 1894), p. 195; A. Holder, *Alt-celtischer Sprachschatz*, II (Leipzig, 1897), 754; W. Walde and J. Pokorny, *Vgl. Wörterbuch d. Indo-germ. Sprachen*, II (1930), 326; T. F. O'Rahilly, "The Goidels and their Predecessors," *Proceedings of the British Acad.*, XXI (1935), 355.

[63] *Mark*, I, 17 (ed. M. Heyne [Paderborn, 1885], p. 20). See S. Feist, *Vgl. Wörterbuch d. got. Sp.* (Leyden, 1939), p. 380.

[64] W. H. Bathurst, *Roman Antiquities at Lydney Park* (London, 1879); R. E. M. Wheeler, *Journal of Roman Studies*, XVIII (1928), 204; XIX, 200–203. Dogs are figured in the temple, and there is the statue of a lady bearing a cornucopia. The lady I would explain as the country (Logres) personified and bearing a cup of plenty like the Grail. This would be the usual idea of a god married to a woman who is virtually the country personified. See also E. Windisch, "Das keltische Brittanien," *Abhandlungen der königl. sächs. Gesellschaft d. Wiss. zu Leipzig*, phil.-hist. klasse, XXIX (1912), 92, 97.

fisherman. Additional evidence that Irish Nuadu was a water god may be found in his connection with the river Boyne. The Boyne "was the forearm of Nuadu's wife." [65] The Boyne sprang from a well owned by Nechtan, who was doubtless the same as Nuadu Necht. Doubtless the real meaning is that Nuadu's wife was Ireland personified. It is not absurd to see in this Nodons, who is Nuadu and a manifestation of Brión,[66] the origin of Chrétien's Fisherman. Both the Fisherman and the *notonier* exhibit characteristics of Charon. I believe that Chrétien's *notonier* is Nodons, a little fallen from his high estate, although he still dwells in a house that "a count might lodge in" (vs. 7475), and altered into a ferryman who exacts passage payment for transporting travelers across the terrible river.

The man of wealth with a silver leg, who sits on a bundle of flags and whittles a stick, at the entrance to Chastel Merveilleus,[67] is, I think, a mere doublet of the *notonier*. *Notonier* is derived from Gaulish * *nauto*, Latin *nauta* or *navita*. Tibullus and others call Charon *navita*.[68] *Navita* sometimes meant "merchant." Probably a British-Latin word * *nauto* gave rise both to Chrétien's *notonier*, and, in its other meaning, to his *eschacier*,[69] namely the man with a silver leg. Both *notonier* and "merchant" may be manifestations of Nuadu. The Irish god's silver arm, *argetlám*,

[65] E. Gwynn, *Metrical Dinnsenchas*, III, p. 26, l. 15. On Nuadu Necht and Nodens, see Rhŷs, *Celtic Heathendom*, pp. 122–129.

[66] Page 292.

[67] Verses 7650 f. The whittling a stick is unexplained. In the *Dream of Macsen Wledig*, Eudaf son of Caradawc sits at the entrance of a marvelous castle carving chessmen, *Mab.*, I, 145. Cf. R. S. Loomis, *Celtic Myth and Arthurian Romance* (Columbia University Press, 1927), p. 167.

[68] Tibullus, I, 10, l. 36; Apuleius, *Metam.*, bk. vi, chap. 17.

[69] Verse 7657; some manuscripts read *eskiekier*. In *Parzival* the word is *krâmære* (vs. 562,23).

has, I suppose, by some accident of transmission, been changed [70] to an *eschace d'arjant* (vs. 7652), or silver crutch. The prose *Perceval* of 1530 gives the man of wealth, instead of a silver leg, a silver club in his hand.[71] This silver club probably points to an original silver arm. The bundle of flags, upon which the man with a silver leg sits (vs. 7650), is another trace of the river of death. The ancient Irish imagined flags or reeds along that melancholy shore. This appears in a tenth-century poem quoted by Kuno Meyer:

> Well I know what they are doing:
> They row and they row
> Over the reeds of the Ford of Alma,
> Cold is the place where they sleep.[72]

As has been remarked, a Hospitable Host is often divided into two or more figures. Here are two figures, the ferryman and the man with the silver leg, both of whom seem to go back to an original Nuadu Argetlám who was a Host and a wounded god.

[70] Welsh tradition probably favored a wounded leg. Bran was wounded in the foot (*Mab.*, I, 66).

[71] Hilka, *Perceval* (p. 597, l. 28): "Il trouverent ung bedeau ou huissier seul, assis sur ung trousseau de jonc tenant en sa main une masse d'argent doré en plusieurs lieux enrichie de pierres precieuses lequel dolloit atout ung coustellet ung petit baston de fresne. Si passerent devant luy sans mot dire et quant ilz furent oultre passez dict le marinier a Gauvain de cest huissier que vous en semble feist il et pareillement de sa masse. Bien m'est advis ce faict Gauvain que la masse n'est pas de bois mais fort riche a ce que je voy."

[72] *Sitzungsberichte der Preussischen Akademie der Wissenschaften*, XXXII (Berlin, 1919), ر43:

> "Is eól dam a ndognïat
> räit ogus darräat
> curchasa Átha Alma,
> Is üar in adba i fäat."

Chastel Merveilleus seems to have borrowed attributes from the famous Irish banqueting hall at Tara. Not all the material in AA, to be sure, is of Celtic origin. The marvelous couch is a piece of international bric-a-brac which, whatever be its origin, seems to have been thrust into the Chastel Merveilleus story before Chrétien's time, probably by a Celtic narrator.[73] The construction of Chastel Merveilleus with its lookout tower and numerous windows is borrowed from a cosmic palace which has its four sides toward the four winds. The topography of the surrounding country with its terrible rivers reflects that of the land of the dead.[74]

Notwithstanding this material of diverse origin, Chastel Merveilleus may have borrowed features from the hall at Tara. That Ireland was formerly fairyland, and that Tara was formerly a fairy castle, are ancient ideas. According to *LG*, the Tuatha Dé conquered Ireland and established their king Nuadu at Tara.[75] After he was wounded, he and his followers withdrew to underground palaces beneath hollow hills, from which abodes they still exerted an influence over affairs in Ireland. The fabulous early history of Ireland in *LG*, with its five successive invasions, was all built up by pseudo-historians round a notion that fairyland is Ireland

---

[73] On the Perilous Couch see Hilka, *Perceval*, vs. 7692 and his note, p. 758; A. Hertel, *Verzauberte Oertlichkeiten*, pp. 69 f.; Margaret Schlauch, *Speculum*, VII (1932), 509 f.; J. Bolte and G. Polívka, *Anmerkungen zu den Kinder- und Hausmärchen der Brüder Grimm* (Leipzig, 1913–1923), I, 23.

[74] On the cosmic palace, see R. Eisler, *Weltmantel und Himmelszelt* (Munich, 1910), pp. 337 f., and on this, and on the land of the dead, see below pp. 363, 368.

[75] In the same way Logres or Arthur's kingdom became regarded in later times as fairyland. Kipling in *Puck of Pook's Hill* calls ancient Britain fairyland.

and the Castle of the Other World is Tara. The hero of a Journey to Fairyland, therefore, after his victory over Fomorian giants, might be thought of as a king at Tara.[76]

According to *CMT*, when Lug arrives at Nuadu's palace at Tara, he takes part in games which are plainly tests of his fitness for kingship. Lug first defeats everyone in the palace at chess. Then, after Ogma has thrown out of the palace a stone that eighty oxen might drag, Lug tosses it back again.[77] The Irish tests for kingship very probably formed a background out of which the tests at Chastel Merveilleus developed. The best account of these Irish ordeals at Tara, *De Síl Chonairi Moir*,[78] is as follows. Although it exists solely in three manuscripts of the fifteenth century, it is undoubtedly very old.

There was a king's chariot at Tara. To the chariot were yoked two steeds of the same color which had never before been harnessed. The chariot would tilt up before any man who was not destined to receive the kingship at Tara so that he could not control it, and the horses would spring at him.[79] And there was a king's mantle (*casal*) in the chariot; whoso might not receive Tara's sovereignty the mantle was ever too big for him.[80] And there were two flagstones (*da liaic*) in

[76] Page 241.

[77] *CMT*, §§ 69–72 (p. 231).

[78] Summarized from the edition and translation by L. Gwynn, *Eriu*, VI (1912), 133–143. The four tests remind one of the Four Jewels of the Tuatha Dé, and of the four corners of the Grail castle.

[79] A modification of this chariot perhaps appears in *Parzival* as a bed that dashes about. This bed stood still for a moment, and Gawain leaped upon it (vs. 567,11). The horses that must be fought may have become in *Parzival* the lion "as tall as a horse."

> "Ein starker lewe sprang derfür:
> Der was als ein ors sô hôch." (vs. 571,12)

[80] A parallel perhaps appears at the Grail castle in the mantle of

Tara: "Blocc" and "Bluigne"; [81] when they accepted a man they would open before him until the chariot went through. And Fál was there, the stone . . . when a man should have the kingship of Tara it screeched against his chariot wheel so that all might hear.[82]

Since the king at Tara was selected by a number of ordeals, these tests may have furnished a starting point from which Chastel Merveilleus with its perilous couch developed.

Not only does there seem to be a connection between AA and Irish Nuadu; the wayward Orguelleuse too has Irish antecedents. A notable feature of AA is the proud, insolent character of the heroine. Chrétien calls her, "la male pucele" (vs. 7145), "la pucele ranposneuse" (vs. 7179), "pucele mesdisant, pucele sanz merci" (vs. 8373), "pucele male et desdeigneuse" (vs. 8637). Only after Gawain has been successful in every adventure does Orguelleuse beg his pardon and become gentle. A group of ancient Irish stories relate the winning of a *fée* who at first is proud,

---

Repanse de Schoie, the Grail queen, that Parzival put on (vs. 228,9). Trevrezent later tells him that this mantle, lent him by his aunt the queen, signifies that he shall be king "of the Grail, and of her, and of me."

[81] These two stones and *Lia Fáil* are in the prose *Dinnshenchas*, *Rev. celt.*, XV (1894), 282–285. *Lia Fáil* and its power to cry out under a true king are in *LL*, p. 9a, l. 13. See R. A. S. Macalister, *Lebor Gabála*, IV, 110; Baudiš, *Eriu*, VIII (1916), 106; J. H. Todd, *Irish Version of Nennius*, Ir. Archaeological Society (Dublin, 1848), p. 201; *Acallam*, l. 7992, *Ir. Texte*, IV, i, 224.

[82] *Lia Fáil* is matched by Wolfram's Grail, which is a stone (vs. 469,3), and which chooses its servants by writings that appear upon it. It seems to me that the barbaric Irish stone, which cried out when the chosen man stepped on it, might have been changed by twelfth-century Frenchmen to a stone that declares by writings that appear on it who shall be chosen.

insolent, and dangerous, but later becomes charming. These Irish stories explain Orguelleuse. In Irish she was virtually Ériu personified; [83] and her waywardness -- she has caused the heads of many brave men to be cut off (vs. 6756) -- is an allegory signifying the perils that await aspirants to royalty. She has fallen into the power of wicked Fomorians with names like Orguelleus, Mal Aguin, Malgiers, and has acquired similar hateful epithets such as Orguelleuse, Male pucele.[84] When the Welsh or the Bretons retold the story, they changed her name from Ériu to Logres (Britain). Chrétien, although it makes no sense, calls her Orguelleuse "de Logres." If this is her title, Gawain by winning her ought to win Logres. Chrétien of course cannot make Gawain ruler of Arthur's kingdom, so he introduces these explanatory verses:

> [Ele] trop est male et desdeigneuse,
> Et por ce a non l'Orguelleuse
> De Logres, ou ele fu nee,
> Si an fu petite aportee.

> (vss. 8637–8640)

"Orguelleuse was carried away from Logres as a child," he says, "and became ruler of Galloway." The object of this of course is to make Orguelleuse ruler of a country that Gawain can perfectly well take without displacing Arthur. Traces that she was once regarded as Ireland personified may be discerned. The Dutch *Lancelot* [85] calls her lover "Orgeleos van Yrlant." In Chrétien's *Erec*, Orguelleus "de la lande," who was at first identical, we may

---

[83] Pages 214, 328.

[84] In *Diu Crône* (vs. 21098), she is Mancipicelle or Maneypicelle, which must be meant for *male pucele*. In *Parzival* (vs. 517,16), the dwarf who accompanies her is Malcrêâtiure.

[85] Edition W. J. A. Jonckbloet ('s Gravenhage, 1846–1849), vs. 40065.

suppose, with this Orguelleus "de la roche," rides upon an Irish horse.[86] This seems to show that Orguelleus and Orguelleuse were originally Irish.

In spite of additions and changes, AA has kept the original supremacy of the *fée* in a remarkable manner; in a better manner even than many Irish stories. It has preserved marks of Irish origin and clearly belongs to the Journey to Fairyland type.

The links which bind Z to Y and AA, and which tend to prove that, if any of the three is of Celtic origin, so are the other two, may now be enumerated. The following resemblances bind together Z and AA. In both the hero comes first to an *angarde* (vss. 2987, 6523). In both stories the Hospitable Host has been split into two figures. In Z, two men in a boat, one of whom is fishing (vs. 3000), correspond to the two men in AA: the ferryman (vs. 7644), and the man with a silver leg (vss. 7650 f.). Both the Grail castle in Z and Chastel Merveilleus in AA appear to be forms of the Castle of Maidens, and both are beside a river. Both castles contain a splendid great hall. In both are many people, especially women who may have been at first *fées*. In both castles the hero is entertained at a feast, although in AA one of the hosts remains sitting outside. At both castles the host, or one of the hosts, is lame. Both castles are under oppression or enchantment, and need to be delivered. The ugly messenger links Z and AA together. On the one hand, she is informed about the Grail castle and rebukes Perceval for not asking a question and thus healing the Fisherman; on the other hand, she is going to Chastel Orguelleus, which is here evidently the same as Chastel Merveilleus.[87]

---

[86] "Et sist sor un cheval d'Irlande," vs. 2176.

[87] *Parzival* supplies additional evidence tending to prove that the Grail castle in Z and Chastel Merveilleus in AA were once adjacent and prob-

Both Z and AA are of course Journeys to Fairyland. It is obvious that, in the Grail episode of Z, ecclesiastical material has been worked in, but there is no reason why this may not have been done by Irishmen. In the tenth-century *Navigatio Sancti Brendani*,[88] an old man in an island lives on one third of a fish a day, and in *Imram Snedgusa ocus maic Ríagala*[89] are monks in a great house on an island celebrating the Mass. These are striking parallels to the Fisher King's aged father, whom Hilka calls the Grail King, and who lives not on fish but on "une sole oiste" (vs. 6422).

The following resemblances bind together Y and AA, and this in spite of the exclusion of everything miraculous from Y, but not from AA. In Y the Fomorian tower has become a tent surrounded by a "flowery plain" (vs. 674), namely a garden; in AA the tower has become a garden (vs. 6715). In Y the tent is beside a spring of water (vs. 640); in AA the garden is across a narrow bridge (vs. 6749).

---

ably identical castles. Parzival visits first the Grail castle and then apparently as a matter of course (vss. 618,20 f.) Schastel Marveile (Chastel Merveilleus). Gawain in Schastel Marveile is cured by an ointment (*salbe*) that comes from Munsalvæsche (Grail castle) and is the same ointment that keeps Anfortas alive (vs. 580,1). Gawain is glad to hear of Munsalvæsche because he thinks he must be near it. Anfortas was once one of Orgelûse's paramours. He gave her Cundrîe and Malcrêâtiure (vs. 519,23). He gave her also a costly tent which she still has (vs. 616,14). Later Anfortas was wounded, apparently in battle, by Clinschor (vs. 479,6), and is still in a death-in-life condition in the Grail castle. This implies that Orgelûse (Orguelleuse) was at first identical with the Grail Damsel, and that the Grail castle and Chastel Merveilleus are essentially the same.

[88] Edition Carl Schröder, *Sanct Brandan* (Erlangen, 1871), p. 33, § 23: "terciam partem piscis manducavi omni die." A. C. L. Brown, *Mod. Phil.*, XIV (1916), 394–401.

[89] Edition W. Stokes, *Rev. celt.*, IX (1888), 14 f., § 25.

In Y the giant is Orguelleus "de la lande" (vs. 3931); in AA the giant is not named, but the heroine's lover is Orguelleus "de la roche" (vs. 8646). In Y the tent damsel refuses Perceval both kiss (vs. 696) and ring (vs. 716), somewhat as in AA Orguelleuse refuses Gawain's advances (vss. 6840 f.). In short, a general parallelism of incident makes it impossible to separate Y, Z, and AA. Either all three have been elaborated by Celts and all three are Journeys to Fairyland or else none is.

According to a device well-known in Celtic storytelling a Hospitable Host is divided into several personnages who at various points on the journey counsel or entertain the hero. This feature appears in several of the stories outlined in Chapter II: in F, Riangabar, Connla *cael corrbarc* ("thin, crooked-hook"), and finally Coipre Cundail receive and lodge Cuchulinn; in E, first Roncu, then Domnall, then "a maiden of beautiful form in a large house," and finally Eochu Bairche entertain Cuchulinn; in G, Kulhwch is lodged first by King Arthur and then by Custennin. This device appears also in the romances of Chrétien which have been outlined in Chapter III: in V, Lancelot is entertained first by a Host who meets him on the road bringing game from a hunt, secondly by a Host who comes in from a hunt with game, and finally by Bademagu.[90]

Regardless of any theory about the origin of the figure, it has been suggested that some of these Hosts were different appearances of a single supernatural being with the power of shape-shifting. Thus the first two Hosts in V are described in almost the same words. Feebleness of human invention might possibly explain this, but there is something more. In *Yvain*, Calogrenant encounters first a Hospitable

[90] Pages 100, 101.

Host who lodges him for a night, and next a monster in a tree, guarding cattle, who tells him the road (vss. 288 f.). When the story of *Yvain* is reproduced some years after Chrétien's time by another writer in the *Livre d'Artus*, he tells us that the monster in the tree is Merlin in disguise,[91] which shows that contemporary readers understood that the monster in *Yvain* is somebody in disguise, and is indeed probably the Host of the night before. In Z, everybody knows that the Fisherman shows himself to Perceval in two forms: first as a fisherman in a boat, and afterwards as a wounded nobleman reclining on a couch in a great hall. From an introductory fragment called the "Elucidation" we learn that the Fisherman is a shape-shifter.[92]

Who is this shape-shifting Host? The three characters who go through a little drama with the hero at each castle visited, although all of them are not always present, are *fée*, Host, and giant. They are in origin always the same three, because, if our hypothesis is right, they are manfestations of (1) the *fée*, who although in origin a goddess became virtually Ériu personified, (2) Brión or Nuadu, the Irish god, and (3) Galam, the aggressor, who has become confused with winter and death. The shape-shifting Host is in origin the Irish god Brión [93] or his earthly avatar, Nuadu.

According to the battle of Lug and Balar in *CMT* and in *LG*, Nuadu is king at Tara and plays the part of a Hos-

[91] H. O. Sommer, *Vulgate Romances*, VII, 125.

[92] See Hilka, *Perceval*, p. 422:

> "Qui moult savoit de ningremance
> Qu'il muast .c. fois sa samblance." (vss. 221–222)

[93] It is hardly necessary to illustrate the shape-shifting power of an Irish god. In *Oided Chloinne Tuirenn* (ed. E. O'Curry, *Atlantis*, IV [London, 1862], 196) Brión changes himself and his two brothers into three hawks and then into three swans.

pitable Host. When Amargen the Milesian invader arrives, he meets in succession three kings called MacCuill, Mac-Cecht, and MacGreine.[94] The wives of these three kings are Banba, Fodla, and Ériu, which are three different names for Ireland. These three kings, therefore, must be merely names for the three different forms of Nuadu or of the god Brión. Like other gods, Brión had many forms and many names,[95] but he appears usually as a triad: Brión, Iuchar, and Iucharba. His three forms are fully attested in Irish documents.[96]

This Irish analogy shows that, just as in *LG* Amargen visited three brothers all kings of Ireland,[97] so in the oldest form of *Perceval* the hero visited in succession three brothers, all Hospitable Hosts and all in origin nothing more than three different manifestations of Brión or Nuadu. In Z the three Hosts are Arthur, Gornemant, and one of two old men at Belrepeire. One of these two old men, I conjecture, is a manifestation of the Fisher King. A notion that such Hosts may be different manifestations of one supernatural being is common in Celtic stories. For example, in "Arthur and Gorlagon," [98] Gorgol, Gorbeil, and Gorlagon are successive Hosts, and in reality the same person in different disguises. Another example is in *Scél Mongáin*,[99] an ancient Irish Journey to Fairyland which has not before been compared to *Perceval*.

---

[94] Pages 256, 265.
[95] Compare the twenty-one names of the Dagda in *CMT*, § 93 (Father G. Lehmacher's translation, *Anthropos*, XXVI [1931], 449 f.).
[96] Page 281.   [97] Page 266.
[98] [Harvard] *Studies and Notes*, VIII (1903), 101, 201.
[99] Edited and translated by K. Meyer, *Voyage of Bran*, I, 52–56. It is in *LU*, ed. Best and Bergin, p. 336; and is certainly far older than Chrétien.

Mongan told a student to go to a fairy-hill, Síth Lethet Oidni, to fetch a jewel and a pound of silver, and he foretold to him his journeys. The youth went first to Síth Cnoc Bane, where he found a noble-looking couple to meet him. They gave a great welcome to a messenger from Mongan. He went on and found another couple in Duma Gránerit, where he had the same welcome. Then he went to Síth Lethet Oidni, where he again found another couple who hospitably entertained him as on the other nights, and in the morning gave him the jewel and the pound of silver that he sought.

In this story, for three successive nights the hero is entertained by a noble-looking couple. Only the last hill is fairyland, but the first two must be foreshadowings of it, and the Hosts, at all three, must be essentially the same.

Our hypothesis that Gornemant and the Fisherman are manifestations of one character, namely the god Brión, explains why neither has a wife. The god has for wife the triple-formed Ériu. Arthur, Gornemant, and the Fisherman, we may suppose, in an earlier form of the story, all three had as wife a triple-formed Ériu or Brigit, who, according to the evidence, was called in Wales Gwenhwyvar. After it was forgotten that Gwenhwyvar had three forms and that she was a *fée*, it was felt improper for her to be Perceval's lady-love. This relationship and that of wife to Gornemant and to the Fisherman were obliterated. Hence, in our romance, Gornemant and the Fisherman remain without wives although they are surrounded by damsels. The situation is particularly noteworthy in the case of the Fisherman, who resembles an Irish "king of the land of women."

Our hypothesis also explains why Arthur sometimes seems to be identical with the Fisherman and yet we know all the time that he is not the Fisherman. At least in *Perceval*, the oldest Grail romance, Arthur, Gornemant, and the Fisher-man are different aspects of the same shape-shifter. They are three manifestations of the triple-formed Brión or Nuadu; all three are thought of as living in the outskirts of the land of the dead, and as old, wounded, and more or less helpless. Andreas Capellanus pictures Arthur as, like the Grail King, the object of a quest, and as living in a kind of dreamland like the land of the dead. The *Wartburg-krieg*, about 1300, puts Arthur and what seems to be the Grail together in a hollow mountain. Long ago Martin saw that Arthur in Avalon is only another form of the Grail King.[100] Both are in fairyland, or, as the romance writers put it, both are enchanted. In general, Arthur corresponds to Irish Nuadu; and Bron, the Fisherman, to Brión.

It is probable that Z, like Y, formerly contained three Hosts, and that in Z these were the Fisherman, the smith, Trebuchet, who made the sword that is given to Perceval at the Grail castle (vss. 3675 f.), and the hermit (called Trevrizent in *Parzival*, vs. 452,15), who tells Perceval about the Grail (vss. 6338 f.). All three are old men whom Perceval visits,[101] and all three have information about the Grail.

The hermit tells Perceval that he is his uncle and that he is brother to the old man (Grail King) who lives on *une sole oiste* (vs. 6422) that is brought in the Grail. This would make the Fisherman, who is the Grail King's son, Perceval's cousin; but in *Parzival*, and in most forms of the

---

[100] E. Martin, *Parzival*, II, lx.

[101] Perceval's visit to the smith is told in Manessier's *continuation* (Potvin's *Perceval*, VI, 36, vss. 41515 f.), where his name is spelled Tribu and Tribuet; and in Gerbert's *continuation* (ed. Mary Williams, I, 17–30, vss. 520–939).

story, the Fisherman is Perceval's uncle. It is probable that
when the hermit calls himself Perceval's uncle, he means to
imply that he is identical with the Fisherman. Both are
Perceval's uncles, because they are two different disguises
of the same shape-shifter.

The shape-shifting Fisherman disguised himself first as
a smith and then as a hermit in order to lure the hero on,
and to help him finally to deliver the Grail castle. If Z
were complete we should probably read that Perceval visited
both the smith and the hermit before his successful visit to
the Grail castle.

That the Fisherman disguised himself as a hermit may
seem probable enough, but some may hesitate to believe
that he shifted his shape to that of a smith. The smith-god
Goibniu appears in Irish mythological references as a different person from Brión or Nuadu. It is worth while,
therefore, to examine Irish evidence to see if Goibniu was
ever regarded as a manifestation of Nuadu.

The first piece of testimony is a folk tale which is known
in many parts of Ireland and which is so often referred to
that it must once have been widely current. The best-
known version,[102] *Glas Gaibhleann* ("The Grey [Cow] of
Goibniu"), runs in brief as follows:

Balar a giant lives on Tory Island. It has been prophesied
that his grandson will kill him. Three brothers, Gavida a
smith, MacSamthainn, and MacKineely, have an all-supplying
cow called Glas Gaibhleann (or Goibhneann). Balar in the
form of a red-headed boy steals the cow. MacKineely carries

[102] J. O'Donovan, *Annals of the Four Masters* (Dublin, 1851), I, 18.
For other versions see *Mod. Phil.*, XXII (1924), 87, n. 4; *Béaloideas*, VII
(1937), 244–246; IV (1934), supplement by É. Ó'Tuathail, "Seanchas
Ghleann Ghaibhle," p. xi; and W. J. Gruffydd, *Math vab Mathonwy*
(Cardiff, 1928).

off Balar's daughter Eithne. Balar slays MacKineely, and Eithne bears a son Lug who later grows up and kills Balar.

The testimony of the *Glas Gaibhleann* story will no doubt be rejected by some who will hold that it has no authority and may be based on Irish printed documents like *LG* and *CMT*. The *Glas Gaibhleann* story, however, is so unlike the older printed documents that it probably preserves independent ancient tradition. If so, it testifies that a smith was one of the forms of Nuadu.

The *Glas Gaibhleann* story has some resemblance to the plot of the Grail legend. Balar the Fomorian is the giant in the story. He takes the shape of a red-headed boy and corresponds to the Red Knight and to Clamadeu. In an older form of the Grail story Clamadeu must have been an enemy not only to Belrepeire but to its duplicate, the Grail castle. The three brothers, Gavida the smith, MacSamthainn, and MacKineely, represent the triple-formed Nuadu and correspond to Arthur, Gornemant, and Fisherman in Y, and to Fisherman, hermit, and smith in Z. Eithne and the cow [103] — for they seem to belong together — correspond to the Grail damsel and the Grail. It has been noticed above that the Grail damsel and Blancheflor were probably once the same. Gavida in this story is certainly Goibniu.

Additional evidence that Goibniu the smith-god was one of the forms of Nuadu exists in O'Mulconry's *Glossary* and in Cormac's *Glossary*. The former calls Nuadu, Mathu, and Goibniu, "three wizards of the heathen." [104] This

---

[103] A. H. Krappe (*Balor*, p. 21) thinks that, in the *Glas story*, Eithne and the cow are interchangeable and were at first the same. The plenty-giving cow is, of course, a talisman or magic treasure similar to the plenty-giving Grail (see Gruffydd, *Math*, pp. 65 f.).

[104] The text is, "Gobæ ocus Goibenn .i. o Goibhninn. iii faithi fis la

means, I think, that Mathu, Nuadu, and Goibniu were three forms of one heathen god. Cormac's *Glossary* [105] says that Brigit had two sisters, "Brigit, woman of leechcraft, and Brigit, wife to Goibniu." Since the triple-formed Brigit or Ériu is wife to the triple-formed Brión or Nuadu, this evidently means that Goibniu is a form of Nuadu and therefore is husband to Brigit.

Evidence that Goibniu was regarded as a host or entertainer of the gods is found in *Fled Goibhninn*, "Goibniu's Feast," the well-known name for the unfailing banquet of the Tuatha Dé.[106] This feast was of course provided by a talisman of plenty, doubtless the Dagda's Cauldron, which generally belongs to Brión. It was truly Brión's feast, and therefore in some sense Goibniu must be the same as Brión or as his manifestation, Nuadu. In ancient times the smith in small villages would generally be the innkeeper or host. This is the reason why Goibniu, like the Greek Hephaistos, was both smith and cupbearer of the gods, and would correspond to the Hospitable Host or the Grail King. That Goibniu was known and doubtless was worshipped in ancient Wales is proved by Gobannium,[107] the

---

geinti .i. Mathu, Nuada, Goibnend" (*Archiv f. celt. Lex.*, I, 265, § 665). Eóin Mac Neill shows that this text is of the ninth or tenth century (*Ériu*, XI [1932], 112). Cf. K. Meyer, *Anecdota*, IV, xvii, note. A poem attributed to Taliessin associates Math Hen and Govannon (W. F. Skene, *The Four Ancient Books of Wales* [Edinburgh, 1868], I, 286, II, 303): "I have been with men skilled in wizardry, with Math Hen, with Govannon."

[105] The text is, "Brigit bē legis ocus Brigit bē Goibne" (*Anecdota from Irish Manuscripts*, IV, 15, § 150).

[106] For example *Acallam*, ll. 6403 and 6806 (*Ir. Texte*, IV, 177, 189, 327); *Altram Tige Dá Medar*, ed. Lilian Duncan, *Ériu*, XI (1932), 188.

[107] On the ending "annon" as the mark of a deity, see Gruffydd, *Math*, p. 145. On Goibniu as ruler of a feast, see d'Arbois de Jubainvaille, *Cours*

ancient name of Abergavenny, a town sixteen miles north of Arthur's residence at Caerleon.

The evidence above makes it probable that Goibniu was, at least sometimes, regarded as a form of Nuadu. In the Grail story, therefore, perhaps a smith was one of the disguises of the Fisherman. Chrétien calls his smith not Goibniu but Trebuchet, and a variant reading is Triboet. Triboet, because it is a *durior lectio*, is probably the older form, and, I think, goes back to an Irish mythological smith Turbe or Tuirbe who, according to the prose *Dinnshenchas*,[108] used to keep back the sea, and who was the father of Gobán Saor. Gobán was the name of a mythical builder, but Dineen's *Dictionary* calls it "a popular form" of Goibniu. The gods have many names, and that Tuirbe was regarded as a manifestation of Goibniu is very possible.

Another entry in the prose *Dinnshenchas* relates that Síd Buidb, a well-known fairy hill, had connected with it a sub-lacustrine smith. Síd Buidb is at some distance, but the *Dinnshenchas* says [109] that a smith called Lén who lived in, or under, Loch Léin (Killarney) made precious vessels for

---

de littérature celtique, II (Paris, 1884), 309. An Old Irish incantation to preserve butter reads, "Fiss Goibnen, aird Goibnenn, renaird Goibnenn" (Stokes and Strachan, *Thesaurus Palaeohibernicus*, II, 248). Patrick's hymn prays, "fri brichta ban ocus goband ocus druad," "against the spells of women, smiths, and druids" (Windisch, *Ir. Texte*, I, 56). By "women" Patrick probably meant *fées* or heathen goddesses, and by "smiths" he meant Goibniu and his heathen devotees.

[108] Edition W. Stokes, *Dinnshenchas*, *Rev. celt.*, XVI (1895), 77. On Gobán Saor see *Béaloideas*, II (1930), 273, and p. 444.

[109] Translation by Stokes (*Rev. celt.*, XV [1894], 450): "Lén Línfiaclach son of Bolgach . . . was the craftsman of Síd Buidb. It is he that lived in the lake [*isin loch*, but Rawlinson B 506, *Folk-Lore*, III (1892), 485, reads *fo (r) loch*, 'under the lake.' The text has been copied by a scribe who did not know that fairy folk live under lakes] making the bright vessels of Fand, daughter of Flidias."

Fand, a *fée* who ruled over Síd Buidb. Lén resembles Trebuchet who lived at a distance from the Grail castle and who yet made for it a marvelous sword. The argument that Trebuchet is the Fisherman in disguise is strengthened by finding that, like the Grail castle, this Irish *síd* had connected with it a sub-lacustrine smith.

Our conclusion is that Trebuchet the smith in *Perceval* is probably the Fisherman in disguise, but the present argument does not depend upon proof that Trebuchet is the Fisherman. Our argument does not oblige us to explain either hermit or smith.

It has occurred to several students of *Perceval* that all the heroines and all the Hosts are the same; [110] to this I would add all the giants. It is worth while to assemble the various names given to *fée*, Host, and giant. The names are collected here from the twenty Irish and Welsh Journeys to Fairyland outlined in Chapter II; from the battle of Lug and Balar in *CMT* and *LG*,[111] which is important because it undoubtedly represents an older model after which other stories were patterned; and from the marvelous episodes in Chrétien's romances, already outlined.

HEROINES

In the Celtic stories the following names for the heroine occur: B, Macha, "plain," which refers without doubt to

---

[110] J. N. Carman, "The Relationship of the Perlesvaux and the Queste del Saint Graal" (*Bulletin of the University of Kansas*, XXXVII, no. 13 [1936], p. 21), finds evidence in the romances he is studying that Chrétien's Fisher King and hermit uncle are identical. R. S. Loomis (*Celtic Myth and Arthurian Romance*, p. 281) reports that Miss Mallon "has demonstrated that Perceval's sister, cousin, wife, and the Grail messenger are one and the same."

[111] Pages 233, 265.

the notion that she was the land personified; C, Fann, "teardrop," and LíBan, "splendor of women"; D, Dergreine, "tear of the sun"; E, Emer; F, Finnchaem, "lovely white"; G, Olwen, "white footprints"; K, Rhiannon; L, Créde; N, Dáirenn; P, Etáin *foiltfind*, "white hair"; Q, BéBind, "white woman"; R, BéBind, "white woman"; S, Delbchaem, "beautiful form"; T, LíBan, "splendor of women"; and Cliodna *cheinnfionn*, "fair head." In the Lug-Balar story, the heroine is Macha, Scota, or Ériu, and is virtually Ireland personified. The element "white" in most of these names would doubtless have suggested to Irish hearers that they were *fées*.

In the marvelous episodes written by Chrétien are the following names for the heroine: W, Laudine and Lunete; Z, Blancheflor; AA, Orguelleuse de Logres! Of these Lunete and Blancheflor contain the element "white" or "shining." Orguelleuse de Logres is like the Irish Macha and is, I think, the country Logres (Britain) personified.

HOSPITABLE HOSTS

In the Celtic stories the following names for the Hosts occur: C, Labraid *luath*, "swift"; Failbe *finn*, "white"; Aed Aebrat, "fire of the eyebrow," and his son, Aengus; D, Fiachna; E, Roncu, "seal head"; Domnall, and Eochu Bairche; F, Riangabar, Connla *cael corrbacc*, "slender, crooked hook"; and Coirpre Cundail; G, King Arthur, Custennin, and his son Goreu, "best"; I, the Dagda and his son, Aengus of the Brug; J, Arawn; O, the twenty-eight sons of the fairy king, Midir, and his queen, Findchaem; P, Aed *uchtgel*, "white breast"; R, Aed *minnbrecc*, "smooth speckled"; Fergus *foltfind*, "fair-haired," and *ilbrecc*, "many-colored"; T, Connla. In the Lug-Balar story the host is the god Nuadu. Several of the above are well-known fairy names, and probably Irish hearers would have put them all into that category.

In the marvelous episodes written by Chrétien are the following names for the Hosts: U, King Evrain; V, two unnamed Hosts and Bademagu; W, unnamed; X, Li Rois de l'Isle as Puceles; Y, King Arthur and Gornemant de Goort; Z, the Fisherman; AA, the Ferryman and the man with a silver leg. The appellation "Rois de l'Isle as Puceles" would fit them all pretty well.

GIANTS

In the Celtic stories the following names for the giants occur: A, Tethra, known as a Fomorian king, whose name has been connected with that of the Old Norse giant Thiasi; [112] C, Senach *siaborthe* (*siabur*, "demon"), Eochaid Iúil, and Eogan inbir, "stream"; D, Eochaid mac Sail, Goll, "blind," mac Duilb, Donn, "dark," mac Nera, and Ecach *amlabair*, "speechless"; E, Forgall *monach*, "shape-shifter," sister's son to Tethra; Cochor, "red," Crufe, "hand," Cuar, "crooked," and Cat; F, Eocho *rond*, "chain," and Eocho *glas*, "green"; Yspaddaden *benn cawr*, "head giant" or "with a giant head," and Gwrnach *gawr*, "giant"; J, Hafgan; K, Gwawl; M, Aillén mac Midhna, also called Aed, "fire"; O, Bodb *derg*, "red"; Q, Cétach *crobderg*, "hundred fighter of the red hand," and his son Aed *alaind;* R, Garb, "rough"; Bé Dreccain, "woman-dragon," and Eolas; S, Morgan and his wife, Coinchend *cendfada*, "doghead longhead"; T, Cathman, perhaps "battle-man" or "warrior," Eochaid and Tuire *tortbhuillech*, "of the heavy blows." In the Lug-Balar story the giants are: Balar, his son, Galam, "warrior,"

[112] Page 41.

Galam's son, Donn, "dark," and Amargen, "grief-born," who is perhaps the same as Marg or Morc. Morc is *drech-deirg*, "red-faced." [113]

In the marvelous episodes written by Chrétien the giants are: U, Mabonagrain, who is clad in red; V, Meleagant, who pretty surely wears red since his seneschal has red armor; W, Esclados *li ros*, "the red"; X, two black kobolds, "fiz de diable, hideus et noir"; Y, the leader of five knights (in *Parzival*, vs. 125,11, called Meljahkanz); Rion, "li rois des isles"; Orguelleus "de la lande," the "vermaus chevaliers de la Forest de Quinqueroi"; Anguingueron, and King Clamadeu "des isles" (*Parzival*, vs. 181,11 f., tells us indirectly that Clâmadê wore red armor); [114] AA, Orguelleus "de la rôche," Guiromelant, and a dreadful, unnamed tyrant called "uns clers sages d'astrenomie," vs. 7548 (in *Parzival*, vs. 548,5, called Clinschor). He is either identical with Guiromelant or Guiromelant is his deputy.

This list of names supports a belief that the Irish before the time of Chrétien conventionally regarded the tower of the dead as red, and expected visitors from that tower to be red giants.

In E the adversary is named Cochor, "red." In H the castle of "shadow land," which because defended by toads and serpents is surely a tower of the dead, is said to be "of a hateful color." This "hateful color" must be red, which so long ago as Virgil's Aeneid was the traditional hue of those belonging to the tower of the dead. [115] In J the dogs of Annwn have red ears, doubtless as a sign that they come

---

[113] Page 400.   [114] Page 179, n. 14.
[115] Compare the glowing red iron walls of the City of Dis in Dante, *Inferno*, VIII, 67.

from the tower of the dead. In M the giant who fights with fire has for one of his names Aed, "fire." In O the adversary is Bodb the red, and in Q the adversary is Cétach Crobderg, "red hand."

In Chrétien's romances the giant is red in *Erec* (U), pretty surely in *Lancelot* (V), certainly in *Yvain* (W), and in *Perceval* (Y); also Wolfram tells us that Clamadeu, another giant in Y, wears red armor.

Of course, black or dusky color may also be a sign of the land of the dead. In *Echtra Laegaire* (D) Donn, "dusky," or "the dark one," *mac Nera* is a giant, and in the Lug-Balar story Donn was leader of the sons of Míl, was wrecked at Tech Duinn, and became the Irish king of the dead.[116] In the romances of Chrétien, in *Pesme Avanture* (X), the rôle of the adversary is played by two black kobolds.

A remarkable testimony to the Irish belief in the red tower of the dead is a ninth-century poem printed by Kuno Meyer in his "Bruchstücke der älteren Lyrik Irlands" which runs as follows:

> House of Donn rich in hosts, fortress of battle,
> Red-cornered rock of security,
> Royal city on the smooth sea, couch of a boar,
> Nest of a griffin of high rank.[117]

---

[116] For Kuno Meyer's proof that Donn was king of the dead, see p. 257.

[117] *Abhandlungen der Preussischen Akademie d. Wiss.*, phil.-hist. Klasse (Berlin, 1919), vii, 59. The poem is also in *Ir. Texte*, III, i, p. 22, § 66; p. 49, § 88; p. 98, § 161. The last line of it is quoted in Cormac's *Glossary*, § 968. The text is as follows:

> "Tech Duinn dámaig, dun Congaile,
> Carrac rúadfáebrach ráthaigthe,
> Ráith ríg fri lán lir féthaigthe,
> Fail nir, net gríphe grádaigthe."

This poem, after applying to the house of the dead the adjective *dámaig*, "rich in hosts," also calls it "red-cornered rock," and "royal city on the sea." The meaning of the word *dámaig* may be better understood if one compares in Máelmura's ninth-century poem [118] the expressions: Bregoin *buidnig*, "Bregond of troops," Amargen *tirech*, "Amargen ruling many lands," and in another poem, Bregaint *bruinig*, "Bregond of large companies." The reference in all these cases is to the great possessions of the king of the dead.

A striking testimony to the Irish belief in red giants who come from the land of the dead may be found in the eighth-century *Togail Bruidne Da Derga*.[119]

King Conaire is journeying to his death at the Bruiden Da Derga, "Hostel of Two Reds," and he sees before him three horsemen riding toward the hostel. "Three red frocks had they, and three red mantles; three red bucklers they bore, and three red spears were in their hands, three red steeds they bestrode, and three red heads of hair were on them. Red were they all, both body and hair and raiment, both steeds and men." King Conaire says that it is a *geis* ("taboo") for him to allow the three reds to go before him *do thig Deirg*, "to the house of Red." Three times he sends his son to try to overtake them and persuade them to turn back. The boy cannot approach them nearer than a spear's length,[120] however much he lashes his horse. At his third attempt one of the riders calls back to him: "Weary are the horses which we ride. We ride the horses of Donn Detscorach from the

[118] Page 256.

[119] Edition Eleanor Knott (Dublin, 1936), pp. 9 f. I summarize and quote from the translation by W. Stokes, *Rev. celt.*, XXII (1901), 36 f., §§ 30–36.

[120] In *Pwyll and Rhiannon*, J, the heroine (a *fée*), outdistances her pursuer in the same marvelous way.

elf mounds. Though we are alive we are dead.[121] Great are the signs: sating of ravens; feeding of crows; whetting of sword-edge; shields with broken bosses after sundown." When the king and his followers hear what the horseman says, they are terrified. Later these three reds appear in the hostel. They are three champions who wrought falsehood *i sídib*, "in the elf mounds." This is the punishment inflicted upon them by the king of the elf mounds, to be destroyed thrice by (or with) the King of Tara.[122]

The name *Bruiden Da Derga* is unexplained. We are told that it was one of the six recognized hostels of Ireland, but it may have become regarded as a Fomorian castle and a red tower of the dead. This is probable enough, because Forgall's *bruiden* in E, which was likewise one of the six hostels, has plainly become a Fomorian tower.

Eleanor Knott [123] prints a passage from *LL* that declares: "Three redheads of the Laigin, sons of Donn Désa, slew King Conaire the Great in Bruiden." Of course Donn Désa is not the king of the dead, but one can hardly help conjecturing that he is a substitution, and that, if we knew the mythological story that lies behind the saga, we should find that King Conaire was slain by the three Reds, sons of Donn, king of the dead, at the red tower of the dead. Such a hypothesis, however, is unnecessary. In any case

---

[121] Eleanor Knott's text is: "Scítha eich imda-rríadam. Im-ríadam eocho Duind Desscoraig a sídaib. Cíammin bí amin mairb" (p. 10, § 35). Stokes' translation is in *Rev. celt.*, XXII, 39, § 35. Thurneysen, *Heldensage,* p. 635, translates *Donn Dētscorach*, "der Dunkle mit Zahn-Ausfall," and adds, "Donn ist der alte Todesgott der Iren." Thurneysen evidently pictures Donn as a skeleton or living corpse.

[122] Edition Knott, p. 40, ll. 1331–1333; Stokes, *Rev. celt.*, XXII, 308, § 134.

[123] *Da Derga*, p. 73.

the passages make perfectly clear that long before Chrétien's time "Red Island" [124] was in Irish a name for the land of the dead.

Recently collected Irish tales introduce a destructive giant called Tomâs *Fuilteach*, "Thomas the bloody," [125] who corresponds to the red warrior of the tower of the dead. Other Irish stories of the Journey to Fairyland type call the giant, who is the guardian of a fairy realm, a red warrior.[126] In the "Children of the King of Norway," the home of hostile giants is called the City of the Red Stream, and in the "Pursuit of Gruaidh Ghriansholus," the City of the Fiery Stream.[127]

An idea that the devil is red, or perhaps black, is very old, and the symbolism of these colors is widespread.[128] In the Irish *Imram Maeile Dúin*,[129] the twelfth island visited is divided by a bronze fence; sheep on one side become black and on the other white. In the Welsh *Peredur* [130] is a valley divided by a river that changes sheep that ford it from

[124] Compare *Erec*, vs. 2192: "Roi de la Roge Cité."

[125] See stories VI–VIII in G. Dottin, *Contes Irlandais* (London, 1901), translated from D. Hyde, *Sgéaluidhe Gaedhealach*. Tomâs has a witch grandmother in the shape of a hare who appears to be the "devil's grandmother" of popular tales.

[126] J. Curtin, *Hero Tales of Ireland* (London, 1894), pp. 183, 423, 463; Patrick Kennedy, *Legendary Fictions of the Irish Celts* (London, 1866), p. 203; J. G. Campbell, *The Fians*, Waifs and Strays, IV (London, 1891), 92.

[127] Douglas Hyde, *ITS*, I (London, 1899), 162–166; and Cecile O'Rahilly, *ITS*, XXIV (London, 1924), 89. See also J. R. Caldwell, *Eger and Grime* (Harvard University Press, 1933), p. 171, n. 131.

[128] F. B. Gummere, "On the Symbolic Use of Colors," *Haverford College Studies* (Haverford, 1889), I, 129; *Handwörterbuch des Deutschen Aberglaubens*, III, col. 1898.

[129] Edition W. Stokes, *Rev. celt.*, IX (1888), 481.

[130] *Mab.*, II, 115.

black to white, and vice versa. That these are symbolic pictures of the valley of death has been noticed by students of the subject,[131] and red more commonly than black is a symbol for the land of the dead.[132]

The same symbolism of red and black appears in the French romances, and observers have interpreted it in the same way.[133]

In Indic mythology the king of the dead appears in red. Siva, the god of the dead in the *Veda*, has one hundred names, one of which is Rudra, "red." He resembles Balar, king of the Fomorians, in having an evil eye.[134] In the *Ramayana*, Râvana, who is Siva under one of his names, came disguised in a red frock as an anchorite and carried off Sîta in his chariot. Sîta's husband, Râma, finally slew Râvana and released Sîta, pale and faint from long imprisonment in a tower.[135] Since Sîta is goddess of the crops, this story is a parallel to the rape of Proserpine.

---

[131] Ella Vettermann, "Die Balen-Dichtungen," *Beihefte zur Zeitschr. f. rom. Phil.*, LX (1918), 293.

[132] Alfred Nutt in D. MacInnes, *Folk and Hero Tales*, pp. 475–477, pointed out the rivalry common in Irish folk tales between the hero and a red or red-haired villain. In Douglas Hyde's *Beside the Fire* (London, 1910), p. 148, a red visitant turns out to be a dead man.

[133] Dr. Arthur Dickson, *Valentine and Orson* (New York: Columbia University Press, 1929), Studies in Eng. and Comp. Lit., XCI, 94, writes: "The red and the black armor in *Lycorne, Atre Perillos*, and Dutch *Lancelot* are to be interpreted . . . as märchen-symbols for death." H. Naumann, *Primitive Gemeinschaftskultur* (Jena, 1921), p. 84, declares: "Die vielen schwarzen Ritter der bretonischen Sage tragen wenigstens die Farbe des preanimistischen Dämons noch, und das Rot wird sich nicht anders erklären." See his pages 47 and 87.

[134] M. Winternitz, *History of Indian Literature*, I (Calcutta, 1927), 185.

[135] G. Courtillier, *La Légende de Râma et Sîta* (Paris, 1927), pp. 114–162.

The red or black warrior with his red city who piques our curiosity in the marvelous episodes in Chrétien's romances provides substantial evidence for a Celtic origin. The materials assembled in this chapter establish to a high degree of probability a Celtic and ultimately an Irish origin for Y, Z, and AA; that is, for the whole of Chrétien's unfinished *Perceval*.

CHAPTER V

Wolfram's *Parzival*

THE hypothesis upon which this chapter is written is that, besides Chrétien's *Perceval*, Wolfram used minstrel versions and perhaps the so-called *Ur-Perceval*, which were closer to Welsh and Irish story. The hypothesis is that Wolfram preserves to some extent a tradition that was independent of Chrétien. This I believe to be the right view, but it should be said that, although Wolfram's *Parzival* strengthens the proof that the Grail legend belongs to the Journey to Fairyland type, it is not necessary to that proof.

Wolfram's story is in general rather close to Chrétien. Sometimes he is further removed from Irish story than Chrétien; but in many passages, where he deviates, he is closer to Irish tradition. To suppose that in these places where he agrees with Irish tradition he had no other sources than Chrétien's *Perceval*, with its continuations, and the other extant romances that were written before his own time lands us in an absurdity. If, to avoid this absurdity, we assert that Wolfram had access to manuscripts of Chrétien that differed extensively from any that have come down to us, or if we assume that he was acquainted with oral versions that rested upon Celtic originals, we are really granting the independent character of Wolfram's narrative, which is all that the present chapter requires. Yet some such admission as this is necessary. Wolfram out of his own fancy could not alter Chrétien's romance in numerous particulars and make it correspond to Irish stories. At the most, chance might account for one or two instances of such agreement, but never for several. Wolfram must have had access to an *Ur-Perceval* (i.e., to Chrétien's source or something like it). He had Irish material that did not reach him through Chrétien.[1] Perceval's story is, of course, retold by Wolfram. It is convenient to divide his *Parzival*, like Chrétien's *Perceval*, into three parts: AB, AC, and AD.

AB. Parzival's Story except for the Grail Castle
(Vss. 1,1 to 224,1) [2]

Parzival's mother, Herzeloyde, brings him up in ignorance of chivalry, in a forest. She is afraid that he will wish to be a knight, will enter tournaments, and get killed. One day Parzival meets three knights (vs. 121,1).[3] Then comes a fourth knight, Karnahkarnanz of Ulterlac, who inquires of Parzival whether he has seen two knights carrying off a maiden. Later he explains that the weeping maiden is Imâne von der Beâfontâne, and that one of the knights he is in search of is named Meljahkanz.[4] Parzival, dazzled by the splendor of the knights,

[1] Professor W. A. Nitze did pioneer work by indicating resemblances between the Grail castle and the hall at Tara in his "Castle of the Grail — An Irish Analogue" (*Studies in Honor of A. M. Elliott*, Baltimore, n. d. [1912], I, 19–51). On the Kiot question see now G. Weber, "Wolfram," *Deutsche Forschungen*, XVIII (1928), 136. The main point is that Kiot did not write a long romance and that Wolfram used several sources, including an *Ur-Perceval*.
[2] Summarized from the edition of E. Martin.
[3] Instead of five, as Chrétien says. Since Perceval takes them for God, three is better than five. See *Mod. Phil.*, XVI (1919), 555. One manuscript of Chrétien reads "three knights."
[4] Both name and character show that this is Meljacanz, son of Poydiconjunz (vs. 344,1), who corresponds to Chrétien's Meleagant,

asks how to become one, and is told by the chief knight that men are made knights by King Arthur. Parzival goes home and tells his mother that he wishes to go to King Arthur's court to be made a knight. She gives the boy a bad horse (*vil boese*, vs. 126,23) and clothes him in a fool's dress of coarse cloth with calfskin leggings, so that people may laugh at him and send him back to her; yet, according to Wolfram, she instills into his mind a vengeance motive.[5] She tells him, "The bold, proud Lähelîn deprived your father's two princes of two kingdoms, Wâleis and Norgâls, and he slew one of the princes, Tûrkentâls." Parzival answers, "I will kill him with my javelin" (vs. 128,4). After Parzival departs, Herzeloyde falls dead of grief. Parzival rides into the forest, Brizljân (vs. 129,6), where he finds beyond a stream a tent gay with three colors. A lady alone in the tent is Jeschûte, wife to Duc Orilus de Lalander (vs. 129,27) (Chrétien's Orguilleus de la lande). Parzival kisses her and takes away her ring.

Soon Orilus returns and accuses his wife of falseness. Then he boasts that he has overthrown eight knights of the Round Table and remarks, "My sister Cunnewâre dwells at Arthur's

son of Bademagus; and perhaps Meljanz de Lîz, who took prisoners from Arthur (vs. 344,15), is a doublet based on some error. Imâne is (as Martin observed in his edition of *Parzival*, II, 287, and Brugger, *Ztsch. f. franz. Sp.*, XXVIII (1905), p. 1, n. 1) one of the *pucelles as puis* who is carried off (as I think) by the king of the dead, whether Amangon as in the *Elucidation*, or Meleagant as in *Lancelot*, and here. The Grail castle and Arthur's castle, as abodes of life and light, are subject to attack from these lords of the dead. Wolfram has preserved more of the original situation.

[5] If the mother wishes vengeance, she ought not to equip Parzival with a bad horse and comical attire. The two ideas are contradictory. That Wolfram kept them both is a hint that he is faithfully following a traditional narrative. At one stage in the development of that narrative, as I suppose, Parzival rode upon the ugly horse of death. Hence the bad horse and poor bridle (p. 350). Later somebody who understood nothing supernatural retold the story and tried to explain the bad mount as a mother's attempt to keep her boy from chivalry.

hall.[6] She will never smile until she sees the bravest of all knights; if that knight shall come, there will be a fight worth watching. Already this morning in a joust I have slain a prince."

After the adventure at the tent, Parzival comes to his cousin, the weeping Sigûne, who holds in her arms her dead lover, Schionatulander. She asks Parzival his name. He replies, "Bon fîz, scher fîz, bêâ fîz" (vs. 140,6). She tells him that his name is Parzival,[7] and says, "Thou art king of North Wales and oughtest to be crowned at Kingrivâls. Two brothers did thee evil. Lähelîn robbed thee of two lands, and Orilus slew my lover, Schionatulander, who was defending thy kingdom."

Next Parzival comes to a fisherman (*ein vischaere*, vs. 142,17), who dwells in a tolerably large house and who refuses lodging until Parzival gives him the gold ring that he has taken from Jeschûte. The next morning the fisherman [8] guides him to

[6] Probably in Wolfram's original Orilus said, "My paramour dwells at Arthur's hall." Wolfram, not comprehending that the tent-damsel, Ginovêr, and Cunnewâre were the same, and that therefore Orilus might call either the tent-damsel or Cunnewâre his paramour, changed this to, "My sister Cunnewâre dwells at Arthur's hall." Cunnewâre was at first a *fée*, and Orilus a giant (see p. 126). Wolfram makes Clâmidê marry Cunnewâre (vs. 326,30). Clâmidê, doubtless, like other Fomorians, wished to seize the Grail maidens. Perhaps Wolfram found something in his original that suggested this marriage.

[7] Sigûne corresponds to the Fisher King's niece weeping over her dead lover, and in Chrétien she does not appear until after the Grail castle visit. Wolfram probably invented this earlier introduction in order to bring in Parzival's name. At the time of his first adventure, a hero learns his name, as, for example, in the "Knight of the Red Shield" (J. F. Campbell, *Pop. Tales of the W. Highlands*, II, 459, a story that has points of contact with the Grail story; compare Lancelot [H. O. Sommer, *Vulgate Version of the Romances*, III, 144 f.], Biaus Desconeus, Finn, and Cuchulinn).

[8] A fisherman is more primitive than Chrétien's *charbonier*. He corresponds to the *notonier* in AA, and to the Fisher King in Z. Like the *notonier* he demands payment, which probably means that he has been confused with Charon.

Arthur's court at Nantes. Parzival's horse has a bridle of hemp and is a wretched beast that stumbles often; his saddle has no new leather in it (vs. 144,23).

Outside Arthur's castle Parzival meets a knight in red armor, Ither von Gaheviez,[9] who claims Arthur's land, and as sign of his lordship has carried away Arthur's golden cup. He is king of Kukûmerlant. He tells Parzival to challenge King Arthur to come and regain the cup. He is Arthur's cousin and has been brought up by Utepandragôn, his mother's brother (vs. 145,12). A damsel, Cunnewâre de Lalant, who is sister to Orilus and Lähelîn, smiles at Parzival, which makes Kay angry and he strikes her. A youth named Antanor, who, because he never speaks, is thought a fool,[10] rebukes Kay and in return receives a blow on the ear. Parzival pursues the red knight, Ither, and slays him with the cast of a javelin that pierces his eye. Parzival remarks, "You might well be Lähelîn, who took away my land." A knight, Iwânet, who has followed Parzival, carries the gold cup back to Arthur. Queen Ginovêr bewails the dead Ither as one who might bear the highest prize of the knights of the Round Table. "His heritage did he claim, for which he was slain. He was beloved of all men" (vs. 160,6).[11]

Parzival puts on the red armor of the slain Ither, rides all day, and towards evening finds sitting under a broad linden tree outside his castle gate a knight, Gurnemanz de Grâharz. Gurnemanz lets go a falcon as a signal to summon his servants, who soon arrive and escort Parzival to the castle. Next morn-

[9] J. H. Scholte (*Neophilologus*, V [1920], 115-121) has argued powerfully that "Ithêr von Gaheviez" is not to be derived from the "Iher Gaheries" of Hartmann's *Erec* (vs. 1658, ed. M. Haupt [Leipzig, 1871], p. 352; and see p. 396).

[10] "Der durch swîgen dûht ein tôr" (vs. 152,24).

[11] Ither is a Fomorian giant, I suppose, who has seized Ginovêr. In the Recurrent Battle he is slain by Parzival. In Wolfram's original, I conjecture that Ginovêr had a kind word for the slain giant, much as in D (p. 45) a heroine says of a slain giant, "I loved Goll mac Duilb," and Wolfram has exaggerated this kindness.

ing several fair maidens prepare Parzival a bath. He is ashamed before them (vs. 166,22). Gurnemanz, besides advising Parzival not to be swift to question, teaches him how to joust; next day in the tourney-field Parzival strikes down five knights. When men see his prowess they suggest marrying him to Gurnemanz' daughter, Lîâze. Gurnemanz bids her kiss Parzival. Parzival tarries fourteen days and, when he takes leave, Gurnemanz tells him how his three sons have been slain: Schenteflûrs in fighting for Cundwîrâmûrs against Clâmidê and Kingrûn, her enemies (vs. 178,2); Lascoyt by Idêr fil Noyt about a hawk; Gurzgrî, when he rode against the castle Brandigan after Schoydelakurt, by Mâbonagrîn. Deeply impressed, Parzival says, "When I win fame, thou shalt give me Lîâze." [12]

Still thinking of Lîâze, Parzival rides away from Grâharz into the mountainous kingdom of Brobarz, where he comes to Pelrapeire, a castle that King Tampenteire had bequeathed to his daughter, Cundwîrâmûrs. A rushing river must be crossed by a slender drawbridge that swings back and forth like a rope on high.[13] More than thirty knights on the other side warn Parzival not to cross, because they mistake him for their enemy Clâmidê. Parzival nevertheless proceeds, and, because his horse trembles with fear, he is obliged to lead it over the bridge.[14] The thirty warriors disappear. Parzival crosses a tourney-field where many have been slain and strikes on an iron ring at the castle door. A maiden answers from a window and, after consulting Queen Cundwîrâmûrs, lets him in. Along the streets of the town he has seen half-starved men, because

[12] Lîâze is not in Chrétien's version, but she may have been in the original story (see p. 195).

[13] This is like the rope bridge of *Tochmarc Emire* (in the older version of *c.* 1050, p. 49), much more so than is Chrétien's bridge. H. R. Patch has noticed this (*PMLA*, XXXIII [1918], 636, n. 118).

[14] Clâmidê wears red armor; consequently Parzival, who is clad in Ither's red armor, is mistaken for Clâmidê.

Clâmidê the king of Brandigan, a city in Iserterre,[15] is besieging the town to win Cundwîrâmûrs (vs. 184,20).

After Parzival has entered the castle the queen appears, escorted by two old men, Kyot von Katelangen and Manpfiljôt, her uncles. Parzival is thinking of Lîâze, as well as of Gurnemanz' warning, and keeps silent till the queen speaks. The two old men, after promising to send provisions and wine, withdraw to their *weidehûs*, "hunting-lodge" (vs. 190,21). Cundwîrâmûrs comes to Parzival's bedside in the middle of the night and tells him that Kingrûn, the seneschal of Clâmidê, is attacking her castle, and has slain Schenteflûrs, the brother of Lîâze, her defender. Parzival promises to champion her against Kingrûn. After Parzival on the next day has fought and conquered Kingrûn, she embraces him and says that she will never be wife to another. Two ships with food arrive, and the citizens take oath to hold Parzival as their lord. That night Parzival leaves Cundwîrâmûrs a maid, but not on the third night (vs. 203,5).

Kingrûn is sent by Parzival to Arthur's court, where he is greeted as a fellow seneschal by Kay (vs. 206,26). Clâmidê, king of Brandigan, comes on his horse, Guverjorz (vs. 210,7) to attack Cundwîrâmûrs, and Parzival conquers him and sends him to Arthur at Löver [16] (vs. 216,4). King Clâmidê declares that he has sought in vain the love of Cundwîrâmûrs, and that his cousin Mabonagrîn is also trying to win her (vs. 220,8).

AC. Parzival and the Grail Castle
(Vss. 224,1 to 256,1)

Next day Parzival takes leave of Cundwîrâmûrs, explaining to her that he hopes to find his way back to his mother. At

[15] By calling Clâmidê king of Brandigan, Wolfram connects him with Mabonagrain, king of Brandigan, who is said to be a cousin, and who appears as a red knight in *La Joie de la cort* (p. 92).

[16] Löver must be a contraction of Lloegr (Britain), although Wolfram may not have understood this.

nightfall he comes to a broad river on which are fishermen in boats. He asks where he can find lodging. A man in a boat who is dressed with peacock plumes in his hat, as if lord of all lands, replies, "No dwelling exists for thirty miles round except one. Ride to the top of the rock and you will see it. I will be your host. Take care not to lose the way." After Parzival finds the Fisherman's castle, he tells the attendants that the Fisherman sent him, rides across a tourney-field, and dismounts. They put a mantle (vs. 228,9) on him which the chamberlain says "has been worn by our queen Repanse de Schoye.[17] She lends it to you till new clothes are ready." A jester summons Parzival to the host's presence in so saucy a way that Parzival almost smites him with his sword (vs. 229,9).[18]

Parzival enters the palace, where hang one hundred crowns and where are many tapers. He sees one hundred couches there, and one hundred cushions; four knights occupy each of these couches. Anfortas, the Fisherman, ruler of the castle, is Frimutel's son (230,4). Three four-cornered fireplaces of marble, supplied with lign-aloe wood, stand in the hall. So great a fire was never seen at Wildenberc. Parzival is invited by his host to sit beside him; the Fisherman host is clad in dark fur with a shining ruby in his cap. The people in the hall are grieving. A lad springs in at the door with a spear from the point of which blood runs. The people now lament loudly. He carries the spear to each of the four walls, and when he departs the outcry ceases.

Two maidens enter, one of whom is Clârischanze, Countess of Tenebroc, carrying golden candlesticks; two more enter carrying stools that they place before the host. All four stand together and are dressed alike. Then eight maidens enter.

[17] Laeg wears a woman's mantle when entering fairyland in F (p. 58). Lancelot dons a woman's mantle on entering a fairy castle (p. 101).

[18] Parzival's readiness to resent affront (cf. his name, *perce+val*) is like Cuchulinn's behavior in F (p. 57).

Four carry tall candles, four carry a jacinth-stone which, when placed across two stools, serves as a table. The maidens are all clad in green. Then enter four more maidens with candles [19] and two with silver knives which they place on the table. Eighteen maidens have now entered, and six more come. Last comes a queen with a face bright as sunshine who carries "the wish of paradise," the object called *der Grâl*. Her name is Repanse de Schoye, and she has been chosen Grail-bearer by the Grail itself. Six balsam lights are borne before the Grail. The queen places it on the jacinth-stone. As Parzival watches her he remembers that he is wearing her mantle (vs. 236,15). Every four knights have a server. There are one hundred tables, and at each table sit four knights. At every table four lads serve the four who sit there. Four wagons are rolled in toward the four walls, and four knights distribute gold dishes from the wagons to the guests. One hundred lads bear bread from *der Grâl* in napkins (vs. 239,4) to the guests. It is *der Grâl* that feeds them, and warm or cold dishes, wild or tame meat, may be had at desire. If one names a drink, his cup is instantly filled. Parzival remembers Gurnemanz' warning and asks no question.

A lad brings in a sword with a magnificent ruby in its hilt. The host, after remarking that he has often carried the sword in battle, gives it to Parzival. Attendants remove the four wagons and bear away the tables. Through an open door in an outer chamber on a couch Parzival sees a noble gray-haired old man [Tyturel].

Parzival is led to a sleeping chamber. Four maidens with tapers before them bring him syrup and wine. Parzival is ashamed before them and springs into bed. The chief maiden kneels down to offer him wine, and he bids her rise (vs. 244,1). The next morning when Parzival awakes, he sees

---

[19] This service by four is exactly like that in the fairy castle in Irish L (p. 76).

his two swords and his armor, but can find nobody. He mounts his horse and rides out across the drawbridge, which rises behind him before his horse has stepped from it. A squire calls out, "Goose, if thou hadst asked concerning the wonders thou hast seen, thou hadst been famous." [20]

Parzival hears a woman's voice, and under a linden tree he finds Sigûne still mourning and holding her dead lover Schîânatulander in her arms. She warns him to flee from this wood, which contains no shelter for thirty miles. He tells her that he has lodged at a castle nearby. "That castle must be Munsalvaesche, which cannot be found except by accident," [21] she said. "This land is Terre de Salvaesche. Tyturel gave it to his son Frimutel (vs. 251,6), who had four children: Anfortas, Trevrizent, Herzeloyde, and Repanse de Schoye. Anfortas is the Fisher who has been wounded so that he must recline on a couch and can neither stand nor sit. Trevrizent is a hermit." Parzival, concerned about the dead Schîânatulander, urges Sigûne to bury him; he does not advise her, as Lunete did Laudine, to marry the man who slew her lord. [22] Sigûne says, "You have Anfortas' sword wrought by Trebuchet. It will break at the second blow, but may be renewed at Karnant, where there is a king called Lac. You did wrong not to ask a question about the Grail and thus heal Anfortas."

AB AGAIN. PARZIVAL'S STORY EXCEPT FOR THE GRAIL CASTLE (Vss. 256,1 to 311,28)

Parzival next meets Orilus and Jeschûte mounted on horses. Orilus has punished Jeschûte, and she is in rags. Orilus has

---

[20] This reproach is not in Chrétien's *Perceval*, and is perhaps not a part of the older story (see p. oo). It comes in with the "frustrated redemption" motive, on which see the story of Potter Thompson (Alfred Nutt, *Folk-Lore Journal*, I (1883), 193). [21] Page 196.

[22] Doubtless in the original she, as a matter of course, married the slayer of her lord. It is thus in *Peredur* (*Mab.*, II, 89).

with him a helmet made by Trebuchet, a spear that comes
from Gaheviez, and a horse that comes from Lake Brumbâne
(vs. 261,27), where Lähelîn his brother has won it for him.
Parzival conquers Orilus in combat and sends him to King
Arthur. They come to the cell of Trevrizent, where Parzival
takes oath that he has not dishonored the lady Jeschûte, and
obtains a bright-colored spear left there by Taurîan, brother
of Dodines (vs. 271,12). When Orilus arrives at Arthur's
court, Cunnewâre de Lâlant welcomes him, "Thou art my
brother, either Orilus or Lähelîn" (vs. 275,24). Kay tells
Kingrûn to wait upon Orilus at table, as he has often waited
upon Clâmidê at Brandigan.

Parzival, while musing one day over some blood drops in
the snow, is assailed by Kay; in the encounter Kay is worsted
and his arm is broken. Segramors and Gawain arrive and take
Parzival with them to Arthur's court.

AD. Gawain and Schastel Marveile
(Vss. 311,29 to 433,1)

King Arthur, holding a feast at Nantes, according to his
custom will not eat till he hears of an adventure (vs. 309,9).
Cundrîe *la surziere*, the ugly Grail Messenger, arrives. She is
clad in a blue mantle and wears a peacock hat. She has a nose
like a dog, tusks like a boar, ears like a bear, and hands like a
lion. She rebukes Parzival for not pitying the Fisherman and
asking a question that would have healed him. To Arthur she
says, "My home is at Schastel Marveile, where are four queens
and four hundred maidens. A noble lady may be won there.
Though the journey be hard, I shall arrive before nightfall"
(318,19).[23] Many knights vow to see the four queens and

---

[23] On this echo of the Irish Journey to Fairyland, see p. 134. The
four queens are: Itonjê, Cundrîe (the messenger herself is probably this
queen in disguise), Arnîve, and Sangîve. The names may be Wolfram's
invention, but the number four is scarcely accidental (see p. 182).

the four hundred maidens. A Greek, Clîas, who is present,[24] tells how he once visited Schastel Marveile and was overthrown there by Florant von Itolac (vs. 334,3).

Gawain rides Gringuljete, a horse with red ears[25] which Orilus gave him, and which came in the first place from Muntsalvâsche (vs. 340,1). Lähelîn took it when its rider, Lybbêâls von Prienlascors (vs. 473,25), fell dead in a joust by Lake Brumbâne. Trevrizent tells Parzival this.

Gawain meets the army of King Poydiconjunz von Gors and of Astor, duc de Lanverunz. With them was Poydiconjunz' son Meljahcanz, who does evil to women (vs. 343,26). Poydiconjunz' brother King Schaut (vs. 386,20) has a son Meljanz (vs. 343,26). Schaut, on his deathbed gave Meljanz to the care of Lyppaut. Lyppaut has two daughters, Obîe, and Obilôt. This Meljanz of Liz is leading the army of Poydiconjunz against the city Bêârosche to win Obîe. Against Gawain fight some of Arthur's men, who have been taken prisoners at the mountain pass of Clûse when they were fighting against Poydiconjunz (to rescue Ginovêr, vs. 387,7). A red knight [Parzival] also fought against Gawain's party. Parzival takes the short-eared steed Ingliârt (vs. 389,26). Gawain, on condition that he undertake the Grail quest,[26] is released from a promise to fight a duel.

[24] Clîas may be a distortion of Girflez. In Chrétien's *Perceval*, vs. 4721, Girflez vows to visit Chastel Orguelleus which is plainly the same as Chastel Merveilleus (see p. 135).

[25] Red ears signify that the horse belongs to the red tower of the dead. The dogs of Annwn had red ears (p. 72).

[26] That the accomplishment of the quest interests not Parzival only but the whole court reminds one of Irish stories, especially of *CMT* (p. 232).

AC AGAIN. PARZIVAL AND THE GRAIL CASTLE
(Vss. 433,1 to 503,1)

Parzival comes to a hermitage built over a spring where Sigûne keeps watch over the dead Schîânatulander. She tells Parzival that the Grail feeds her. Cundrîe *la surziere* brings her food from the Grail every Saturday (vs. 438,29).[27] Sigûne says, "Duke Orilus slew my lover. Cundrîe left me but a short time ago. Follow and she may lead you to the Grail castle." Parzival jousts with a Grail knight. He loses his own horse and wins the Grail knight's horse.

An old knight named Kahenîs and his lady, who are doing penance, reproach Parzival for riding on Good Friday. Parzival comes to Fontân la salvâtsche, where the hermit Trevrizent dwells. He remembers that he has once taken a bright-colored spear from here. It was Taurîân's spear, and he has used it well. Trevrizent tells Parzival about the Grail. No man who sees it can die for a week.[28] On Good Friday a dove brings an *oblât*, which it lays upon the stone to renew its power. The stone (Grail) feeds its servants and, by means of writings that appear upon it, chooses men and women to serve it.[29] Anfortas rules at Muntsalvaesche, but is punished because he sought forbidden love. "I think you are Lähelîn because you ride a Grail horse." Parzival replies that he is son to Gahmuret and that he once killed Ither von Kucûmerlant (vs. 475,9). Trevrizent tells him that this was a sin and another sin was his causing his mother's death by leaving her so hastily. "I am your mother's brother. Another brother is Anfortas. Tschoysîane,

---

[27] Cundrîe's relations with both the Grail castle and Schastel Marveile suggest that originally the two castles were different aspects of the same fairy abode.

[28] This life-giving power resembles that of the "well of healing" in *CMT* (p. 232).

[29] The power of choice belonging to the Grail is like that exerted by *Lia Fâil*, and by other objects in the Irish ordeals.

who married Kyot, is a sister. Her daughters are Sigûne and Repanse de Schoye. Anfortas fought for a lady, Orgelûse, and his battle cry was Amor (vs. 478,30). A heathen from the land, Ethnîse, that borders on Paradise, wounded him in the groin with a poisoned spear and thought to win the Grail (vs. 479,19). The Grail keeps Anfortas alive.[30] A writing on it says that if a knight shall come and ask a question, he will win the kingdom and Anfortas will be healed, but no one may warn a visiting warrior, and he must ask the question the first night that he arrives at the castle" (vs. 484,1). Parzival confesses that he has been there and has failed. The hermit goes on to say that Anfortas's wound is worse when Saturn ends his course. "Then the spear must be laid on the wound. Trebuchet has made two knives to cut the ice that forms on the spear when placed in the wound [vs. 490,22]. Twenty-five maidens stand before Anfortas [vs. 493,16].[31] King Castis wooed Herzeloyde and gave her Wâleis and Norgâls when he died. When Repanse de Schoye lent you her mantle she meant that you were to be king [vs. 500,30]. The old grey man you saw was your great-grandfather Tyturel [vs. 501,22]." [32]

AD again. Gawain and Schastel Marveile

(Vss. 503,1 to 827,30, the end)

The story of Gawain's approach to the land of Schastel Marveile follows closely that in Chrétien's *Perceval*, except that the wounded knight (Greoreas in *Perceval*) is named

---

[30] Anfortas comes from *infirmitas*, as Martin says (in his note on vs. 472,22), but perhaps by way of Irish *Ainfectnach*, a name for Nuadu doubtless referring to his wound (see Eóin Mac Neill, *Celtic Ireland*, p. 54). Nuadu had a son, Anbechtach (p. 305).

[31] The Fisher King is clearly king of a Castle of Maidens, and a parallel figure to "li roi de l'isle as puceles" (see p. 113).

[32] This succession of kings is like the list of kings in *Baile in Scail* (p. 220). Tyturel is a displaced king.

Urjâns, and that he has been wounded by Lischoys Gwell-jus of Gowerzîn, one of Orgelûse's knights. The city where Gawain finds Orgelûse which has no name in *Perceval* is here called Lôgroys (507,29). Orgelûse is mirroring her face in the water of a spring.[33] She is the ruler of Lôgroys.

The dwarf who brings the wretched nag is here called Malcrêâtiure, which is an appropriate name for the companion of Orgelûse whom Chrétien calls *male pucele*. Malcrêâtiure is brother to Cundrîe *la surziere*. Anfortas, when he was wooing Orgelûse, gave her these two deformed creatures who came at first from India (vs. 519,23).[34] In place of the "nephew of Greoreas," who in *Perceval* fought Gawain at the river, Wolfram substitutes Lischoys Gwell-jus,[35] whom he has already mentioned, and who, he says, fights for the love of Orgelûse. To the ferryman, whose house is so stately that Arthur at Nantes would have needed none better, Wolfram gives a name, Plippalinôt.[36] He has

[33] Wolfram, by putting the encounter with Orgelûse, who is the nymph of the place, at a spring, is closer to folklore than Chrétien, and probably preserves a trace of an older form of the story before it was attached to King Arthur.

[34] To make the nag belong to Orgelûse is a primitive feature, because it is a means of transport to fairyland and ought to be sent by a *fée*. Cundrîe and the dwarf may have belonged together in the source, but to make them brother and sister and bring them from India is surely an invention by Kyot or Wolfram. Is the story of Orgelûse's *amour* with Anfortas primitive? If so, she must in origin have been the ruler of both the Grail castle and Schastel Marveile. The two castles must be different aspects of the same place, and Blancheflor only another aspect of Orgelûse.

[35] *Diu Crône* (ed. Scholl, vs. 20185) calls this "nephew of Greoras," Ansgü. This might stand for Anguin or Aingen, which are Irish variants of Amorgen (see p. 376).

[36] Probably a deformation of Palinurus, who is mentioned in the account of the land of the dead in the *Aeneid*, vi, 337 (quoted on p. 16).

two sons and a daughter named Bêne. To continue with a summary:

The daughter would have given Gawain her love had he desired it. When Gawain awakes the next morning he is surprised to see the ladies still looking from the windows of Arnîve's castle. Arnîve is Arthur's mother, called Ygerne in *Perceval*. Had the ladies been at the windows all night? [37] He falls asleep, and when he awakes Bêne is at his side. He inquires who the ladies are. Bêne shrinks in terror. "Ask me not. If I knew, I might not tell." Her father, when he comes in, is likewise terrified. "You are in Terre Marveile and Lît Marveile is here. No one has overcome the dangers of Schastel Marveile. If you win, you shall rule this land and free the ladies. You conquered Lischoys Gwelljus, who is braver than anybody except Ither of Gaheviez. Parzival, who slew Ither, travelled in my boat yesterday, and gave me the horses of five knights that he had conquered." "Did he hear of this adventure so near?" asked Gawain. "I did not tell him, nor would I have told you," said the ferryman, "unless you had asked. If you conquer and rule this land, then my poverty shall end."

The man who in *Perceval* has a silver leg is here pictured as a merchant at the door of Schastel Marveile, to whom Gawain entrusts his steed. He is a wealthy merchant [38] and has a booth of samite, square, wide, and high (vs. 563,2). All his treasure shall belong to Gawain if Gawain wins. The castle roof glitters like peacock's feathers.[39] The hall containing the Lît Marveile has a glass floor. The bed runs on four rollers made of rubies. It is dashing about, when Gawain leaps upon

[37] They are ghosts as we presently learn.

[38] Wolfram's "merchant" may go back to some manuscript of *Perceval* that read *eskiekier*. That the merchant takes pay from Gawain may be a trace of Charon's fee.

[39] Feather roofs occur in Irish Journey to Fairyland stories (see pp. 76, 83).

it. It strikes against the four walls of the hall and finally stands
still in the center. Five hundred slings shoot stones, and five
hundred crossbows shoot bolts. A big *bûr* now enters, who
carries a club and is dressed in a sea-otter's skin.[40] He threatens
Gawain, and then lets in a lion as tall as a horse. Gawain slays
the lion and drops senseless.

The maidens put Gawain on a couch before a fire. Arnîve,
with the help of Cundrîe *la surziere* cures him. Arnîve applies
a salve which comes from Munsalvaesche where it keeps Anfortas alive. When Gawain hears of Munsalvaesche he is glad,
for he thinks he must be near it (vs. 580,3).[41] Then Arnîve
gives him a root that makes him sleep. Many ladies stand by
and keep silence. Gawain wakes and looks at them. He has
never seen anything so splendid as the hall. A winding stair-
case leads to a dome with windows of adamant, amethyst, topaz,
and carbuncle. Presently Arnîve comes with her daughter
Sangîve, and her granddaughters, Itonjê and Cundrîe, Gawain's
sisters. None of these four queens, thinks Gawain, equals in
beauty Orgelûse. Here is a pillar that shows everything for six
miles around. Gawain sees in this pillar a lady leading a knight
by a rein. He looks out of the window and sees Orgelûse
(here called the Duchess of Lôgroys), leading Flôrant von
Itolac (Orguelleus de la Roche in *Perceval*), her *turkoyte* who
was never conquered.

After Gawain has conquered the *turkoyte* and given him
over to Plippalinôt, he goes with Orgelûse through Clinschor's
forest. She tells him that if he will fetch her a garland from a
tree beyond a *grabe* ("ditch") she will grant him her love.
The ditch is named Sabbîns. The tree is guarded by King
Gramoflanz, who will fight only two at once. Gramoflanz is

[40] Although Wolfram turned Nuadu into a merchant, he here on the
contrary preserves a trace of the sea god. This *bûr* appears to be Nuadu,
or one of his emissaries, in disguise.

[41] Could this be a trace of an original identity of the Grail castle
and Schastel Marveile?

unarmed. He wears a peacock hat and a long green robe. To Gawain he says, "I slew Orgelûse's lover, Cidegast, and three other warriors. I carried her off and offered her my land and crown. I kept her for a year, but she would not yield to me. You have now become lord of this terre marveile. Since Orgelûse refused me, I love Itonjê" (Clarissant in *Perceval*). Gramoflanz has never seen Itonjê, but he sends her a ring, as in *Perceval*. King Irôt, his father, was treacherously slain by King Lot, Gawain's father. When Gawain reveals himself they arrange a battle for the sixteenth day at Jôflanze. "I can bring fifteen hundred ladies," says Gramoflanz, "and you can bring a host from Schastel Marveile. Your uncle, King Arthur, can bring people from Löver, his country." Gramoflanz, after declaring that no bridge over the Sabbîns exists, except at his city, Rosche Sabbîns (vs. 610,26), unsuccessfully invites Gawain to go thither.

After Gawain has leaped the Sabbîns and returned to Orgelûse, she explains, "Gramoflanz slew my knight Cidegast. My insulting words were only meant to prove your steadfastness." Gawain then asks for her love. She says, "No!" But she promises to accompany him to Schastel Marveile. "Anfortas sent me the costly tent [42] that stands without," she continues. "His wound saddened me. After Cidegast, I chose him. When Anfortas was forsaken of joy, I was afraid of Clinschor, and I gave him the tent on condition that, if any knight should conquer here, to this knight I would offer my love, and, if he refused, this tent should belong to me. I am eager to have Gramoflanz conquered. No man ever refused to serve me, except one who wore red armor, who came hither from Lôgroys and overthrew five of my knights. He had a wife, he said, the queen of Pelrapeire, who was fairer than I. His name is Parzival."

[42] Compare the marvelous tent given by the *merfeinne* to the hero in *Lanzelet*, vs. 4690. These tents may be of oriental origin (K. G. T. Webster [Harvard] *Studies and Notes*, XVI [1934], 225, n. 96).

Gawain and Orgelûse are ferried over the river by Plippalinôt and his daughter Bêne. Orgelûse secures the release of both Lischoys Gwelljus and Florant, her *turkoyte*, who are Plippalinôt's prisoners. King Arthur is at the city Bems bî der Korcâ in the country of Löver (vs. 610,18). Arnîve and Bêne conduct Orgelûse to Gawain's chamber, and she gives herself to him without ceremony.

The next day Gawain delivers to his sister, Itonjê, the ring and message from Gramoflanz. Gawain's grandmother, Arnîve, tells him that in Schastel Marveile men and women are separate and do not see each other. Clinschor, a magician, devised this castle and carried off to it Arnîve as his prisoner. It will belong to the man who conquers it. Next, King Arthur and his company arrive at Joflanze. Gawain, accompanied by the four queens, visits him. Arthur has attacked Orgelûse's troops, and Meljanz de Liz has captured and made prisoners several of Arthur's knights. To see the battle between Gramoflanz and Gawain, the former's uncle, Brandelidelîn (vs. 682,10),[43] comes from Punt, a waterlocked city. Arthur sends to Rosche Sabbîns to summon Gramoflanz. Bêne takes a ring from Itonjê across the river to Gramoflanz. As she and he return, they encounter Gawain and Parzival fighting. Some of Gramoflanz's people call Gawain by name. Thereupon Parzival, who had not recognized his antagonist, stops fighting in sorrow, and Gawain falls in a swoon. Bêne, after speaking bitterly to Gramoflanz, springs from her horse and helps to revive Gawain. Gramoflanz postpones his combat with Gawain till the morrow. Parzival wishes to fight in Gawain's place, but Arthur forbids.

The next morning Parzival steals out secretly and fights with Gramoflanz, who mistakes him for Gawain. When Gawain arrives, Gramoflanz is being worsted, and he is allowed to defer further fighting until the next day. Itonjê, with Bêne as messenger, finally persuades Arthur to make peace

---

[43] Brandelidelîn, I conjecture, stands for *Brun de l'isles*.

between Gramoflanz, her lover, and Gawain, her brother. Many weddings follow: Gramoflanz and Itonjê, Lischoys and Cundrîe, Sangîve and Florant. Gawain and Orgelûse celebrate a feast, but Parzival steals away out of love for Cundwîrâmûrs. The next incident is a tremendous battle between Parzival and his heathen half-brother, Feirefîz. After this, at Arthur's feast, Cundrîe *la surziere* appears to announce that Parzival has been chosen to the Grail kingship. He and Cundwîrâmûrs and their son Loherangrîn set out for Munsalvaesche. By asking the fateful question Parzival heals Anfortas and reigns in his stead.

Doubtless Wolfram now and then deviated from Chrétien merely to pursue some fancy of his own. Occasionally he is less close to what must have been the traditional story than is Chrétien. Some cases of Wolfram's inferiority may be mentioned first. The Sore Pucele should send the hero the sword as Chrétien makes her do (vs. 3145). Wolfram ought not to have omitted Greoreas's statement that Galvoie is a land "from which nobody returns" (vs. 6604), nor the remark of Orguilleus that he attacks Gawain for having passed the gates of Galvoie (vs. 8385). Wolfram's merchant is less primitive than Chrétien's man with a silver leg (vs. 7652). The swift motion of the Perilous Couch about the hall in Schastel Marveile, the mirrors, the shining pillar that showed what was happening for six miles around, and Gawain's bringing a garland instead of flowers, from a tree beyond the *grabe*, "ditch" (vs. 604,8), are all points in which Wolfram seems to be less primitive than Chrétien. Wolfram also omits a primitive statement that Gawain must remain always in Chastel Merveilleus (vs. 8024). This is all natural enough, if Wolfram handled his material freely, and contradicts in no way the hypothesis advocated in this chapter, which is that he used, along with *Perceval*, other sources (minstrel versions or the *Ur-Perceval*) which were closer to Irish story.

Some of the points in which Wolfram deviates from Chrétien's *Perceval* and agrees with Irish Journeys to Fairyland are as follows. They are numerous enough to destroy any theory that all these coincidences may have resulted from the fortuitous operation of Wolfram's fancy.

1. Meljacanz, who carried off Imâne von der Beâfontâne (vs. 125,11), is evidently the same as Meleagant who appears in Chrétien's *Lancelot* and elsewhere as a king of the dead. Thus, at the very outset, Wolfram introduces depredations made by enemies [kings of the dead] upon Arthur's people [*fées*], a motive that corresponds to the strife between Tuatha Dé and Fomorians in Irish stories. Wolfram refers to this strife every now and then. In 135,7 f., Orilus, who is evidently a Fomorian, boasts that he has overthrown eight knights of the Round Table. Arthur fights Orgeluse's soldiers (vs. 673,11) and is repulsed by Meljanz von Lîz. Although Wolfram probably did not know it, this Meljanz must be the same as Meljacanz. This background of strife resembles the war in the prose *Lancelot* between King Arthur and Galeholt with his five generals, but it cannot conceivably be based on *Lancelot*. It is a survival, I suppose, from the minstrel version of *Perceval* of a background of strife that has been minimized in Chrétien's work.

2. Parzival's bad horse (vs. 126,23) and his poor bridle (vs. 144,22), although not so understood by Wolfram, are, I conjecture, traces of an original *char de la mort*.[44] Chrétien

---

[44] Page 350.

gives Perceval a good horse (vs. 78), which, unless we are entirely on the wrong track, is less original.

3. The fisherman who exacts payment before he will entertain Parzival (vs. 142,17) is a parallel figure to the Fisherman who is seen first in a boat, in Y, and to the ferryman who exacts payment, in Z. Because he is more like Charon, he is probably more primitive than Chrétien's *charbonier*.[45]

4. Parzival's love affair with Lîâze, the daughter of his host, Gurnemanz, is a part of the love-making of Mag Mell and is doubtless connected with the custom mentioned above.[46] Chrétien tells no such incident.

5. When Parzival, wearing the red armor that he had taken from Ither, crosses the bridge at Pelrapeire, thirty knights guarding the other shore mistake him for Clâmidê. This proves that Clâmidê was a red knight.[47] Chrétien lacks this point.

6. The Fisher is dressed as if he were lord of all lands and in his hat wears peacock plumes (vs. 225,9). This attire resembles the splendor of the fairy king in Irish stories. One may compare Labraid in C. Peacock feathers may or may not be a sign of Irish origin, but they are a sign that the wearer belongs to the realm of the dead. A peacock's feather signified the evil eye.[48] In *Yvain*, at the castle of the Hospitable Host, Calogrenant is given a mantle spotted with peacock plumes (vs. 233). In *Parzival* the

---

[45] *Perceval*, vss. 3007, 7379, 835 (see p. 125).

[46] *Parzival*, vs. 175,21 (see p. 106).

[47] Page 179.

[48] A. H. Krappe, *The Science of Folk-Lore*, p. 255; *Myth. Univ.*, pp. 174–175. On the evil eye in Irish one may compare *milliud* in Cormac's *Glossary*, *Anecdota*, IV, 73; *Togail Bruidne Dá Derga*, § 62, ed. E. Knott, p. 16, and Stokes, *Ir. Texte*, IV, i, 323.

ugly messenger Cundrîe has a peacock hat (vs. 313,10).
Gramoflanz wears a peacock hat (vs. 605,8). The roof of
Schastel Marveile glitters like peacock's feathers (vs. 565,9).
Chrétien does not describe the Fisherman's costume.

7. Wolfram's three fires in the center of the Grail hall
(vs. 230,9) are like the three fireplaces in the hall at Tara.[49]
Chrétien mentions but one fire.

8. The Grail castle, according to Sigune, cannot be
found except by accident (vs. 250,26). This is a well-
known characteristic of the castle of fairyland.[50] Chrétien
does not mention it.

9. Gawain's love affair with Bêne (vs. 549,8), like Parzival's with Lîâze, is a part of the love-making of Mag Mell
and probably a reflection of the custom referred to. Chrétien mentions no love affair with Bêne.

10. The roof of Schastel Marveile glitters like peacock's
feathers (vs. 565,8). This resembles the fairy palaces
roofed with bird's feathers in Irish stories, as in L, and
Echtra Cormaic.[51] No such roof is mentioned by Chrétien.

11. Clinschor who carried off Queen Arnive as prisoner
to Schastel Marveile (vs. 656,11), acts more like Eochu
Glas in F than does Chrétien's clers sages d'astrenomie,
who was brought by Queen Ygerne to build Chastel Merveilleus (vs. 7548). Clinschor, who in other stories is sometimes a musician, has long been recognized as a king of the

---

[49] Dr. Nitze noticed this (see above, p. 175). See also G. Petrie, "On
the History and Antiquities of Tara Hill," Royal Irish Academy, Transactions, XVIII (1838), 211, n. 20; and R. A. S. Macalister, Tara (New
York, 1931), pp. 64–65.

[50] See W. Hertz, Parzival (Stuttgart, 1927), p. 507. Compare St.
Brendan's Isle, which cannot be found by searching, and the rath of
King Ailill, "to be seen from afar but not to be found on the spot"
(J. Rhŷs, Arthurian Legend, p. 117, n. 1).

[51] Pages 76, 222.

dead.[52] Both Chrétien and Wolfram wish to explain everything as a result of magic, but Wolfram's account of
Clinschor is closer to Irish stories.[53]

12. The slender drawbridge that swings back and forth
like a rope at the entrance to Pelrapeire (vs. 181,3) is like
the rope bridge in E.[54] Chrétien merely remarks that the
bridge is *foible* (vs. 1713).

13. That Parzival wore the mantle of Repanse de Schoye
(vs. 228,9) is more like the protection afforded by a *fée*
in Irish story. So also (in vs. 552,20 and vs. 621,28) is
Bêne's lending her mantle to Gawain. In the first incident
Chrétien merely says that a servant brought Perceval a
scarlet mantle (vs. 3073), and in the Gawain incidents
he says nothing.

14. Service by four at the Grail castle is developed
more fully than in Chrétien's *Perceval*, and is more like the
service at Créde's castle in L.[55]

15. In Clinschor's castle men and women live apart
from each other (vs. 637,20), as in the land of the dead.
Chrétien does not mention this, although he hints at it
in vs. 7588.

16. Perhaps the strongest reason for believing that Wolfram had access to some story which was closer to Irish
tradition than is Chrétien appears in the way in which he
has kept Orgelûse's supremacy. This is truly remarkable,

---

[52] See "Klinsor" in Ersch and Gruber, *Allgemeine Encyklopädie*, § 2,
Theil 37 (Leipzig, 1885); W. Hertz, *Parzival*, p. 539.

[53] Chrétien may possibly have kept something older than Wolfram
in one point, namely in making the *clers sages* act at the order of Queen
Ygerne instead of vice versa. This could be a trace of the original
supremacy of the *fée*.

[54] Page 49.

[55] Page 76.

considering that even in Irish stories the original dominance of the *fée* often becomes obscured. Wolfram, to be
sure, in accordance with the taste of his day, formally
ascribes all the wonders of Schastel Marveile to the magic
of Clinschor. Several incidents, however, bear witness to
Orgelûse's former control over the action. It is her warrior,
Lischoys, for example, who has wounded Urgâns when he
tried to penetrate her kingdom.

17. That Malcrêâtiure and his nag belong to Orgelûse
(*la male pucele*, vs. 7145) is doubtless a primitive idea,
because a *fée* ought to control the means of transport to
her land.[56] This is not in *Perceval*.

18. Orgelûse, as has been shown above, was in origin
virtually the country personified. In Ireland she was Ériu.
Since Lloegr was an ancient Welsh name for Britain, in
Wales she was called Lôgroys. Wolfram is closer to this
original than Chrétien, because he calls her "herzoginne
de Lôgroys," and the city where Gawain finds her he calls
"Lôgroys." Chrétien to be sure keeps Orguilleuse's title
"de Logres," but he explains that she was born there and
was brought to Galvoie while small.[57] She brings Gawain
the sovereignty of Galloway. "Grey Galloway" was regarded by dwellers to the southeast as a land of the dead,
and Chrétien could make Gawain become prince of this
little-known land without displacing King Arthur.[58]

---

[56] In the same way the *fée* at first probably controlled the glass ship
in A (p. 40), the bronze ship in C (p. 17), the beast like a lion in E
(p. 48), and the ship guided by a charm in F (p. 56). A dwarf sometimes acts as the servant of a *fée* as in V (p. 100). On dwarves and the
land of the dead, see Krappe, *Science of Folk-Lore*, p. 88.

[57] Page 152.

[58] William of Malmesbury (*Gesta Regum Angliae*, Rolls Ser., XC,
ed. W. Stubbs, II [1887-1889], 342) and other early writers make Gawain
ruler of Galloway. In *Erec* (vs. 6815 f.) Gawain and the King of Gallo-

19. Wolfram makes it evident that Lischoys and Florant are in the service of Orgelûse by causing her to deliver them from Plippalinôt's prison. This must have been in the older story. Chrétien fails to make clear that the corresponding figures, "li niés Greoreas" (vs. 7302), and "Orguelleus" (vs. 8646) belong to Orguelleuse.

20. Orgelûse's paramours (husbands) are in succession as follows: Cidegast (vs. 616,2), Gramoflanz who after slaying Cidegast kept her prisoner for a year (vs. 606,8), Anfortas the Fisherman (vs. 617,7), Clinschor (vs. 617,11; since she "feared shame" she must have been in Clinschor's power), and Gawain (vs. 642,29); not to mention Florant, her *turkoyte* (vs. 594,3), and Lischoys who fought "for love of her" (vs. 543,3). A lack of realism in this list of lovers is obvious. The explanation is that she is not an ordinary heroine of romance, but is virtually Logres personified, an immortal,[59] and, like Ériu and Medb, is always young and desirable. Chrétien's list of paramours is not so clearly given nor so long.[60] He makes Guiromelant say that he once slew a lover of Orguelleuse:

> a un suen ami la toli
> Qu'ele soloit mener o li,
> Si l'ocis et si l'an menai.
>
> (vss. 8569–8571)

---

way appear together. Did Chrétien invent this connection? See Hilka's note to vs. 6602 (*Perceval*, p. 745); E. Brugger, *L. E. Kastner Miscellany of Studies in Romance Languages* (Cambridge, 1932), p. 102; Bruce, *Evolution*, II, 98, n. 7.

[59] Wolfram omits all reference to Anfortas's age; Cidegast, however, is associated with Utepandragun and Lôt, and seems to belong to an older generation. The picture, I believe, is that of an old and discarded lover with a perpetually youthful *fée*. One thinks of the Fisherman as an old man, perhaps because Chrétien tells us that his hair is mixed with grey (vs. 3087).

[60] Does the story of Gawain's horse, Gringuljete, illustrate this alterna-

Chrétien does not tell us that one of her lovers was the Fisherman.

21. A haughty and imperious *fée*, when her conditions are fully met, gives herself at once to her lover as Orgelûse does in *Parzival* (vs. 642,29); nothing is said of any wedding ceremony. That this surrender of herself to Gawain was in Chrétien's source is almost certain. It is the natural outcome of the situation, and Chrétien's has kept Orguelleuse's consenting words. She begs Gawain's pardon and says:

> Vostre volanté d'outre an outre
> Ferai sire.
>
> (vss. 8972–8973)

After this, she drops out of Chrétien's story without any reason, which is certainly not primitive, for common sense demands some sort of explanation. Chrétien evidently did not comprehend that she is virtually the sovereignty personified, mother earth, a goddess. For him she is *la male pucele*.

22. Wolfram is right in calling Gramoflanz' castle Rosche Sabbins — that is, Roche de Sanguin, "castle of blood" — because according to the Irish picture of fairyland it would be a Dolorous Tower. The other castle he rightly calls Schastel Marveile, because according to the

---

tion in kings? This horse belonged to Lybbêâls of Prienlascors (vss. 473,25 f.), who by his name "li beals" must have belonged to the Tuatha Dé. Lybbêâls was slain by Lähelîn who took the horse (vs. 261,29). Lähelîn who wounded Anfortas (vs. 479,8) was, of course, a Fomorian. Lähelîn handed over Gringuljete to his brother Orilus, and Orilus "gave" the horse to Gawain (vs. 545,28). Probably in an older form of the story Gawain took it from Orilus. In any case the horse belonged alternately to a friendly warrior of the Tuatha Dé and to a Fomorian captor.

same picture it would be a Castle of Maidens. Chrétien by an easy blunder bestowed the name Roche de Sanguin upon the wrong castle. Wolfram could not have corrected Chrétien's blunder unless he had a source closer to folklore.

These numerous points in which Wolfram is closer to what must have been the traditional original seem to supply plenty of evidence that he had access to material ultimately of Irish origin and not transmitted by Chrétien.

CHAPTER VI

The Welsh *Peredur* and the English *Sir Perceval*

THE argument of this book is confirmed by *Peredur* and *Sir Perceval*, but they are not necessary to the argument. It is convenient, therefore, to discuss them by themselves.

The independence of *Peredur* is a part of the vehemently debated Mabinogion question.[1] Undoubtedly there are two sides to this question, but those who insist that the Welsh stories have no sources other than Chrétien's romances have not brought forward any telling argument to support their view, except that it is simpler and can be grasped by a beginner. Many students of literature will find it reasonable to believe in the independent character of the Welsh stories and will consider that *Peredur* Ia,[2] *Owein*, and *Gereint* are based chiefly upon French minstrel or oral versions of the stories represented by Chrétien's *Perceval*, *Yvain*, and *Erec*.

Mary R. Williams has shown[3] that *Peredur* consists of three parts. Thurneysen[4] in a review of Mary Williams's

---

[1] For bibliography see Bruce, *Evolution of Arthurian Romance*, I, 342 f., II, 59 f.; and add L. Mühlhausen (*Ztsch. f. rom. Philologie*, XLIV [1924], 465–543), who attacks the independence of the Welsh versions.

[2] I omit *Peredur*, Ib, II, and III, as some urge a different origin for them, and they are not important to the present argument.

[3] *Essai sur la composition du roman Gallois de Peredur* (Paris, 1909).

[4] ZCP, VIII (1910), 185.

thesis has named these parts, Ia, Ib + II, III,[5] and has ascribed them to three different authors. Part Ia corresponds
from beginning to end to our Y (*Perceval*, vss. 1–4602).

No one has overthrown the demonstration that was made
by me some thirty years ago [6] of the persistence of an original order of events in *Owein* as against Chrétien's *Yvain*.

My first point is that *Owein* puts the Yvain-Gawain combat in the right place, at the time of Arthur's arrival at the
Fountain. This is the correct place for it [7] because in
Chrétien's *Yvain* the hero has been afraid from the first
(vss. 687 f.) that Gawain will forestall him by demanding
from Arthur the privilege of the combat at the Fountain.
In *Yvain*, the Yvain-Gawain combat has been transposed
to the end of the romance (vss. 5991 f.), where it serves
no purpose and reveals that it is out of place by interrupt-
ing the helpful-lion theme.

My second and more important point is that *Owein*
makes the *Pesme Avanture* episode, our X, which, as we
have seen above, is a Journey to Fairyland, a separate story,
after the main tale W is ended.[8] This must be the older order
of events, for nobody who understood that both tales are
Journeys to Fairyland would have thrust the shorter tale
as an episode into the framework of the longer, as Chrétien,

---

[5] Ia (*Mab.*, II, 72–104) as far as the words "and they return towards
Caerleon"; Ib + II (*Mab.*, II, 104–123) as far as the words "for fourteen
years as the story tells"; III (*Mab.*, II), pp. 123 to the end.

[6] "The Knight of the Lion," *PMLA*, XX (1905), 681; and "On the
Independent Character of the Welsh Owain," *Romanic Review*, III
(1912), 150–157.

[7] R. H. Griffith (*Sir Perceval of Galles*, p. 114), working independently,
made the same deduction.

[8] I have not seen the manuscript, the Red Book of Hergest, but
apparently (see ed. Rhŷs and Evans, II, 191) by the use of a large initial
letter it marks this *Pesme Avanture* episode as a separate story.

or some French predecessor, in his search for an external appearance of unity, has done in *Yvain*.

If *Owein* is independent of *Yvain*, *Peredur* Ia may be independent of Y (Chrétien's *Perceval*). As I have argued elsewhere,[9] *Peredur* Ia and Wolfram's *Parzival* agree in a number of particulars against Y (*Perceval*, vss. 1–4602), showing, as I think, that they both knew a minstrel version which was independent of it. This is somewhat the view about *Peredur* Ia, *Owein*, and *Gereint*, which R. Zenker has elaborately defended in numerous articles.[10] My view, however, is not so rigorous as Zenker's, because I do not attempt to prove that *Peredur* Ia is uninfluenced by Chrétien. All that I suppose is that it retains, as against Chrétien, a more original order of the scenes. That *Peredur* Ia may be superior to Y in the order in which the scenes are presented [11] is the line of thought which will be adopted in this chapter.

Peredur Ia, just as has been argued above in the case of Chrétien's *Perceval*, evidently at first contained three Hosts: Arthur, who was the hero's uncle, and a second and a third uncle. The heroine was doubtless at first wife to the third uncle; but, as soon as it was forgotten that she was a *fée*, this relationship was eliminated, thus leaving Arthur, who is an uncle, a second uncle, and the heroine. This is the stage reached in the English *Sir Perceval*.[12] A third step

[9] *Mod. Phil.*, XVI (1919), 553 f.

[10] See especially "J. D. Bruce und die Mabinogionfrage," *Ztsch. f. franz. Sp. u. Lit.*, Supplementheft, XIII (Behrens Festschrift, 1929), pp. 218–230. Compare his earlier articles ZFS, XLVIII (1926), 1–102, 386–410; LI (1928), 225–254; *Ztsch. f. d. Altertum*, LXII (1925), 49–66; *Germ. rom. Monatsschrift*, XI (1923), 240–254. Compare also E. Brugger, ZFS, XLVIII (1926), 325–345.

[11] Leo Weisgerber has found that all manuscripts of *Peredur* agree in the order of scenes (ZCP, XV [1925], 186).

[12] Page 207.

was to split both the second uncle and the heroine into two figures, making a total of five Hosts. This is what we find in *Peredur* Ia, namely: (1) Arthur's court; (2) first uncle; (3) second uncle, who has talismans; (4) first heroine, who is oppressed by an earl; (5) second heroine, who is oppressed by nine witches. In Chrétien's *Perceval* the Hosts are: (1) Arthur's court; (2) Gornemant, who is an uncle; (3) Blancheflor the heroine; and (4) the Fisher King, who is a cousin or an uncle.

Between *Peredur* and Chrétien's *Perceval* the chief difference in order of events is that Peredur puts the visit to the heroine's castle last, whereas Chrétien, by transposing the heroine to a penultimate place, destroys the thread of the story. In *Peredur*, what the hero saw at his uncles' castles, although marvelous, was not meaningless. At the castle of his first uncle, Peredur was taught to wield a *ffonn*, "single-stick," and at that of his second uncle, a *cleddyf*, "sword." This of course meant that his uncles needed a hero to fight for them and to drive away their foes. At the second uncle's castle Peredur saw a bleeding spear and a bloody head on a dish. This no doubt meant that blood had been shed and cried out for vengeance.

From the second uncle's castle Peredur went to the castle of the first *iarlles*, "countess," and delivered her from her oppressors, who were an earl and his two subalterns. Then he went on to the castle of a second *iarlles*, whom he rescued from her assailants, the nine witches of Gloucester. Since, according to the conjecture made above, these four castles grew out of one castle, Peredur, by delivering the last two, in effect delivered all four, and returned successful to Arthur's court.

In Chrétien's *Perceval*, the hero after visiting his first uncle, Gornemant, comes next to Blancheflor's castle, where he is successful and delivers her from her foes, Clamadeu and Anguingueron. Then he comes to the Grail castle, which in *Perceval* has been combined with the second uncle's castle and transposed to the end. Here he is given a sword, which is of course an invitation to him to deliver the castle, and he sees carried in procession a bleeding spear, a Grail, and a platter, but he does nothing, and returns unsuccessful to Arthur's court. Arranged in this way, the different castles are a succession of disconnected pictures. *Peredur* Ia shows an earlier stage of development in which the incidents meant something to the hearers.

Peredur Ia comes nearer to the original three Hosts, who, as the preceding chapters have attempted to show, were three forms of the Irish god Brión, than does Chrétien's *Perceval*. In Peredur are three Hosts: King Arthur, and two grey men who are the hero's uncles. The text does not say that Arthur was also his uncle, but perhaps this is implied.[13] If King Arthur is his uncle, Peredur visits in succession three uncles, that is, three brothers. They correspond doubtless to three forms of the Irish god Nuadu, or to Brión, Iuchar, and Iucharba.

Peredur Ia keeps fairly well the original four talismans of the Tuatha Dé. The Dagda's caldron has become King Arthur's gold cup which the Red Knight carried away. Nuadu's sword is with the second uncle. It is the sword that he gives to the hero to cut the staple with. Lug's spear is also with this uncle. It is the profusely bleeding lance. Only *Lia Fáil*, or the "Stone of Destiny," is missing, and its place is taken by a bloody head in a dish. For this important change, a peculiarity of Welsh tradition may well be responsible. My hypothesis is, not that *Peredur* Ia repre-

[13] In *Sir Perceval*, vs. 1050, Arthur is the hero's uncle.

sents Chrétien's source, but that it is a Welsh offshoot from that lost source. Now a belief that Brión, who is called in Welsh Bran, existed as a head in a sort of death-in-life condition seems to have prevailed in Wales.[14] The belief appears in *Branwen*, where Bran's head furnished good company and a feast lasting many years.[15] My hypothesis is that Welsh tradition has here changed the Irish talisman *Lia Fáil* to a head in a dish.

In the English *Sir Perceval* the story is at an earlier stage than in *Peredur* Ia. The three fairy castles here are: (1) the castle of King Arthur, who is Perceval's uncle; (2) the castle of a second uncle; and (3) the castle of the heroine Lufamour. The four talismans of the Tuatha Dé are considerably changed. Lug's spear is here the short spear that Acheflour carried to the woods and gave to her son (vs. 191). The place of Nuadu's sword has been usurped by a ring taken from the Hall Damsel by Perceval (vs. 474), which renders him invulnerable (vs. 1860). (Nuadu's sword made the bearer invincible.) The Dagda's caldron both here and in *Peredur* Ia has become King Arthur's golden cup (vs. 617). A trace of the magic of *Lia Fáil* appears in the "drynk" that cures Acheflour of insanity, and which Perceval finds at the second giant's castle (vs. 2245). This healing medicine probably comes from some magic object like *Lia Fáil* carried off by the giant. This is a reasonable explanation, because in Wolfram's *Parzival* Gawain is healed by an ointment that comes from the Grail castle. It is the same ointment (*salbe*, vs. 579,30) that keeps

---

[14] This is altogether more likely than a notion held by some opponents of Celtic origins, who explain this head in a dish as a borrowing from John the Baptist (see L. Mühlhausen, *ZRP*, XLIV (1924), 509 f.).

[15] *Mab.*, I, 67.

Anfortas alive. Evidently it comes from the Grail, which according to Wolfram was a stone, like *Lia Fáil*.

In *Sir Perceval* the Red Knight has a witch mother who can restore her son to life and who must be slain. She is not mentioned in *Peredur* Ia, but in *Peredur* Ia the castle of the second heroine is under siege by the witches of Gloucester. Peredur fights these nine witches and delivers the countess. The Perceval story evidently at one stage told of witches, who were doubtless the Red Knight's mother and aunts, and who must be fought. Chrétien has eliminated the witches, probably because the courtly tradition which he followed felt it improper to describe a combat between a knight and witches.

Both *Sir Perceval* and *Peredur* Ia show a trace of the Dümmling motive, but they confine it to the hero's first contact with the world, and do not allow it to confuse the invincibility of the hero after he has acquired victory-bringing talismans. Chrétien carries the Dümmling motive forward in the story and allows it to become entangled with the invincibility motive.

Peredur Ia makes the Tent Damsel welcome the hero and give him a ring, and *Sir Perceval* says nothing that is at variance with this. Chrétien's *Perceval*, on the other hand, by making the damsel surprised and terrified at the hero's approach, has obscured her fairy superiority. In Chrétien's *Perceval* the mother advises Perceval to take a ring from any fair lady that he met. This is crazy advice unless, as was probably true in an earlier form of the story, the mother knew that her son was destined to meet first the *fée* who was the sovereignty of the country, and to receive from her the ring that would enable him to conquer.

Some moralizer (probably the redactor of Count Philip's book) changed the story, as we have seen, to make Perceval

fail. This redactor explains later that Perceval failed because of his crime in leaving his mother so suddenly, but
his leaving his mother would not be a crime in early story.
It is not a crime in *Sir Perceval*, and hardly even in *Peredur* Ia.[16] This same moralizer did not understand that the
four talismans belong together. He separated the sword
from the Grail, spear, and platter, and invented a short
procession for the last three objects.

If Chrétien had any explanation for the Grail castle, he
doubtless regarded it as under a *deablie*, "spell," cast by a
wicked enchanter. Now it is characteristic of persons
under a spell that they must not ask for help. They have to
wait and watch till some visiting hero grasps the situation.
Such, in *Perceval*, must be the condition of the Grail castle
and the Fisher King.

Chrétien followed the conventional twelfth-century explanation of marvels, which was that they are the work of
evil spirits or of magicians. Thus his Chastel Merveilleus,
which had at one time been thought of as having fallen
into the power of the King of the Dead, is represented by
him as being under the spell cast by *uns clers sages d'astrenomie* (vs. 7548; Clinschor in *Parzival*, vs. 658,19).

In this chapter it has been pointed out that the English
Sir Perceval represents the Grail story at an early stage of
development before the Grail had become an important
feature. We have seen also that the Welsh *Peredur* Ia preserves an original order of events better than Y, the first
part of Chrétien's *Perceval*, and we have found evidence
that both *Sir Perceval* and *Peredur* Ia represent an independent tradition and are very slightly if at all influenced
by Chrétien.

---

[16] Except that Peredur's foster-sister calls him "excommunicate" for
being the cause of his mother's death (*Mab.*, II, 88).

CHAPTER VII

The Hateful *Fée* Who Represents the Sovereignty

THE Irish and Welsh Journeys to Fairyland which have been outlined above do not represent the *fée* as sinister or destructive, and therefore the heroines in these stories do not resemble Orguelleuse. Is it necessary to conclude that Gawain's malevolent lady-love in *Perceval* [1] cannot be of Celtic origin? To argue in this way would be demonstrably wrong. Malevolent and ugly *fées* like Orguelleuse are described in ancient Irish literature. In England there was a story current about an adventure of Sir Gawain with a *fée* of hideous appearance. It is told in the Middle English romance "The Wedding of Sir Gawayn," and in the ballad "The Marriage of Gawain." In Irish there exists a number of tales dealing with the sovereignty of Ireland that introduce a *fée* of this malevolent and haughty type. I summarize here several of these tales. [2]

The first, *Temair Breg, Baile na Fían*, is a poem written by Cúan ua Lothcháin who died in 1024: [3]

King Eochaid Mugmedón has by Queen Mongfind four sons, and by Cairenn Casdubh, whom he has brought captive from

---

[1] Page 136.

[2] Stories of this type have been studied by G. H. Maynadier, *The Wife of Bath's Tale* (London, 1901). There is an unpublished dissertation in the Harvard University Library by J. W. Beach entitled "The Loathly Lady" (1907).

[3] Edition Maud Joynt, *Ériu*, IV (1910), 92–111.

Alba, another son named Níall (later "of the Nine Hostages"). Queen Mongfind forces Cairenn to toil as a slave at Tara, and Mongfind's sons compel her to expose the infant Níall. The baby, however, is found and brought up at a distance by the poet Torna. When he is nine years old [4] and has golden locks, Torna brings him back to Tara. His first exploit is to persuade his father to release Cairenn from her toil. After this the five brothers go hunting and kill a boar near Loch Erne. Brían the eldest says: "Go one of you to seek a drink to the border of bright-crested Banba." [5]

Fiachna sets out and finds a fountain with "water of virtues," [6] but it is guarded by a dreadful hag. "A mouth she has into which a hound would fit. Her spiked tooth-fence about her jaws is more hideous than all the goblins of Ireland." As the price of a drink she demands a kiss. Fiachna withdraws in terror and tells his brothers that he can find no water. Two of the other brothers go but are scared away by "the spectre of the cliff." Then Brían goes, and, for a drink of water, gives the hag a hasty kiss. "Since hasty is the kiss thou hast given me," says she, "thou shalt have a hasty visit to Tara." [7]

When Níall goes, the ugliness of the hag is described at length, but he throws his arms around her "as if she were forever his wife." Thereupon she grows beautiful. "Blooming

[4] Compare the forest rearing of Lug, Finn, and Perceval.

[5] "Do brú Banba barrgile." The adjective *barrgile*, "bright-topped," probably referring to trees, suggests that the actual earth of Ireland is thought of. Banba is a name for Ireland.

[6] The *fée* guarding "marvelous water" may be a parallel to the damsel guarding the Grail.

[7] Only a persistently brave hero wins the ugly-appearing *fée*. The same motive of persistence may be seen at the Castle of Maidens in Wauchier's continuation, ed. Potvin, *Perceval*, vss. 26519 f., where a hero not persistent enough to keep on beating a gong will be shut out all night and go away shamed. This motive may be traced at Belrepeire, *Perceval*, vss. 1720 f., in *MaelDuin* (p. 274), and at the Fountain Perilous in *Yvain* (p. 111).

her face in hue as the crimson lichen of Leinster crags." "The fearsomeness thou sawest in my face, since it repelled not thy desire," she exclaims, "thou art the princely heir of Tara." She then tells him to refuse water to his brothers till they promise to let him speak first in the assembly. They agree, and, when they all return to Tara, King Eochaid says that by this agreement they have given away the kingship to Níall. Queen Mongfind is still hostile, and the five brothers go to Elg's (Ireland's) foremost smith for a test. He sets fire to his smithy over their heads. Brían bears away the sledge hammers, Ailill the coat-of-mail, Fiachna the drinking vat, Fergus the dry wood, but Níall takes bellows, hammer, anvil, and anvil-block. Then Eochaid declares that Níall shall be king.

The next story, *Echtra mac Echdach Mugmedóin*, is a prose version of that last summarized. The chief variations are as follows: [8]

The test by the smith comes before the test by the hag. When the hag transforms herself she says to Níall:

'Misi in flathius' or si, ocus asbert andso:
'A ri Temra, is me in flathius.'

"As at the first," she continues, "thou has seen me ugly but in the end beautiful, even so is royal rule. Without battles it may not be won, but in the end, to anyone, it is comely and handsome."

In the next story, *Lughaid Laighe*, the abode of the fée corresponds strikingly to the Grail castle. Both are found by accident at nightfall; both contain light and fire with brilliant surroundings and self-serving dishes; in both the hero is tested; both disappear overnight (in Chrétien's castle only the inhabitants disappear, but the entire castle dis-

[8] Edition S. H. O'Grady, *Silva Gadelica*, I, 327–330; II, 369–373, from *BB*; edition W. Stokes, *Rev. celt.*, XXIV (1903), 190–203, from *YBL*.

appears in Pseudo-Wauchier's story).[9] Blancheflor, who must in origin have been the same as the Grail damsel, brought Perceval the sovereignty of her land somewhat as the hag did Lughaid Laighe.[10]

Daire, because of a prophecy that a son of his named Lughaid shall rule Ireland, names all his six sons Lughaid. When he is holding the Tailtiu assembly he asks his druid which son shall be king. The druid replies: "A golden fawn shall come to the assembly and whoever captures it shall rule."

When a fawn appears, the six brothers pursue it to Benn Edar. Lughaid, who from this is named Laighe, catches the *laegh*, "fawn." They are now lost in a magic mist and snow-storm. One of them finds a "great house with a big fire, with victual and liquor in plenty, silver dishes, bedsteads of white bronze, and a dreadful hag. The hag will grant food to him only who will sleep with her. He refuses. "Thou hast missed of royalty," she cries.[11] He goes back to his brothers. One after another, the others come. She names each by a nick-name, but they all refuse her. At last comes Lughaid Laighe who is brave enough to enter her couch. She forthwith be-comes beautiful and says to him: "Thine is an auspicious jour-ney, for I am royalty and thou shalt have Ireland's rule."

"[Then they] have meat of the freshest, liquor of the oldest, drinking horns of themselves [i.e., automatically] pouring to them, and of royalty so he makes his own. On the morrow the six find themselves without house, without fire, without anything but the open plain, smooth and level, and their wolf-dogs tied to their spears." They return to Tailtiu and tell the adventure.

Lughaid Laighe's adventure is also told in *Cóir Anmann*,

---

[9] Potvin, *Perceval*, vss. 20303 f. (cf. p. 274).
[10] Edition O'Grady, *Silv. Gad.*, II, 489–490; 537–538, from *BB*.
[11] A previous adventurer fails, like Calogrenant in *Yvain* (p. 110).

"Fitness of Names." [12] Here, when the ugly hag changes into a beautiful *fée*, all exclaim, "Who art thou?" *Missi banflaith hErenn*, "I am the sovereignty of Ireland," says she, "and the kingship of Ireland shall belong to thee, O Lughaid."

The most picturesque of these stories is a poem called the *Dinnshenchas of Carn Máil*, the first stanza of which [13] shows that its unknown author was conscious that he was writing about an occult heathen myth:

> "Pleasant is the theme that falls to my care.
> It is not the (mere) knowledge of one place,
> While my spirit sheds light eastward
> On the mysteries of the world.".

Daire has seven (six is probably right) sons named Lughaid. He also owns an enchanted fawn which they hunt. They take refuge in a house from the storm. "When the men were in the house . . . there entered a hag, a loathly offence; she was hideous and unsightly. Taller was she than a mast upright, bigger than a sleeping-hut her ear, blacker than any visage her form. She set upon them in the strong house where sat King Daire's sons. . . . A change fell upon the nature of the tender youths before that obese, lustful horror; sooner than look upon her they had chosen to be buried under earth alive . . . the sons of Daire gave themselves over to a death of shame. She addressed them with an evil saying: 'One of you must sleep with me tonight, or I will devour you all, unaided, hound and strong man alike.' [14] When he saw the danger plain, Lughaid Laighe spoke: 'I will sleep with her — unwelcome task: enough for you to lose me only.' As the

---

[12] Summarized from *Ir. Texte*, III, ii, 317-323, § 70.

[13] Edition E. Gwynn, *Metrical Dinnshenchas*, IV, 135 f.

[14] Something like this aggressively evil hag must lie at the basis of Chrétien's Orguelleuse.

firelight fell dim, she changed to another wondrous shape; she took on a radiant form, beyond praise." Lughaid asks her who she is and she replies:

> "I will tell thee gentle youth;
> With me sleep the High Kings:
> I, the tall, slender maiden,
> Am the kingship of Alba and Ériu.[15]

To thee I have revealed myself this night, but nothing more shall come of our meeting: The son thou shalt have, he it is that I shall sleep with — happier fate. I will tell thee thy son's name — lucky his lot; Lughaid shall his name be, and MacCon thereto."

Here is an unmistakable instance of a *fée* consorting first with a father, Lughaid Laighe, and then with a son, Lughaid MacCon. A *fée* has the gift of perpetual youth. This agelessness explains the successive lovers of Orguelleuse, who in *Perceval* are an unnamed lover slain by Guiromelant,[16] Guiromelant, Orguelleus de la Roche, and Gawain. In *Parzival* they are Cidegast, Gramoflanz, Anfortas, Clinschor, and Gawain.[17] Orguelleuse is plainly of the race of immortals. She is Orguelleuse de Logres,[18] a name that suggests that she is virtually the sovereignty of Logres (Britain) personified.

The Irish sovereignty stories outlined above, which are older than the rise of French romance,[19] pretty surely repre-

---

[15] The text is:

> "Atbér-sa fritt, a meic mín:
> Limm-sa fóit na haird-ríg:
> Is mé ind ingen seta seng,
> Flathius Alban is Hérend."

[16] Verse 8571.

[17] Pages 35, 199, 452.

[18] Verse 8639 (see p. 152).

[19] *Lughaid Laighe* from *BB* may not be so old, but it seems untouched

sent the source of Chrétien's taunting and malevolent Orguelleuse.[20] Like the sovereignty, she appears at first in
hateful guise, but in a romance of chivalry Chrétien did not
wish to make his heroine physically repulsive. He contented
himself by representing her as mocking and cruel. The
physically ugly *fée*, however, does appear in *Perceval*, as the
hideous messenger.[21] The close verbal resemblances between Chrétien's description of this ugly messenger and
the Irish account of the appearance of the sovereignty as
set forth in *Carn Máil* may be shown in parallel columns.

Perceval	*Dinnshenchas of Carn Máil*
La dameisele estoit treciee	
A deus treces tortes e noires;	Taller was she than a
E se les paroles sont voires	mast upright, bigger than a
Teus con li livres les devise,	sleeping-hut was her ear,
Onques riens si leide a devise	blacker than any visage her
Ne fu neïs dedanz anfer:	form, a weight on every
Einz ne veïstes si noir fer	heart was the hag. Broader
Com ele ot le col a les mains	her row of teeth than a
Mais ancore estoit ce del mains	board set with draughts-
A l'autre leidesce qu'ele ot:	men; her nose stood out far
Que si oel estoient dui crot,	before her; it was longer
Petit ausi come oel de rat;	than a ploughshare. Bigger
Ses nés fu de singe ou de chat,	than a basket full of sheaves
Et ses levres d'asne ou de beuf;	was each fist of the mis-
Si dant sanbloient moël d'uef	natured woman; bigger
De color tant estoient ros,	than rough-hewn stone in

by French influence. Recently collected Irish and Gaelic tales that tell
of *fées* who assume an ugly disguise are studied in Maynadier, *Wife of
Bath's Tale*, pp. 21 and 33 f.

[20] Chrétien calls her *la male pucele*, vs. 7145; *la plus male riens del
mont*, vs. 7258; *la puciéle sans merci*, vs. 8373; *la male dameisele*, vs. 8469.

[21] Page 132.

Et si ot barbe come bos;
Anmi le piz ot une boce,
Devers l'eschine sanbloit croce
E s'ot les rains e les espaules
Trop bien feites por mener
  baules,
S'ot boce el dos e jambes tortes
Qui vont ausi con deus reortes:
Bien fu feite por mener dance.
  (vss. 4614–4637, ed. Hilka)

rampart, each of her black bony knees. A paunchy belly she bore, Ï trow, without rib to the armpits; a scabby black crown with a crop of wens like a furzy hillside upon her.
(*Met. Dinn., IV*, 139; Gwynn's translation)

In the above description of the ugly messenger, the grotesque exaggeration of Chrétien's language suggests an Irish source. Perhaps *li livres* to which he refers was a French or Latin book based upon Welsh and ultimately upon Irish sources. Wolfram calls the ugly messenger Cundrîe *la surziere*.[22] According to him, Gawain's sister, one of the four queens at Schastel Marveile, was named *die süezen* Cundrîe.[23] E. Martin conjectures that Wolfram followed a source in which the two Cundrîe's were identical.[24] A *fée* took an ugly shape in order to test the greatest of all knights.

Eóin MacNeill[25] has pointed out that most kings named

[22] *Parzival*, vs. 312,26.

[23] Verse 591,10.

[24] *Parzival*, II (1903), lxii. In Wauchier's continuation (Potvin, *Perceval*, vss. 25569 f.), the hero meets a hideous damsel who is described in much the same terms as those Chrétien uses of the ugly messenger. Her name is Rosete, and she transforms herself into a beauty. Some manuscripts add: "Je ne sai s'ele fu faée" (vs. 25744). Miss Mallon, according to R. S. Loomis (*Celtic Myth and Arthurian Romance*, pp. 273–281), has proved that "Perceval's sister, and cousin, and wife, and the Grail messenger were one and the same." It is not incredible that all these personages were originally different manifestations of one supernatural earth-mother who controlled the plot.

[25] *Celtic Ireland*, p. 61.

Lughaid are merely faded pictures of the god, *Lug mac Eithne*. It is therefore probable that Lughaid Laighe, in the poem of *Carn Máil* above, has borrowed his adventure from the god Lug. We may even go further and infer that all the Irish stories just outlined probably began in stories about Lug. As Lug was the winner of the sovereignty, it is natural that he should appear in some versions as lord of the great house where the sovereignty dwells.

The oldest story of this type, which must therefore take us back to something rather primitive, is the *Baile in Scáil*, "The Spectre's Prophecy." This text, which is mentioned in both of the ancient lists A and B, and which is referred to by Flann Mainistrech, who died in 1056, runs as follows: [26]

(§§ 1–3) Conn with his three druids and his three poets was upon the royal rath at Tara before sunrise. He stepped upon a stone there that screamed under his feet. Conn asked his poet, "Why did the stone scream?" After obtaining a delay of fifty-three days the poet replied: "*Fál* truly is the name of the stone, and from *Fál* it was brought. . . . In the Land of Tailtiu here it shall remain forever, and it is in this place there shall be a meeting of games by thy race as long as there shall be sovereignty in Tara. And on the last day of the week of the Assembly of Tara which the sovereign does not see, there

[26] This outline and translation I have made from Pokorny's printing of a copy of manuscript, Rawlinson B 512, found among Meyer's papers, (ZCP, XIII (1921), 371–382, §§ 1–40), from which extracts are printed below. I have compared Thurneysen's copy (ZCP, XX [1935], 213–227. On the date, see p. 213). The last part of Rawlinson B 512, §§ 41–65, was printed by Meyer, ZCP, XII (1918), 232–238. E. O'Curry in his *Lectures on the Manuscript Materials* (Dublin, 1861, pp. 618–622), translated from Harleian MS. 5280, which varies considerably. The Harleian text, which includes §§ 1–40 only, has been printed by Meyer, ZCP, III (1901), 457–466.

shall be leanness in that year. *Fál* screamed on that account
under your feet." This is what the poet said, and he prophesied, "The number of groans that it uttered is the number
of kings who shall be of your seed over Ireland forever."

(§ 5) As they were there after this they saw a great mist
all round so that they knew not where they went from the
greatness of the darkness which had come. And they heard
the noise of a horseman approaching them. "It would be a
great grief to us," said Conn, "if this mist should carry us
into an unknown country." After this the horseman let fly
three casts [of a spear] at them, and the last cast came with
greater speed than the first cast. "It is the wounding of a
king indeed," said the druid, "whoever shoots at Conn in Tara."
The horseman desisted from shooting, came to them, bade
welcome to Conn, and took them with him to his house.

(§ 6) They went on after that till they passed a plain and
a golden tree. A house under a roof tree of white bronze
[was there]. Thirty feet was its length. They went thereafter into the house until they saw a young maiden in a glass
chair with a gold crown on her head and a cloak with borders
of gold round her. A bowl of silver with four golden corners
before her, full of red beer. A cup of gold on the ground. A
beaker or cup of gold at her lips.[27]

And they saw the *scál* himself in the house before them in
his royal seat. And great was his dignity. This was proper
because there was not found in Tara before him a man of his
size, nor of his beauty, in respect to the nobility of his form,
and his appearance, and in respect to his wonderfulness. (§ 7)
He spoke to them and said: "I am not a *scál* [shadow] and I

---

[27] The text of § 6 is: "Docótar íarum ass condarala assa mag ocus
bile n-órda ann. Tech foa ochtaig findruine and. Deich traigid fichit
a mét. Lotar íarum issa tech co n-accatar ingen maccthacht i catháir
glanidi ocus barr órdhai for a mullach ocus brat co srethaib di ór impe.
Dabach arcait co cethraib cernaib órdaib ar a bélaib, lán di dergflaith.
Escra óir ar a óu, airideog nech [no-ech] di ór, ar a bélaib."

am not a phantom. . . . After my death I am come, and I am of the seed of Adam. This is my name, 'Lug mac Ethnen' [here he tells his genealogy]. And it is for this reason that I have come that there mightest be seen by thee the duration of thy reign, and of every reign that shall be after thee in Tara forever."

(§ 8) And the maiden who was in the house before them was the sovereignty of Ireland, and 'twas she that gave a meal to Conn, namely an ox rib and a boar's rib. Twenty-four feet were in the ox rib, eight from its arch to the ground; twelve feet were in the boar's rib and five between its arch and the ground. (§ 9) "When the maiden went to the distribution, she said to them: 'To whom shall be given the beaker with the red beer?' And the *scál* answered her name, and he named every sovereign, one after another, from the time of Conn forever." [After this the *scál* and his house disappeared, but the bowl, the cup, and the beaker remained with Conn.]

The evident paganism of this tale is broken by Lug's statement that he is of the race of Adam. This is of course an interpolation made by some redactor to prove that he did not himself believe in pagan gods. Lug in this story, "with his great dignity," corresponds to the majestic Fisher King. The lady, who is the sovereignty or the land personified, and who from first to last is not ugly, corresponds to Blancheflor. The splendid house, which is found with difficulty, is like the Grail castle and, like it, vanishes at the end. The *dabach arcait*, "silver bowl," corresponds to the Grail.

It is to be observed that this rather brief Irish piece, although it does not explicitly connect the different objects which it locates at Tara with each other, does in the short space of a few lines mention the Games of Tailtiu, who is

Lug's queen, and is virtually the sovereignty of Ireland personified, and *Lia Fáil*. *Lia Fáil* is one of the "Four Jewels" of the Tuatha Dé which are the apparent originals of the four talismans of the Grail castle.

The next story, *Echtra Cormaic i Tír Tairngire* ("Cormac's Adventure in the Land of Promise), exists in no manuscript older than the fourteenth century, but nobody supposes it to be influenced in any way by French romances. It contains no malevolent *fée* but ought to be considered here because it combines a Journey to Fairyland with an account of the twelve ordeals of Ireland and connects these ordeals or talismans with Tara. In the summary [28] I mention all twelve ordeals but give a description of numbers 6, 11, and 12 only:

Ordeals 1, 2, and 3 are Morann's three collars. No. 4, Mochta's adze. No. 5, Sencha's lot-casting. No. 6, Badurn's *leastur*, "vessel," which was brought by his queen out of a well that led down into fairyland. If three false words were spoken, it would separate into three parts; then, if three true words were uttered, it would unite again. No. 7, three dark stones. No. 8, the cauldron of truth. No. 9, the old lot of Sen. No. 10, Luchta's iron. No. 11, waiting at an altar. The proof was "to go nine times around the altars, and afterwards to drink water over which a druid's incantation had been uttered. Now if [the accused] were guilty, the token of his sin was manifest upon him. But if he were innocent, [the water] would do him no harm. Now Cai Cainbrethach [was] the pupil of Fenius Farsaid. . . . It was that Cai who brought this ordeal from the land of Israel when he came to the Tuatha Dé. . . . It was that same Cai, moreover, who first ordained in Erin the law of the four tracks, for only two of the school

[28] Summarized from the edition and translation of Stokes, *Ir. Texte*, III, i, 188–198, 206–216.

came to Erin, namely, Amergen Whiteknee the poet and Cai the judge; and Cai remained in Erin till he had outlived nine generations." [29]

No. 12, Cormac's cup. One morning at dawn at Tara Cormac saw a grey-haired warrior having a branch of silver with three golden apples. When the branch was shaken it made music so sweet that men sore wounded would fall asleep at it.[30] "I come," he said, "from a land where there is neither age, nor decay, nor gloom, nor sadness, nor envy, nor jealousy, nor hatred, nor haughtiness. Cormac makes a *caradradh*, "alliance," with the man, who agrees to give Cormac the branch, saying: "In return you must grant me the three boons which I shall ask in Tara." "They shall be granted," says Cormac. After a year the warrior returns and demands as his first boon to carry away Cormac's daughter. When "the women of Tara utter loud cries, Cormac shook the branch at them so that he banished grief . . . and cast them into sleep." After a month the warrior demands his second boon, namely to carry off Cormac's son. Finally he comes and takes away Cormac's wife. "That thing Cormac endured not." He goes after them, and everyone then follows Cormac.

A great mist is brought upon them in the midst of the plain of the wall. Cormac finds himself upon *Mag Mór*, (great plain) [31] alone. "In the midst of the plain (is) a large fortress with a wall of bronze around it. In the fortress is a house of white silver and it is half-thatched with the wings of white birds. . . . Then he sees another fortress, vast and royal, and another wall of bronze around it. There were four houses [32] therein. He enters the fortress. He sees a vast palace with its beams of bronze, its wattling of silver, and its thatch of the

[29] This Cai associated with Amargen must be the Kay of the Arthurian romances.

[30] Music is sometimes a lure to the land of the dead (p. 271).

[31] A name for the land of the dead.

[32] Compare the insistence on the number four at the Grail castle.

wings of white birds." [33] He sees also a fountain inhabited
by magic salmon, and he comes finally to a palace where water
for bathing is supplied by invisible hands. "There was one
couple inside awaiting him. The warrior's countenance was
distinguished owing to the beauty of his shape and the come-
liness of his form and the wondrousness of his countenance.[34]
The girl along with the warrior . . . yellow-haired . . . is the
loveliest of the world's women." A pig is boiling in a cauldron. Four true stories have to be told in order that the pig
may be boiled. (Since Cormac must tell one of these stories,
he actually undergoes an ordeal to test his truthfulness.) His
distinguished host tells him that he is Manannán mac Lir. He
says to Cormac "until today neither thy wife nor thy daughter
has seen the face of a man since they were taken from thee out
of Tara, and thy son has not seen a woman's face." [35] He gives
Cormac a marvelous truth-testing golden cup. "Now on the
morrow morning when Cormac arose, he found himself on
the green of Tara, with his wife and his son and daughter, and
having his branch and his cup. Now that was afterwards
'Cormac's cup,' and it used to distinguish between truth and
falsehood with the Gael. Howbeit, as had been foretold Cormac (by Manannán), it remained not after Cormac's death."

The *Echtra Cormaic* show traces of having been worked
over in later times. Manannán, who is of the Tuatha Dé,
ought not to carry off Cormac's wife and daughter. The
author has forgotten the distinction between the friendly
people of fairyland (Tuatha Dé) and the hostile people
(Fomorians). There is no reason, however, to distrust the
antiquity of the main thread of the story.

[33] For houses thatched with birds' wings, see p. 189.
[34] Compare the dignified appearance of the Fisher King.
[35] This separation of the sexes occurs in Chastel Merveilleus. It suggests the land of the dead (p. 139).

The stories outlined above confirm the inference that the *fée* in a Journey to Fairyland might be virtually the sovereignty, so that the hero by winning her becomes king of the land. The stories show that a *fée* of this sort was often difficult and dangerous to win. It seems safe to infer from this that AA, the Chastel Merveilleus part of *Perceval* with the malevolent Orguelleuse, goes back to an essentially Irish original.

CHAPTER VIII

The Boyhood Exploits

PRECEDING chapters have established a probability
that Irish and Welsh Journeys to Fairyland furnished
a basis for most of the incidents in Chrétien's *Perceval*.
None of the Journeys hitherto outlined, however, describe
the hero's upbringing. In Chrétien's *Perceval* the boyish
exploits of the hero are told at considerable length (vss.
1–864). Is this account of Perceval's youth a French invention, or may it be, like the rest of Chrétien's romance,
based upon a Celtic original?

Our business in this chapter is to examine ancient Irish
and Welsh stories in search of *enfances* or boyhood exploits. If these exist, it would be a reasonable hypothesis
that Chrétien took the boyish deeds of Perceval from the
same sources from which he appears to have taken the
rest of Perceval's story.

At the outset we discover in Irish that the *macgnímrada*
or "youthful exploits" of Cuchulinn and the *macgnímartha*
or "boyish deeds" of Finn are well known; and that in
Welsh the word *mabinogi* probably meant "youthful exploits" and referred to the youthful exploits of Pryderi.[1]

[1] J. Rhŷs, *Arthurian Legend*, p. 2 ("*Mabinogi Jesu Grist* translates
De Infantia Jesu Christi"); W. J. Gruffydd, *Transactions of the Hon.
Society of Cymmrodorion* (London, 1912–1913), p. 39; E. Windisch,
Abhandlungen d. k. Sächsischen Gesellschaft d. Wiss. zu Leipzig (1912),
p. 227. J. Loth, however, has urged that *mabinogi* did not acquire this
meaning until the fourteenth century (*Contributions à l'étude des
romans de la Table Ronde* (Paris, 1912), p. 30).

More decisive evidence for the Irish origin of Perceval's youthful deeds is the occurrence of youthful deeds in the story of Lug, because he seems throughout his career a parallel figure to Perceval. Our main business in this chapter, therefore, is to outline the story of Lug, giving due attention to his youthful exploits.

The parallelism between the *Macgnímrada ConCulaind*, the *Macgnímartha Finn*, and the *enfances Perceval* has been studied elsewhere,[2] and it will be unnecessary to do more than print a few striking incidents from these stories in parallel columns:

Macgnímrada ConCulaind	*Macgnímartha Finn*
1. He was swift enough to run down deer, and he shot swans in a lake.	1. He ran down two deer and shot a duck in a lake.[3]
2. He killed some of the boy troop with whom he played.	2. He drowned nine youths with whom he played.
3. He was taught skill in weapons by amazons or fairy women.[4]	3. He tried his strength at his uncle Fiacal's house and was given a remarkable spear.
	4. He avenged a weeping woman and slew a man who had helped to kill his father.

Lug was a god, and, since his story belonged to Irish mythology, it is probable that his youthful exploits were older in some form or other than the exploits of Cuchulinn and Finn, and that exploits told of Cuchulinn and Finn

[2] A. C. L. Brown, *Mod. Phil.*, XVIII (1920), 210 f., 227 f.
[3] *Ériu*, I (1904), 180–190.
[4] *Táin Bó*, ed. E. Windisch, *Ir. Texte, extraband* (1905), pp. 106–171, and *Tochmarc Emire* (see p. 50).

were borrowed from his. A reason for feeling confident of this is that the seventh invasion, outlined below from *LL*,[5] mentions that Lug was brought up in a forest by a foster-mother, Tailtiu. At least this much of Lug's story is as old as the oldest version of *LG*. Moreover, since Tailtiu is a name for Ireland, this makes it certain that the story is one of those that tell how a youth was brought up by a *fée* who was virtually the land personified. Lug, therefore, had *enfances féeriques*. It is probable that these were the source of the *enfances* of Cuchulinn and of Finn,[6] especially as Lug was Cuchulinn's divine father and it would be natural to transfer the exploits of the father to the son. We may be pretty sure that the exploits in the above table, although not now told of Lug, were once attributed to him.

All of these incidents find more or less close parallels in the Perceval story, except the killing of boy companions; and this may once have been told of him, for it suits well his headstrong disposition as a youthful Hercules or pierce-vale. Killing of companions, if, as is probable, it once belonged to the Perceval story, would, as a matter of course, have been omitted by French redactors as uncourtly.

By a piece of luck a longer account of the invasion of the Tuatha Dé has been preserved under the title *Cath Maige Tured* (*CMT*). In an older and better version it was evidently the source of invasion 7 in *LG*. It is the best preserved of Irish mythological sagas, and on account of its importance will be outlined here. *CMT*, as we have it, is a conflation of several pagan stories, all of which have been rationalized by Christian scribes. Nevertheless, the

---

[5] Page 265.
[6] *Enfances féeriques* may be transformed into *enfances humaines* but not vice versa (E. Philipot, *Romania*, XXVI [1897], 299).

original mythological story may be dimly discerned, and by the aid of *LG* to some extent safely reconstructed. *CMT* was probably composed in the ninth century,[7] but was rewritten in the eleventh and exists in a fifteenth-century manuscript.

§ 1. The Tuatha Dé were in the northern islands of the world where they learnt knowledge, witchcraft, magic, sorcery, and enchantment until they surpassed the sages of the heathen arts. § 2. In four cities they learnt knowledge, sorcery, and infernal lore: Fálias, Gorias, Murias, and Findias. § 3. Out of Fálias was brought *Lia Fáil* that was at Tara. It used to roar under every king that took Ireland.[8] § 4. Out of Gorias was brought the spear of Lug. In battle no one could resist it, or him who bore it. § 5. Out of Findias was brought the sword of Nuadu. No one escaped it when it was drawn out of its terrible sheath, and it was irresistible. § 6. Out of Murias was brought the Dagda's cauldron. No company went from it unsatisfied. § 7. Four druids were in those four cities. . . . From these four *filid* "poets" the Tuatha Dé learnt knowledge and sorcery.[9]

[7] The opinion of Robin Flower, *Catalogue of Irish Manuscripts in the British Museum*, II (London, 1926), 319. *CMT* occurs in only one manuscript, Harleian 5280. Its full title is *Cath Maige Tured an scelsa sis ocus genemain Bres meic Eladhain ocus a righe*. It is translated by Gustav Lehmacher, S.J., *Anthropos*, XXVI (1931), 435-460, and my summary follows Lehmacher. An incomplete edition and translation by W. Stokes is in *Rev. celt.*, XII (1891), 56-130. Portions of the text omitted by Stokes are printed by Thurneysen (*ZCP*, XII [1918], 401 f.). Vernam Hull brings evidence to date *CMT* before 908 (*ZCP*, XVIII [1930], 81 and 89).

[8] *Lia Fáil* [stone of *Fál*] indicated by roaring that the man standing on it should be king. See Vernam Hull, "The Four Jewels of the Tuatha Dé," *ZCP*, XVIII (1930), 73-89.

[9] Sorcery is obviously the remark of a Christian rationalizer, but the four cities and four jewels must be old, although d'Arbois de Jubainville (*Cours de litt. celtique*, V [Paris, 1892], 394), thought that the account

§ 8. Next is mentioned the *gein mbúadha,* "wonder-child," Lug, whose mother was Eithne daughter of Balar, and whose father was Cian son of Dian-Cécht.[10] Then comes the invasion and the battle. § 9. "The Tuatha Dé came with a great fleet to take Ireland from the Fir Bolg. They burned their ships . . . the smoke filled the air. Therefore it was imagined that they came in clouds of mist." § 10. In the [first] battle of Moytura they defeated the Fir Bolg and slew their king, Eochaid son of Erc. § 11. Nuadu's hand was struck off in that battle by Sreng son of Sengann, but Dian Cécht aided by Creidne made him a silver hand. §13. Such of the Fir Bolg as escaped from the battle went in flight unto the Fomorians.[11] § 14. The women of the Tuatha Dé, after Nuadu lost his hand, urged that he was disqualified to be king. The kingdom was therefore bestowed on Bres. Bres had a Fomorian father and a Tuatha Dé mother. § 15. The paternity of Bres is thus related. § 16. Éru, a woman of the Tuatha Dé, was one day beside the sea when she saw a golden-haired man in a silver ship which the stream of the wave bore to the land.[12] § 17. He won her love, and she wept when he departed. § 21. He told her that he

---

of the four cities was an interpolation made after the year 1000. The number four, as we shall see, runs through this story and other analogues of the Grail story. We expect to be told that the Tuatha Dé won a victory by the aid of the four talismans, but they are not mentioned again. From this point *CMT* follows a different recension in which the four talismans are supplanted by a well of healing. This well, which is operated by four physicians, is described in § 123. To the four jewels and four physicians may be compared the harp of the Dagda called "four-angled-music," § 163. The account of the four jewels of the Tuatha Dé is printed in full above. These four jewels, I believe, as was pointed out by Alfred Nutt (*Studies* [1888], p. 184), are the source of the four talismans of the Grail castle.

[10] Only because he is the hero of the story is Lug named here.

[11] Fir Bolg and Fomorians are not distinguished from each other. At this point begins the second part of the story, *genemain Bres,* etc., "The Birth and Reign of Bres."

[12] Fairies, whether Fomorians or Tuatha Dé, have self-moving ships.

was Elathu, son of Delbaeth, king of the Fomorians, and that she should bear him a son to be called Echid Bres, "Echid the Fair." [13] § 23. After his birth Bres developed so fast that in seven years he had attained a growth of fourteen years of age. § 24. The sovereignty of Ireland was given to him. § 25. When Bres took the kingship,[14] three Fomorian kings, Indech, son of Dia Domnann; Elathu, son of Delbaeth; and Tethra, laid tribute upon Ireland. Their *trén fir*, "champions," were made servants to Bres. Ogma carried firewood, the Dagda built forts.[15] § 39. After the Tuatha Dé had been in bondage for some time [16] to the Fomorians, Bres, their representative, was driven from the kingdom in consequence of a satire pronounced upon him by Cairpre son of Etain, *file* of the Tuatha Dé.[17] § 43. Bres fled to the Fomorians and came to *mag mór co n'airechtaib iomdaib*, "a great plain with many assemblies." [18] Upon the request of Bres, Balar grandson of Néit, king of the Islands, and Indech, the son of Dia Domnann, king of the Fomorians, made a bridge of ships *o indsib Galld*, "from the isles of the foreigners," in order to enforce their tribute and their rule upon the Tuatha Dé.

[13] The lady Éru is, I conjecture, Ireland personified (Ériu), and the story is an allegory to signify that the Fomorian, Elathu, seized the sovereignty.

[14] In § 124 Ruadán is son of Bres and of Bríg the Dagda's daughter. Bríg was evidently wife of Bres. Bríg is a personification of Ireland, and this is another allegory signifying that Bres took possession of Ireland.

[15] Here follow other matters, §§ 26–35, especially the Dagda's choice of a heifer, concluded in § 165, which is a Märchen formula thrust into our saga. See Lehmacher, *op. cit.*, p. 458.

[16] No time is mentioned. According to *LG* it was twenty-seven years (see p. 265).

[17] Cairpre's satire, which occurs as a separate anecdote, has been edited by Vernam Hull, ZCP, XVIII (1930), 63–69.

[18] Mag Mór is the land of the dead; by the pseudo-historians it was interpreted as Spain. To Balar king of the isles, compare Clamadeu *des isles*, Rion *rois des isles*, Galaholt *li sires des estraignes isles*. These last are the *indsi gall* mentioned above, and are commonly explained as the Hebrides, but all are doubtless islands of the dead.

§ 55. The story now turns to Lug, called *lonn-ainsclech*, "furious fighter."[19] He was a foster-son to Tailtiu daughter of Mag Mór, king of Spain, and to Echid the Rough son of Duach. (From *LG* we know that Tailtiu cleared land in the Forest of Cian where she brought up Lug.) § 53. Nuadu, now again in sovereignty over the Tuatha Dé, after the expulsion of Bres, held a great feast at Tara. A fair young warrior (Lug) who was called *Samildánach*[20] presented himself and asked the porter for admittance. § 56. He was tested, first by being questioned about the different arts he knew, and second by being asked to play *fidchell*, "chess," and was triumphant in both trials. § 70. Thereupon King Nuadu commanded to admit him, and he "sat in the sage's seat [third test] because he was a sage in every art." § 72. Ogma tossed outside the palace a stone that required eighty oxen to draw (fourth test). Lug threw it back and restored the piece that had been knocked out of the palace. § 73. Lug was then asked to play the *crot*, "harp" (fifth test). He played the *súantraige*, "sleep-strain," that put them asleep till the morrow; the *goltraige*, "mourning-strain," that made them weep; and the *gentraige*, "laughing-strain," that made them laugh.

§ 74. After Lug had passed all the tests, Nuadu resigned the

[19] In OCT (*Atlantis*, IV, 163), he is *lamfada*, "of the long arm." This seems the origin of Peredur's epithet *paladyr-hir*, "of the long lance" (see A. C. L. Brown, *Mod. Phil.*, XXII [1924], 84). Our manuscript of CMT (Harl. 5280, fol. 69r., *Rev. celt.*, XII [1891], 127) calls Lug, *lonn-bemnech*, "furious striker." The manuscript calls the foster-mother "Taillne," which I take to be the genitive case of Tailtiu. She is Ireland personified (cf. *talam*, gen. *talman*, "earth"). She is called the daughter of Mag Mór, I suppose, because of confusion based on the idea that the fruits of the earth come from the land of the dead. Tailtiu's burial-place is modern Telltown. Games founded by Lug in her honor took place there every *Lugnasad* (August first).

[20] "Possessing many arts" or, as J. Loth translates it (*Revue archéologique*, XXIV [1914], 211), "summer with many gifts." Loth believes that Lug's marriage with the Earth was celebrated at *Lugnasad*. The *Lugoves* were earth-mothers.

throne to him for thirteen days in order that Lug might over-throw the Fomorians. § 75. Lug met for a year in secret con-verse with the Dagda, Ogma, Goibniu, and Dian-Cécht (a statement which implies that when Lug had gained the throne he kept it for more than thirteen days). § 83. Lug, the Dagda, and Ogma went to the three gods of Danu,[21] who secured for Lug the *gréssa an cathae*, "contrivances" or "talismans for battle," and seven years they were preparing for it and making their weapons. §§ 84–92. Then follows a discussion of the enchantments used in the battle. § 93. The Dagda gives a list of his names: *Fer Benn, Bruach*, etc., twenty-two in all, which illustrates the difficulty of identifying mythological charac-ters. § 95. Because of Lug's knowledge an attempt was made to keep him out of the battle to prevent his being slain.[22] They put him in charge of nine fosterers to protect him.

§ 121. After the (second) battle of Moytura began, (§ 122) the Tuatha Dé had their weapons renewed every day by Goibniu the smith, and their dead men restored by a magic well so that they could fight again the next day. § 123. "The mortally wounded became whole through the might of the chant of the four physicians who were about the well." The four physicians were Dian-Cécht, his two sons Ochttriuil and Miach, and his daughter Airmed. § 126. The Fomorians at length destroyed this magic well by filling it with stones. The stone heap was called Carn Octhriallig.

§ 128. The kings and chiefs of the Fomorians were Balar, son of Dot and grandson of Néit; Bres, son of Elathu; Tuire *Tortbuillech*, "giving heavy blows," son of Lobos; Goll and Argoll; Loiscenn Lomm, "naked frog," son of Lommglúnech; Indech; Ommne; and Bagne; Elathu son of Delbaeth. § 129. Lug escaped from his nine fosterers and entered the battle.

[21] The "three gods" are Brión, Iuchar, and Iucharba. Their quest for talismans is an independent story (p. 276).

[22] An attempt to spare Cuchulinn by keeping him out of battle is made in *Tochmarc Emire* (p. 51).

He went round the men of Ireland on one foot with one eye closed, singing an incantation.[23] § 133. In the battle, Nuadu Argeclám, "silver hand," and Macha [24] daughter of Ernmas were slain by Balar. "Balar had a *suil milldagach* [evil eye].[25] The eye was never opened except on a battlefield. Four men raised the lid of the eye with a polished pole that went through the lid. An army that he looked at through that eye though it numbered many thousands could make no resistance." § 135. "The lid was raised from Balar's eye. Then Lug cast a *lia talma*, [sling stone] at him, which carried the eye back through his head. It looked at his own army. It fell among the host of the Fomorians so that twenty-seven of them died beside it."

§ 138. Thereafter the Fomorians were defeated. § 149. The Tuatha Dé captured Bres. § 150. "If you spare me," said Bres, "the kine of Ireland shall always give milk." [26] This ransom was refused. "For sparing me the men of Ireland shall reap a harvest in every quarter of the year," said Bres. This also was refused. § 160. Then Lug asked, "How shall the men of Ireland plough, sow and reap?" Bres replied, "On Thursday shall they plow, sow and reap." By this *celg*, "trick,"[27] Bres secured his release.

§ 162. Ogma found Orne the sword of Tethra king of the Fomorians which related all that had been done by it, for demons used to speak from swords at that time. § 163. Lug, the Dagda, and Ogma went in search of the Dagda's harp. It had two names, *Dair dá blá*, "oak of two fields," and *Coir*

[23] On this incantation see *corrguinecht* in O'Davoren's *Glossary*, § 383 (ed. W. Stokes, *Archiv f. celt. Lexikographie*, II [1904], p. 257).

[24] Macha was evidently Nuadu's queen. Macha is a name for Ireland, and here is another allegory to signify that Nuadu took the sovereignty of the island.

[25] Balar is, I conjecture, a god of the dead whose look kills.

[26] Fairies, both Fomorians and Tuatha Dé, control prosperity.

[27] Father Lehmacher thinks (*op. cit.*, p. 456, n. 75) that this word implies a contempt felt by Christians for a heathen custom.

Cetharchoir, "four-angled music." § 164. This harp which had been stolen by Fomorians returned of itself to the Dagda when he called, killing nine Fomorians on the way. § 165. The Dagda's heifer is then mentioned and finally (§ 167) the Morrigan daughter of Ernmas makes a prophecy about the end of the world.

Only a full outline, such as that above, can give the reader an idea of the tangled threads that make up the saga. For comparison with the Perceval legend one of these threads, the career of Lug, may be disentangled as follows:

Cath Maige Tured	*Chrétien's "Perceval"*
1. Lug was a wonder-child or destined hero.	1. Perceval was a destined hero, as is proved by the damsel who was not to laugh till she saw the best of knights (vs. 1059).
2. Who was brought up in the absence or death of his father.	2. Perceval's father was dead (vs. 74).
3. Lug was brought up by a foster-mother at a distance from the king's court.	3. Perceval was brought by his own mother in the "waste forest" (vs. 80).
4. She lived in a forest that she cleared or planted.	4. She cultivated fields in the forest (vs. 82).
5. Lug was called a fair warrior.	5. Perceval was called *biaus filz* (vs. 347).
6. Lug came to Nuadu's palace at Tara.	6. Perceval came to Arthur's palace at Carduel (vs. 863).
7. A feast is being held.	7. Arthur is at a feast (vs. 902).

8. Lug was called by his nickname, "samildanach." (*CMT* mentions his real name, but this cannot be primitive, *Mod. Phil.*, XVII (1919), 379.)

8. Perceval did not guess his real name till he met his cousin after leaving the Grail castle (vs. 3575).

9. Lug underwent several tests at Tara.

9. Perceval at Arthur's castle passed a test when the damsel laughed, "because he was the best of all knights" (vss. 1059 f.).

10. Lug took the place of the wounded Nuadu for thirteen days.

10. Perceval fought the Red Knight, thus in a sense taking Arthur's place, while Arthur seems helpless.

11. Lug's followers tried to keep him out of the battle.

11. Arthur feared that Perceval might be slain by the Red Knight.

12. Lug slew Balar by hitting him in the eye with a sling-stone.

12. Perceval slew the Red Knight by hitting him in the eye with a javelin (vs. 1092).

This table shows that the events of Lug's career, including his killing of Balar, can be matched by events in Perceval's story from the beginning up to his slaying the Red Knight. Since the incidents occur in the same order, some literary connection between the stories must exist.

The account of Lug's arrival at Tara is confused. He took Nuadu's throne for thirteen days (§ 74) and then went to the three gods of Danu to secure talismans and weapons. They spent, we are told, seven years (§ 83) in preparing talismans and weapons for the battle of Moytura in which Lug killed Balar. Seven years must, therefore, have elapsed from the coming of Lug till his killing of Balar.

The passage about the three gods preparing and procuring weapons for the battle is an allusion to the chief transaction of *Oided Chloinne Tuirenn* (*OCT*). Now *OCT* adds one important incident to what we know from *CMT*, for it declares [28] that Lug, immediately upon arriving at Nuadu's castle, slew Fomorian tax-gatherers and so brought about the battle. Fomorian tax-gatherers would, like other Fomorians, be red giants. If Lug killed a red giant (the Ith of *LG*) upon arriving at Nuadu's fort, this would be an exact parallel to Perceval's slaying the Red Knight (Ither in *Parzival*) upon arriving at Arthur's court.

Despite the survival of *OCT* in a manuscript of the eighteenth century only, we may accept as ancient this statement that Lug, upon his arrival at Nuadu's court, slew a Fomorian and thus provoked an invasion. It seems safe to accept this statement because Lug's slaying a Fomorian is evidently another version of the account in *LG* which tells that Ith was the first to visit Ireland, was slain there and his body carried back to Spain to arouse vengeance. According to *LG*, Ith was brother to Bile, or Balar, the father of Galam, or Míl. *LG* does not say that Ith and his men went to Ireland to collect taxes, and perhaps their purpose at first was to secure wives, but anyhow their visit was resented and Ith was slain by the Tuatha Dé. The invasion of Ireland by the sons of Míl was to avenge Ith's murder. Ith corresponds to the Red Knight who in *Perceval* is unnamed, but in *Parzival* is called Ither.

[28] Printed and translated by E. O'Curry (*Atlantis*, IV [1863], 164 f.). The only manuscript is of the eighteenth century.

In *Perceval* the Red Knight demands that Arthur hold his lands in fief, which is nearly the same thing as asking tribute:

> diras au mauvés roi:
> Se il ne viaut tenir de moi
> Sa terre, que il la me rande.
>
> (vss. 889–891)

It is not said that the assaults of Anguingueron and Clamadeu upon Blancheflor's castle later, and we may suppose upon the Grail castle, for it is merely another aspect of Blancheflor's castle, are in revenge for the Red Knight's death, but we may surmise that such was the original situation. In the Irish, war on the Tuatha Dé was precipitated by their slaying of Ith; in the French, war on the Grail folk was precipitated by Perceval's slaying the Red Knight (Ither). Not to push this resemblance unduly, the following parallels may safely be added to those tabled above:

Cath Maige Tured	*Chrétien's "Perceval"*
13. Balar was a Fomorian, "king of the isles" (§ 50).	13. Clamadeu who besieged Blancheflor's castle wore red armor (*Parzival*, vs. 181,17) and was "king of the isles" (vs. 2005).
14. Lug, by his victory, freed Ireland from some sort of curse or wasting.	14. The lands of Blancheflor and of the Grail castle were wasted, and were to be restored by Perceval's success.
15. Lug obtained talismans.	15. Perceval received a sword at the Grail castle (vss. 3130 f.).

Perceval's destiny is obviously to marry Blancheflor [29] and rule over her castle, which is virtually identical with the Grail castle. Nothing is said in *CMT* about Lug's marriage, but, on general principles, we can be sure that he is to marry Nuadu's queen, Macha, who is virtually Ireland personified, and reign in Nuadu's stead. Moreover, the Irish had a tradition that Lug was wedded after the battle of Moytura.[30] That this tradition is older than the rise of French romance is proved by a reference to it in the later version of *Tochmarc Emire*,[31] which has been assigned by Thurneysen to the middle of the twelfth century. We may then add the following to the above list of parallels:

Cath Maige Tured	*Chrétien's "Perceval"*
16. Lug was wedded to his foster-mother Tailtiu, who is the sovereignty, and in mythology is probably a form of Nuadu's queen, Macha.	16. Perceval was married to Blancheflor, who represents the sovereignty of Belrepeire (vss. 2104 f.).

Lug's career is parallel to that of Perceval throughout, except that from his story the usual signposts of a Journey to Fairyland, such as the man who tells the road and the

[29] Chrétien's unfinished *Perceval* does not tell this, but, according to Wolfram, Parzival married Cundwîramours.

[30] Rhŷs, *Celtic Heathendom*, p. 416.

[31] Cuchulinn is explaining to his charioteer a cryptic remark that he had made to Emer: "The Remnants of the Great Feast [*Tresc in mârimdill*] I said, that is Taillne. It is there that Lug Scimaig gave the great feast to Lug son of Ethle to comfort him after the battle of Moytura, for that was his wedding feast of kingship. For the Tuath Déa made this Lug king, after Nuadu had been killed." The place of the feast is Tailtiu today. Kuno Meyer's translation is in *Archaeological Review*, I (1888), 231. The Irish text is in Van Hamel, *Compert Con Culainn*, pp. 41 f. On the date see Thurneysen, *Heldensage*, pp. 381 and 669.

dangerous river, are missing. Lug's journey to Tara is not narrated at all. A reason for this omission is easily found. *LG* purports to be history, and the pseudo-historians who constructed it could not picture Tara as fairyland. The same synthetic historians have evidently worked over *CMT*, and, because they aimed at realism, have obliterated all traces of a Journey to Fairyland. It is from wonder tales and not from pseudo-history that the incidents of the Journey to Fairyland have been deduced in our Chapter II.

The well-known youthful exploits of Cuchulinn and of Finn are presumably borrowed from the mythological exploits of Lug. Lug's youthful deeds are lost, but that he was brought up by a fairy foster-mother in a forest is attested by the old manuscript *LL*. The Perceval *enfances* resemble those of Cuchulinn and of Finn. It is therefore reasonable to believe that the Perceval *enfances*, like the rest of Perceval's exploits, are borrowed from the life story of the god Lug.

CHAPTER IX

The Enslaving of Fairyland

MANY of the twenty Irish and Welsh Journeys to Fairyland outlined in Chapter II presuppose that fairyland has fallen into the power of Fomorian giants and needs to be delivered, but none of them asks the question, "How did fairyland become enchanted?" Hitherto nobody seems to have concerned himself with this question; nor has anybody put much stress on a corresponding query about the Grail castle, "How was the Fisher King wounded and his land laid waste?" The story of the ruin of fairyland has never before been compared to the Grail story. The answer to the question about fairyland clearly is that hostile invaders called Fomorians conquered the isle of women; and it would be interesting to find out whether the same kind of answer explains the ruin of the Grail kingdom. For the present our concern is with the ruin of fairyland.

The story of the ruin of fairyland by giants is lost, but is believed to be the basis out of which the five invasions of Ireland in the fabulous history, *Lebor Gabála Érenn*, "Book of the Taking of Ireland" (*LG*),[1] were constructed. The

[1] After this chapter was first written, Parts I–IV of an edition of *Lebor Gabála* by R. A. S. Macalister reached me (*ITS*, vols. XXXIV, XXXV, XXXIX, and XLI [Dublin, 1938–1941]). Later volumes I have not seen. Macalister distinguishes three redactions: "R¹," which goes back in some form to the eighth century; "R²," about 1000; "R³," twelfth century. Important articles on *LG* are: R. Thurneysen, "Zum Lebor

following pages are a pioneer attempt to untie the knot
wrought by the pseudo-historians, and to reconstruct out
of *LG* [2] the myth of friendly and hostile fairies, Tuatha Dé
and Fomorians, upon which the five invasions are thought
to be founded. It is first necessary to trace the growth of
LG, and to ascertain from various documents just what
details in it are certainly older than the time of Chrétien.
The action of the myth we must suppose was in fairyland,
and the people all fairy folk: the women friendly fairies
or Tuatha Dé, and the men hostile fairies or Fomorians.
The pseudo-historians, since they knew that the Tuatha
Dé were ancient gods of the country, identified the land
of women with Ireland of long ago, and the invaders with
giants of old time who seized upon the women and the
riches of the island. By a natural development the women
acquired a king, a more or less friendly leader, and a battle
for possession of Ireland between him and the chief giant
arose. A notion of alternation between a friendly king
and a hostile invader evidently entered the story, transform-
ing it into a Recurrent Battle (type V),[3] so that Ireland
and the women are ruled alternately by a friendly king,

Gabála," *ZCP*, X (1915), 384–395; A. G. Van Hamel, "On Lebor Gabála,"
ZCP, X (1915), 97–197.

[2] Kuno Meyer warned against using *LG* as a "source book for mythology" (*Sitzungsberichte der Preussischen Akademie d. Wiss.*, Berlin,
XXXII [1919], 546). On p. 538 he wrote, "Wir in Lebor Gabála in der
Hauptsache nicht mit volkstümlicher Sage und Überlieferung zu tun
haben, die sich, wie leider noch oft geschieht, ohne weiteres zu mytho-
logischen Zwecken benutzen liesse [Meyer was probably thinking of
d'Arbois, *Cours* II], sondern mit bewusster und planmässiger Erfindung
klassisch gebildeter Gelehrten." No doubt the compilers knew their
Bible and their Orosius, but, as I think, the real story they had to tell
came from their own mythology.

[3] Page 31.

a king of the Tuatha Dé, and by a hostile fairy, a king of the Fomorians. By repetition of this battle the five invasions of Ireland, it is thought, were built up and told in LG as shown in the table on page 243.

The following pages attempt to trace the building up of the five invasions out of the myth of the ruin of fairy-land.[4] The invader as a symbol of his victory marries, in every case, a queen who, under different names, is virtually a personification of Ireland.

This is very nearly the explanation of LG adopted by Dr. R. A. S. Macalister in his new edition, the main difference being that he derives the mythological materials from summer and winter games in Ireland. I am as yet unconvinced of the existence in Ireland of these games, although I agree that a Recurrent Battle formed a part of Irish myth. More influential and older than the Recurrent Battle is, I think, the myth of Amargen and Banba — that is of an island of women, ruled over by a triple-formed god, Brión, but destroyed by a giant, who in the beginning was one of a race of monsters called Fomorians, having one eye, one leg, one hand, and sometimes a goat or a dog head. The famous five invasions were, I think, developed

---

[4] The historical character of the invasions has already been destroyed, as, for example, by A. G. Van Hamel, "Aspects of Celtic Mythology" (British Academy, XX [1934], 222). In general I agree with Van Hamel except in one page of his "On Lebor Gabála" (ZCP, X [1915], 180), where, contrary to his usual procedure, he attempts to derive Amargen in the mythological sagas from the Ulster saga. Possibly certain details in LG may have been influenced by the Cuchulinn saga, but the core of the mythological cycle, including the story of Amargen and Eriu, is surely older than the Cuchulinn cycle, and to some extent the source of it. Irish mythological tales, despite the late and degraded forms in which they are preserved, contained the ruins of pagan mythology which are no doubt older than the heroic sagas.

TABLE OF THE FIVE INVASIONS

King of Friendly Fairies	Queen	King of Hostile Fairies	Reference
4. Partholon*	Delgnat [Elga]	Cichol grigenchos	LG, II, 253
5. Nemed	Macha	Conaing	LG, III, 115
6. Cesarb, Luamh, Luacchra	Tailltiu	Eochaid	LG, IV, 6
7. Nuadu [triple-formed]	Macha	Balar	LG, IV, 106
8. Mac Cuill, Mac Cecht, Mac Greine	Ériu [triple-formed]	Galam [Mil] and his sons: Donn, Amargen	O'Clery I, 271

THREE EARLIER INVASIONS

King of Friendly Fairies	Queen	King of Hostile Fairies	Reference
1. Three heroes: one is named Ladra Iúam	Banba	Amargen	Page 250
2. Ladhra, Bith, Finntan, or Luam, Medar, Mel	Cessair, or Cessair, Barriu, Banba		LG, II, 191
3. Three fishermen: Capa, Laigne, Luasat			LG, II, 185

* To save the reader trouble I adopt Macalister's numbers. On the right is the page in his edition. After his edition fails I give the reference in O'Clery, *Leabhar Gabhála*, ed. R. A. S. Macalister and Eóin Mac Neill, vol. I (Dublin, 1916).

out of this myth by different writers, in different places, and later, in accordance with a well understood practice of Irish story tellers,[5] were attached one to another to build up our present *LG*.

That our *Lebor Gabála* derives its name from a story of the *gabál*, "taking," of Ireland by the sons of Míl;[6] that the invasion of the sons of Míl (Macalister's *Liber Occupationis*) was at first a separate document from the five invasions (Macalister's *Liber Praecursorum*) is probable enough; in addition, the invasion of the sons of Míl may well have been modeled, as Macalister thinks,[7] on the ancestry of the Israelites, and on Moses viewing the Land of Promise. A suggestion to combine the myth with the Bible story may have developed out of a remark in Genesis 6: 2–4, about the sons of God and the daughters of men; the passage mentions "giants," and the Fomorians were giants.[8]

The notion that the sons of Míl came from Spain seems to have arisen from an identification of the mythological tower of the dead, which I suppose was Amargen's home, with a lofty tower in Spain mentioned by Orosius:

> Secundus angulus [Hispaniae] circium intendit, ubi Brigantia Gallaeciae civitas sita altissimum farum, et inter pauca memorandi operis ad speculam Brittanniae erigit.[9]

Another passage in Orosius may have been misunderstood by Irish compilers to mean that Ireland was visible from Spain:

[5] Page 118.

[6] Míl is supposed to be from *miles*, and a translation of the Irish name Galam (cf. *gal*, "valor"). According to Van Hamel (ZCP, X, 122), Míl, not Míled, is the oldest form of the name.

[7] Macalister, I, xxx; II, 166, 231, and 249 f.

[8] Giraldus Cambrensis translates Fomorians, "gigantes" (p. 262).

[9] *Adversum paganos*, ed C. Zangemeister (Leipzig: Teubner, 1889), I, 2, p. 11, ll. 72 f. See Van Hamel, ZCP, X (1915), 173.

Hibernia insula inter Britanniam et Hispaniam sita longiore ab Africo in boream spatio porrigitur. Huius partes priores intentae Cantabrico oceano Brigantiam Gallaeciae civitatem ab Africo sibi in circium occurrentem, spatioso intervallo procul spectant, ab eo praecipue promuntorio, ubi Scenae fluminis ostium est et Velabri Lucenique consistunt.[10]

More influential than the Bible and Orosius, however, was, I think, the myth of Banba and Amargen. Macalister has not noticed that most of the important names in invasion eight — Ith, Bile, Galam (Míl), Donn, and Amargen — come not from the Bible or Orosius but from the heathen myth of Banba and Amargen.

Unlike the summer and winter games, this myth of an island of women is not hypothetical. From a study of three fragments which were in Cin Droma Snechta, a lost tenth-century manuscript, a rather good idea of it can be obtained. These pseudo-historical fragments have been printed but not translated by R. Thurneysen [11] in a collection made by him of all known direct quotations, thirteen in number, from this lost manuscript. Thurneysen's extracts 4, 6, and 9 relate to the island of women myth. The first (no. 4) I translate as follows:

Who now first found Erin after the creation of the earth? This is what says the book Druim Snechta, that Banba was the name of the first maiden who found Erin before the Flood so that it is from her would be [the name] Banba upon Erin. She came with one hundred fifty maidens and three men. Ladra, the navigator, was one of the three men. He is the first

---

[10] *Adversum paganos*, I, 2, p. 12, ll. 82 f. Eóin Mac Neill (*Phases of Irish History* [Dublin, 1919], p. 94) supposed *Scena* was in Spain, but Macalister (I, xxxi) thinks it may be the River Shannon.

[11] "Zu irischen Handschriften und Literaturdenkmälern," Ser. I, *Abhandlungen d. k. Gesellschaft d. Wiss. zu Göttingen*, phil.-hist. Klasse, XIV (1912), ii, 23 f.

who died in Erin then, and it is from him Ard Ladrann is named. Forty years were they here. There came to them after that a disease so that they all died in one week. For two hundred years thereafter Erin was without one person alive. So afterward came the Flood. For a year and forty days Erin was under the Flood. At the end of three hundred years after the Flood, Partholon took possession of Erin. His seed inhabited it for five hundred fifty years till the Dogheads [mythical giants, a variety of Fomorians] slew them, so that there did not escape one of his children alive. For thirty years thereafter there was no living person in Erin.[12]

In this story it is reasonable to explain Banba with her one hundred fifty maidens as a fairy queen of the Re-current Battle (type V) surrounded by her followers of the Tuatha Dé; and it is natural to believe that the three men are Brión, Iuchar, and Iucharba, the triple-formed god of the Tuatha Dé. Since gods have many names, it is no objection to this interpretation that the name given to one of the men is not Brión but Ladra. The oldest manuscript,

[12] Macalister (II, 17) translates this from his text which belongs to his redaction "R¹." Thurneysen's text, based on manuscripts *BB* (p. 21, col. b, l. 21), Lecan (folio 271ᵛ), Fermoy (folio 8), is as follows: "Cia didu ciata rogab Érinn iar tusmid talman? Is ed asbert lebar Droma Snechta comad Banba ainm na cét ingine fo gabad Érinn ría n-dílind ocus comad úaithi nobeth Banba for Érinn. Tri .l. og (Lecan trichaechad) dodechaid ocus triar fer. Ladra (Laghra B. Ladra lúam L) in tres fear. Is é cetmarb Érinn insin ocus is uad ainmnigther Ard Ladrann [Ardmine, co. Wexford]. Cethorcha blíadan bádar isinn indsi. Dos-(n)-ainic íarom galar conerbailtar uili a n-áen-shechtmain. Da cét-bliadan íar sin bái Ériu can óenduine béo. Conad íarum táinic díliu. XL lá ocus bliadain robái Ériu fo dílind. I cinn tri cét mbliadan íar n-dílind rogab Parthalón Érinn. Trebsat a shíl .l. blíadan ar u.c. condaselgadar Conchind, conna-terno nech dia chlaind i m-bethu. Tricha blíadan íar sin cen duine i m-bethaid i n-Érinn."

LL, reads Ladra *lúam*, "navigator," an epithet that points directly to Brión, for he is usually a fisherman or navigator who ferries people across the river of death, or who voyages from earth to fairyland. In this extract, fairyland is identified with the Ireland of a long past, golden age. Banba is virtually Ireland personified, and, as will be seen, was often triformed.

Prefixed to the *Liber Originum*, but not known to Nennius, is the invasion that I have numbered two, that of Cessair. According to R[1] [13] Cessair, daughter of Bith son of Noah, took Ireland before the Flood. The early scribes interpreted Cessair as another name for Ireland, and regarded her story as a variant of the Banba story. R[2] gives Cessair's story in two versions. As evidence of an isle-of-women myth, lying behind these stories I summarize the longer of these versions from Macalister's edition.[14]

Cessair brought with her to Ireland two women leaders, Bairrind and Banba, together with fifty maidens and three men, Bith, Ladra navigator, and Finntan. The men quarreled about dividing up the maidens. Finntan took seventeen, including Cessair. He gave Bith seventeen, including Bairrind, but Ladra only sixteen, including Banba; so that Ladra was dissatisfied. Ladra died of excess of women.[15] Then Bith and Finntan

---

[13] The oldest of the redactions of *LG* (Macalister, II, 177).

[14] II, 184–193.

[15] "*Do furail banaich*," Macalister, II, 188. This is a survival from some myth about amorous *fées*. Love-making is apparent also in Thurneysen's no. 9 (p. 251). Islands of women are told of in many parts of the world and are invariably devoted to love-making. One needs only recall the islands of Circe and of Calypso. See W. Hertz, *Spielmannsbuch* (1931), p. 385; L. A. Paton, *Studies in the Fairy Mythology of Arthurian Romance* (Boston: Radcliffe College Monograph, 1903), p. 43; H. R. Patch, *PMLA*, XXXIII (1918), 624, n. 81. Love-weariness is a well-known motive. In the oldest of the Irish voyage stories, *Imram*

each had twenty-five. Later Bith died, and Finntan had all the women. Finally he fled from them to Tul Tuinde near Loch Dergleirc.

Another version of the Cessair myth appears in a poem called "Forty Questions," which is attributed to Eochaid ua Cérin, an eleventh-century poet:

> Three brothers of Cessair came one night before the Flood to Ireland, and they did not speak to Cessair. Lúam, Medar, and Mel were their names. They were in bird shape on Benn Boirche.[16]

Lúam "navigator," Medar, and Mel, like Bith, Ladra "navigator," and Finntan in the first version, are apparently names for the triple-formed Brión. That he sometimes manifested himself in the form of three birds is known from other channels. In *Cath Mucríma*, Brión seems to appear as a triple-headed bird.[17] In the Welsh *Branwen daughter of Llyr*, the three birds of Rhiannon that awake the dead and put to sleep the living [18] and that sing during the feasting of Bran's head are pretty surely a manifestation of the god Bran (Irish Brión).

One manuscript of R¹ [19] contains a short statement, which

Brain, Nechtan wished to return to Ireland, which hints that a love-making island might grow tiresome (p. 272). In *Imram Maeile Dúin* (p. 275) departure from an isle of women is definitely "an escape." Some trace of this is in D, in the Calypso episode, and in Chrétien's *Yvain* (pp. 111, 114).

[16] Edited by Thurneysen, ZCP, XIII (1921), 130 f.

[17] Edited by Stokes, *Rev. celt.*, XIII (1892), 448 f. The Tuatha Dé appear to the sons of Míl in bird form, according to a gloss in *Liber Hymnorum* (ed. J. H. Bernard and R. Atkinson [London: Henry Bradshaw Society, 1898], I, 103; II, 186).

[18] *Mab.*, I, 67 and 204.

[19] Macalister, II, 179; see pp. 199 and 215.

I have numbered invasion "three," about three fishermen from Spain, Capa, Luasad, and Laigne, who came to Ireland before the Flood, and adds: "Howbeit Lebor Gabála does not reckon them, for they did not settle in the land of Ireland."

This old story of three fishermen must be a fragment of the myth about the triformed Brión and the island of women. Spain in Irish fable is often the land of the dead. The three fishermen from Spain are, I think, clearly the triple-formed Brión, crossing the river of death. The different names here, Capa, Luasad, and Laigne, need bother nobody. My interpretation is, I think, supported by a famous passage preserved by Tzetzés [20] which relates that fishermen, dwelling opposite to Britain, ferry souls across, in the darkness of the night, to an island, which, though called "Britain," is manifestly an island of the dead. This passage is probably a Roman misunderstanding of the old myth of Brión and the Tuatha Dé, which we are trying to reconstruct.

Extract no. 4 does not imply a battle. The most interesting of Thurneysen's extracts is his no. 6, because it introduces Amargen who is later the leader in battle of the sons of Míl. I have numbered this invasion "one," because very likely it affords our oldest glimpse of the underlying myth. My translation of Thurneysen's text (no. 6, first part) [21] is as follows:

[20] Quoted on p. 134.
[21] His text (from *BB*, p. 40, col. a, ll. 15 f.) runs: "Adbert leabur Droma Sneachta gorfiarfaigh Amargéin di [i.e. Banba] a céineal. 'Do cloind Adhaimh' or si. 'Cia ceinel do macaibh Noe duit?' ol se. 'Am sine sea nas Noe' ol si. 'For rínd slcbhe robhadhasa isin dílind gosa teal sa anois' ol si, 'do dhecháin tonda dilind.' Is desin dogairthear Tuínde. Acht cheana ingnathach in seal sin anuas. Canaid iarum dichealta furri,

The *Book of Druim Snechta* said that Amargein asked her (Banba) about her descent:

"From the children of Adam," says she.

"From which of Noah's sons are you descended?" says he.

"I am older than Noah," says she. "I have been on the top of a mountain in the Flood until this present time," says she, "to look upon the waves (*tonda*) of the Flood."

Hence comes the name Tuinde. But also that space of time mentioned above is surprising! Afterwards [Amargein] chants spells over her, and Banba is driven [?] from them.

Thurneysen's comment is: "It would appear from this that extract no. 4 was an inexact copy from manuscript Druim Snechta, because according to no. 4 one would understand that Banba as well as her companions died of the disease, while, according to no. 6, she survived the Flood." It is, however, no longer necessary to believe with Thurneysen that extract 4 was an inexact copy. The following pages contain abundant evidence to prove that Banba is virtually Ireland personified, the earth goddess, and so could not possibly perish in a pestilence. Irish readers probably saw no contradiction between 4 and 6. They doubtless knew that Banba was one of the "ever-living ones," and that like Ériu and Cessair she was virtually the earth of Ireland personified.

After some omission Thurneysen continues with extract 6 (second part) [22] as follows:

---

ocus ataghar Banbha uaidhibh. . . ." No part of Thurneysen's extracts nos. 6 and 9 are in the four volumes of Macalister's edition of *LG* that have appeared.

[22] The text (from *BB*, p. 40, col. a, ll. 35 f.) is as follows: "Atbert leabur Droma Sneachta conidh i Sleibh Mís roagaill Eríu íad ocus gordhealbh sluagha mora fa chomair combadar i-cathughudh friu íad. Corochansat a n-druidhe seon ocus a filidh dicealta doibh. Conaccadar mbatir

The Book Druim Snechta said that it is in Sliab Mis that
Ériu conversed with them, and that she fashioned great hosts
before him [them?], so that they were doing battle with them.
So their druids chanted a charm, and their poets [chanted] spells
for them so that they saw that [the hosts] were [only] sods
of turf of the mountain. Hence the name Sliab Mis. And Fotla
conversed with them at Uisnech.

Here for the first time is mentioned the battle fought
between the sons of Míl and Ériu by phantom armies. This
battle is thus described in the prose *Dinnshenchas*: [23]

Sliab Mis or Sliab-Mí-fis, because the magical army there
devised by Fodla, and Banba, and Ériu, was a *mí-fis* (a mis-
knowledge) that is, it was a delusion to the sons of Míl.

This description evidently retains features borrowed
from an underlying mythological battle of gods and giants,
which, whatever it may have been at first, had adopted
traits from the battle of summer and winter or of wind and
clouds. It is like the Welsh *Cad Goddeu*, "battle of the
trees," which was fought between Amathaon and Arawn,[24]
and like Partholon's battle against Fomorians in invasion
four which is said to have been "a magic battle in which
nobody was slain." [25]

Thurneysen's extract 9,[26] so far as is relevant, I translate
as follows:

(níbatir MS.) foid mona slebe. Conad de ata Sliabh Mís. Ocus Fodla
roagaíll iad a n-Uísneach."

[23] Edited and translated by W. Stokes, *Rev. celt.*, XV (1894), 446.
[24] See W. F. Skene, *Four Ancient Books*, I, 205–206.
[25] Macalister, III, 13.
[26] Thurneysen, *Abhandlungen d. k. G. zu Göttingen*, XIV, 25, prints
nothing but the title of this extract. It has been edited and translated by
Vernam Hull ("The Milesian Invasion of Ireland," ZCP, XIX [1932],

Historians say that there were exiles of Hebrew women in Erin at the coming of the sons of Míl, who had been driven by a sea-tempest into the ocean from the Mediterranean Sea so that they landed in Erin. They were in Erin before the sons of Míl. Then they said to the sons of Míl that their own country was dearer to them, and that they would not abandon it without receiving dowry for mating with them. It is from this that the men purchase wives in Erin forever, whilst in the rest of the world couples [who marry] buy each other [i.e., exchange gifts].

This text has evidently been preserved by some jurist, who has adapted it to illustrate the doctrine of *tindscra* or dowry. It indicates plainly enough that a desire of Amargen and his men to secure wives was a part of the story, but it has been altered to suit a notion that the inhabitants of Ireland came from Biblical peoples. Amargen has become "the sons of Míl," and he meets, not Banba and her maidens, but "exiles of the Hebrew women." Of course they are the Tuatha Dé, who according to some manuscripts of *LG* are said to have come from the northern islands of Greece. The search for wives is a plain hint that the story has been developed out of a myth of the island of women.

A fragment of an early version of *LG* called by d'Arbois de Jubainville, *Orgain Tuir Conaing*,[27] has been edited and translated by Vernam Hull under the title, "The Invasion of Nemed." [28] Enough exists to show that the sons of

155–160). My translation is independent of Dr. Hull's, and I print it merely because it embodies a suggestion or two kindly made me by the late Edward Gwynn, Provost of Trinity College.

[27] *Essai d'un catalogue de la litt. épique de l'Irlande* (Paris, 1883), p. 192.

[28] *Mod. Phil.*, XXXIII (1935), 119–123. More recently Macalister

Nemed fought Conaing, king of the Fomorians, and broke down Tor Conaing. Conaing's deputy, Morc mac Deiled, did battle for the tower. Many on both sides perished in the sea, and only the crew of one Fomorian ship and thirty warriors of the Tuatha Dé escaped. This story was certainly known to Nennius, who repeats everything except the proper names.

Important to our discussion because it shows how much of *LG* existed in 826 is the Latin history of Nennius or Nemnius. I quote the relevant passage: [29]

Novissime autem Scotti venerunt a partibus Hispaniae ad Hiberniam. Primus autem venit Partholomus cum mille hominibus de viris et mulieribus et creverunt usque ad quattuor milia hominum et venit mortalitas super eos et in una septimana omnes perierunt et non remansit ex illis etiam unus.

Secundus venit ad Hiberniam Nimeth, filius quidam Agnominis, qui fertur navigasse super mare annum et dimidium et postea tenuit portum in Hibernia fractis navibus ejus et mansit ibidem per multos annos et iterum navigavit cum suis et ad Hispaniam reversus est.

Et postea venerunt tres filii militis Hispaniae cum triginta ciulis apud illos et cum triginta coniugibus in unaquaque ciula et manserunt ibi per spatium unius anni.

Et postea conspiciunt turrim vitream in medio mari et homines [MSS. M and N read "et quasi homines"] conspiciebant super turrim et quarebant loqui ad illos et numquam respondebant et ipsi uno anno ad oppugnationem turris properaverunt cum omnibus ciulis suis et cum omnibus mulieribus

(III, 155–156) prints his own text and translation. The fragment is preserved in a fourteenth-century manuscript, but since it is mentioned in both lists of epic tales, A and B, it may reasonably be regarded as old.

[29] Edition T. Mommsen, *Mon. Germ. hist.*, p. 154. Macalister (II, 249–250) translates this passage from Nennius.

excepta una ciula, quae confracta est naufragio, in qua erant viri triginta totidemque mulieres. Et aliae naves navigerunt ad expugnandam turrim, et dum omnes descenderant in litore, quod erat circa turrim, operuit illos mare, et demersi sunt et non evasit unus ex illis. Et de familia illius ciulae, quae relicta est propter fractionem, tota Hibernia impleta est usque in hodiernum diem. Et postea venerunt paulatim a partibus Hispaniae et tenuerunt regiones plurimas.

Novissime venit Damhoctor[30] et ibi habitavit cum omni genere suo usque hodie in Brittania. Istoreth Istorini filius tenuit Dalrieta cum suis; Builc autem cum suis tenuit Euboniam insulam et alias circiter; filii autem Liethan obtinuerunt in regione Demetorum et in aliis regionibus, id est Guir Cetgueli, donec expulsi sunt a Cuneda et a filiis ejus ab omnibus Britannicis regionibus.

Van Hamel[31] has shown that in the above extract from Nennius the paragraph "Et postea venerunt" is out of place and interrupts the story of Nemed. The next paragraph, "Et postea conspiciunt," refers back to the sons of Nemed. It was they who fought at the glass tower. The sons of Nemed are the Tuatha Dé, and the people on the tower are Fomorians. That the tower is the land of the dead is shown by several bits of evidence: It is of glass; the

---

[30] *Dám-hoctor* means "a company of eight men" (H. Zimmer, *Nennius Vindicatus* [Berlin, 1893], p. 222) and evidently refers to the Tuatha Dé. They are, I suppose, identical with the seven companions who feast with Bran's head in "Branwen" (*Mab.*, I, 67; see p. 302). In the Nemed invasion (Macalister, III, 128), "Nemed-ochtar" means eight men including Nemed. In the Partholon invasion, according to the *Metrical Dinnshenchas* (edition E. Gwynn, III, 418), Partholon's band was called *dám ochtair*. All three invasions, that of Partholon, of Nemed, and of the Tuatha Dé, are in origin one invasion. Probably "dám ochtair" were eight chief gods of the Tuatha Dé (see Macalister, II, 251).

[31] ZCP, X (1915), 157. *The Irish Nennius*, and the poem *Ériu ard*, support Van Hamel's interpretation (see pp. 261, 262).

people on it do not speak; [32] and two good manuscripts say that the people on the tower were *quasi homines*, i.e., supernatural beings or ghosts.

Invasions 1–3, including Cessair, were lacking in the copy of *LG* used by Nennius. Invasions 4 and 5 were doubtless there, but invasions 6–7 must have been greatly compressed, or else lacking and supplied by oral tradition, because Nennius would scarcely have cut down a plain account of the Fir Bolg and the Tuatha Dé to the short enigmatic sentences beginning: "Novissime venit Damhoctor" with which he winds up his story. Nennius's mention of Spain probably implies that he knew the whole story of the sons of Míl, but we cannot be sure.

The oldest dated account of invasion eight to contain the names Bregond, Ith, Bile, Galam, Donn and Amargen is a poem of eighty-five quatrains by Máelmura of Othan [33] who died in 887. The poem, *Canam bunadas na n-Gaedel*, [34] runs in outline as follows:

The Irish were descended from Japheth son of Noah. Their leaders were successively: Nembroth; Fenius Farsaidh out of Scythia; [35] his son Nil who knew all languages and married Scota; the son of Nil and Scota called Gaedhal Glass; Sru son of Esru; Brath son of Deatha; and finally Bregond *ua Deatha ruaid*, "grandson of the red Deatha." Bregond built a tower in Spain:

[32] On the dead as the silent folk, see p. 128.

[33] Fathain, now Fahan, near Loch Swilly in Inishowen, county Donegal.

[34] Edited by J. H. Todd, *The Irish Nennius*, pp. 220–271, from *LL*, p. 133, col. b, l. 12–p. 135, col. a, l. 28; with variants from the Book of Lecan, a fifteenth-century manuscript.

[35] A wrong connection with *Scotti* was here at work. *Scythi* was erroneously supposed to be the origin of *Scuit* and *Scotti* (Van Hamel, *ZCP*, X (1915), 127, 173).

Northeast from the tower was seen Eri
. . . On a winter's evening was it discovered
By Ith mac Bregoin *buidnig*.[36]
It was at Brentracht he landed.
He was the first of his conquering tribe who died.
. . . He died at Slemnaib.
South-eastwards Ith is carried to Spain,
Iar na brigaib, "after his strength." [37]
The sons of brave Míl [*Lecan* reads "sons of Bile"]
Returned to avenge him,
Dond, Colptha, Amairgen *Glungel* ("white-knee"),
A hero mighty, *tirech* ("wide ruling").
Ír and Éber, Herimón,
The six sons of Miled.

With them were Lugaid son of Ith and many others. "Cruithne son of Cing had taken their wives from them except Tea, the wife of Herimón. . . . They fought Banba at Sleibh Mis . . . Fothlá at Ebhlinn, and Ériu at Uisneach. . . . The Tuatha Dé by the laws of war, repelled them beyond nine waves. Donn went round the south and was drowned.

There was raised a cairn with the stone of his race
Over the broad sea,
An ancient, stormy dwelling; and *Tech Duinn*
It is called.

[36] "Son of Bregond of troops"; *buidnig*, "full of troops," probably refers to the many subjects of the king of the dead. In the next verses Amairgen *tirech*, "landed," probably means that he ruled the extensive lands of the dead. In a poem printed by Macalister, II, 112, we read of Bregaint *bruinig*, "Bregaint of large companies," which I conjecture means that Bregantia is in the land of the dead (Spain).

[37] The Book of Lecan reads, "iar mbas mbrigaich," "after a becoming death," which is doubtless correct. As old as the year 900 is this story that Ith was slain by the Tuatha Dé, and that his companions carried his body back to Spain and showed it to his relatives (to excite them to revenge) (Van Hamel, ZCP, X (1915), 168–169).

This was his great testament
To his numerous children:
"To me, to my house, come ye all
After your deaths." [38]
They made an alliance with the Fir Bolg
And with the sons of Nemed.
They had no wives,
The women having been stolen
They made alliance with the Tuatha Dé.

The sons of Míl took half of all the land; [39] Herimón the
north and Eber the south of Ireland.

In this poem the remarkable stanza about *Tech Duinn*,
"Donn's House," beginning "This was his great testament,"
drew the attention of Kuno Meyer, who wrote that this
stanza affords "einen Blick in eine ganz andere Welt, die
Welt wirklicher irischer Überlieferung und religiösen Glau-
bens." [40] There was a conspiracy of silence, Meyer believes,
that prevent scribes from writing down anything about
heathen beliefs, although all Irishmen knew about them.
I put into English the rest of Meyer's remarks on Donn's
House. "Donn son of Míl has nowhere any children assigned to him. Máelmura by forgetting this reveals that

[38] The Irish text is:

> "Ba h-ésin a h-edact adbul
> Dia chlaind chetaich
> Cucum dom tic tissaid uli
> Iar bar n-écaib."
>
> (*LL*, p. 134, col. b, ll. 12 f.)

[39] *Mesca Ulad* (ed. W. M. Hennessy, *RIA*, Todd Lect. Ser., vol. I,
pt. 1 [1889], pp. 2–3) explains that this means that the Tuatha Dé were
driven to the underground half of Ireland beneath lakes and hills, while
the sons of Míl kept the surface of the land.

[40] "Der irische Totengott und Jer Toteninsel," *Sitzungsberichte der
Preussischen Akademie d. Wiss.*, Berlin, XXXII (1919), 538.

he knows another Donn, the ancestor of the Irish, and the god of the dead, who ruled over the island of the dead, *Tech Duinn*. . . . If Máelmura *ríg-file*, 'king-poet,' in 887, knew and expected his hearers to know about Donn, the learned compilers of *LG* must have known. They suppressed Donn, the god of the dead, because it was a heathen belief." That the pagan Irish placed their land of the dead somewhere off the Kerry coast, and therefore no doubt at *Tech Duinn*, is proved, Meyer shows, by an ancient tale [41] that relates the coming of Cailte's spirit over river and mountain from the southwest corner of Ireland.

In support of his explanation of Donn as king of the dead Meyer quotes the following passages. The eighth-century *Togail Bruidne Da Derga* has the statement: "Atmbía bás . . . for tráig maitne do Thig Duind matin moch a mbárach," "Death will strike them on the strand on the journey to Donn's House at break of day." [42] Not mentioned by Meyer is another passage in the same text [43] about three red horsemen who ride the horses of Donn. To the ninth century probably belongs a poem printed by Meyer which calls *Tech Duinn* a "red-cornered rock in the sea." [44] To the tenth century belongs *Airne Fingein*,[45] where *Tech Duinn* is mentioned as the southwestern limit of the realm of Conn: "Co Teach nDuind frisndailit mairb," "to *Tech Duinn* where the dead have their tryst." To the same century also belongs the *Reicne Fothaid Canainne* [46]

[41] This tale is printed in Meyer and Nutt, *The Voyage of Bran*, I, 47.
[42] Edition Eleanor Knott, p. 22, l. 717, § 79.
[43] Page 10, l. 329, § 35.
[44] This and the red-horsemen passage are quoted above (p. 168).
[45] *Anecdota from Irish Manuscripts*, II, 8, § 12.
[46] K. Meyer, "Fianaigecht," *RIA*, Todd Lect. Ser. (Dublin, 1910), XVI, 16.

in which the spirit of Fothad declares: "M'anum do píenadh la donn," "my soul shall be delivered to Donn for punishment."

In support of Meyer's view about Donn may now be quoted the remarkable *Dinnshenchas* of *Tech Duinn* which has been printed by Gwynn: [47] "Is aire sin adellad na hanmanda peccacha co teach n(D)uind ría techt a n-ifearn, do reír na ngennti, cédus, co tabraid a mbendachtain for anmain Duinn. . . . As i sin tra cédfaidh na ngénnti," "Tech Duinn is so called because, according to the heathen, the souls of sinners visit Tech Duinn before they go to hell, and give their blessing, ere they go, to the soul of Donn. . . . Such, at least, is the belief of the heathen." The apologetic way in which the author of this *Dinnshenchas* introduces the superstition about Donn, twice explaining that only heathen believe it, is strong evidence for Meyer's view that a taboo rested upon Middle-Irish scribes forbidding them to write anything about heathen gods. Another *Dinnshenchas* in the same manuscript mentions *Tech Duinn*: [48] "Cairpre chotutchind shall be drowned at length north of Bui" [Dursey Island]. . . . "Over his body a rock shall rise, in the ocean by *Tech Duinn*." This rock shall float "till it touches ground at Bentraige."

That Donn was king of the dead seems amply proved by the quotations given above, many of which were first pointed out by Meyer. The educated Irish, of course,

[47] *Metrical Dinnshenchas*, IV (1924), 310–311, from MS. Stowe D. ii. 2., which was probably written in the fifteenth century.

[48] Gwynn, *Metrical Dinnshenchas*, IV, 306–307. Gwynn says Bentraige is Whiddy Island, opposite Glengariff, near the head of Bantry Bay. This island is now called Faoide. See *Acallam na Senórach* (*Ir. Texte,* IV), i, l. 737.

repressed the belief, but there are traces of it in Modern Irish.[49]

The evidence that Donn, "dark," was the ancient Irish god of the dead seems convincing; no trace, however, of Donn's sinister origin has been allowed to appear in *LG*, which has been rigorously euhemerized to look like history. The oldest dated account to call the Tuatha Dé "invaders of Ireland" is a poem of eighteen stanzas [50] by Eochaid ua Flainn who died in 1004. The value of Eochaid's poem to us is that it reveals the original divine character of the Tuatha Dé: "Although we tell about them, we do not pray to them." [51] To be sure, in an earlier verse Eochaid expresses his personal opinion that they were "descendants of men." [52] He calls the Fir Bolg also "murderous men," [53]

---

[49] "Dar Donn!" and "Donn a dúine!" as mild oaths (see Dineen's *Dictionary*) are doubtless survivals from a time when Donn was believed to be a god. Patrick Kennedy (*Legendary Fictions of the Irish Celts* [London, 1866], p. 345) introduces *Fear Dhoirche* as a fairy king who once visited a smith near the Shannon; see his *Fireside Stories* (Dublin, 1870), pp. 131–133. Carl Marstrander (in *Miscellany Presented to Kuno Meyer* [Halle, 1912], p. 397) says that this is Donn, who, though shipwrecked at *Tech Duinn*, according to one story escaped and took taxes from the Tuatha Dé. Tuatha Dé and Fomorians were not very different in nature. By the time our stories were written, Ireland had long been Christian, and the distinction was sometimes forgotten. Donn sometimes, for example, appears as a fairy king. In J. C. Mangan, *Poets and Poetry of Munster* (ed. J. O'Daly [Dublin, 1850], p. 20), is the statement: "It is traditionally believed that Donn is chief of the Munster fairies." A. MacCurtin, an eighteenth-century poet, quoted by D. Hyde (*Lit. Hist. of Ireland* [London, 1899], p. 49), calls Donn a fairy in a fairy hill.

[50] *Ériu co nuaill co nidnaib*, ed. G. Lehmacher, S.J., ZCP, XIV (1923), 173–178; also in Macalister, IV, 212 f.

[51] Page 178, stanza *n*.

[52] Page 175, stanza *d*.

[53] Page 175, stanza *c²*.

but his remark, "they snorted like cows," [54] discloses their original, monstrous, and superhuman character. He calls the giants, Fir Bolg, but neither here nor in *LG* can the Fir Bolg be kept apart from Fomorians.

The next account of the Tuatha Dé is in an Irish version of Nennius, *Lebor Bretnach*,[55] made by Giolla Coemhain, who died in 1072. I summarize as follows:

Giolla Coemhain mentions Nemed and his people (§ 12), adding that they fled from Ireland because of tribute imposed by Fomorians. He refers to the Fir Bolg, Fir Gaileoin, and Fir Domnann, and to our surprise calls them "of the seed of Nemed." He introduces the *plebes deorum* or Tuatha Dé, and names eleven leaders, including "Goibnenn *faber*" and Lug mac Eithne. "These people," he continues, "defeated in a great battle the marine folk or Fomorians so that they fled into their tower." He adds: "It was the Tuatha Dé, or according to others the descendants of Nemed with Fergus Leithdearg, son of Nemed, that destroyed the tower." Then he remarks (§ 13), "the children of Gaileoin around the sons of Hercules, namely Istoreth son of Istoirine, son of Aigine [56] . . . seized the Orkney Islands." After this came the sons of Míl to Ireland in thirty ships (§ 14). "Donn their king was drowned at *Tig Duind*." Three goddesses held the sovereignty of Ireland: Fodla, Banba, and Ériu; and three battles were won

---

[54] "Buaibthe," p. 174, stanza *b*.

[55] Edition A. G. Van Hamel (Dublin, 1932). An earlier edition is by J. H. Todd, *The Irish Nennius*. On the date 1072, consult Zimmer, *Nennius Vindicatus*, p. 14.

[56] By popular etymology the Orkneys were associated with *Orcus* (Hades); the Fir Gaileoin are evidently a sort of Fomorians; and the "sons of Hercules" must be giants. Aigine is probably a mythical ancestor of the Fomorians or of the kings of the dead. By metathesis Aigine corresponds to Aingen, and it may be a by-form of Amargen (see p. 372).

over them by the sons of Míl. Amergin the poet divided Ireland; Eber took the northern half, and Herimon the southern half.

This same Giolla Coemhain was one of the synthetic historians who, in his time, worked over *LG*. He also wrote a poem, *Eriu ard, inis na ríg*,[57] in which he mentions "Nuada, Lug," and others, but does not name the Tuatha Dé. The *Chronicle of the Scots*[58] in 1127 does not mention them as opponents of the sons of Míl. Probably the expression Tuatha Dé was avoided because it belonged to a race of heathen gods. Even so late as 1188, Giraldus Cambrensis [59] avoids Tuatha Dé and translates Fomorians into "gigantes."

Having sketched their development, and having satisfied ourselves that they are older than the twelfth century, we may now run through the five invasions [60] endeavoring to reconstruct the underlying myth and to examine the proofs that in every invasion the chief actors are in origin the same three figures: Brión, Ériu, and Amargen.

Invasion Four [61]

Partholon, the leader, whose name is a puzzle, may very well represent Brión. His wife is Elgnat or Delgnat, which

[57] Edition B. MacCarthy, *RIA*, Todd Lec. Ser., III (1892), 142-213.

[58] Edition W. M. Hennessy, Rolls Series (1866), pp. 5-15. On the date 1127, see p. xl.

[59] Edition J. F. Dimock, *Topographia Hibernica*, Rolls Series (1867), V, 141, dist. iii, chap. 2.

[60] Page 243. The summaries of the five invasions contain no detail that is not in *LL*, a manuscript written within seven or eight years of 1160. Everything in these summaries is therefore older than Chrétien. On the date of *LL*, see Thurneysen, *Heldensage*, p. 35.

[61] Macalister, II, 268 f. Van Hamel (*Rev. celt.*, L [1933], 217-237) interprets Partholon as a "corn spirit." This does not contradict his being an hypostasis of Brión.

is a name for Ireland.[62] The Fomorian leader is Cichol
Grigenchos, which may mean "the footless." The epithet
refers, I conjecture, to the single foot [63] which along with
a single hand and a single eye is often attributed to Fomorians. Cichol's mother is Lot *Luamnach*, "destruction the
active." She is probably the hag who in the Recurrent
Battle revivifies slain giants. In invasion 5 she is turned into
a man and is Loth father of Dela, parent of the Fir Bolg.
Loth belongs to a class of Fomorian names that signify evil,
and is probably the source of Loth, king of the Orkneys,
in the romances. Cichol is perhaps from the Greek *Cyclops*
and refers to the monster's one eye. I conjecture this because in *Togail Bruidne Da Derga*,[64] Fer Cailli, who has
"one arm, one eye, and one leg," has a wife Cichuil. Our
Cichol is son of Goll, "blind," or "one-eyed," son of Garb,
"rough," which are descriptive Fomorian names. Topa, a
servant who seduced Partholon's wife Elgnat and was slain
by Partholon, is, as the text says, "the same as Ith" — clearly
the Ith of invasion 8.

The battle with Cichol was a *cath druidecht* or "battle
of magic" in which "not a man was slain." In this battle
Partholon was wounded, but he lived twenty-seven years
longer. Probably this wound, like that of Nuadu in invasion 7, left Partholon and his people in subjection to
Fomorians.

Invasion Five [65]

Nemed, "sacred," the leader, is a doublet of Nuadu in
invasion 7 and like him a hypostasis of Brión. His wife is

[62] Elg means Ireland (Cormac's *Glossary*, § 510; *Anecdota*, IV, 42).
[63] Macalister (III, 13) translates "clapper-leg."
[64] Edition Eleanor Knott, p. 11.
[65] Macalister, III, 120 f., 146.

Macha, which is a name for Ireland. He fights the Fomorians, Gann and Sengann, and the Fomorian king Conaing son of Faebur [66] at his tower. The tower is, of course, the tower of the dead, and identical with the tower of glass in Nennius. Conaing's deputy is Morc son of Dela or Deled. He and Morc collect from the people of Nemed a tribute of two-thirds of their grain, milk, and children at *Mag Cetne,* "same plain," which is very likely the plain of the dead.[67]

Invasion Six [68]

The invaders are the Fir Bolg, and their leader is Eochaid mac Eirc. His antagonists are Cesarb, Luamh, and Luachra, three sons of Nemed, who represent, I think, the triformed Brión and who rule over the Tuatha Dé. The heroine, Tailtiu of the Tuatha Dé, which is a name for Ireland, is said to be Eochaid's wife. The meaning of Eochaid's marriage to her is, of course, that he has conquered the island. Eochaid, who corresponds to Amargen, is finally slain by the Tuatha Dé.

Other leaders of the Fir Bolg are Gann and Sengann, who in invasion 5 were called Fomorians. In invasion 5, Morc the Fomorian was "son of Dela"; here the Fir Bolg are "children of Dela." Dela is here son of Loth, which con-

[66] This is evidently the Anglo-Saxon *cyning,* which shows that this Fomorian has been identified with a Germanic pirate. The "o" in *Conaing* is due to the influence of genuine Old Irish names with *con-* (J. Pokorny, *Hist. Reader of Old-Irish* [Halle, 1923], p. 29).

[67] Macalister (III, 117) suggests that Morc may be the name of the idol Crom spelled backward. No doubt names of heathen gods were obliterated or concealed; and it is true that one-third of produce, flocks, and children are said to have been sacrificed to Crom at Mag Slecht (Gwynn, *Metrical Dinnshenchas,* IV [1924], 21).

[68] Macalister, IV, 6 f.

nects this with invasion 4, where Lot was mother of the Fomorian Cichol. The Fir Bolg cannot be differentiated from the Fomorians.

Invasion Seven [69]

The Tuatha Dé are here pictured as invaders, and their king, Nuadu silver-arm, is an hypostasis of Brión. In the first battle of Moytura between the Fomorians and the Tuatha Dé, Nuadu's arm is cut off. In consequence of this wound Bres enforces Fomorian tyranny for seven years, till Diancecht and Credne make a silver arm for Nuadu. He then resumes the throne, apparently under tribute to the Fomorians, and reigns at Tara for twenty years.

Lug son of Cian by Eithne daughter of Balar the Fomorian is brought up in the forest of Cuan by a foster-mother, Tailtiu of the Tuatha Dé (called "Queen of the Fir Bolg" because in invasion 6 she married Eochaid), who clears land there.

Lug fights the second battle of Moytura in which Nuadu is slain by Balar, and he kills Balar by a stone from his sling. Lug becomes king, and institutes games called Lugnasad on August first in honor of his foster-mother Tailtiu. Between the two battles of Moytura twenty-seven years elapse.

Invasion Eight [70]

The invaders are sons of Míl or Galam, and the leaders are Donn and Aimirgin. They are opposed by three kings of the Tuatha Dé: Mac Cuill, Mac Cecht, and Mac Greine,

---

[69] Macalister, IV, 106 f.

[70] LL, p. 12, col. a, l. 27; col. b, l. 49. Cf. O'Clery's LG, ed. Macalister and Mac Neill, I, 271 f.

who are clearly the three-formed Brión. Their three queens, Banba, Fodla, and Ériu, are the three-formed Ériu, and are virtually Ireland personified.

The narrative begins by tracing the pedigree of the sons of Míl in Spain back through Breogan to Noah. Among Breogan's sons are Ith and Bile. Bile has a son Galam, who because of his success in battle is called Míl. Ith sees Ireland from Breogan's tower in Spain and with others goes thither. He settles a dispute about treasure between kings of the Tuatha Dé, recites a poem in praise of Ireland, and is mortally wounded by the Tuatha Dé. On the homeward voyage Ith dies, and his companions show his body to the sons of Míl: Donn, Emer Finn, Aimirgin, Eremon, and others, who invade Ireland to avenge his death. Banba with hosts of druidry meets them in Sliabh Mis, and asks that her name be given to the island. So does Fodla in Eblinne, and Ériu in Uisnech. In every case Aimirgin, *file*, "poet," asks the queen's name and promises to grant her request. The silence of the older brother Donn is remarkable, and perhaps proves that Aimirgin was the original leader. They meet three kings, Mac Cuill, Mac Cecht, and Mac Greine.[71] Donn advises battle but decision is left to Aimirgin, who recites a poem. The druids of the Tuatha Dé raise a storm against the invaders. The wind drives Donn's ship apart from the others and sinks it. "He is buried at the *Dumhacha* ['sand banks'] so that from him *Tech Duinn*, 'Donn's House,' is named." Aimirgin speaks another poem, and a calm ensues. He puts his right foot on shore at Inbher

---

[71] That these are concocted names seems evident. They mean "son of hazel," "son of plowshare," "son of the sun." The three are called "grandsons of the Dagda," which reveals, I think, that they are identical with Brión, Iuchar, and Iucharba (see Macalister, IV, 104).

Colptha and recites two more poems. They fight the Tuatha Dé, first at Sliabh Mis, and then at Tailtiu. They kill the three kings, the three queens, and drive the rest of the Tuatha Dé into the sea.

In mythology persons carried off by kings of the dead are often said to have died.[72] Here probably some monkish transcriber has taken delight to record that pagan gods are dead. The usual belief is that the Tuatha Dé did not die but retired into palaces beneath hills or lakes and left the surface of Ireland to the sons of Míl.[73]

Evidence of an unhistorical basis for the invasions may be found in the love-making motive which appears in three of the oldest versions.[74] This motive was, of course, minimized by the compilers of LG. Evidence that the leader of the friendly fairies is always the same may be found in the term *dám hoctor*, "a company of eight," applied in invasions 4, 5, and 7 to him and his confederates; also in the wound from which the leader suffers in invasions 4 and 7.

Invasions 6 and 8 are told from the point of view of the hostile fairies. In all five invasions the hostile folk are giants and have at one time been confused with kings of the dead, but in the last invasion their gloomy origin has been obscured. The point of view in invasion 8 is that they are ancestors of the Irish. Thus the Fomorians, who in the first invasions were monsters having dog or goat heads, or giants with one eye, one arm, and one foot, become in the last invasion the ancestors of the Irish. It is a great change,

[72] See *Entführung* in *Handwörterbuch des deutschen Märchens*, I, 541 f.

[73] Page 257.

[74] Pages 245, 247, 252.

perhaps suggested by an ancient belief of the Celts that they were descended from the god of the dead.[75]

Although in invasion 8 the sons of Míl are ancestors of the Irish, two of them, Donn and Amargen, retained too much of their gloomy character to be desirable as ancestors. No pedigree begins with either name.[76] The king of the hostile fairies in all the five invasions, whether called Cichol, Conaing, Balar, Galam, Morc, or Amargen, is always the same giant, who is virtually death personified. His names are descriptive epithets. Cichol is perhaps "cyclops"; Conaing is "king"; Balar may be from the stem in *atbail*, "he dies"; Galam was connected with *gal*, "valor," translated into Latin as Míl [from *miles*, "soldier"]. Donn, "dark," Amargen, "grief-born," Mairg or Morc, "grief," are names referring to a gloomy Fomorian origin.

In this chapter it has been shown that the five invasions in *LG* are older than the time of Chrétien and that they are based on an old myth about an island of women. The king of this island was Brión, the queen Ériu, and the invader Amargen. Brión was wounded in battle and withdrew to a hiding place. In invasion 7 we get the sequel, namely that a youthful hero Lug conquered the invaders.

In invasion 8 the names of the chief invaders are Ith, Bile (Balar), Galam, and Amargen. If we transfer this plot to Chrétien's *Perceval*, Brión will be the wounded

[75] Julius Caesar (*De bello Gallico*, VI, 18): "Galli se omnes a Dite patre prognatos praedicant idque ab druidibus proditum dicunt."

[76] Professor Eóin Mac Neill, to whom I read my statement that no pedigree begins with Amargen, kindly furnished me with one exception: pedigree no. 150 in the collection in the Book of Lecan, which begins on p. 449, col. b, runs in part as follows: "Aimirgen Gluingeal a quo Coraidi et Orbraidi et Corco Athrach Ele."

Fisher King (called Bron by Robert de Boron), and Ériu, the Grail damsel (and her doublet Blancheflor). The invaders will be the foes of the Grail folk: Ith is the Red Knight (Ither in *Parzival*); Balar (king of isles), is Rion, "king of isles," Arthur's enemy; Galam is Clamadeu who wishes to carry off Blancheflor; Amargen is Anguingueron.

By itself the similarity of names would have small force, but, combined with the way in which characters having similar names play similar rôles in the two plots, the resemblance becomes impressive. The conclusion indicated is that the sources of *Perceval* are connected in some definite way with the sources of invasion 8, that of the sons of Míl, in the Irish *LG*. None of the names in *LG* coming from the Bible and Orosius appear in any form in *Perceval*. The connection, of course, is not with *LG* but with some form of the underlying myth.

CHAPTER X

Pagan Survivals in Arthur and Guenevere

BRIÓN'S VOYAGE

THE story of Brión's voyage and wound and the coming of Lug must have been paramount in pagan Irish religion for the pseudo-historians to choose it as a basis out of which to construct their account of the early settlements of Ireland. The battle and the wound were important for their purpose, and they minimized, as has been seen in the last chapter, the voyage and the love-making. The Irish *imrama*, "rowings around," or voyage stories, invite our attention. These *imrama* appear to be based upon the same story of Brión and Lug, but they ignore the battle and the wound, and confine themselves to the first part, the voyage and the love-making. An examination of the *imrama* will round out our picture of the lost myth of Brión's voyage, which we have endeavored to reconstruct from the pseudo-historical documents *CMT* and *LG*. The wonder stories will supplement the fabulous histories.

The following pages are written on an hypothesis that the story of Brión's voyage was always vividly present to the imagination of the ancient Irish Christian scribes, but that these scribes avoided mentioning the pagan god Brión, although, like the pseudo-historians, they used materials from his voyage to build up their own inventions. By far the oldest of the *imrama* is the *Imram Brain*.[1]

(§§ 1–3) Bran sets out on his voyage because of alluring music made by a fairy branch which is the gift of a *fée*.[2] (§§ 6–7) She describes the island to which she invites him as supported on four feet. (§ 17) It contains a tree with singing birds and a music-making stone. "Then they row to the conspicuous stone, from which arise a hundred strains."[3] (§ 25) She tells Bran that one hundred and fifty islands exist in the western ocean, twice or thrice as large as Ireland. (§ 30) She invites him to *Tír na m-Ban*, "Land of Women." (§ 32) The next day Bran sets out. "The number of his men was three companies of nine. One of his foster-brothers and mates was set over each of the three companies of nine." After sailing two days and nights, Bran meets Manannán mac Lir driving his chariot across the sea, who tells him that he is near his destination. (§ 60) "Emne[4] with many hues of hospitality thou wilt

[1] Summarized from the edition and translation by Kuno Meyer, *The Voyage of Bran*, I (1895); he says (I, xvi) our text "was originally written down in the seventh century" (see p. 39).

[2] Music is sometimes a lure to the land of the dead. Gandîn is a musician in Gottfried (*Tristan*, ed. F. Ranke [Berlin, 1930], vss. 13121 f.). In *Diu Crône* one reads, "durch die Gaudîn" (ed. G. H. F. Scholl, vs. 3413). In *Diu Crône* (vs. 13180), Igern is lured by music: "Igern diu bluome, Künec Artûses muoter: Die minnet aber Gansguoter, Die er mit videlen erwarp, Dô Uterpendragôn starp, Und vuorte si gein Madarp." See Gertrude Schoepperle, *Tristan and Isolt*, II, 420; A. H. Krappe, *Rev. celt.*, XLVIII (1931), 107, 111.

[3] This suggests the stone, *Lia Fáil*, that had a voice (p. 228).

[4] Emne is one of the numerous names here applied to *Tír na m-Ban*. Many of the names are compounded with *mag*, "plain," and suggest Mag Mór or the plain of the dead:

Mag Findargat	"Plain of White Silver"
Mag Argatnél	"Plain of the Silver Cloud"
Mag Réin	"Plain of the Sea"
Mag Mon	"Plain of Sports"

reach before the setting of the sun." (§ 61) Next day they come to *Inis Subai*, "Island of Joy," where one of Bran's men lands and falls to laughing like the other people in the island. So they leave him behind.

(§ 62) Upon their arrival at *Tír na m-Ban*, Bran is welcomed by a queen and twenty-seven damsels to match his twenty-seven men. Supernatural dishes supply whatever food each man desires. They stay many years, but it seems but one year. (The place, however delightful, must be beyond the grave, because return is impossible.) (§ 63) Homesickness seizes one of them, even Nechtan mac Collbrain, and he begs the others to take him home to Ireland. The Queen forbids any of them to land in Ireland. (§ 65) Nechtan, however, springs out of the ship, but when he "touched the earth of Ireland, forthwith he was a heap of ashes, as though he had been in the earth for many hundred years. . . . And from that hour (Bran's) voyages are not known."

The next *imram* in importance is *Imram Maeile Dúin* [5] ("The Voyage of MaelDuin"), the text of which is not later than the eleventh century. In the following summary I omit a good many of the islands.

MaelDuin with a crew of sixty men put to sea to find his father's murderers. They come to many islands. (§ 6) In the sixth island they find a great house, "and the sea waves were

Mag Mell	"Plain of Happiness"
Cluche Mag	"Plain of Sport"
Mag Aircthech	"Bountiful Land"
Mag Ciuin	"Gentle Land"
Mag Imciuin	"Very Gentle Land"
Mag Ildathach	"Many-Colored Land"

[5] Summarized from the edition and translation by Stokes, *Rev. celt.*, IX (1888), 447–495; X (1889), 50–95. On *Imram Maeile Dúin*, see A. C. L. Brown, *Iwain*, pp. 60–69; a number of the islands are different pictures of fairyland.

flinging salmon into the midst of the house." They find also cups of liquor in the house, and they dine off that food and liquor. (§ 11) They come to an island where is a great white rampart round a *dún,* and snow-white houses. In the largest of the houses they see no one except a small cat that is "playing upon four stone pillars that were there." Within are precious jewels and a feast prepared. They eat and sleep, and after that MaelDuin's third foster-brother takes one of the necklaces. Thereupon "the cat leapt through him like a fiery arrow, and burnt him to ashes." MaelDuin replaces the necklace and they depart.

(§ 13) In the thirteenth island is a great mountain. Diuran and Germán, two of MaelDuin's companions, go to visit the mountain and find before them a broad river. "Into this river Germán dipped the handle of his spear, and at once it was consumed as if fire had burnt it. So they went no farther. Then they saw on the other side of the river great hornless oxen lying down, and a huge man [6] sitting by them. Germán after this struck his spear-shaft against his shield to frighten the oxen. 'Why dost thou frighten the silly calves?' saith the huge herdsman. 'Where are the dams of those calves?' saith Germán. 'They are on the other side of yonder mountain,' saith he. So they went thence."

(§ 16) In another island "were four fences which divided it into four parts: a fence of gold, another of silver, the third fence of brass, and the fourth of crystal. In the four divisions were kings, queens, warriors, and maidens." [7] A maiden comes to meet them, brings them to land, and gives them food. "They likened it to cheese, and whatever taste was pleasing to anyone he would find it therein. And she dealt [liquor] to them out of

[6] This is doubtless the river of death. A similar giant herdsman is in *Yvain* (p. 110).

[7] This island with its supply of whatever food is desired is an analogue to the Grail castle. Its division into four parts is perhaps a form of the cosmic palace idea that appears in the four-sided Grail castle.

a little vessel so that they slept an intoxication of three days and three nights. . . . When they awoke on the third day they were in their boat at sea. Nowhere did they see their island or their maiden." [8]

(§ 17) In another island "was a *dún* with a brazen door and brazen fastenings thereon. A bridge of glass [was] by the door. When they went up on the bridge they fell backwards. With that they espy a woman coming out of the *dún* with a pail in her hand. . . . After this they struck the brazen fastenings . . . and the sound which they made was a sweet soothing music that sent them to sleep till the morrow." The same thing happened on the second day and the third day. On the fourth day she let the men in, and told them that their coming had long been foretold.[9] They feast in the great house, and each man tastes whatever food he desires. Then the men propose that MaelDuin sleep with the queen; but she refuses, and the next morning they find themselves in their boat, and their island has vanished.

(§ 19) In another island are many trees with singing birds. An aged hermit, whose clothing is his hair, tells them that the birds are the souls of his kindred [10] and that he is fed daily by the ministry of angels. (§ 26) In another island is a great silver column. It has four sides, and a silver net hangs from its top. (§ 27) The twenty-seventh island "stood on a pedestal, to wit, one foot supported it."

(§ 28) In the twenty-eighth island they find "a *mag mór* [great plain] and on this a great tableland, heatherless but grassy and smooth. In that island near the sea was a *dún* large, high, and strong, and a great house therein adorned and with good couches. Seventeen grown-up girls were there preparing a bath." Presently the queen rides up on a horse. They are

[8] On disappearance overnight, see pp. 212, 220.

[9] Here are several familiar motives of the Journey to Fairyland: protection by a *fée*, fairy music, and a destined hero.

[10] This is doubtless a Christianization of fairies appearing in bird form.

invited to enter. They are bathed and feasted. At night the damsels pair off with MaelDuin's seventeen men, and he sleeps with the queen. "They abode in that island for the three months of winter. . . . His people began to murmur greatly against MaelDuin, and they said this, 'Great is the love which MaelDuin hath for his woman.' . . . One day they went on board their boat" and began to flee. "Then she comes . . . and flings a *certle* [clew] after them, and MaelDuin catches it, and it clung to his hand. A thread of the clew was in her hand, and she draws the boat unto her by means of the thread back to the harbor. So then they stayed with her thrice three months." When they start to flee again MaelDuin appoints one of his men to mind the clew. "Diuran cuts off his hand and it fell with the clew into the sea." When the queen sees this she begins to wail. "In that way they escaped." [11]

(§ 32) The thirty-second island has a fiery rampart around it. "And this rampart used to revolve round the island. There was an open doorway in the side of that rampart. Now whenever the doorway would come in its revolution opposite to them, they used to see the whole island and all that was therein and all its indwellers, even human beings, beautiful, abundant, wearing adorned garments and feasting with golden vessels in their hands. And the wanderers heard their ale-music." [12]

The remaining *imrama* are perhaps not older than Chrétien, although they seem to be made up of older materials. Some incidents from them are here summarized for illustrative purposes, but no argument is based upon them. The first is *Imram Snedgusa*.[13]

---

[11] The men are obviously weary of the amorous *fées* (see p. 248).

[12] This is doubtless a Castle of Maidens, and the fiery rampart is a trace of a Dolorous Tower.

[13] Summarized from an edition and translation by Stokes, *Rev. celt.*, IX (1888), 19 f.

The heroes visit many islands. (§ 15) "Then they came to another island with a fence of silver over the midst thereof, and a *cora éisc* [fish-weir] therein. And that weir was . . . a plank of silver, and against the weir huge salmon were leaping. Bigger than a bull-calf was each of those salmon and thereof were they satisfied." (§ 17) "Thereafter the wind wafts them to an island wherein was a great tree with beautiful birds." (§ 18) "Melodious was the music of those birds a-singing psalms and canticles praising the Lord. For they were the birds of the plain of heaven and neither trunk nor leaf of that tree decays." (§ 19) "Thereafter they . . . voyage to a fearful land wherein dwelt men with dogs' heads."[14]

In the next *imram*, *Imram Curraig hua Corra*,[15] the description of one island ought to be quoted for comparison with *Imram Maeile Dúin*.

"An island was shewn to them with four sets of various men therein. They divided the island into four, to wit a folk sedate, fair-grey, in the [first] place in it; royal lords in the second place; champions in the third place; servants in the fourth place. Beautiful and bright were they all. Play without resting they had."

Further light on the lost "Brión's Voyage" can probably be obtained from the late prose tale called *Oided Chloinne Tuirenn* (*OCT*).[16] In this tale Brian, Iuchar, and Iucharba go on a voyage as a penalty for having slain Lug's father.

[14] Christian influences have altered this *imram*, but it is easy to see that § 18 once described a Castle of Maidens and § 19 an adjacent Dolorous Tower. Fomorians are called Dogheads, pp. oo, oo. In the *Serglige* the king of the Tuatha Dé fought a Doghead (p. 20).

[15] Summarized from the edition and translation by Stokes, *Rev. celt.*, XIV (1893), 42 f. This island shows a trace of the four-sided cosmic castle motive observed in MaelDuin, § 16 above.

[16] Printed and translated by E. O'Curry, *Atlantis*, IV (1863), 158 f.

This penalty, and the pathetic story of their death upon their return to Ireland, cannot be primitive. We may be sure that gods did not die,[17] although monkish redactors of the old stories, in their wish to force paganism back into the past, enjoy telling of the death of gods. I quote from O'Curry's translation:

The three gods, Brian, Iuchar, and Iucharba, voyaged on the sea to obtain talismans, and finally searched for the Island of Finnchoire. Iuchar and Iucharba remained in the ship, but "Brian put on his water-dress . . . and he made a water-leap; and it is said that he was for a fortnight walking in the salt water seeking the island of Finnchoire. . . . He found in it but a troop of one-hundred-and-fifty women engaged at embroidery, and he obtained from them the cooking-spit," which was the talisman that he sought. He then went back up through the water to his comrades in the ship.

The main plot of *OCT* is preserved in a poem which, according to its editor Thurneysen,[18] arose as early as the year 1100. It occurs as an insertion in certain manuscripts of *LG*, and is accompanied by a prose account which is not much later than the poem. Here are briefly the objects sought in the poem, and in *OCT*.

Poem of 1100	*OCT*
1. Two immortal horses.	1. Three apples from the Garden of Hisbeirne (Hesperides?).
2. The unerring Spear of Assals, that returned of itself.	2. The pig's skin of Tuis that healed wounds.

[17] Could this penalty be an intrusion from later *imrama*? MaelDuin's voyage was to avenge his father's death, and the Ua Corra went as a penance for their sins.

[18] "Tuirill Bicrenn und seine Kinder," ZCP, XII (1918), 243 f.

3. A pig's skin that cured wounds.	3. The blazing Spear of Pisear.
4. Six never-failing pigs.	4. The steeds and chariot of Dobar.
5. A dog of the smith of Hiruaid that turned water into wine.	5. Seven never-failing pigs.
6. The dog of Luchra Lia.	6. The dog (called Fáilinis) of the King of Ioruaidhe.
7. The apples of the apple tree of Finnchoire.	7. The cooking-spit of the women of the island Finn-choire.

In the last and most important quest, the prose is notably inferior to the poem. Apples are a good old characteristic of fairyland,[19] whereas the cooking-spit looks like a degenerate form of the cup-of-plenty motive. *OCT* is almost everywhere inferior to the poem, and has been influenced by Latin stories and perhaps by French romances.[20] The full title of the poem is *Imthechta Tuirill Picreo ocus a mac .i. Brían, Iuchar, Iucharba*. The word *imthecht*, "going round," sometimes refers to a sea voyage, and we shall probably not be wrong if we regard the poem as an *imram*. The third line of the poem says, "Tuirill Piccrenn was the father of the gods of plunder." [21] The fifth line declares

[19] See Hertz, *Spielmannsbuch* (1931), p. 360, and p. 39, above.

[20] R. A. S. Macalister (*Bealoideas*, I [1927], 20) urges that the "Spear of Pisear" in *OCT* shows the influence of the French Grail romances. He believes that Pisear comes from *le riche pecheor*. Even if he is right, the "Spear of Assals" in the poem of 1100 must represent older tradition. It is too old to be influenced by French romances.

[21] "Tuirill Piccrenn ba bechta Athair na ndee nairc (h)elta." It is astonishing to find Brión, Iuchar, and Iucharba called "gods of plunder," but we know too little about their true character to be sure that this is

that Ethliu was Lug's father. According to other authorities, Eithne daughter of Balar was his mother, Cían or Céin his father, and Brión's father was Delbaeth. The prose introduction to the poem says that Tuirill was a name for Delbaeth. Evidently the author of the poem was confused and did not well understand the traditions which he was retelling. Both *OCT* and the poem have lost any original amorous incentive for the voyage, although they keep Finnchoire,[22] the Isle of Women.

From this brief survey it seems probable that "Brión's Voyage" did not, like *Imram Maile Dúin*, tell of many islands, but resembled *Imram Bran*. In the latter, as Nutt showed,[23] the Isle of Laughter is almost surely an interpolation and there is but one original island, namely the Isle of Women. It is probable, in short, that the lost "Brión's Voyage" is best represented by *Imram Brain*.

What does the similarity of names mean? Bran mac Febal is otherwise unknown, and, of course, Bran is an entirely different name from Brión. Thurneysen suggests that the hero of *Imram Brain* was at first anonymous and got his name by mistake from that of a promontory called *Srúb Brain*,[24] "raven's beak," which was misunderstood to mean "Bran's promontory." Thurneysen's explanation is probable enough; only I would add that there must have been a reason why this, rather than some other place-name, was chosen for the hero. The reason I suggest is that the original hero was the god Brión. Brión, to monkish copists,

an error. In the story of Cessair, her consort (who ought to be a form of Brión), is called Ladra, which might be for *latro* (p. 247).

[22] "White whirlpool." Compare *Findargat*, "white-silver plain" (p. 271).

[23] *Voyage of Bran*, I, 171.

[24] ZCP, X (1915), 424; cf. K. Meyer, *Voyage of Bran*, I, 32, n. 2. Srúb Brain in Kerry must be meant, not Srúb Brain in Donegal.

doubtless had disgusting associations; so they changed it to the innocent Bran mac Febail. It may also have been known to them that a Welsh pagan god corresponding to Brión was named Bran. My theory, therefore, is that both *Imthechta Tuirill Picreo* and *Imram Brain* are largely re-tellings of the lost "Brión's Voyage."

This theory will explain a number of points. Both Brian and Bran are associated with Manannán, for in *OCT* Brian had Manannán's boat *Scuaba tuinne*,[25] and in *Imram Brain* the hero met Manannán upon the sea. Both Brian and Bran come to Mag Mell; Brian to an underwater island called Finnchoire, where there was only a troop of women, and Bran to the Isle of Women.[26] Brian's two brothers, Iuchar and Iucharba, reappear in *Imram Brain* as Bran's two foster-brothers. Mention is made of but one ship, but there were three companies, because we read: "Three nines was Bran's number; one man over the three nines of his foster-brothers and equals in age."[27] Although many pagan details have doubtless been suppressed, the mortal Bran has inherited the story of the god Brión.

This investigation leads us into the field of pagan Irish beliefs. It is a marvelous thing that any distinct traces of heathen mythology remain in Irish manuscripts, which have all been copied and recopied in Christian monasteries by Christian scribes; and indeed in some respects Germanic mythology is better preserved than Irish mythology. Without doubt every Irish story here summarized has been rewritten more than once with a determined effort to oblit-

---

[25] *Atlantis*, IV, 192.

[26] ZCP, XII, 246; *Atlantis*, IV, 218.

[27] "Trí nonbuir a lín. Óinfer forsnaib tríb nonburaib dia chomaltaib ocus comáisib," § 32.

erate anything that shocked Christian morality. In spite of difficulties caused by this destruction of evidence we may try to put together all details that we can about the god Brión.

The name was in Old Irish dissyllabic, Brión or Briún, for which was everywhere substituted later the monosyllabic Brían. This form Brían is not older in Ireland than the tenth century.[28] Brión was one of three brothers who are called "three gods of the Tuatha Dé Danann." Their names are: Brión, Iuchar, and Uar; or Brión, Iuchar, and Iucharba; and they are, as d'Arbois has shown,[29] three different manifestations of one supernatural being who was the chief god, or one of the chief gods, of heathen Ireland. According to the "Colloquy of the Two Sages," which goes back to the year 900, the three together begat one son, Ecne, "wisdom,"[30] and *LL* adds that the three were the sons of Bres and Brigit. Other documents quoted by Thurneysen[31] from *LL* and other manuscripts give this parentage. Different authorities, however, give different fathers. Thus Thurneysen quotes from a later text in *BB*[32] which gives

[28] Kuno Meyer (*Ériu*, IV [1908], 68–71). The form Brían, he thinks, comes from Brittany.

[29] *Cours de litt. celtique*, II, 373.

[30] *Immacallam in dá thuarad*, ed. Stokes, *Rev. celt.*, XXVI (1905), 30. The text is: "Ecna mac ma trí nDea nDana (tri maic Brigti banfhili .i. Brian et Iuchar et Uar, tri maic Bressi maic Eladan: et Brigit banfhile ingen in Dagdai móir rig Herenn, am máthair)." The part in parentheses occurs in one MS. only (*LL*, p. 187, col. c, ll. 53 f.).

[31] *ZCP*, XII (1918), 241 (he refers to *LL*, p. 30, col. d).

[32] *Verslehre*, *Irische Texte*, III, i, 58 (from *BB*, p. 35, col. a, l. 5): "Badar iad na tri Dee Danand o-nainnmigther íad (sc. the Tuatha Dé Danann) .i. tri meic Breiss meic Ealathan .i. Triail et Brian et Cet; (l-)no tri meic Tureill Bigreo .i. Brian et Iucháir et Iucharba tri Dee Danand .i. na tri druídhe o nainmnigter (naínmthíther MS) Tuatha Dé Danann."

either Bres or Tuirill Bicreo as the father, and calls the three gods (once), "Triall, Brian, and Cet." [33] *LL* in another place says that the three *dée Danann* are sons of Delbaeth mac Ogma.[34]

That Bríg or Brigit was Brión's mother is the usual statement, and she is often virtually Ireland personified. Ireland, moreover, was often Brión's wife. In the battle of Moytura, according to *LG* and *CMT*, the tri-formed Brión appeared as Mac Cuill, Mac Cecht, and Mac Greiniu, and the wives of these three kings were Banba, Fodla, and Ériu, three names for Ireland. In Irish mythology then Brión was Brigit's son and afterwards her husband. This would be a reason for Christian scribes to avoid mentioning him. For reticence about this great heathen god another reason existed. Heathen scribes probably avoided the name through fear; the use of the appellative "three gods of the Tuatha Dé," instead of Brión, Iuchar, and Iucharba suggests this. A saga like *CMT* that avoids the name Brión testifies indirectly to his importance by saying that all the Tuatha Dé, including the great Dagda, go for aid in securing talismans to "the three gods."

Some considerations that testify to Brión's importance and mark him as one of the chief gods of Ireland may be mentioned. Ireland is sometimes called "Brión's Land." [35]

---

[33] *Tochmarc Étáine* goes all wrong and calls the three gods: "Lug, the Dagda, and Ogma" (*Ériu*, XII [1938], 154).

[34] *LL*, p. 10, col. a, l. 26. The scribe here notices a difficulty and tells us that Delbaeth is another name for Tuirill Bicreo.

[35] Ireland is so called in a poem edited by K. Meyer (*Abhandlungen der Preussischen Akač. d. Wiss.*, phil.-hist. Klasse [Berlin, 1919], VII, 24; also in Univ. of Illinois *Studies in Lang. and Lit.*, II, iv [1916], 43). Meyer thinks it is older than the eleventh century. *Banba Bhriain*, "Brión's Ireland," occurs in a poem quoted by D. Corkery in *The Hidden Ireland* (Dublin, 1925), p. 114.

He is sometimes spoken of as if lord of the sea. In *OCT* his
sister Eithné addresses him thus: [36]

> Thou salmon of the quietly flowing Boyne
> Thou salmon of the stream of Liffey
> Thou horseman of the wave of Tuaidh.

Brión is often connected with talismans. *Echtra Nerai* [37]
which is a tenth-century text, tells of *barr Briuin*, "Brión's
helmet" in Síd Cruachna, which, along with the mantle of
Laegaire in Armagh and the shirt of Dunlaing in Kildare,
is "the third most wonderful gift in Erin." *Airne Fingein*,[38]
a text almost as old, mentions as the three *primaig[d]i*,
"chief-fabrics," of Erin: *barr Breoin a sidhaibh Cruachan*,
"the helmet of Brian from the fairyhill of Cruachan,"
which Breó son of Smeathru, the smith of Aengus mac
Umor, made; and the chessboard of Crimthann Nia Narr;
and the diadem of Laegaire mac Luchta. A poem printed
by Kuno Meyer declares that Brión fashioned the stone with
which Lug slew Balar. The verses that mention the stone
are as follows: [39]

> Briuin the son of Betha, no mean warrior,
> Who on the ocean's eastern border reigned.
> It was he that fused and smoothly formed.
> It was he that fashioned the *tathlunn*, "sling-stone."

In Gaelic-speaking regions many traces of a belief in
Brión as a god survive.[40] No room seems to be left for doubt

---

[36] *Atlantis*, IV, 216–217.

[37] Edition K. Meyer, *Rev. celt.*, X (1889), 212 f. On the date see
Thurneysen, *Heldensage*, p. 312.

[38] *Anecdota*, II, 3, § 5.

[39] *ZCP*, V (1905), 504.

[40] George Henderson (*Survivals in Belief among the Celts*, Glasgow,

of his importance or of the importance of his voyage story.

A derivative from the lost Brión's voyage, of a somewhat different character from the regular *imrama*, survives in the *Dinnshenchas of Inber Ailbine*.[41] This tells of Ruad's voyage with three ships and his discovery of an island of maidens beneath the Irish Sea.

Rúad, son of Rígdonn, son of the king of Fir Murig, mustered the crews of three ships to go over sea to have speech with his foster-brother, the son of the king of Lochlann. When they had got half-way across, they were unable to voyage in any direction, just as if an anchor were holding them. So then Rúad went out over the ship's side that he might know what it was that was stopping them, and he turned under the vessel.

1911, pp. 66 f.) quotes from a Badenoch poet, Lachlan Macpherson of Strathmashie, who was born about 1723, and who, in describing a wedding, remarks, "When all had assembled they of Brian entreated." Henderson also quotes a poem of the reign of James VI which speaks of "Brian" in a context where strength of sun and sea is involved, and a note explaining that "Brian" means "divine power." In John Gillies, *Collection of Gaelic Poetry* (Perth, 1786), p. 21, occurs the expression, "Counsel Brian did give me." In Douglas Hyde, *The Religious Songs of Connacht* (London, 1906), II, 409, are the words, "I shall not lie down with Brian," where Brian seems to be an evil power akin to Satan. In A. Carmichael, *Carmina Gadelica* (Edinburgh, 1900), I, 200, one reads, "Thou didst take the steed of Brian Michael. He was without a bit in his mouth," which seems to be the description of a sea-god like Manannán. One reads also, "Brian gives good counsel"; he is of "virgin birth"; native speakers use an expression, "*A Bhrian!*" meaning "Thou god!" Eleanor Hull (*Folklore of the British Islands* [London, 1928], p. 108) writes: "A dedication of a church to what seems to be a pagan deity is to be seen in the name Templebrian, or Church of Brian, in the parish of Kilgariff. No Christian saint of the name is known, but the god Brian was one of the oldest and greatest of pagan deities. . . . A stone circle proves the place was one for pagan worship."

[41] Summarized from Stokes' edition and translation of the prose *Dinnshenchas, Rev. celt.*, XV (1894), 294. Compare the version in *Tochmarc Emire, ZCP*, III (1899), 243; and also Thurneysen, *Heldensage*, p. 395.

Then he sees nine women, the loveliest of the world's women, detaining them, three under each ship. So they carried Rúad off with them, and he slept for nine nights [one] with each of the women on nine bronze ships. And one of them became with child by him, and he promised that he would come again to them if he should attain his way.

The rest of the story which tells how Rúad returned across the sea but failed to keep his tryst with the women seems of later invention. Rúad's three ships suggest the tri-formed Brión.[42]

What must be a Christianized form of the same story tells how St. Bridget obtained a "Rule" for her convent from an undersea city named Plea. The story of Bridget's Rule is briefly as follows: [43]

Bridget sends messengers to Rome to obtain a Rule. As they voyage across the Irish Sea their anchor is held. Bridget's "blind boy" goes down, and spends a year under the sea [in what appears to be a nunnery] learning the Rule. The messengers leave the boy and continue on their errand. On their return, when crossing the Irish Sea, they are stopped again. They receive the blind boy into their ship and bring him to Bridget. This is the origin of Bridget's Rule.

Christianization in these voyage stories is progressive. *Imram Brain* contains, among other Christian interpolations, a reference to the birth of Christ.[44] In *Imram Maeile*

[42] The story of Inber Ailbine is also in the *Metrical Dinnshenchas*, ed. Gwynn, II, 26, and a somewhat similar tale about a hero named Rot is in III, 190.

[43] See *Liber Hymnorum*, ed. J. A. Bernard and R. Atkinson (London, 1898), I, 113; II, 191; *Félire Óengusso*, ed. W. Stokes (London, 1905), p. 64 (both are in the Henry Bradshaw Society); and *Thesaurus Palaeo-hibernicus*, II, 328.

[44] *Voyage of Bran*, I, 14, "A great birth will come."

Dúin one of the islands has been transformed into a hermit's abode.[45] In this story of Bridget's Rule it appears that a Castle of Maidens has become an undersea nunnery. The same change has occurred in French continuations of Chrétien's *Perceval*. Wauchier describes in detail a Castle of Maidens; Manessier transforms it into a nunnery; and Gerbert makes the change more decided.[46]

St. Brendan

The ecclesiasticization of Irish pagan stories is well known[47] and one notable example, St. Bridget's borrowing of adventures from the heathen goddess Brigit, has been fully recognized by R. A. S. Macalister[48] and others. I venture to point out that St. Brendan has in like manner borrowed Brión's voyage. That St. Brendan's Isle of Promise is a Christian variant of the pagan *Tír na n-Óg* has been pointed out. Charles Plummer has observed resemblances between the *Navigatio Sancti Brendani* and the *Imram Brain*, and has noted the similarity of names.[49] The dependance of St. Brendan on Brión, however, goes farther than this, and I suggest that it was a desire on the part of the Christian Irish to keep as near as possible to a familiar name, without actually introducing a pagan god, that led

[45] Page 274.

[46] Potvin, *Perceval*, vss. 26470–27004, 36447–37010; Gerbert's *Perceval*, ed. Mary Williams, vss. 3008–3241.

[47] A. C. L. Brown, "From Cauldron of Plenty to Grail" (*Mod. Phil.*, XIV [1916], 385–386 f.), gives references.

[48] *Tara*, p. 197.

[49] "There are several parallels to the Brendan story in Bran: the island supported by four feet (*Voyage of Bran*, I, 5), the birds singing the hours (I, 7), the 150 islands (I, 13). Here the resemblance of names may have helped the mutual assimilation of the two legends" (*Vitae sanctorum Hiberniae* [Oxford University Press, 1910], I, clxxxvii, n.).

them to ascribe the marvelous voyage to Brendan, an otherwise unimportant saint, rather than to the better known Columba, who was historically a voyager. Brendan is a marine saint, if not a fisher saint. He is seen on the back of a fish; [50] he turns seals into horses; [51] he is nourished by a fish. He is almost as much a Christianization of Brión as St. Bridget is of Brigit.

Stories preserved on the continent of Europe afford additional testimony that St. Brendan is only Brión dressed up as a saint. Der Striker in *Pfaffe Amis*, a thirteenth-century poem,[52] makes his hero persuade religious folk to give him money by telling them that he has in his possession a very precious relic, the head of St. Brendan, which has commanded him to build a cathedral. Talking heads are common in folklore, but this seems a borrowing from Bran's head in the Welsh *Branwen*, which is likewise a companion to his friends. Nicholas of Bibera in a Latin satiric poem of the thirteenth century [53] says that the Irish when drunk affirm that St. Bridget is St. Brendan's mother. This must mean that the Irish knew St. Brendan to be a substitute for Brión, and when off their guard returned to their old belief in Brigit as mother of the god Brión.

That the triple-formed Brión was transformed into a saint is shown by a prayer attributed to Cuimmíne the Tall, who died in the year 661. The prayer is as follows: [54] "My

[50] W. J. Rees, *Lives of the Cambro-British Saints* (Llandovery, 1853), pp. 132–133.

[51] "Stair ar Aedh Baclámh," *Silva Gadelica*, I, 67; II, 72.

[52] Hans Lambel, *Erzählungen und Schwänken*, Deutsche Classiker des Mittelalters, XII (Leipzig, 1872), 35–36.

[53] Theobald Fischer, *Die Geschichtsquellen zu Provinz Sachsen* (Halle, 1870), I, 16.

[54] Cormac's *Glossary*, § 513, *Anecdota*, IV, 43.

three Brans, to God they send up a prayer — Bran of three plains, Bran of Leinster, Bran Find near Feimin." Brión's four talismans seem to have been inherited by Brandub mac Eochaid, King of Leinster, probably on account of the resemblance in name. The *Bóroma* [55] relates that Maedoc brought to King Brandub four presents: a flesh-hook, a marvelous caldron, a shield, and a sword. These are but faded copies, perhaps, of the "Four Jewels" of the Tuatha Dé.

BRAN

The Irish god Brión appears in Welsh as Bran. As has been seen above, the Irish *CMT* and parts of *LG* are concerned with a tale of strife between gods and giants, pictured as two supernatural clans. A similar, although somewhat confused, Welsh tale of strife between two clans of demigods runs through the four *Branches of the Mabinogi*. A parallel between the two tales is easy to follow when once it has been pointed out.

In Welsh, as in Irish, one of the clans is pictured as benevolent (Irish, Tuatha Dé), and its leaders are members of one family, namely Bran, his brother Manawyddan, his half-brothers Nissyen and Evnissyen, and his sister Branwen. The malevolent clan (Irish, Fomorians) consists of Matholwch, King of Ireland, and his followers, namely Caswallawn son of Beli son of Manogan, who conquered the Island of Britain, and others like Llwyd son of Kilcoed, and Gwawl son of Clud, who are clearly malevolent, but whose relation to Caswallawn is not defined. In *CMT*, Ireland is thought of as fairyland, and is the home

---

[55] *Silva Gadelica,* I, 370–371; II, 408–409 (from *LL* and other manuscripts).

of the Tuatha Dé. The invading Fomorians come from the Northern Isles. In *Branwen*, Wales is fairyland, and the invaders come from Ireland, which is here vaguely made equivalent to the land of the dead.

In both Irish and Welsh the warring clans at first make an alliance by marriage, and the great battle arises out of this alliance. Bres, a Fomorian, marries Bríg of the Tuatha Dé, and their son Ruadan [56] is slain in a quarrel that leads up to the battle. In *Branwen*, Matholwch marries Branwen, and their son Gwern is slain in a quarrel that begins the battle. In both stories some, both of the malevolent and of the benevolent clan (e.g., Bran; the Dagda), are of gigantic size. In both, success in battle depends upon a well-of-regeneration, or a caldron. In *CMT*, the Tuatha Dé have a well which restores deadly-wounded men. In *Branwen*, Matholwch has a caldron that restores men to life. It is a difference that in Irish the well belongs to Brión's people, the Tuatha Dé, whereas in Welsh the caldron belongs to Matholwch. It had been given, however, to him by Bran, so that this difference is probably of no importance. Both stories mention the use of other talismans: those brought by the "three gods"; Ruadan's spear; [57] a poisoned dart that wounded Bran in the foot; a veil of illusion worn by Caswallawn. [58] In both, the king of the benevolent clan, called Nuadu in the Irish and Bran in the Welsh, although wounded, remains alive for a long time. In both, a sign of the enchantment that rests upon the benevolent clan after the battle is that their leaders, in Irish the Dagda and Ogma, in Welsh Manawyddan and Pryderi,

[56] *CMT*, § 124 (see p. 232).
[57] *CMT*, §§ 83, 124.
[58] *Mab.*, I, 66, 68.

are forced to do manual labor. In both, the malevolent clan puts enchantment upon crops and fields, and in neither tale is this spell released till one of the evil clan (namely Bres in the Irish and the wife of Llwyd in the Welsh) is taken prisoner and threatened with death.

Although these parallels are sufficiently apparent, the main thread of the Welsh story, which runs through two *Branches of the Mabinogi*, is confused, and is told from at least three points of view: the *Branwen* point of view, the enchantment of Britain, the mice that destroyed the wheat. The last point of view is entirely different from the others, because it rationalizes the magical destruction of crops by explaining that the havoc was wrought by troops of mice who were the fairies transformed into animal shape. In spite of these difficulties, however, I think that the parallelism indicated above proves that the Irish and the Welsh stories have similar origins, or are in some other way definitely connected.

In view of this similarity of plot, it becomes probable that Bran in Welsh is identical with Brión in Irish or has been confused with him. Other reasons for believing this are as follows:

Manawyddan in Welsh is either identical with Manannán in Irish or was early confused with him. In Welsh, Bran and Manawyddan are brothers. Likewise in Irish, Brión and Manannán, as for example in the *Dinnshenchas of Carn Amalgaid*,[59] are brothers, although they are more often cousins or close associates.[60] In both stories the whole company of people about Bran or Brión and Manawyddan or Manannán are magicians and demigods.

[59] E. Gwynn, *Metrical Dinnshenchas*, III, 424.
[60] Geoffrey Keating represents them as cousins (*History*, ed. D. Comyn, *ITS*, IV, 216–217).

In both stories Bran or Brión is not merely a leader of the benevolent clan. He is something more, and stands on a higher plane than the rest. Bran's epithet "blessed" is probably the epithet of a pagan god,[61] and is not to be explained away, as one of the later triads tries to do, by declaring that it was this Bran who first brought Christianity to Britain. In much the same way Brión and his brothers Iuchar and Uar are always referred to as the "gods of the Tuatha Dé," which must imply that Brión is in some special sense their leader. In both Welsh and Irish, Bran or Brión is associated with the water world. In Welsh he wades through the sea from Britain to Ireland.[62] His caldron was brought out of a lake by two giants. In Irish his chief exploit is a voyage, and epithets applied to him connect him with the sea.

In both Welsh and Irish, Bran or Brión has control of the talismans upon which victory depends. In Welsh he has the caldron of regeneration, which was brought to him by two giants out of a lake. In Irish he secures possession of talismans of victory and plenty by his marvelous voyage. A poem in the Black Book of Carmarthen [63] calls Bran "Iweryd's son." This makes Bran equivalent to Brión, for

[61] Rhŷs suggests this (*Arthurian Legend*, p. 262). For the triad see Loth, *Les Mabinogion*, II, 308 (quoting from *Myvyrian Archaiology*, ed. Owen Jones, Edward Williams, and W. O. Pughe [Denbigh, 1870], p. 404, triad 35).

[62] The difficulty of this crossing probably implies that it was formerly a crossing of the river of death. The vast house built for Bran was probably *Tech Duinn*, the house of the dead.

[63] Edition J. G. Evans, Series of Old Welsh Texts, V (Pwllheli, 1906), 99, fol. 50. Gwynn son of Nudd is speaking:

"I have been where Bran fell   Mi awum in lle-llas bran
Iweryd's son the far famed."   Mab ẏwerit clod lydan.

See Rhŷs, *Transactions of the Society of Cymmrodorion* (London, 1894–1895), p. 30; *Celtic Folklore, Welsh and Manx*, I, 204.

Brión was son of Ériu, and Ériu is Ireland or "Iweryd." These seem to be sufficient reasons for regarding Bran and Brión as essentially the same. Both in Ireland and Wales he is lord of talismans and leader of the benevolent folk in a battle fought by enchantments. He is the chief beneficent god of the Irish, and many of their kings and heroes were regarded as manifestations or hypostases of him.

NUADU

The chief of the manifestations of Brión was Nuadu, who as we have seen in *LG* and *CMT*, was thought of as an actual king reigning at Tara. Brión never reigns at Tara, but he and Nuadu are essentially the same divine being. Like Brión, Nuadu is a triad,[64] and like him Nuadu was known in Wales where he was worshipped under the name Nodons.[65] Rhŷs finds in the *Annals of the Four Masters* three kings named Nuadu, whose reigns are spaced about nine hundred years apart: Nuadu Argetlám, Nuadu Finnfáil, and Nuadu Necht.[66] He thinks that the chroniclers manufactured these three kings out of the three forms of the god Nuadu. Nuadu *Argetlám*, "silver hand," is Nuadu on earth, Nuadu *Finnfáil*, "white light," is Nuadu in the sky, and Nuadu *Necht*, "water," is Nuadu in the sea. It has already been pointed out that Goibniu the smith was probably one of the three forms of Nuadu. Several triads or sets of three brothers who are probably hypostases of Nuadu ought to be considered.

Three Fothads, who appear in the royal pedigrees as sons

[64] Rhŷs, *Celtic Heathendom*, pp. 122 f. Eóin Mac Neill, *Celtic Ireland*, p. 55.

[65] Page 146.

[66] These kings are dated 1866, 970, and 80 B.C.

of Lughaid MacCon and reigning at one time, are clearly a divine triad,[67] as is proved by their epithets: *Oendia,* "one god," *Caindia,* "comely god," and *Trendia,* "mighty god.' They stand at the beginning of some pedigrees. It is logical to conclude that they are Brión, Uar, and Iucharba under another name, *Fothad,* "foundation." This conclusion is, I think, rendered certain by the following considerations:

The father of the three Fothads, according to *Coir Anmann,* is Lughaid MacCon, or Conmac,[68] that is, in reality the god Lug. Fothad Canann's wife was the Hag of Beare, who, as is shown on another page,[69] is virtually a personification of Ériu. Now the husband of Ériu, or Brigit, in mythology is Brión. It is reasonable to infer that Fothad is a manifestation of Brión. Fothad Canann's head spoke [70] after it was cut off, which is the same motive as Bran's talking head in the Welsh *Branwen,* and he had a set of talismans like Bran and like Brión.[71]

Another divine triad consists of three Findeamna: Breas, Nar, and Lothar, whose story has horrified pedestrian readers. They are probably under different names a distorted reflection of Brión, Iuchar, and Uar. They were sons of Eochaid Feidleach who were born at one birth, and together they had by their own sister, Clothra, a son,

[67] Eóin Mac Neill, *Celtic Ireland,* p. 50; Pokorny, ZCP, XII (1916), 354. Compare the entry in *LL,* p. 146, col. a, l. 49: "Na tri Fothad: Oendia ocus Endia ocus Tendia."

[68] Some pedigrees, however, call the father Fedlimid.

[69] Page 334.

[70] Kuno Meyer, *Fianaigecht, RIA,* Todd Lect. Ser., XVI (Dublin, 1910), p. 8.

[71] For more about these talismans and their connection with the talismans of the Grail castle, see p. 228.

Lughaid Red Stripe. Then Lughaid had by his own mother, Clothra, a son, Crimthain. Astonishment at this story subsides when it is recalled that these people are gods. Clothra was sister to Medb Cruachna, who, as will be shown on a later page, is virtually the sovereignty of Ériu personified. Three sisters are mentioned: Clothra, Deirbriu, and Medb. Their father must have been in origin not Eochaid Feidleach but Eochaid Ollathar or the Dagda. The three sisters are in origin the triple-formed Brigit or Ériu, and their husbands are Brión, Iuchar, and Uar, under other names. The one son, Crimthain, corresponds to the one son, Ecne, in the myth.

Another faded picture of the divine triad, Brión, is probably preserved as Lomna in Cormac's *Glossary*.[72] By some error Lomna has been made Finn's jester. Thurneysen calls attention[73] to a common interchange in the manuscripts of *druid*, "druids," and *drúith*, "fools." My suggestion is that Brión was called "Finn's druid," and then by a mistake in the word became "Finn's jester." The account in the *Glossary* runs as follows:

The forests frequented by Finn and his men were inhabited by "woman-hosts," who supplied them with food in return for protection. Lomna was Finn's jester. He revealed an intrigue between Coirpre and one of Finn's concubines. Coirpre, at the woman's insistance, slew Lomna and cut off his head. Later Finn found Coirpre in an empty house, cooking fish . . . "and Lomna's head was on a spike by the fire." The head spoke twice. "Put out the head," said Coirpre. Then it spoke a third time "from outside." What prompted these speeches, we are then told, was Coirpre's neglect to give the head even one morsel of the fish. (§ 1018)

[72] See § 1018, *Anecdota*, IV, 86.
[73] *Heldensage*, p. 659.

Years ago Rhŷs conjectured [74] that we have here the god Brión or Bran fallen from his high estate, and degraded to be the fool or jester of Finn. The head was offended, Rhŷs thinks, because it was a pagan custom to offer the first morsel at a feast to the god Brión. Rhŷs's conjecture is probably right, for a talking head at a feast is like Bran's head in the Welsh *Branwen*, and Lomna grandson of Donn Désa is elsewhere [75] said to be one of three brothers, and is therefore possibly a faded manifestation of the triad, Brión. The story of Lomna, if it preserves something of the god Brión, has interesting suggestions. The eating of fish [76] may remind us of the Fisher King, Bron. The forest frequented by damsels who supply food is like the forest of the Grail damsels who surround the Fisher King.[77]

Another probable offshoot of the Brión myth, although the resemblance is not sufficient to put the matter out of doubt, is the episode of Donn-bó in the *Battle of Allen*.[78] This mentions a separated head that talks, and, indeed, is later restored to its trunk and comes to life again.

King Fergal of Connaught and King Cathal of Leinster prepared for battle. Fergal's men said to him: "If Donn-bó go with thee, I will go. Now Donn-bó's mother was a widow, and he had never gone for a day or a night out of his mother's

[74] *Celtic Heathendom*, pp. 98–99.

[75] See Gwynn, *Metrical Dinnshenchas*, III, 116 (the references in *Togail Bruidne Dá Derga* are based on this, Thurneysen, *Heldensage*, p. 654). See also the prose *Dinnshenchas*, § 29, *Rev. celt.*, XV (1894), 330; but according to § 35 (p. 421), Donn Désa had seven sons.

[76] Finn's dissevered head spoke while a fish was being cooked, according to MS. Egerton 92 (ed. Meyer, ZCP, I [1896], 462–465). Compare Kittredge, *Gawain and the Green Knight*, pp. 178 f.

[77] Page 422.

[78] Edition Stokes, *Rev. celt.*, XXIV (1903), 41–70. Cf. J. O'Donovan's edition, *Annals of Ireland, Three Fragments* (Dublin, 1860).

house. Donn-bó was in this wise: the brightest and hand-somest and dearest boy in Erin was he. Not in all Erin was there one who was pleasanter or cleverer than he, and from him came the best *rainn espa ocus rigscéla*, 'wanton-staves and king stories,' in the world. 'Tis he who was best to train horses, to set spears, to plait hair, and whose wit was clearest in his countenance. His mother did not let him go along with Fergal until the king had given Columcille guarantees and bonds for him, that he should come back safe." Fergal asked Donn-bó to play music on the night before the battle. Donn-bó refused, but promised to play the night after the battle. The heads of both Fergal and Donn-bó were cut off in the battle. A warrior sent by Murchad son of Bran of the Leinster-men went to the battlefield and found Donn-bó's head making music for the slain king. He brought Donn-bó's head and re-placed it on the trunk. Thereupon Donn-bó came alive again and returned safe to his mother.

According to the storyteller, this was one of St. Colum-cille's miracles, but it is plainly founded on pagan mythol-ogy. Columcille saw Bridget above the army of Leinster terrifying the men of Connacht. One manuscript [79] re-lates that "Mo-Dichu son of Amargen" helped the Connacht men and "Murchad son of Bran" helped the Leinstermen. This appears to be only a distorted reflection of the mythi-cal battle between Amargen, king of the giants, and Bran, king of the gods, who are here represented by their sons Mo-Dichu and Murchad. Mo-Dichu and Amargen on the one hand fight against Murchad and Bran or Brión on the other.

In Irish the battle of *Mag Tuired*, "plain of the towers," which means no doubt "plain of the tower of the dead," is

---

[79] Brussels MS., edition Stokes, *Rev. celt.*, XXIV (1903), 57, n. 4.

evidently based upon a mythical battle of fairies and giants. The story of how Nuadu, king of fairies, was wounded in this battle and withdrew to a place of refuge, where he lived for a long time in weakness surrounded by *fées* until he was rescued by the youthful Lug, evidently dominated Irish story and attached itself to the traditional accounts of several Irish kings. As has been shown, three kings named Nuadu are told of at different dates. Three Fothads, who are said to have reigned at one time, are apparently Nuadu under another name, and likewise three Findeamna.

The most renowned in story of the early kings were Conchobar and Cormac. Like that of Nuadu, the reign of each of these was a golden age. Like Nuadu, each suffered a disabling wound, and, like him, each survived for a number of years.

King Conchobar was wounded by a missile that lodged in his brain. "He was not capable of action but remained in his seat." [80] This disability continued for seven years till the news of the crucifixion of Christ reached Ulster, when he died from the shock.

King Cormac, who rebuilt the banqueting hall at Tara about 350 A.D. at the height of his prosperity, was blinded in one eye by Aengus "of the terrible spear." "Now it was a *geis* for a man with a blemish to be king at Tara. Cormac was therefore sent to be cured to Aicill close to Tara." From Aicill he gave counsel and aid to Coirpre, his son and his successor on the throne, and after seven years he died.[81]

---

[80] Kuno Meyer, "Death Tales of the Ulster Heroes," *RIA*, Todd Lect. Ser., XIV (Dublin, 1906), 9.

[81] Summarized from *The Ancient Laws of Ireland, Senchus Mór*, ed. J. O'Donovan and others (Dublin, 1865–1901), III, 82–84. See A. C. L. Brown, *PMLA*, XVIII (1910), 53 f.

His giving aid after his retirement is like Nuadu after his wound, from his underground palace, exerting control over the crops of Ireland.

Proof that King Cormac has taken over the belongings of the god Nuadu is found in the possession by both of the four jewels of the Tuatha Dé: spear, sword, caldron, and *Lia Fáil*. The spear with which Aengus put out Cormac's eye was evidently the spear of Lug, called the *Luin*. Aengus found it in Cormac's palace and it may be traced back to the battle of Moytura.[82] *Echtra Cormac* [83] says that Cormac had at Tara the *Coire ansicc*, "caldron of restitution," which was so named because it "would deliver to any company its suitable food." Cormac also had Cuchulinn's victory-bringing sword and a fairy cup that could distinguish between truth and falsehood. As we have seen this cup did not remain in Ireland after Cormac's death but, like the Grail, returned to fairyland. Cormac's treasures are evidently the same as the "Four Jewels" of the Tuatha Dé, a cup that acts as a test having been substituted for *Lia Fáil*, the stone that had a voice.

Further information about stories that attached themselves to Cormac may be obtained from vision literature. In 1149 an Irishman named Marcus wrote *The Vision of Tundale*.[84] In his vision of the land of the dead, Tundale saw King Cormac on a golden throne in a splendid palace which had no doors or windows but was full of light and bright with jewels. Nevertheless Cormac was obliged to spend three hours daily in pain, in fire up to his waist. This

[82] Edition Eleanor Knott, *Togail Bruidne Dá Derga*, p. 37, l. 1242.
[83] *Ir. Texte*, III, i, 205 f. (see p. 221).
[84] Edition A. Wagner, p. 42; cf. C. S. Boswell, *An Irish Precursor of Dante* (London, 1908), p. 221.

Cormac whom Tundale saw was no doubt his contemporary Cormac mac Carthaig, king of Desmond, who died
in 1138.[85] It is probable, however, that Cormac mac Carthaig
has been confused with Cormac mac Airt and that this
part of the vision is a borrowing from the story of Nuadu.
It copies Nuadu's retirement to the land of the dead, and
Cormac's suffering resembles the suffering of the Fisher
King from his wound.

That the wound of Conchobar and the wound of Cormac
were suggested by a popular identification of them with the
god Nuadu is a reasonable explanation of the phenomena
and likely to be generally accepted. I venture to propose
a more hazardous theory of borrowing from the myth of
Nuadu's wound.

The famous King Conchobar had another disability
which is not called a wound but which rendered him and
his warriors incapable of fighting from November first to
February first. Readers of the *Táin Bó Cuailgne* will remember the disability that afflicted Conchobar and all
Ulster at the time when Ailill and Medb, king and queen
of Connacht, and their allies, made their great attack. It
was this mysterious enfeeblement which forced the youthful Cuchulinn, who came from a distance and was exempt,
to fight single-handed the hosts of Ailill and Medb for
three winter months.

No satisfactory explanation for this disability has been
proposed. It has been interpreted as a trace of an old
couvade,[86] but a *couvade* does not plunge all the men of a
province into illness at once, nor does it persist for three

[85] J. F. Kenney, *Sources for the Early History of Ireland*, Records of
Civilization (New York: Columbia University Press, 1929), I, 742.
[86] Rhŷs, *Celtic Heathendom*, pp. 627, 677.

months. The traditional explanation, which goes back to an eighth-century text, is that the weakness was a punishment inflicted upon King Conchobar by a *fée* whom he had mistreated,[87] but this looks like an explanation invented after the origin of the story had been forgotten. My hypothesis does not in the least deny an historical basis for the *Táin Bó* but it supposes that the story of a real war between Ulster and Connacht was, in the course of centuries of retelling, so confused with a mythical battle of gods and giants that it now conforms somewhat with the story of Nuadu. My hypothesis supplies for the first time a reasonable explanation for the strange incapacity of Ulster for three months. It is the enchantment which in a story of the Journey to Fairyland type is fastened by the giants, after their victory, upon the Hospitable Host and his people.

The characters in the *Táin Bó* fit well into their places in the Journey to Fairyland plot. King Conchobar is the wounded Hospitable Host and corresponds to Nuadu and to the Fisher King. Queen Medb, who is virtually a personification of a province of Ireland, corresponds wonderfully to Queen Macha, and to Orguelleuse in *Perceval*. Her daughter Finnabair is also a personification of the sovereignty, and this explains why the daughter is offered in the *Táin Bó* as a bait or lure to warriors ambitious of power. Her name is the same as that of Arthur's queen. King Ailill is the Fomorian adversary, and corresponds to Balar or to Clamadeu in *Perceval*. He is supposed, of course,

---

[87] See p. 44. The name of the vengeful *fée* is Macha. This story may possibly preserve, greatly distorted, a trace of an old tradition that made Conchobar a hypostasis of Nuadu, and thus associated him with Macha (Ireland, Nuadu's wife).

to be a historical king of Connacht, but there are traces of another origin. The name means "demon" or "elf." To make the correspondence exact he should steal Queen Medb from Conchobar, and, according to *Cath Boinde*,[88] Conchobar had been Medb's husband. Fergus the good-natured ancient whose throne Conchobar has occupied, corresponds to the Fisher King's aged father. Cuchulinn, the youthful hero, corresponds to Lug, or to Perceval. This is the closest correspondence of all, for Lug is Cuchulinn's divine father, and in the *Táin Bó* he comes invisible and takes Cuchulinn's place for three nights and days in the battle. For three days, therefore, Lug plays in the *Táin Bó* the same rôle of youthful rescuer that he does in the mythical battle.

This hypothesis that I suggest about the *Táin Bó* has good evidence in its favor, but its acceptance is not necessary to the argument of this book. Whatever be the explanation of the *Táin Bó*, it is clear that any king in ancient Ireland who became a national hero was likely to have the Nuadu story ascribed to him. This is the meaning of the three kings named Nuadu, and of the legends about Cormac.

Did this same situation obtain in ancient Wales, and was their national hero Arthur likely to attract to himself the story of Nuadu? Reasons for thinking that Welsh popular tradition would ascribe the Nuadu story to King Arthur are as follows. First, and most important because not understood by some critics, a community of tradition and saga going back to heathen times existed between the Irish and the Welsh. The Celts had a feeling of unity resting perhaps upon the uniform *disciplina* of the druids which Caesar mentions. What the Irish did the Welsh did. Second, al-

---

[88] Edition Joseph O'Neill (*Ériu*, II [1905], 176 f.). Cf. J. Rhŷs, *Celtic Heathendom*, p. 138.

though no sagas about him have been preserved, Nuadu in
the form Nodons was worshipped, evidently as a sea god,
in Wales not far from the time and place of Arthur.[89] Whatever legends about Nodons existed in Wales must have been
known to those who first told the story of Arthur. Finally,
it is certain that the story of the wound, although attached
to Bran instead of Nuadu, was known in ancient Wales.
Bran is the Irish Brión who is personified in Nuadu. *Branwen Daughter of Llyr*, one of the four genuine branches
of the *Mabinogi*, which are surely older than French Arthurian romances, tells the story of Bran's wound as
follows.

Bran, king of Britain, is wounded in a great battle in which
all but seven of his companions are slain. His adversary, Caswallawn son of Beli,[90] seizes the throne of Britain. Bran,
wounded in the foot, commands his seven surviving friends
to cut off his head. The seven, with Bran's head as an eighth
companion, spend seven years, in a palace with three doors,
at Harlech listening to the song of three fairy birds. Thereafter they spend eighty years in company with Bran's head at
Gwales, an island, where was music and good fellowship.[91]

---

[89] At Lydney Park, about twenty miles from Caerleon, Arthur's favorite
residence, and not much more than one hundred years before his time
(p. 146). That Nuadu was worshipped in Ireland is shown, I think, by
names like *Mag Nuadat*, "plain of Nuadu" (now Maynooth), *Tobar
Nuadáin*, "well of Nuadu," *Disert Nuadáin*, "cell of Nuadu" (see
E. Hogan, *Onomasticon Goedelicum*, Dublin, 1910); and by the name
Mog Nuadat, "slave of Nuadu," which was assumed by Eoghan, King
of Munster, about the year 200.

[90] Caswallawn is explained on p. 389 as a compound name: *Cas*, "evil,"
+ "gallon" = Irish Galam, or Míl, the leader of the Milesian invaders.
His father Beli is, I think, Balar, king of the Fomorians.

[91] *Mab.*, I, 66 f. Gwales may or not be the island Grassholm, but it is
surely fairyland and like the *síd* to which Nuadu retired.

Bran wounded in the foot in this Welsh story corresponds to Nuadu wounded in the arm in the Irish *LG*. The Welsh, I suppose, changed an arm into a foot. The seven companions who feast with Bran's head correspond to the eight chief gods of the Tuatha Dé who by Nennius are called *damhoctor*, "a company of eight." [92] The palace with three doors may hint that Bran was a three-faced god like the Gaulish Cernnunos; and the three fairy birds may be one of his manifestations.

Years ago Alfred Nutt [93] recognized this eighty years' feast in Gwales as the Grail feast, and Bran wounded in the foot as the Fisher King. The song of the birds and the supernatural lapse of time are matched in other analogues to the Grail story. *Branwen Daughter of Llyr* goes on to relate an enchantment of Britain like that which devastated the Grail country.

Bran's head defending Britain against invasion looks like a variant of Nuadu's exerting control over Ireland after his retirement to a hollow hill. A Welsh triad relates that Arthur, because he did not wish to have the island defended by any power but his own, dug up the head.[94]

KING ARTHUR

The Arthur who dug up Bran's head seems to regard himself as his successor and heir. Probably Arthur was like the famous Irish heroes Cuchulinn and Finn, who not only borrowed exploits from the gods, but were sons of

---

[92] Page 254.
[93] *Legend of the Holy Grail* (1888), p. 219.
[94] This is one of the old and good triads in the Book of Hergest (J. Loth, *Les Mabinogion*, II, 242; Rhŷs and Evans, *The Text of the Red Book*, I, 300).

the gods. Cuchulinn was the son of Lug, and according to some accounts a rebirth of the god. Finn was grandson of Nuadu, and there is a suggestion that the relationship was closer. On the father's side the pedigree of Finn is variously given,[95] but on the mother's side it runs: Finn mac Muirne ingin Tadg mac Nuadu. Like Nuadu, Tadg was a god. The Hill of Allen or Almu, five miles north of Kildare, where Finn had his principal seat, was named from Finn's mother, Almu, and Finn doubtless inherited it from her. In Irish mythology, Almu is generally Nuadu's wife. L. C. Stern,[96] therefore, thought it a good tradition that made Finn son to Nuadu, and drew a conclusion that the Irish Finn mac Nuadu was confused with the Welsh fairy king Gwynn ab Nudd. Stern also pointed out that in some stories Arthur behaves like Gwynn ab Nudd. Eóin Mac Neill [97] speaks of Finn's ruling his mortal followers on the Hill of Allen while his grandfather Nuadu ruled immortals in the *síd* beneath.

Just as Cuchulinn and Finn were fabled by the Irish to be sons of the gods, Arthur was, I think, believed by the Welsh to be a son and a rebirth of Bran. In Welsh *bran* means "raven." That Arthur was believed in Cornwall to be in the form of a crow is mentioned by Cervantes.[98] This perhaps means that Arthur took the shape of his divine

---

[95] In *LL*, p. 311, col. c, l. 13: "Finn mac Cumall mac Trenmor mac Sualt mac Eltan mac Baeiscne mac Nuadu" (*Sil. Gad.*, II, 474, 519). In a twelfth-century account of Finn's death: "Finn mac Cumall mac Sualtach mac Baeiscne mac Nuada" (*Sil. Gad.*, I, 92; II, 99). Invented links seem present here (*Trenmor*, "very strong"; *Sualtach*, "well-fed").

[96] *ZCP*, VII (1910), 233.

[97] *Duanaire Finn*, pt. I (*ITS*, VII [London, 1908], lix).

[98] E. K. Chambers, *Arthur of Britain* (London, 1927), p. 229. See *ZCP*, VII, 226.

father Bran. In *Branwen Daughter of Llyr* Bran has not a raven's shape, but rather the shape of one of those crouching gods consisting of little but a head, statues of which have been dug up in France. Some redactor of *Branwen Daughter of Llyr* who did not understand pagan idols has drawn a striking though incredible picture of Bran as a living, talking head that has been severed from its body. Bran, I believe, was by the Welsh called *pen,* "head," and was thought of as a living corpse. He is described as *gorlassar,* "livid." [99] Evidence for this is that, in Irish saga, Donn king of the dead was called *détscorach,* "with teeth missing," [100] and Anbechtach son of Nuadu, who is the probable original of Wolfram's Anfortas, was called *glas,* "green were his face and his countenance usually." [101] The illness of a Hospitable Host in a Journey to Fairyland, which in the case of Nuadu and of the Fisher King was a wound, is sometimes an enchantment, and sometimes, as here, a trance, or death-in-life.[102]

Preiddeu Annwn [103] in the Book of Taliesin is little more than a retelling of Bran's Feast, with Arthur substituted for Bran as leader. As in *Branwen,* only seven return. Who these seven are, is not told, but Taliesin, who recites the poem, and Pryderi are among the number, and they are also among the seven to escape in *Branwen.* All translations

[99] The meaning of *gorlassar* has been disputed (Loth, *Rev. celt.,* XLII (1925), 318). On the general idea, see p. 340.

[100] Page 170.

[101] *Cóir Anmann,* § 7, ed. W. Stokes, *Ir. Texte,* III, ii, 291.

[102] In *Diu Crône* the Fisher King says that he is dead (p. 345).

[103] Translated by J. Rhŷs in his preface to Malory's *Morte Darthur,* Everyman's Library, XLV (1906), xxii. Compare W. F. Skene, *Four Ancient Books,* I, 264; II, 181. The manuscript is of the thirteen century, but the poem is far older. See now R. S. Loomis, *PMLA* (1941), pp. 889 f.

of *Preiddeu Annwn* are partly conjectural, but it pretty surely tells of a voyage to the land of the dead in quest of talismans.[104] Because only seven return, it has been supposed that a battle is fought, but no fighting is mentioned.[105] One ship only is referred to, but perhaps the often discussed refrain: "Three shiploads of Prydwen we went into it" hints that there were originally three ships and three brothers to command them, as must have been the case in the lost "Brión's Voyage" to which this is certainly another analogue.

The romances testify that the Fisher King had one or more brothers. Chrétien, to be sure, gives this relationship to the Fisher King's father, who is the hermit's brother and Perceval's uncle.[106] Wolfram, however, makes the Fisher himself brother to the hermit, Trevrizent, and uncle to Perceval, and this is the usual relationship. It has been shown above that three men (Gornemant, one of the old men at Blancheflor's castle, and the Fisher King) seem to have taken over the function of three forms of the mysterious Brión. In Chrétien's *Perceval*, when the hero approaches the Grail castle he sees two men in a boat. In the prose *Perceval*, according to the Modena manuscript,[107] he sees first three men, and then one. According to the Didot manuscript also, he sees three men. It is reasonable to be-

---

[104] Page 360.

[105] Rhŷs suggests that the episode in *Kulhwch and Olwen* (*Mab.*, I, 223) where Arthur with a small company in his ship Prydwen carried off the caldron of Diwrnach the Irishman, and fighting does take place, is a variant of this story, Ireland being put for the land of the dead.

[106] *Perceval*, vs. 6416.

[107] Jessie L. Weston, *The Legend of Sir Perceval* (London, 1906–1909), II, 57: "Vit enmi le riviere iii homes en une nef. Lors les aproisma Percevaus, et vit enmi le batel i molt viel home."

lieve that the three men were in origin different manifestations of the Fisher King, who is a shape-shifter.[108] They
are Brión, Iuchar, and Uar. Another manuscript, as quoted
by J. L. Weston,[109] refers more than once to *roi Alain,
roi Pellenor, roi Pelles*. All three sit at the Grail table;
sometimes they are cousins, and sometimes they are brothers.
In the *Perlesvaus*,[110] *roi Pescheor, roi Pelles, et li rois du
chastel mortel* are three brothers.

We have seen that Brión was in Irish mythology a voyager after talismans, a son and husband of Ériu, and a lord
of a fairy castle with its talismans. He was, we infer, the
origin of the Fisher King. In Chrétien and his continuators
the Fisher is unnamed, but Robert de Boron calls him
Bron,[111] a name that Nutt identified with Bran of the
Welsh *Mabinogion*. It was first pointed out by me [112] that
the Welsh Bran is the same as the Irish Brión, who is usually
called the "god of the Tuatha Dé." If objection be made
that in *OCT* and *CMT* Brión is always in quest of talismans, and that we have no good picture in Irish of him as

---

[108] The *Elucidation*, vs. 222 (see p. 427).

[109] *Sir Perceval*, II, 259. The manuscript is B.N. 337.

[110] Edition W. A. Nitze and T. A. Jenkins (University of Chicago
Press, 1932), p. 24.

[111] The longer form *Hebrons*, which Boron also uses, is no doubt due
to the influence of the Biblical *Hebron*. See Nitze, "The Identity of
Brons," *Gertrude Schoepperle Loomis Volume* (London and New York,
1927), pp. 135 f. A difficulty is (as Bruce said, *Evolution of Arthurian
Romance*, II, 130, n. 12) that proper names are often shortened in the
romances, but never expanded. Here I offer a new suggestion. In
Middle Irish, *ebrón* meant "caldron" (Edward Gwynn, *Hermathena*,
XX [1930], p. 62). Was Brión, the Lord of the Magic Caldron,
called in Irish by popular etymology *Ebron*, "caldron"? This could
give in French the expanded foim *Hebron*.

[112] A. C. L. Brown, *Mod. Phil.*, XXII (1924), 131; cf. Alfred Nutt,
Studies on the Legend, p. 211.

lord of a fairy palace, the answer is plain. The quester for fairy treasures in Irish regularly becomes a lord of fairy-land.[113] Thus Conle of A appears in F and in T and in the *Dinnshenchas* [114] as such a lord. Lug, who in *CMT* is in search of talismans, in *Baile in Scáil* is in settled possession. Moreover, in the Welsh *Branwen* we do have a picture of Bran in possession of talismans. We may therefore consider it certain that Brión is the origin of Bron and the prototype of the Fisher King.

Uther Pendragon as the name of Arthur's father is a blunder, as was suggested long ago by Edwin Guest,[115] a view that is now rather generally accepted. Two thirteenth-century manuscripts of Nennius contain a gloss as follows: [116] "[Artur] mab uter Britannice, filius horribilis Latine." *Mab uter*, "terrible youth," was misunderstood by Geoffrey and others to mean "Arthur son of Uter." Kuno Meyer has shown that by a similar error the Irish Cuchulinn, son of the god Lug, has gained a mortal father, as follows: the phrase, *Cuchulinn mac soalte*, "well-nourished youth," has been misunderstood to mean "Cuchulinn son of Soalte" (also written Sualtach). That this mistake was natural Meyer proves by showing that "Madog *mab uthyr*" has been misread "Madawc son of Uther." [117]

What Geoffrey misread in an older manuscript which

[113] Nutt, *Studies*, p. 265. In *Sir Launfal* the hero becomes lord of a fairy realm.

[114] Pages 39, 57, 86, 42; Gwynn, *Metrical Dinnshenchas*, III, 286, 292.

[115] *Origines Celticae*, II (London, 1883), 263. See now J. J. Parry, *Speculum*, XIII (1938), 276-277.

[116] T. Mommsen, *Mon. Germ. hist.*, III, 156. Of course, Geoffrey never saw these manuscripts, but they are probably copied, glosses and all, from an older manuscript which he saw.

[117] *University of Illinois Studies in Lang. and Lit.*, II, iv (1916), 9-11; J. Loth, *Rev. celt.*, XLIX (1932), 137.

was the source of our thirteenth-century copies was probably the phrase: *Artur map uther ben,* "a son of the terrible
(or venerable) head." This to the Welsh meant "a son
of the god Bran." The feast of seven companions with
Bran's head, referred to above, is called *yspydawt urdawl
ben* or, in English, "the entertainment of the honorable
head." [118] Geoffrey, who of course understood nothing
about *uther ben,* "venerable head," imagined for Arthur
a father *Ben* or *Pen.* How he expanded *Pen* into Pendragon
is less clear. Perhaps he had read of a Welsh magician,
Uther Pendragon, who is mentioned in a triad.[119]

The circumstances under which I suppose that stories
about the god Nuadu may have been transferred to Arthur,
and that Bran, the "venerable head," of mythology may
have been fabled to be Arthur's father, were doubtless like
those that existed in Brittany according to the *Cartulaire
de Redon,* a manuscript of about 1050. Here the names
Bran and Arthur are signed together as witnesses to four
ninth-century documents.[120] Three more documents of
this period contain the name Nodent as a witness. At this
time in Brittany the names Arthur, Bran, and Nodent
flourished side by side.

People who were loath to let a good story die, when
they no longer dared to attribute it to the old heathen
god Nodent, kept the story but told it of the new Christian
hero, Arthur. Arthur "son of the venerable head" sounded
heathenish and was dropped, but Arthur "son of *Pen*"
(dragon) was unobjectionable. Arthur bore an image of

---

[118] *Mab.,* I, 70; Rhŷs and Evans, *Red Book,* I, 42.

[119] J. Loth, *Les Mabinogion,* II, 252; Rhŷs and Evans, *Red Book,* I, 302.

[120] A. DeCourson; *Cartulaire de l'abbaye de Redon* (Paris, 1863); Bran
and Arthur are on pp. 19, 42, 60, 188; Nodent is on pp. 14, 99, 129. The
names Bran and Arthur occur together in Ireland before this (see p. 316).

the Virgin Mary on his shield, according to Nennius, and was therefore a Christian hero who could not be objected to by the clergy.

The ordinary man is frustrated and finds his plans demolished by the arrival of death. He consoles himself by imagining a national hero who, after accomplishing wonders in this life, finally fights and conquers death so that he may return some day for future triumphs; in other words, the ordinary man imagines a superior hero of his race who becomes a god. My hypothesis is that this was the reaction of the Welsh to Arthur. They exalted him to the position of the god Nuadu and regarded him as Nuadu's son and successor. They transferred to him the story of Nuadu's wound and of his expected return from fairyland.

That King Arthur has borrowed exploits from heathen gods in the same way that saints borrowed an occasional miracle from heathen mythology [121] has been understood for some time, but direct testimony to this borrowing has, of course, not been found. Borrowing was not made by scribes or by people who could read and write. It was made by the folk who were unwilling to let a good story die, and who, at a time when heathen names like Bran and Nuadu were taboo, told an ancient story and then attributed it to King Arthur.

In this way the story of Arthur's being wounded in the battle of Camlan, of his voyage to Avalon, and of his expected return, was borrowed from Nuadu. How long ago was this story transferred to Arthur? Arthur's expected return is not mentioned by Nennius (826). The Laon canons (1113) found Cornishmen ready to quarrel

[121] See Charles Plummer, *Vitae sanctorum Hiberniae*, I, cxxxii.

with any who doubted that Arthur was still alive.[122] The story, therefore, of Arthur's going to Avalon must have arisen after 826 and have been widespread by 1113. Nennius refers to twelve battles of Arthur. The battle of Camlan between Arthur and Medraut is first mentioned in the tenth-century *Annales Cambriae*.[123] Camlan is a copy, I think, of the Irish battle of Moytura, so Arthur's borrowing from Nuadu had probably begun by the tenth century.

It was doubtless the taking-over of this wonderful story and the development of Arthur into a successor or substitute for Nodons that elevated him to the rank of chief hero of Wales, Cornwall, and Brittany, and laid foundations for his being regarded as a world conqueror. A commentary on Geoffrey's *Prophecies of Merlin* which was written by Alain de Lille (1167–1183) declares that Arthur's return is so firmly expected in Brittany that anyone who should go thither and deny it might expect to be cursed and stoned.[124] The commentary goes on to declare that the Arthur story was known throughout the world, and that palmers report having heard Arthurian stories even in Armenia and Palestine.[125]

[122] J. S. P. Tatlock, "The English Journey of the Laon Canons," *Speculum*, VIII (1933), 454–465. Early references to Arthur are assembled by R. S. Loomis, "The Arthurian Legend before 1139," *Rom. Review* (1941), 3–38.

[123] E. K. Chambers, *Arthur of Britain*, pp. 15 and 241.

[124] *Prophetia Anglicana Merlini Ambrosii* (Frankfort, 1603), bk. i, p. 17: "Quod si mihi non credis, vade in Armoricum regnum, id est, in minorem Britanniam, et praedica per plateas et vicos, Arturum Britonem more caeterum mortuorum mortuum esse, et tunc certe re ipse probabis, veram esse Merlini prophetiam, qua ait: Arturi exitum dubium fore. Si tamen immunis evadere inde potueris, quin aut maledictis audientium opprimaris, aut certè lapidibus obruaris."

[125] *Prophetia Anglicana*, p. 22: "Quò enim Arturi Britonia nomen fama

Arthur's reign, like Nuadu's, was a golden age; both ended in a great battle. Arthur was wounded, as was Nuadu, and was carried to fairyland to be healed. Doubtless Arthur's wound produced the enchantment of Britain referred to in the *Elucidation* and other texts, just as Nuadu's wound brought debility on Ireland. Arthur's expected return to help the Britons is something like Nuadu's exerting control, even after his retirement to his fairy hill, over the crops of Ireland. Finally, Arthur has inherited the "Four Jewels" of the Tuatha Dé, which were associated with Nuadu, and which consisted of a sword, spear, stone, and cauldron.

Nuadu's chief attribute was a sword. The same is true of Arthur. The importance of this sword to Arthur's fame has been caught by Wordsworth in the well-known lines:

> Of Arthur, — who, to upper light restored,
>   With that terrific sword
> Which yet he brandishes for future war,
> Shall lift his country's fame above the polar star!
>
> "Artegal and Elidure," vss. 53–57.

Excalibur, which comes from the Irish *Calad-colc*, is, I think, in origin the same as the sword of Nuadu.

The spear of Lug reappears as the *Luin* of Celtchar and of Cormac, and as Arthur's spear, *Ron*.

---

volans non pertulit et vulgavit quousque Christianum pertingit imperium? Quis inqum Arturum Britonem non loquatur, cum penè notior habeatur. Asiaticis gentibus quam Britannis; sicut nobis referunt palmigeri nostri de orientis partibus redeuntes? Loquuntur illum orientales, loquuntur occidui toto terrarum orbe divisi. Loquitur illum Aegyptus Bosforus exclusa non tacet. Cantat gesta ejus domina civitatum Roma nec emulam quondam ejus Carthiginem, Arturi praelia latent, celebrat actus ejus Antiocha, Armenia Palaestina."

Lia Fáil reappears, I suppose, as that stone from which Arthur drew the sword and thus vindicated his right to be chosen king. *Lia Fáil* acted as an ordeal in Ireland and selected the man to be king by crying out when he stepped upon it. The polished French writers of the twelfth century, I suppose, changed the barbaric Irish stone that had a voice into a stone that contained a sword. To draw out the sword was an ordeal that, according to the romances, confronted Arthur when he aspired to be king.

Finally, the caldron of the Dagda reappears as the Grail. Both supply whatever food a company desires. In Irish this caldron is never closely connected with Nuadu but rather with his older and mysterious double, Brión. So, in Arthurian romance, the Grail is not connected directly with Arthur but with the enigmatical Fisher King. Probably it was the Fisher King that tradition first made son of Nuadu. *Cóir Anmann* [126] calls Anbechtach Nuadu's son. *Anbechtach* seems to represent the original of Anfortas, Wolfram's name for the Fisher.

The Finn saga grew up in Gaelic lands at about the same period that the Arthur saga arose in Welsh-speaking countries; there was no borrowing between them except in recent times, and yet the two sagas are parallel in many points. Neither Finn nor Arthur was a king, but a leader of battles; Finn's warriors, the *fian*, had rules and admission ceremonies, as did the knights of the Round Table; Finn and Arthur, like other Celtic and Arthurian chieftains, adhered to the primitive custom of the unspecified boon. [127]

[126] (See p. 305.) *Anbechtach* could mean "wounded"; cf. *becht*, "complete," and *Ainfectnach*, a name for Nuadu (p. 187). On Arthur's spear and other marvelous belongings, see A. C. L. Brown, *PMLA*, XVIII (1910), 30 f.

[127] Finn had a custom of engaging a retainer with a promise to give

Finn's wife had a love affair with one of his warriors, as Guenevere did with Lancelot. Finn's battles were mostly against giants and dragons, so that he is almost a fairy king; the same is true of the Arthur of the romances. Finn made songs on summer and winter; Arthur was much occupied with seasonal festivals. Finn's warriors sought a quadrangular cup; Arthur's knights sought the Grail. Finn's relatives seem to be gods or fairies. His father, Tadg, and his grandfather, Nuadu, were gods, his wife Grainne and his nephew, "Diarmuid of the women," seem like fairy folk. The statement just made is even more true of Arthur. Arthur's sister, according to Geoffrey, was Anna.[128] In Ireland, Ana is the mother of the three gods — that is of the triformed Brión. She is the goddess of abundance and is often virtually Ireland personified.[129] Arthur's sister, according to Chrétien, is Morgan the *fée*. Arthur's wife, Guenevere is the Irish Finnabair, "white enchantress," and certainly a *fée*.[130] The company of Finn's warriors was dissolved at

---

at the end of a year whatever wages are asked ("The Pursuit of the Gilla Dacker," in P. W. Joyce, *Old Celtic Romances* [London, 1879], p. 230). Arthur in *Kulhwch and Olwen* promises Kulhwch anything, with a few exceptions, that Kulhwch may ask (*Mab.*, I, 179). Queen Guenevere and Arthur, at the beginning of Chrétien's *Lancelot*, promise Kay anything to keep him at their court, and learn too late that his boon is for the queen to accompany him and Meleagant to the forest (p. 99). This is a variety of the custom called "potlatch," namely, a savage's notion that a chieftain must prove his greatness by extravagant gifts or boons. See H. Hubert, "Le Système des prestations totales dans les littératures celtiques," *Rev. celt.*, XLII (1925), 330–335, and *The Greatness and Decline of the Celts* (London, 1934), p. 193. See also Cross and Nitze, *Lancelot*, p. 49, n. 3.

[128] *Historia regum*, edition A. Griscom (New York, 1929), bk. viii, chap. 20, p. 427.

[129] Page 318.

[130] See Chrétien's *Erec*, vs. 4220, and p. 337.

the battle of Gabhra, where almost all were slain, just as the fellowship of the Round Table came to an end at the battle of Camlan. Unlike Arthur, Finn was not wounded in the last battle, but, like him, Finn lives on beneath a hollow hill. It is expected in some places that Finn will return with his warriors to rescue Ireland,[131] just as it is believed in Wales that Arthur will return to fight for the Welsh.

The theory that in Celtic lands King Arthur was popularly regarded as a son of Bran or Nuadu or Nemed receives corroboration by the sudden appearance of "Arthur son of Nemed" in the Irish *LG*. The first redaction, which Macalister calls R[1], contains no Arthur in any form. The second redaction, R[2], introduces "Artoat son of Nemed" as slain in the battle of Cnamros by Conaing, king of the Fomorians. The name also appears as "Artach" among the thirty men who escaped from Conaing's tower.[132] R[2] was probably, although it cannot be proved, put together about the year 1000. The oldest manuscript that contains "Artoat son of Nemed" was written about 1400. Macalister explains Artoat as a misreading of Iarbonel, who was son to Nemed.[133]

It seems to me that to change Iarbonel into Artoat a scribe must have had running in his head a notion that Arthur was son of a god. This guess finds some confirmation in the third version, R[3], which was probably put together in the twelfth century, although our oldest manuscript dates from about 1500. R[3] reads: "Artúr son of

[131] J. Mac Dougall, *Folk and Hero Tales from Argyllshire*, Waifs and Strays, III (London, 1891), 263.

[132] R. A. S. Macalister, *LG*, III, 135, 143.

[133] Macalister, *LG*, I, xv; III, 195.

Nemed," [134] and in O'Clery's *LG*: "Artúr the Great, son of Nemed." The older scribe and O'Clery probably both knew Celtic traditions that made King Arthur son to Nemed. One of the earliest occurrences of the name Arthur, as will be seen, traces his pedigree back to *Nimet*, which is Old Welsh for Nemed.

The widespread and sudden appearance of the name Arthur shortly after 500 in all Celtic lands is, as Zimmer saw,[135] a proof of the outburst of an Arthur saga in those lands. The first occurrences of the name Arthur in Celtic documents are as follows:

1. WALES. "Mongan ab Artúir filio Bicoir Pretene [Bicor the Briton] . . . interit" (*Annals of Tigernach* at the year 624, edited by W. Stokes from a fourteenth-century manuscript, *Rev. celt.*, XVII [1896], 178. Cf. Meyer and Nutt, *Voyage of Bran*, I, 84, 137).

2. IRISH IN SCOTLAND. Artúr mac Aedein mac Gabráin, slain in 596. One of this Artur's brothers was named Bran (*Annals of Tigernach, Rev. celt.*, XVII, 160). In Adamnann, *Life of St. Columba* (ed. W. Reeves, Dublin, 1857, bk. I, chap. 9), the date is 606, and the spelling is Arturius.

3. IRELAND. Feradach, grandson of Artúr, was one of the guarantors of the Law of Adamnann in 697 (Kuno Meyer, *Cáin Adamnáin*, Oxford, 1905, p. 16, l. 30).

4. IRISH IN WALES. Arthur map Petr, in a pedigree tracing the line back to Nimet (ed. E. Phillimore, *Y Cymmrodor*, IX [1888], 171 f.). This Arthur reigned from about 550 to 600. In the Irish *Migration of the Dessi*, written about 750,[136] this Artúr mac Petuir, but not his descent from Nemed, appears.

[134] Macalister, *LG*, III, 135, footnotes.
[135] *Nennius Vindicatus*, pp. 284–285.
[136] Edition Meyer, *Ériu*, III (1907), 136, l. 39. E. Faral (*Légende Arthurienne*, I [Paris, 1929], 136) erred in believing this Welsh pedigree to be no older than Nennius.

5. IRELAND. Artúir son of Muiredach, king of Iarthar-Lifi in 846 (*Annals of Ulster*, ed. W. M. Hennessy, Dublin, 1887, I, 355).

6. BRITTANY. Arthur, in six documents of the second half of the ninth century in the *Cartulaire de Redon*, a manuscript of about 1050. (See above p. 309, and J. Loth, *Rev. celt.*, XLIX [1932], 140.)

7. IRELAND. *Aigidecht Artúir*, in a lost tenth-century story of Arthur's boar hunt (Kuno Meyer, "Eine verschollene Artursage," *Festschrift für E. Windisch*, Leipzig, 1914, pp. 63 f.).

8. IRELAND. Artúr mac Muiredeig who died in Leinster in 1052 (*Annals of the Four Masters*, ed. O'Donovan).

9. IRELAND. Artúr amra, "the famous Arthur," in a poem attributed to Finn (*LL*, p. 205, col. b, l. 5).

10. IRELAND. Artúir mac Benne Brit, in *Acallam na Senórach* (ed. Stokes, l. 170). This Arthur was taken prisoner and made one of the Fenians.

11. IRELAND. Artúir mac Coscraig, MS. *Rawlinson B. 502*, 125a, 41.

12. IRELAND. Suitheman mac Artúir in Leinster in the year 858 (*Annals of Ireland, Three Fragments*, ed. J. O'Donovan, Dublin, 1860, p. 138).

13. IRELAND. Artúir mac Brain, "Artur son of Bran." "From this Artúr the Húi Artúir are named" (*BB*, p. 184, col. b, ll. 35, 39). This probably implies a belief that King Arthur was a son of Bran.[137]

BRIGIT

Brigit was mother of the three gods Brión, Iuchar, and Uar.[138] The common expression, Tuatha Dé Danann,

[137] The last three references I copy from K. Meyer, *Sitzungsberichte der Preussischen Akad. d. Wiss.* (Berlin, 1919), p. 399. Most of the other references above were collected by Meyer, *op. cit.* (1912), p. 1156. See also Thurneysen, ZCP, XX (1933), 134.   [138] Page 281.

"peoples of the goddess *Dana*," appears to make *Dana* (gen., *Danann*) mother of the gods.[139] Cormac's *Glossary* says that *Anu* or *Ana* (gen., *Anann*) is mother of the gods. Clearly Brigit, Dana, and Ana were three names for the same divine mother. Another entry in Cormac's *Glossary* [140] testifies that there were three sisters, Brigit the goddess of poets, Brigit the woman-physician, and Brigit wife to Goibniu; and so important were they that "all Irishmen call any goddess a Brigit." From the evidence collected in preceding pages it is clear that Brigit was, like her son Brión, a triad. These three Brigits are really one Brigit. They resemble the three fates and the triformed Diana.

In preceding pages we have seen that Brigit is virtually the land personified, at first perhaps fairyland, but by an easy transition Ireland. She is the same as the three queens, Banba, Fodla, and Ériu, whose husbands were, under other names, Brión, Iuchar, and Uar. Irish records, of course, obscure the fact that Brigit was in origin both Brión's mother and his wife. In them, for the most part, Brión, like the Fisher King, has no wife but is surrounded by troops of maidens who are the Tuatha Dé.

Brigit, Ana, and Dana are hypostases of Ériu. Evidence that Ana was virtually the earth of Ireland personified is the existence of two small mountains in Kerry which are

[139] Thurneysen, *Heldensage*, p. 63. Cf. d'Arbois, *Cours de litt. celt.*, II, 145; and J. Vendryes, *Rev. celt.*, L (1933), 85.

[140] *Anecdota*, IV, 11, § 104; IV, 15, § 150; "Brigit .i. banfile ingen in Dagdae. Isí insin Brigit the female sage that is the goddess whom poets adored. For great and famous was her protecting care. Ideo eam deam uocant poetarum. Cuius sorores erant Brigit bé legis ocus Brigit bé Goibne ingena in Dagda, de cuius nominibus pene omnes Hibernenses dea Brigit uocabatur."

called even today "two paps of Ana." They are so described in Cormac's *Glossary*:

Ana mother of the Irish gods. It was well that she nursed the gods. Concerning her name Ana, it means "plenty," and from her are named the two paps of Ana west of Luchair, as the story goes, i. e., as it is told in the histories. Or ana is *anyon* [?] in Greek, which means dapes, i. e., food.[141]

They are called sometimes "the paps of the Morrígu." In this there is no contradiction, for the word Morrígu, whether it originally meant "great queen" or not, came to be an epithet for a goddess [142] and does not necessarily refer to the battle-goddess Bodb. O'Clery's version of *Leabhar Gabhála* [143] explains this use of Morrígu, and testifies to the identity of Dona and Ana.

Ana is described in the last quotation from Cormac's *Glossary* as a plenty-goddess. Reference seems to be made to some story like that preserved in the *Elucidation* in which a goddess and her maidens supplied travellers with food and drink, perhaps at fountains in the forest. Such a story is partly outlined at the beginning of the extract from Cormac's *Glossary* about Lomna, summarized on an earlier

---

[141] *Anecdota*, IV, 3, § 31. This Ana is probably the same as Arthur's sister, Anna (cf. A. H. Krappe, *Archiv f. d. Studium d. Neueren Sprachen*, CLXVII (1935), 175).

[142] Thurneysen, *Heldensage*, p. 63; Lucy Paton, *Studies in the Fairy Mythology*, p. 11.

[143] Edition Macalister and Mac Neill, I, 153, § 103: "Badb, Macha, and Moir-Rigan, the three daughters of Dealbaeth, son of Ned, son of Ionda. Ernbas, daughter of Eatarlamh, son of Ordan, son of Iondae, son of Alldae, was mother of all those women. Mor-Riogan had another name, Ana; from her are named the Paps of Anann in East Luachair. Dona, daughter of Dealbaeth, son of Oghma, son of Ealathan, was mother of Brian, Iucharba, and Iuchar, and they are called the three gods of Dona; from them are the Tuatha De Danann called."

page.[144] Another section in the same ancient document mentions Ana [145] and still another explains *ana* as a name for cups at wells. This is perhaps a trace of a lost story about *fées* who served food at wells in an enchanted forest.[146]

St. Bridget

St. Bridget is believed to be an historical saint who died in the year 525. That she has borrowed attributes from the heathen goddess has long been well understood. It has been recognized that the Irish quietly identified St. Bridget with the Brigit whom we have seen to be the mother of their great god Brión — the Earth-Mother, in fact, some of whose names were Ana, Dana, and Ériu. The saint has been substituted for the goddess [147] just as we have seen above that St. Brendan has been substituted for Brión.

The partial identification of St. Bridget with the pagan Brigit accounts for the astonishing epithets given to the saint in the oldest Irish hymns. In *Brigit bé bithmaith* she is called "the mother of Jesus." [148] In *Ní car Brigit* we read

[144] *Anecdota*, IV, 86, § 1018. The passage mentions *ban-brugaid*, "women-hosts," in a forest (see p. 294). Andreas Capellanus speaks of a meadow with tables containing meat and drink (see p. 347).

[145] *Anecdota*, IV, 11, § 104, reads: "Búanand nurse of warriors .i. bé n-Anand from their similarity to each other. For as Ana was mother of the gods *sic Búanand quasi mater erat na fían*."

[146] *Anecdota*, IV, 5, § 48: "Ana .i. stába beaca bítis for tiprataib isnaib cánaibh dlúthib." Compare in Kuno Meyer, *Contributions to Irish Lex.*, p. 89: *án*, f., "a drinking vessel," pl. *ána*; O'Davoren's *Glossary*, §§ 119, 150, 174; and O'Mulconry's *Glossary*, § 87; both glossaries were edited by Stokes, *Archiv f. celt. Lex.* (1900–1906).

[147] Macalister, *Tara*, p. 197. Macalister thinks that the chief priestess of the cult at Kildare was called Brigit; that the last priestess accomplished the wonderful feat of turning the heathen temple into a Christian convent and is remembered as St. Bridget.

[148] *Thesaurus Paleohibernicus*, II, 325.

that she "slept a captive's sleep for the sake of her Son," [149]
where the context proves that the reference is to Christ.
She is *máthair mo rurech*, "Brigit mother of my Lord,"
and *oen máthair Maicc Rig máir*, "the unique mother of the
Great King's Son," and again "Brigit's Son brought to
her," [150] where the context indicates Christ, or a supernatural helper. A Latin commentator explains, "Brigit was
the Mary of the Irish," [151] and no doubt St. Bridget was
sometimes identified with the Virgin. St. Bridget's Day,
February first, is the eve of Candlemas, the Feast of the
Purification. Perhaps a partial identification with the Virgin
was allowed by early missionaries.[152] The only adequate
explanation, however, of the extraordinary epithets just
quoted is that the Irish country folk would not give up the
old title of the pagan Brigit, "mother of the gods." This
epithet had to be interpreted by the missionaries in a
Christian sense, by partly identifying Brión with Christ.

The pagan association of Brión and Brigit and their connection with the sea has passed over to St. Brendan and
St. Bridget. A prose introduction to the poem *Brigit bé
bithmaith* runs in brief as follows:

When St. Brendan was sailing in search of the Land of
Promise he heard one sea-beast calling on Brendan and the
other saints of Ireland to protect it from another beast. The
other kept up its attack till the first beast called on Bridget

---

[149] *Thesaurus Paleohibernicus*, II, 327.

[150] *Thesaurus Paleohibernicus*, II, 327, 342, 344.

[151] W. Stokes, *Lives of Saints from the Book of Lismore* (Oxford,
1890), p. 51.

[152] Ana the heathen goddess, and Anna the cousin of the Virgin are
confused in Welsh pedigrees of the thirteenth century. See J. Rhŷs and
D. Brynmore-Jones, *The Welsh People* (New York, 1900), p. 42.

for help. Then it cried, "Since you have called on Bridget, I cannot injure you." Brendan afterwards made the poem *Brigit bé bithmaith* in praise of Bridget, and went to Kildare to find out why she was honored above other saints.[153]

This story appears also in the notes to *Ní car Brigit* with a picturesque addition that Brendan once saw Bridget hang her cloak on a sunbeam. He tried to do likewise with his cloak, but did not succeed till the third attempt. St. Bridget's power over the sea is illustrated in another story. The Book of Lismore relates [154] that St. Bridget once sent a man to the shore to secure food. The man was carried by a seal across the channel to Britain. In Britain a helpful fisherman gave the man a marvelous boat in which he returned to Ireland to Bridget bringing the seal.

James Mooney in his article "The Holiday Customs of Ireland" says that Candlemas was probably part of a general European celebration with which the Irish Brigit was connected:

In ancient Rome torches were carried about on that day in honor of Februa. . . . In Ireland the eve of Candlemas is called Oidche Brigide (prn. Ekha Vreja). On it wives used to bake a cake for Bridget (prn. Breej), and send it round with ale. . . . Young girls used to dress up the churn-dash to represent St. Bridget and carry it in procession. . . . In Limerick a broom is dressed up and called "Miss Bridget." In Galway, men carry a rope known as Crios Brigide (prn. Cris Vreja) or girdle of Bridget. . . . In Galway (not in the north or south-west, however) people pass through the rope which is made of rushes. . . . The next morning — that is, on St. Bridget's Day

[153] *Thesaurus Paleohibernicus*, II, 324.
[154] R. O'Flaherty, *A Chorographical Description of the West of Connaught*, Irish Arch. Soc. (Dublin, 1846), p. 96.

— all the animals are made to go through it. . . . The men who carry around the *Crios Brigide* sing verses, a part of which is: 'Give me something and pass through my girdle. And may you be 7000 times better, a year from tonight.' In Galway boys gather rushes and on the eve of St. Bridget's Day go to every house and shout seven times, 'Let Bridget enter.' The reply is, 'Enter and one hundred welcomes before you.' In Donegal the bringer of the rushes is a girl who is called Bridget for the occasion.[155]

Maud E. Sargent, in her paper on "Vanishing Customs and Superstitions of Rural Ireland," [156] writes:

On Biddy's Day (February first) in a few remote places . . . a huge and very ugly rag-doll resembling a Guy, or the 'Morena' of Hungarian children, and supposed to represent St. Bridget or 'Bride,' is carried round by little girls. . . . In the north of Ireland and in Scotland 'Bride' is a common form of the name. . . . On St. Bride's Day a silk ribbon is still occasionally placed on the window-sill in honor of the saint, and left out all night. It is afterwards kept as a cure for headaches. . . . The women and girls of each house often made a circlet of green rushes with a cross inside composed of the same material, on 'Biddy's Day.' This was known as 'St. Bridget's Ring' (or 'Cross'), and was pinned to the interior of the thatched roof, a fresh one being added every anniversary.[157]

Martin Martin in his *Description of the Western Islands of Scotland*, 1703, wrote:

Another ancient custom observed on the second of February, which the Papists there (Islay, or more probably, Colonsay)

---

[155] *Proceedings of the American Phil. Soc.*, XXVI (1889), 380–427.

[156] *New Ireland Review*, XXVIII (1907), 207 f.

[157] A word *Brídeog*, defined as "an image of St. Bridget used for domestic ceremonies on the eve of her festival," is in Dinneen's *Dictionary* (Dublin, 1927).

yet retain, is this: The mistress and servants of each family take a sheaf of oats, and dress it up in women's apparel, put it in a large basket, and lay a wooden club by it, and this they call Briid's-bed; and then the mistress and servants cry three times, 'Briid is come, Briid is welcome!' This they do just before going to bed, and when they rise in the morning they look among the ashes, expecting to see the impression of Briid's club there; which, if they do, they reckon it a true presage of a good crop and prosperous year.[158]

These ceremonies on the eve of St. Bridget are apparent survivals of the worship of the pagan Brigit. A survival of the plenty characteristics of the heathen goddess Brigit or Ériu seems indicated in a hymn ascribed to St. Bridget:

> I should like a great lake of ale
>   For the King of Kings.
> I should like the family of heaven
>   To be drinking it through time eternal.[159]

The perpetual fire of Kildare is another piece of evidence showing that St. Bridget fell heir to the worship of a heathen goddess. Giraldus Cambrensis, about 1190,[160] tells of the perpetual fire at Kildare which was guarded by nineteen nuns. A different nun guarded the fire each night till the twentieth night, when Bridget cared for the fire herself. The fire was surrounded by an enclosure which no male could pass without incurring supernatural vengeance.

[158] Quoted from a reprint in J. Pinkerton, *General Collection of Voyages*, III (London, 1809), 613.

[159] E. O'Curry, *Lectures on the MS. Materials*, p. 616:
> "Ropadh maith lem corm-lind mór
>   Do righ na righ," etc.

[160] Edition J. F. Dimock, *Topographia Hibernica* (1867), dist. ii, chap. 34–36.

Sir James Ware records,[161] on the authority of an anonymous Dominican monk who wrote about 1314, that this fire was extinguished in 1220 by order of Henry of London, Archbishop of Dublin, on the ground that it savored of paganism. It was, however, rekindled, on the plea that it was useful to guests, and was kept up till the time of Henry VIII.

From this testimony it is clear that almost down to the present day a dim recollection of Brigit as an Earth-Mother, and the mother of a chief god, Brión, persisted in Ireland. Brión's name, however, considering what must have been his importance as the god of the Tuatha Dé, is seldom mentioned. A taboo against writing down heathen names probably kept references to Brión, and to the heathen side of his mother Brigit, out of literature.

Queen Medb

Medb is, strictly speaking, a parallel figure to Brigit, not an hypostasis, for she represents Connacht, one of the five provinces, not Ireland as a whole; but it will give rise to no mistake to call her an hypostasis of Brigit. Her story is of interest because it shows the succession of husbands required by a *fée* who is virtually the sovereignty, and because her daughter, Finnabair, who is likewise the sovereignty, and who in the *Táin Bó* is used as a lure to attract ambitious warriors, gave her name to Arthur's queen, Guenevere. Arthur's queen brought him the Round Table and was probably originally the sovereignty.

Everybody in Ireland today talks of Queen Medb as a historical ruler of Connacht. The *Táin Bó* is believed to

[161] *De Hibernia et Antiquitatibus disquisitiones* (Dublin, 1658), p. 96, chap. 17, § 6.

tell of an actual foray made by the men of Connacht
against Ulster. Medb, the leader of this foray, lived at
Cruachan [162] at about the time of the Christian era, and is
today regarded as a bad lot because she had so many lovers
and husbands. Nothing in what follows weakens the historical basis of the *Táin Bó*, or disproves the existence
of a historical Queen Medb. My point is that this historical queen was named from, and borrowed exploits from,
a fairy queen or earth-goddess who was virtually the province of Connacht personified.

The first piece of evidence tending to prove that the
actions of Queen Medb are partly unhistorical is the existence of another Queen Medb who lived some two hundred and fifty years later, and who was likewise noteworthy
for the number of her lovers and husbands. This is Medb
Lethdearg, after whom a *rath* at Tara is named.

In truth, Queen Medb, whether Medb of Cruachan the
instigator of the *Táin Bó* or Medb Lethdearg the reputed
builder of the *rath* near Tara, is a *fée* disguised by rags of
history thrown over her shoulders by the synchronizers.
Several pages that I had written on this topic are here
omitted because they have been anticipated in an excellent
paper by Tomás Ó Máille.[163] He shows that "Queen
Medb" generally stands for "the sovereignty of Ireland"
personified. From the *Ferchuitred Medba*, "Husband Al-
lowance of Medb," [164] he demonstrates that Medb Chru-
achna had in succession four husbands, Conchobar, Tindi,

---

[162] An ogamic inscription on a stone found near Cruachan was interpreted by J. Rhŷs as follows: [Stone] "of Fraech son of Medvv" (*Journal
of the Royal Hist. and Arch. Assoc. of Ireland* [1898], pp. 231, 409).

[163] ZCP, XVII (1927), 129–146.

[164] Edited under the title *Cath Boinde* by Joseph O'Neill in *Ériu*, II
(1905), 174 f.; and from another manuscript by Kuno Meyer in *Anecdota*,
V (1913), 18 f.

Eochaid Dala, and Ailill; and that the unhistoric character of this account is proved by her bearing Ailill seven sons,[165] although she had been his foster-mother when he was a child, and was his great-aunt. Here I would add that Medb procured the death of Eochaid Dala at the hands of Ailill his successor, and that this is a parallel to Chrétien's *Yvain*, where Laudine was originally a *fée*, and must have instigated the killing of her husband, Esclados, by Yvain, his successor. The account in *Cath Boinde* is as follows:

> After Medb had reared Ailill he became her lover, and "he fought Eochaid (Medb's husband) for his kingdom and his wife, and Eochaid fell by Ailill through the *imdill*, 'wiles' of Medb." [166]

In regard to Medb Lethdearg, Ó Máille quotes an ancient document as follows:

> Medb Lethdearg had in succession four kings as husbands: CúCorb, Feidlimid Rechtaid, his grandson Art, and Art's son Cormac. "She did not allow anybody in the kingship of Tara with whom she was not mated." Like Medb Cruachna, she encouraged her lover to displace and slay her husband. "Medb Lethdearg was mother of Cúcorb's two sons (i.e. she was married to Cúchorb). The Medb mated with Feidlimid Rechtaid. Medb left Cúchorb before that, and she was wife to Feidlimid when he killed Cúchorb." [167]

He next quotes from a poem, *Cnucha cnoc os cionn Life*, which has been edited by Maura Power, the following verses:

---

[165] The sons are all named "Maine." J. Rhŷs (*Celtic Heathendom*, p. 368) has attempted to explain them as personifications of the days of the week.

[166] *Ériu*, II (1905), 183.

[167] ZCP, XVII (1928), 137 (from LL, p. 380, col. a, ll. 53 f.).

The Leinstermen of the blades
Gave the kingship to the son of the king of Ireland.
Until Medb mated with that son
(He) Cormac was not king of Ireland.[168]

His conclusion is, "According to this series of traditions, Medb means nothing else than the sovereignty of Ireland." Ó Máille further shows that the metaphor of the "marriage" of a king to Ireland is common throughout Irish literature. Of his examples I will reprint two quotations from the Book of Leinster.[169] The first is: "The husband of Macha with great pride was the battle-head [i. e. Cimbaeth] of the Red Branch"; and the second: "Macha afterwards took Cimbaeth unto her as a husband." Later, as Ó Máille shows, she is called "Macha wife to Nemed." Cimbaeth and Nemed were successive conquerors of Ireland (Macha).[170]

The metaphor of Ireland as a lady married to a ruler is even more widespread in Irish literature than Ó Máille has shown. She appears under many different names: Caitilin ni Uallachain (as in Yeats's first play), Sighile ni Gara, Cailleach Bheara, etc. In the already quoted anthology by J. C. Mangan, *Poets and Poetry of Munster*,[171] she appears many times: For example (p. 101), Timothy O'Sullivan encounters a girl in a wood and kisses her. He asks, "Art thou Helen or Deirdre?" She replies, "My name is Éire." On page 118 Conor O'Riordan finds a damsel sleeping in a wood. "Banba and Éire I am called," she says. Conor O'Sullivan (p. 256) sees a lady who declares, "I am the

[168] Maura Power edits the verses from the *RIA* transcript of the Book of Lismore (*ZCP*, XI [1916], 43, 48).

[169] *LL*, p. 21, col. a, l. 43, and p. 20, col. b, l. 26.

[170] Pages 263, 44.

[171] Page 260.

wife of the long banished chiefs of this island." Donogh
O'Sullivan (p. 258) tells him, "That lady that spoke to
you was Banba." Kuno Meyer quotes King Diarmait mac
Cerbaill [172] as saying:

> I was the lawful bridegroom
> Of the beautiful daughter of Erimon.
> Clerics have thrust me
> From the rule of highland Fotla.
> Young, unlawful kings
> Will wash their shoes in her house.

It is clear that in this personification of Ireland as a lady we
have an ancient, and probably a distinguishing, characteristic of Irish fancy.

Medb's name is connected with the word "mead" and,
as Ó Máille shows, may mean "the intoxicating one." [173]
It is an appropriate name for an earth-goddess who is also
a goddess of plenty. Thurneysen has argued [174] that place-
names, such as Bile Medba, mentioned in the older text of
the *Táin Bó*, prove that she was anciently a goddess who
was worshipped under a *bile*, "great tree." Since he prints

[172] *Vision of MacConglinne* (London, 1892), p. 135 (quoting from *LL*,
p. 149, col. b). Diarmait reigned from 539 to 558. "To wash one's shoes"
meant to "make one's self at home." The idea is that other kings will
make themselves at home in Fotla's realm.

[173] This is W. Stokes' etymology (*Urkeltischer Sprachschatz* [Göt-
tingen, 1894], pp. 207–208 and note on p. 336). A. Holder (*Alt-Celtischer
Sprachschatz* [Leipzig, 1897], II, 528) connects Medb with * *medu(v)os*,
and quotes from a Gaulish inscription, *De(abus) Vercane et Medun(a)e*,
"to the goddesses of anger and of mead" (*Corpus inscrip. Rhenarum*,
ed. G. Brambach, p. 709).

[174] "Göttin Medb?" *ZCP*, XVIII (1930), 108. I would compare Kildare, "cell of the oak," which preserves the memory of a tree at the
shrine of the goddess Brigit. See also Thurneysen, *ZCP*, XIX (1933),
352.

the title of his article with a question mark after it, additional evidence may be assembled.

O'Davoren's *Glossary*, although warfare rather than food is under discussion, seems to connect Medb of Cruachan with abundance. The passage is:

> Sruth i. e. 'abundance,' that is 'a woman that turns a stream of warfare behind her' i. e. a princess . . . like Medb of Cruachan.[175]

Proof that Medb of Cruachan was essentially a *fée* may be found in the description of her palace and of her way of entertaining visitors. In the *Táin Bó Fraich*,[176] the account of Medb's palace, especially in two details — that it was illuminated by precious stones so brilliantly that night was like day, and that time passed in a supernatural way — corresponds to the description of an Irish *síd*. In *Fled Bricrend*, when Cuchulinn, Conall, and Laegaire arrive at Cruachan they are received exactly as at a fairy palace:

> Each hero chooses such as he prefers of one hundred and fifty girls, and all are brought into houses fitted with beds of surpassing magnificence. . . . Finnabair daughter of Ailill and Medb was brought to Cuchulinn. . . . Medb herself was wont to resort to Cuchulinn.[177]

Medb's palace is evidently an island of women like those described in the *imrama*.[178]

On the next day the heroes who have come to be judged

---

[175] Edition Stokes, *Archiv f. Celt. Lex.*, II, 449, § 1416.

[176] Edition Mary E. Byrne and Myles Dillon, Med. and Mod. Irish Series, V (Dublin, 1933), 3–5, §§ 8–12.

[177] Edition G. Henderson, *ITS*, II (London, 1899), 68, § 54, and 80, § 63.

[178] See pp. 271, 275.

by Medb are sent by her to Ercol, by Ercol to Samera, and by Samera, *cusna genitib glinni,* "to the evil spirits of the glens." Presumably all these creatures are subject to Queen Medb. In like manner the famous cats of Cruachan [179] which are "let loose upon the heroes" would seem to be under her control.

In the *Táin Bó* [180] Queen Medb consulted a prophetess who said: "I am a bondmaid among thy people, Feidelm, out of the *síd* of Cruachan, am I." This puts the *síd*-dwellers among Medb's subjects. It is true that the author of this passage regarded Medb as an historical person and did not make her live in the *síd.* Also in other places a distinction is drawn between Ailill and Medb, and the fairy folk. In *Echtra Nerai,*[181] Nera met the fairy king of Cruachan, who is plainly not Ailill, because Nera has just come from Ailill. Also in the *Táin Bó Fraich* the hero is carried by his mother and sister from Ailill and Medb into Síd Cruachan, which is thought of as a fairy palace. All this is true, but it in no way invalidates the evidence for the existence of a goddess or *fée* named Medb, from whom the historical Medb of Cruachan borrowed many of her exploits.

Perhaps the most conclusive evidence that Medb was in origin a *fée* may be gathered by anyone who will go through the *Táin Bó* and notice the marvelous part played by that stormy personage. Like Fergus and Manannán, and like the enormous horse in the *Dinnshenchas of Tuag Inber,*

---

[179] "Tri bíasta druidechta" (*Fled Bricrend,* p. 72, § 57; p. 84, § 66). Three she-wolves in the *Acallam* (ed. Stokes, ll. 7677 f.) are evidently the same. Modern stories make the "King of Cats" live at Cruachan.

[180] Edition Windisch, ll. 219–221.

[181] Edition Meyer, *Rev. celt.,* X (1889), 212 f.

she was of gigantic size. She gave names to natural objects and caused lakes to burst forth.[182]

According to the *Aislinge Aenguso*, a story of the ninth or tenth century,[183] the Dagda once went for help to Ailill and Medb. It is true that the help he received was in storming an elf mound; but, although this detail may not be primitive, the notion that the great Dagda should resort to Medb at all implies that she was in origin a goddess. The *Dinnshenchas of Snám dá én* [184] tells how Remur and Cael, two sons of Ailill and Medb, appeared in bird shape, and again in dog shape, shifting their form like fairy children. Medb has the all-compelling beauty of a *fée*. In the *Dinnshenchas of Fert Medba* it is said: "Such was the glory of Medb, and such the excellence of her form, that two-thirds of his valor was quelled in every man on beholding her." [185]

Like the Dagda and like Nuadu, Medb and Ailill stand in the first place in a number of Irish pedigrees. The Connaicne were descended from Fergus and Medb, and Thurneysen regards Fergus, whose name signifies "manly strength," [186] as a kind of "fertility god." The association of Medb and Fergus is probably mythological.[187] Fergus,

---

[182] Gwynn, *Met. Dinn.*, IV, 67; cf. *Táin Bó*, ed. Windisch, ll. 6082–6084, "siblais Medb a fual uathi co nderna tri tulchlassa mora de."

[183] Edition Ed. Müller, *Rev. celt.*, III (1876–1878), 344. On the date see Thurneysen, *Heldensage*, p. 301.

[184] Edition C. Marstrander, *Ériu*, V (1911), 222–225. Also Gwynn, *Met. Dinn.*, IV, 350–366.

[185] Gwynn, *Met. Dinn.*, IV, 366 (from *LL*, p. 203, col. b).

[186] ZCP, XVIII (1929), 108.

[187] Compare a passage in *Aided Ailella ocus Conaill Cernaig*, a text edited under the title *Goire Conaill* by Meyer in ZCP, I (1896), 104: "Mor tra cumachta ocus armitin ocus ordan inti Medba ocus ba mor a hacobur im gach ni .i. tricha fer cach lai do claemclodh di nó tagall Fergus(a) aonfecht."

a good-natured giant who had the strength of seven hundred men, and who owned the marvelous sword Caladbolg which could expand like a rainbow,[188] seems to be an older god, who was displaced by Conchobar, as Cronus was by Zeus. Fergus is, I suggest, the original of the old man at the Grail castle, the father of the Fisher King. The story is that Fergus married Nessa and promised Ulster to her son Conchobar for one year, and Conchobar retained the kingdom.[189]

Finally the Irish-speaking country folk preserve a memory that Medb was once a queen of the fairies. The figure that appears to Irish country folk today is no earthly queen, but brings with her splendors from another world.[190] These orally transmitted stories retain, I believe, the true doctrine about Queen Medb, which hardly appears in written Irish at all — at least not for hundreds of years. Queen Medb was one of "the ever-living ones," after

[188] *Táin Bó*, ed. Windisch, pp. 48, 872.

[189] See W. Stokes, *Lismore Lives*, p. xxxiv.

[190] W. B. Yeats, *Beltaine*, II (Feb., 1900), 16: "Maive (Medb is the Irish spelling) is continually described as the queen of all the western fairies. . . . But neither Maive, nor any of our Irish fairies are like the fairies of Shakespeare; for our fairies are never very little, and are sometimes taller and more beautiful than mortals. The greatest among them were the gods and goddesses of ancient Ireland, and men have not yet forgotten their glory. I recently described in the *North American Review* (Dec., 1899), pp. 169 and 862, a vision of Queen Maive that came to an old Mayo woman: 'She saw . . . the finest woman you ever saw traveling right across the mountain. The old woman covered her eyes. . . . The neighbors were wild with her for not waiting to see if there was a message, for they were sure it was Queen Maive who often shows herself to the pilots.' " Another vision of Queen Maive, seen by one Mary Battle near Knocknarea, is recorded by Yeats in *Autobiographies* (New York, 1926), p. 329. At Knocknarea near Sligo is a heap of stones which is called "Medb's Grave." (These references were kindly pointed out to me by Seán O'Faoláin.)

whom various historical queens were named. Medb was a
fée, like Etáin, the story of whose existence for more than
a thousand years is well known.[191]

THE HAG OF BEARE

It has not been, I think, before observed that *Cailleach
Bheara*, "The Hag of Beare," is another personification of
Ireland. The *Banshenchas* makes her "the wife of Fothaid
Canaan," [192] one of three Fothads, who, as has been shown,
are Brión, Iuchar, and Uar, under other names. "She had
seven periods of youth one after another, so that every man
reached death by old age before her." [193] Her many husbands have caused her to be defamed just as Queen Medb is
defamed. Meyer thought that the poem ascribed to her
in this manuscript indicated that she had been a courtesan
and was bewailing her former evil life. The poem begins:

> Once I was with kings
> Drinking mead and wine;
> Today I drink whey water
> Among withered old hags.

After what has been said it will be clear to everyone, I
suppose, that she is Ireland personified, and is lamenting
the kings of old time and contrasting them with contemporary loss of sovereignty in Ireland.[194]

[191] Thurneysen, *Heldensage*, pp. 598–616. See now *Ériu*, XII (1938),
154 f.

[192] Edition M. C. Dobbs, *Rev. celt.*, XLVII (1930), 302, 327. According to H. 3. 18, fol. 42, her name is Digdi.

[193] Meyer, *Vision of MacConglinne*, pp. 208–210; cf. Vernam Hull,
ZCP, XIX (1932), 174.

[194] Rhŷs and Brynmor-Jones (*The Welsh People*, pp. 58–60) say
that *Cailleach Bheara* "is probably to be identified with the *Beare* whom

Like other mythological characters, and like Queen Medb in the *Táin Bó*, the Hag of Beare gave names to natural objects. The cairns and inscribed stones on Lough Crew, a hill west of Kells, are said to have been built by her:

The Hag brought stones in her apron. She dropped one cairn on Carnbane, then jumped to the summit of *Slieve na Cailliagh*, "hill of the Hag," a mile distant and dropped another cairn there; then on to another hill in the neighborhood.[195]

Father O'Growney, after referring to this incident,[196] which he locates near Oldcastle, mentions other stories about the Hag, and about a stone called her "Bull," near Slyne Head in Connemara. Eleanor Hull also writes:

The Hag is equally well known in Scotland as a mountain-builder. All the hills of Rossshire were built by her, and Ben Wyvis was formed of rocks carried in her creel. . . . Once her creel upset . . . and formed Little Wyvis.[197]

---

certain stories make the daughter of a king of Spain, and wife of Eogan Mór or Mog Nuadat." Her name is often written Moméra. Since the wife of Nuadu is Ériu, this hints that the Hag of Beare is a personification of Ireland.

[195] Eleanor Hull, *Folk-Lore of the British Isles*, p. 52.

[196] K. Meyer, *Vision of MacConglinne*, pp. 132–134.

[197] *Folk-Lore*, p. 52. Eleanor Hull conjectures that the Hag of Beare was a goddess of winter, and Brigit of spring. Brigit and the Hag are mentioned together in MS. H. 3. 18. The Hag, Eleanor Hull thinks, became "The Nun of Beare," and Brigit "The Nun of Kildare." A preface to a poem printed by Meyer on the page referred to in the last note says: "The Hag of Beare was of the Corcaguiny. Of them was also Brigit daughter of Iustan." This association of Brigit and the Hag may be reminiscence that they were both once personifications of the land, and therefore, in a sense, identical. Douglas Hyde (*Legends of Saints and Sinners* [Dublin, 1915], pp. 183–185) says the Hag is called *Aine an chnuic*, "Aine of the hill," lives in *Teach Mór*, and is queen of the Limerick fairies. Elsewhere he says that the Hag is a terrible antagonist but may be subdued by the aid of her daughter. This daughter is very

The sisters Ériu, Banba, and Fodla were like the three sisters: Medb, Clothra, Deirbriu, and like Ana, Macha,[198] the Hag of Beare, Caitilin ni Uallachain and others, all virtually personifications of Ireland. Medb and her daughter Finnabair belong to Connacht, but were not always kept apart from the others.

QUEEN GUENEVERE

The three sisters, Medb, Clothra, and Deirbriu, with their three brothers, Breas, Nár, and Lothar, are merely the triple-formed Brigit, Ériu, Banba, and Fodla, and the triple-formed Brión, or Nuadu, under other names. King Arthur took over Nuadu's story, but he did not take over his three-formed queen, doubtless because Ériu, Banba, and Fodla rather definitely meant Ireland. Queen Medb of Connacht was also too well-known to become queen of Britain, but her daughter, Finnabair, was borrowed and became the Welsh Gwenhwyvar.

A Welsh triad [199] testifies that there were three Gwen-

ugly but Donnchadh Mór loves her and she becomes beautiful. J. Curtin (*Hero Tales*, p. xli) tells of another hag, Mór, wife to Ler, who, like Medb, made ravines on Mount Eagle.

[198] That Macha, wife of Nuadu, was a figure like Medb who personified the sovereignty, is shown by the account in *Tochmarc Emire* (ed. A. G. Van Hamill, *Compert Con Culainn*, etc., pp. 33–34, § 30). This tells that Macha, after the death of her father, seized the kingdom for herself for seven years. Later she exalted Cimbaeth to be her husband and king, and finally disguising herself as a leper (transformation of herself into a hag) subdued her other suitors. Stories like those told of the *Cailleach Bheara* are told in Wales of a giantess named Corwena, who is also said to have dropped piles of rocks from her apron.

[199] Loth, *Les Mabinogion*, II, 250; Rhŷs and Evans, *Red Book*, ᵀ, 302: Triad 21 reads: "Three principal ladies of the court of Arthur: Gwenhwyvar daughter of Gwryt Gwent; Gwenhwyvar daughter of Gwythyr ab Greidiawl; Gwenhwyvar daughter of Ocvran Gawr, 'the giant.'"

hwyvars. This statement finds so little support in Arthurian romance that it is probably old — a trace of an early Welsh legend that Queen Gwenhwyvar was three-formed. A later story about a true and a false Guenevere (in the Vulgate *Merlin* and the prose *Lancelot*) may have had its inception in the three Gueneveres of the Welsh triads.

Arthur's queen is as implacable and as fickle as the Irish Medb. She is best understood by being regarded as virtually the sovereignty or Logres personified, just as the Irish Medb was Connacht personified. That Finnabair is virtually the sovereignty personified explains the astonishing way in which in the *Táin Bó* she is offered by her mother, Medb, as a lure or bait to induce warriors to fight against Cuchulinn.

Finnabair is made up of *finn*, "white," and *siabar*, "phantom." Welsh Gwenhwyvar is a translation, composed of gwen, "white," and *hwyvar*, "phantom." The second part, *hwyvar*, was formerly doubted by Thurneysen [200] and others because it had never been observed as a word in Middle Welsh. Thurneysen, having found *hwyvar* written separately, has withdrawn his doubt,[201] and I think the

---

Triad 22 reads: "His three mistresses were: Indec daughter of Arwy Hir, 'the long'; Garwen daughter of Henen Hen, 'the old'; Gwyl daughter of Endawt."

[200] Thurneysen, ZCP, XII (1918), 282, n. 2. Cross and Nitze, *Lancelot and Guenevere* (1930), p. 58, n. 1.

[201] "Zu Nemnius (Nennius)," ZCP, XX (1933), 133, n. 1. "Zweitens ist mein Bedenken, ein selbständiges mkymr. hwyvar (ir. siabar) anzunehmen, geschwunden wegen der poetischen Trennung: 'agud gwenn hoewvud hwyfar' in einem Gedicht von Gronw Gyryoc, auf die Parry-Williams (*Bull. Board Celt. Stud.* I, 110) aufmerksam gemacht hat." Gronw Gyryoc died in 1360, and his poem is printed in the *Myvyrian Archaiology*, p. 332, col. 2.

derivation of Gwenhwyvar from Finnabair may be regarded as established.

This chapter shows that Nuadu, called Nodent by the Welsh, was an hypostasis of Brión, called Bran by the Welsh, a god and king of fairies. The story of Brión's voyage, or Nuadu's voyage, dominated Irish storytelling and was transferred to several Irish kings. St. Brendan has borrowed the adventures of Brión, just as St. Bridget has of Brig, or Brigit. King Arthur inherited the voyage story of Brión or Nuadu and was probably regarded by the Welsh as son and successor to the god. King Arthur was suddenly glorified by the Welsh into a sort of god and was given the adventures of a god.

This chapter also shows that a personification of Ériu as a lady was ancient and widespread. She was identified with Brigit who was Brión's mother and wife, and both were triformed. She was fought for by various claimants to the throne, was sometimes identical with the *fée* or heroine in Irish sagas, and bore many names: Banba, Fodla, Medb, Ana, Macha, the Hag of Beare, etc. Queen Medb's daughter, Finnabair, likewise represented the sovereignty and was the origin of Queen Guenevere. Guenevere inherited Medb's fickleness and was perhaps in popular lore her daughter.

CHAPTER XI

The Land of the Dead

LOCATION

WHAT was the location of the land of the dead in ancient Irish and Welsh story? A very old account is that of Plutarch, who on the authority of a traveler named Demetrius reported that the inhabitants of Great Britain located the land of the dead in adjacent small islands. After mentioning that the death of a great man caused a tempest among the islands Demetrius said: "There is one island where Cronus (τὸν Κρόνον) is prisoner, being guarded in his sleep by Briareus; for sleep has been devised as a chain to bind him, and there are many deities about him as satellites and attendants."[1] Sir E. K. Chambers has conjectured[2] that Cronus here may be Cernunnos, the three-headed squatting divinity who appears on Gallo-Roman altars with a cornucopia,[3] and who seems to be a kind of plenty-divinity like the Fisher King.

Although no part of the main argument, it is my conjecture that by some accident Cernunnos has given rise to the form Gornemant, which is the name that Chrétien

[1] Plutarch, De defectu oraculorum, chap. 18 (ed. Zwicker, Fontes historiae religionis Celticae [Berlin and Bonn, 1934–1936], I, 65). The antiquity of Plutarch's story seems to be proved by Pliny's mention of "Mare Cronium" (Hist. naturalis, IV, 27 [Leipzig: Teubner, 1906], I, 344).

[2] Arthur of Britain, p. 230.

[3] E. Espérandieus, Recueil gén. des bas-reliefs (Paris, 1907–1928), IV, 3133, 3210. See also d'Arbois, Cours, II, 384.

applies to Perceval's second Host. Cernunnos is then one of the three forms of Nuadu or Bran who in *Branwen Daughter of Llyr* is only a head. It is a part of this conjecture that the Welsh Bran was at first not a mere head but a wounded person like the Fisher King. Bran was, I suppose, represented in a crouching position like the Gaulish gods and like the Buddha. The notion that he was a dissevered head was introduced by some narrator who sought in this way to explain Bran's short stature.

Plutarch's account as quoted above may be a very old form of the Grail story.[4] If so, Cronus asleep on a couch would be Nuadu, or the Fisher King, and Briareus would be the Fomorian giant, Balar.

Another ancient writer, Procopius,[5] relates that "fishermen, farmers, and merchants" dwelling on the sea are sometimes awakened at midnight and compelled to ferry boatloads of souls over to an island which he calls Βριττία which is divided into two parts by a wall:

West of this wall the air is so unwholesome that no man can live there half and hour. Serpents, adders, and evil beasts dwell there. The most remarkable thing is that, as the natives say, if a man goes for a walk on the west side of the wall he falls dead at once, because he cannot endure the pestilential air;

---

[4] A lost Gawain story, all too briefly outlined by Pierre Bersuire (c. 1360), may possibly be another glimpse of the Grail castle. As quoted by Kittredge (*Gawain*, p. 180), it is in brief: Gawain found himself by chance in an underwater palace from which he could see no exit; before him was a table set, but when he would eat, the head of a dead man stuck on a pike, and a giant lying on a couch before a fire, appeared and forbade him. Bersuire is too brief to be clear, but the head on a pike might be Bran, and the giant might be forbidding Gawain to eat, just as in a story quoted below from Andreas Cappelanus a giant forbids a visitor to eat (see p. 347).

[5] *De bello Gothico*, IV, 20 (ed. Zwicker, *Fontes*, II, 170–172).

likewise if beasts go there, at once death seizes upon them. . . .
To this region, say the natives, the souls of the dead are brought.

Procopius appears to say that the souls are carried from
France to Great Britain. The wall is doubtless a confused
reminiscence of the Wall of Severus, and is probably a
later addition which has confused the geography.

The source of Procopius' story is doubtless to be found
in a fragment of Plutarch's commentary on Hesiod, in
which there is no wall. This fragment, which is preserved
by Tzetzès,[6] runs as follows:

On the ocean strand opposite Βρεταννίαν dwell certain fishermen. They hear a voice calling them and a knock at the door.
Rising from their beds, they find at the shore unfamiliar boats
heavily laden. They grasp the oars and in one hour are across,
although their own boats would require a day and a half. When
they arrive, although they see nobody, they hear a voice calling
out the names of those who disembark.

That the dead are received at once by name, in an island,
by those whom they formerly knew is a Celtic idea,[7] but it
would naturally imply an island smaller than Great Britain.
This story probably reflects an Irish belief that the souls
were ferried to a small island. The fishermen who transport
the souls in this story are in all probability a confused
reminiscence of the Irish myth of the triple-formed fisherman or navigator, Brión, who managed a boat on the river
of death. This myth was no doubt a part of Celtic pagan
religion and was known to everybody. Another reminis-

[6] Zwicker, III, 271 (see p. 134).
[7] E. Brugger (ZFS, XXVIII [1905], 66 f.) remarks about this passage
that, although Procopius is not good authority on Celtic history, he invented none of his legends and must certainly have had a Celtic basis
for this account.

cence of it is the story already mentioned [8] which is preserved in the Irish *LG* and which tells of "three fishermen from Spain, who came to Ireland before the Flood." These fishermen are, I think, the triformed god, Brión, who like Charon, ferried visitors over the river of death and afterwards entertained them.

Chrétien's Fisher King who, as has been argued above, was in origin the Irish Brión, gives Perceval directions from a boat and afterwards entertains him. In the Chastel Merveilleus part of *Perceval*, AA, a *notonier* [9] ferries Gawain over a dreadful river and then entertains him. Heinrich calls this ferryman Karadas,[10] which is a probable Welsh corruption of the name Charon. In the rather late Irish story, P, outlined above,[11] Teigue on visiting the islands of the dead finds his own brother Eogan ferrying visitors across from one island to another. In the later Finn saga, Conan becomes a kind of Charon who ferries visitors to the land of the dead.[12]

The ancient Irish put the land of the dead at *Tech Duinn*, a little island southwest of Kerry,[13] where Donn, the leader of the sons of Míl was buried, or, according to some, where he still ruled. It is shown south of Ireland on the map, page 343. Donn was the Irish king of the dead and was, or became, a Fomorian. By the time that Giolla Coemhain

---

[8] Page 249. Of course, stories of ferrying souls across a water are widespread. For example, a fisherman at Speier on the Rhine one night ferried over mysterious persons dressed like monks (J. L. and W. Grimm, *Deutsche Sagen*, no. 276, 3d ed. [Berlin, 1891], p. 187).

[9] Page 138.

[10] Edition Scholl, *Diu Crône*, vs. 16726.

[11] Page 87.

[12] D. MacConmara, *Eachtra Ghiolla an Amárain* (ed. T. Flannery [Dublin, 1901]).

[13] Page 257.

LOCHLANN
OR
NORWAY

ORKNEY

(ALBANIA)

GORRE

LOTHAIN

TORY IS.

GALLOWAY ×××××× HADRIAN'S
WALL

.TARA

ERIU

LOGRES

.CAERLEON

TECH DUINN

GALLIA

wrote (c. 1072) the land of the dead had been moved to Tory Island. It is shown north of Ireland on the map (page 343). Sometimes the land of the dead was put in the Orcades, which popular etymology connected with Orcus or Hades, and more commonly in Lochlann or Norway because the Norwegian pirates had been identified with the hateful Fomorians. Irish stories H and R summarized above [14] call Fomorian land, or the land of the dead, Lochlann.

The early Welsh or British put the land of the dead north of the Roman Wall in Galloway, Lothain, and Gorre. A reference to the supposed deadly character of the country north of the wall has been quoted. They also, like the Irish, located the land of the dead in the Orcades or in Norway. Loth, according to different authorities, was king of Lothain, of the Orkneys, and of Norway. His son Gawain was ruler of Galloway. Lot ("destruction") was apparently a mythical king of the dead. In *Perceval*, AA, Galloway is the land of the dead and Arthur is holding court in the Orkneys.

It is worth remarking that for the Irish the land of the Tuatha Dé was Ireland, and for the Welsh the land of Arthur was Logres, or Britain.

ARTHUR AND THE LAND OF THE DEAD

Evidence was brought forward in Chapter IV, above, to show that Arthur, Gornemant, and the Fisher King, in the first part of *Perceval*, are three forms of the god Nuadu or Brión. They are different manifestations of one supernatural being. Since the Fisher King is generally recog-

[14] Pages 66, 81.

nized to be under an enchantment resembling death,[15] it follows that Arthur must be likewise at times thought of as a ghost or dream king.

Light on this elusive relationship existing between Arthur and the Fisher King may be found in two stories told by Andreas Capellanus (c. 1174–1186). In these stories Arthur and the god of love are doublets. Each lives in a similar mysterious palace, and each gives out the laws of love. Arthur is not the god of love, and yet in the second story he seems to have taken his place. The thirty-one rules were dictated by the god of love, it is said, but they are given out in Arthur's palace.

These stories are Journeys to Fairyland, and, although they were probably known to Chrétien, they have never been used to clarify our idea of what the scenario of such a story was like when it came into his hands. The first may be based entirely upon Continental allegory. The second must have had for its immediate source something from Welsh or Irish. The palace in the first story is in the land of the dead; presumably in the second story it is in fairyland. In both stories the palace is rectangular and is inhabited by a great multitude of women. If Andreas did not mean the square-cornered palace in the two stories to be the same palace, it is clear that anyone retelling the stories might easily confuse them. The first story I may call "The Twelve Precepts of Love": [16]

---

[15] Heinrich in *Diu Crône* makes his Fisher King say to Gawain:

> "Ich bin tôt, swie ich nicht tôt schîn
> Unde daz gesinde mîn
> Daz ist ouch tôt mit mir." (Ed. Scholl, vss. 29532–29534)

[16] My summary from the text of *De amore*, ed. E. Trojel (Copenhagen, 1892), pp. 89–107, 296–312. Cf. ed. Amadeo Pagès, Latin text (Castellón de la Plana, 1929), pp. 45–54, 152–161. A translation by

A man tells the story as follows. In the center of the world is a palace [17] having four fronts and a gate in each front. In the palace dwell the god of love and an assembly of ladies. The east gate belongs to the god of love alone; the south gate to those ladies that love wisely, the west to those who love immodestly, and the north to those who love not at all.

The man goes on to say: One day I was on horseback with my master, Knight Robert, in the royal forest of France and lost my way. I saw a great train of folk. First rode a man wearing a diadem, followed by a band of ladies splendidly dressed and attended; then a second band of ladies without magnificence; finally, a third band wretchedly mounted. I spoke to a lady of the last band. She said: Hic, quem vides, est exercitus mortuorum. I was terrified, but she reassured me, explaining that the leader was the god of love and the three trains of ladies were identical with the three companies of the south, west, and north gates of the palace.

The story then narrates at length, in episodes that seem imitated from visions of purgatory, the punishments of those ladies who do not love. Finally the god of love gives the man the Twelve Precepts of Love.

The second story I may call "The Thirty-one Rules of Love":

A Brittanniae miles goes into the royal forest to find King Arthur [18] and meets a damsel of wonderful beauty on horseback. She knows his errand and tells him that he can obtain it only by her help. At his request she tells him his errand,

---

J. J. Parry (New York: Columbia University Press, 1941) comes to me too late to be used. W. A. Neilson has compared to these "Twelve Precepts," the "Laws of Arthur's Round Table" ("The Origins and Sources of the Courts of Love," [Harvard] *Studies and Notes*, VI [1899], 201).

[17] This is the rectangular cosmic palace facing the four winds.

[18] Like the Grail King, Arthur is here the object of a quest.

namely: "A domina Brittaniae has promised him her love if
he will fetch her a hawk that sits upon a golden pole in Arthur's
hall," and adds, "To get the hawk you must prove in battle
that you have a more beautiful lady than has any knight in
Arthur's hall. To enter Arthur's hall you must have the
chirotheca [gauntlet] belonging to the hawk. To get the
gauntlet you must subdue two warriors." The damsel then gives
the knight her horse which will carry him to the desired place
and bestows on him a kiss so that he can say that he has the
love of a more beautiful lady.

He comes to a wide deep river over which he finds a golden
bridge. The bridge rests upon the water in the middle and at
each end is a hostile warrior. He slays the first defender. The
second, who is a giant, shakes the bridge so that it is for the
most part under water, but the knight, trusting to his horse,
crosses and finally drowns the giant. In a flowery meadow is a
round palace with no entrance. Scattered about the meadow
are silver tables upon which are all kinds of meat and drink
and *gausapes* ("white napkins"). There are also silver bowls
containing food and drink for horses. He lets his horse feed
and walks round the palace. Seeing nobody, he begins to eat.
Forthwith a door opens with a thunderous clang and a giant
brandishing a copper club assails him:

"Who are you, O man of such presumption that you were
not afraid to intrude into this royal palace and boldly and
impudently to eat from the royal table of the warriors? . . .
O foolish one! What madness possessed you, Briton! For
sooner could you be dead ten times and come to life again
than obtain those things which you mention."

The knight and giant fight. The knight cuts off the giant's
arm and forces him to relinquish the gauntlet which is hanging upon the central pillar of the palace. The knight goes
forward on his horse to another meadow where is a golden
palace six hundred cubits long and two hundred wide; it has
many rooms and is adorned with precious stones. On a golden

throne sits Arthur and about him countless beautiful ladies. In the palace are the hawk and two tied dogs which are guarded by twelve warriors. The knight shows the gauntlet and is admitted, but must fight to prove his lady is the most beautiful. After his victory he takes the hawk and the dogs, and a voice bids him take the rules of love "quas ipse amoris rex ore proprio amatoribus edidit."

He returns with these treasures to the damsel of the forest, who gives him a kiss and declares that any time he will come alone to the forest she will appear to him. Finally he delivers the hawk and the Thirty-one Rules of Love to the lady who sent him, who rewards him.

In this second story the marks of the land of the dead are the death-horse which knows the way and which corresponds to Gawain's *roncin* in AA and to the cart in *Lancelot*; [19] the wide, deep river which is crossed by a perilous bridge; the giant at the bridge corresponding to Cerberus; the round tower with no entrance; and the meadow with food guarded by a giant, which is the garden beside a Dolorous Tower. Arthur's rectangular palace corresponds to a Castle of Maidens. With its many rooms, its precious jewels, and its countless ladies, it is doubtless the cosmic palace of the dead.

Numerous references to Arthur in the years following Chrétien imply that he belongs to the land of the dead, and has established for himself a kingdom there. Such are the accounts of his leading the wild hunt, and those of his living beneath Mount Aetna,[20] where he issues commands

[19] Pages 137, 100.

[20] Gervase of Tilbury, *Otia imperialia*, decisio II, cap. 12, ed. F. Liebrecht (Hannover, 1856), pp. 12–13. Caesarius of Heisterbach, *Dialogus miraculorum*, dist. XII, cap. 12, ed. J. Strange (Cologne, Bonn, and Brussels, 1851), II, 325.

like a god whom it is death to disobey. Such is, I think, a plain inference from the belief that Arthur was lord of the Antipodes.[21] Such is also the story of his dwelling in a hollow hill with Juno, Felicia, and St. Brendan.[22]

Chaucer knew that King Arthur was in fairyland, and that Britain of long ago was considered identical with fairyland. He writes in his *Canterbury Tales:*

> That Gawain, with his olde curteisye,
> Though he were come ageyn out of Fairye.

> In th' olde dayes of the King Arthour
> Al was this land fulfild of fayerye.

He also knew that fairyland was confused with the land of the dead:

> No man but Launcelot, and he is deed.

> Pluto, that is the king of fayerye.

> Pluto, and his quene Proserpina, and al her fayerye.[23]

Dunbar, writing a little later, called Pluto "an elrich incubus in cloak of green," [24] and thus refused to keep the underworld apart from fairyland.

THE DEATH-HORSE

In most of the Irish and Welsh stories outlined, the hero goes to fairyland by boat. In the only story in which he

---

[21] This belief has recently been well set forth by R. S. Loomis, although he does not infer as above ("King Arthur and the Antipodes," *Mod. Phil.,* XXXVIII (1941), 289–304).

[22] *Wartburgkrieg,* ed. Karl Simrock (Stuttgart, 1858), stanzas 83–87.

[23] W. W. Skeat, *The Complete Works of Chaucer* (Oxford University Press, 1900), IV, 464, 345, 469, 454, 449; F95, D857, F287, E2227, and E2038.

[24] Edition J. Small, *Scottish Text Society* (Edinburgh, 1893), II, 5.

travels mounted, he is mocked by the bystanders. This is in *Tochmarc Emire*, E, where Cuchulinn rides upon "a dreadful beast like a lion," and youths at play "laugh at the sight of a hurtful beast doing service to a man." [25]

In Chrétien's romances, however, in most of the episodes summarized, the hero rides toward fairyland upon a horse and is derided by the spectators:

U. "Disoient tuit: Haï, Haï, chevaliers!" (*Erec*, vs. 5705)

V. "Ainz le huient petit et grant." (*Lancelot*, vs. 409)

X. "Hu! Hu! maleüreus, ou vas?" (*Yvain*, Pesme avanture, vs. 5131)

AA. " 'Ha! certes, or va bien la chose!'
        Fet la pucele ranposneuse." (*Perceval*, vss. 7178–7179)

The last quotation is of great interest because in it Gawain on his way toward a dreadful river is forced to ride upon an exceedingly wretched nag. The beast was thin and bony, "his crupper was emaciated . . . his bridle was made of string and there was no saddle-cloth." [26] To explain this detestable nag my hypothesis is that the animal has borrowed traits from death's skeleton horse [27] and from the ugly death-cart of popular superstition.

My hypothesis will explain the wretched horse upon which in several romances the hero rides on his way to fairyland. In *Graelent*, for example, the hero on setting out is derided by the people on account of his miserable mount: [28]

---

[25] Page 48.

[26] *Perceval*, vss. 7170–7174.

[27] Compare the emaciated horses in illustrations to Petrarch, *Triumph of Death* (*I Trionfi* [Firenze, 1599], facsimile [Rome, 1891]).

[28] Edition E. Margaret Grimes, *Desiré, Graelent, and Melion*, Inst. of French Studies (New York, 1928), p. 82.

Cil et celes qui l'esgarderent
L'escarnirent moult et gaberent.
(vss. 201–202)

Much the same thing happens in the English *Sir Launfal*: [29]

He rood with lytyll pryde;
Hys hors slod and fel yn þe fen,
Wherefore hym scornede many men
Abowte hym fere and wyde.
Pouerly þe knyght to hors gan sprynge;
For to dryue away lokynge,
He rood toward þe west.
(vss. 213–219)

In both romances it is explained that extreme poverty prevents the knight from procuring proper equipment. This
interpretation is inadequate, whereas my hypothesis of a
borrowing from the bony horse of death will account both
for the bad horse and for the derision of the spectators.[30]
In *Eger and Grime* the hero rides to the abode of Lillias on
a horse which he finds ready for the journey and which
vanishes at the journey's end.[31] The horse is thus described:

He was right lean but he was wight
He had gone bridled dayes nine,
For fault of food was like to tine.
(vss. 230–232)

[29] Edition French and Hale, *Middle Eng. Met. Romances*, p. 352.
[30] Evidently in the French *Lanval* a similar bad horse bears the hero
to fairyland, for there is one line, "Sis chevals tremble forment" (ed.
K. Warnke, *Die Lais der Marie de France* [Halle, 1925], p. 88, vs. 46),
which in the context is unintelligible, unless it be a reference to a
miserable horse like those in *Graelent* and *Sir Launfal*.
[31] Edition J. R. Caldwell, p. 195; compare p. 120.

In the late Irish story, *Gilla Decair*, Conan and fourteen others are borne away to fairyland on the back of a great bony horse: "Shambling upon weedy legs, and wearing a rude iron halter. . . . The Fianna guffawed with a shout of mockery, flouting Conan." [32]

In *Perceval* the hero has a good horse, but not so in *Peredur* or *Parzival*. In *Peredur* when the hero rides into Arthur's hall on a bony horse, Cai exclaims: "You come too ill-furnished with horse and arms" and "the bodyguard began to deride and hurl sticks at him." [33] My hypothesis would explain Peredur's imitation bridle "made out of twigs" [34] and Parzival's "rough, hempen bridle," [35] as derived originally from the rude iron halter of the death-horse.

Emaciated horses harnessed to the death-wagon are often described in Breton tales. A workman returning late met the dreaded vehicle:

Il vit déboucher les chevaux, puis la charette. Ils étaient terriblement maigres et efflanqués, ces chevaux. . . . Quant à la charette, elle avait pour fond quelques planches disjointes; deux claies branlantes lui servaient de rebords.[36]

THE DOLOROUS TOWER

In Journey to Fairyland stories the Dolorous Tower and the Castle of Maidens are borrowed from the land of the

---

[32] Edition and translation by S. H. O'Grady, *Silva Gadelica*, I, 259, 262; II, 294, 297.

[33] *Mab.*, II, 78; compare pp. 143 and 149.

[34] *Mab.*, II, 78, 140.

[35] Wolfram, *Parzival*, vs. 144, 23.

[36] A. LeBraz, *La Légende de la Mort chez les bretons armoricains*, (Paris, 1922), I, 121. Compare P. Sébillot, *Traditions et superstitions de la Haute-Bretagne* (Paris, 1882), I, 208. A similar belief exists in Ireland (LeBraz, I, 115, n. 2) and in Celtic Spain (C. Cabal, *La Mitologia asturiana*

dead. In regard to the first it is probable that the heads on pikes, sometimes seen at the Dolorous Tower, connect themselves with the *char de la mort*. Let us read another Breton account of that terrible vehicle:

Un char de structure grossière. . . . Les montants étaient à claire-voie; entre les barreaux pendaient au dehors des jambes, des bras, voire des têtes, des têtes humaines, jaunes, grimançantes, hideuses.[37]

This wagon with heads protruding suggests the heads projecting above the walls of the tower of the dead.[38]

Not unlike this is the superstition that death or Charon retains the horse of a victim as payment.[39] In AA the *notonier* at the dreadful river is accustomed to keep the horse of a vanquished knight as his perquisite.[40] He is persuaded, however, to accept, in lieu of Gawain's steed Gringalet, the knight conquered by Gawain (Greoreas' nephew) as prisoner. In *Yvain*, Calogrenant's horse is taken from him by the red giant Esclados, who, as we have seen,

---

[Madrid, 1925], I, 67). See also W. B. Yeats, *Irish Fairy and Folk Tales* (London, 1907), p. 108 (introductory note to *banshee* chapter).

[37] LeBraz, *La Légende*, I, 128.

[38] In R.N.S. Ralston, *Russian Folk-Tales* (London, 1873), p. 153, the Baba Yaga (female devil or principle of evil) has her house fenced round by the bones of men she has devoured. On top of the fence are stuck "human skulls with eyes in them." In A. Amelung and O. Jänicke, *Deutsches Heldenbuch*, II (Berlin, 1873), *Wolfdietrich*, D VI, 8 f, "Beliân der rîche" is lord of a castle bristling with heads on spikes. Beliân has an idol "daz heizt der Tod" which Wolfdietrich demolishes. The name probably hints that it is a castle of the dead.

[39] In German tales, dwarves pay a cowherd for ferrying them across a river by giving him a dead horse or the leg of a horse (A. Kuhn, *Norddeutsche Sägen* [Leipzig, 1848], no. 291, p. 260). Cf. H. Plischke, *Die Sage vom wilden Heere im deutschen Volke* (Eilenburg, 1914), p. 72.

[40] *Perceval*, vss. 7372–7447.

represents the king of the dead. In *Le Bel Inconnu*,[41] Lanpars retains the horses of vanquished knights.

More common is the notion that Charon retains a part of the body as his payment. It was a pagan custom to bury wooden hands and feet with a corpse for the ferryman to take instead of the real ones.[42] A watchman demands hand and foot as price of admission to Laurin's Rosengarten.[43] A ferryman makes a similar demand at Gibich's Rosengarten.[44] Sir Grey Steel in *Eger and Grime*[45] cuts off the little fingers of those knights, including Sir Eger, whom he has conquered. Sir Grey Steel is a red knight, and his mysterious land has borrowed features from the land of the dead.

It is my suggestion that the heads on pikes at the Dolorous Tower were in origin a form of this tribute of a part of the body. The demand for a head may have been softened in later times to an arm, a finger, or even, as I venture to suppose, to a beard. That the demand for a beard is an attenuation of the exaction of a hand or foot seems to me to be proved by the account in *Perlesvaus* of the castle of the beards.[46] It appears that at this castle some knights have lost, not a beard, but a nose, an eye, a hand, a foot, or even have been beheaded. The place seems to be a castle of the dead.

The well-known castle of the beards told of by Geoffrey[47] belonged to the giant Ritho who demanded King

---

[41] Edition G. P. Williams (Paris, 1929), vs. 2535. Cf. *Yvain*, vs. 544.

[42] J. Grimm, *Deutsche Mythologie*, 4th ed. (Berlin, 1878), III, 404; "Indiculus . . . de ligneis pedibus vel manibus pagano ritu."

[43] *Germania*, I (1856), 433.

[44] W. Grimm, *Rosengarte* (Göttingen, 1836), p. lxxiv.

[45] Edition J. R. Caldwell, pp. 192–193, vss. 190 f. See also p. 189, vs. 137.

[46] Edition Nitze and Jenkins, ll. 2714, 2767, 6439 f.

[47] *Historia*, bk. x, chap. 3, p. 473.

Arthur's beard. Ritho, as is shown on a later page,[48] is the same as Chrétien's Rion, king of isles, and must be identical with the Irish Balar, king of isles. Balar was king of the dead, and no doubt Ritho also, which corroborates my suggestion that the castle of beards was a Dolorous Tower.

Chaucer introduces both the round Dolorous Tower and the square Castle of Maidens into his *House of Fame*, but he brings in his square "House of Fame" first, and describes his revolving "House of Tidings" later. He also makes the revolving castle sixty miles long, which is evidence, no doubt, of some confusion.

The *Elucidation* mentions the two castles, but calls the tower of the dead not Castel Doloreus but Castel Orguel-lous: [49]

> Et fisent pour les damoseles
> Le rice Castel as Pucieles;
> Cil fisent le Pont Perellous
> Et le grant Castel Orguellous.
>
> (vss. 407–410)

Geoffrey of Monmouth in his *Historia* mentions the two castles, although perhaps he regarded them as identical: "Oppidum montis agned quod nunc castellum puellarum dicitur et montem dolorosum." [50] It did not occur to Geoffrey, of course, that these places were in the land of the dead. He locates them at Edinburgh, which is beyond the Roman Wall in Lothain, and therefore, according to ancient British belief, was in the land of the dead.

The oldest known reference to the tower of the dead is in Pindar: ʹΕτειλαν Διὸς ὁδὸν παρὰ Κρόνου τύρσιν. "[The

---

[48] Page 404. See Chrétien's *Perceval*, vs. 851.

[49] A. Hilka, *Perceval*, p. 427.

[50] Bk. II, chap. 7, p. 259: see p. 374.

dead] pass by the highway of Zeus to the tower of Cronus"
[on the way to the blessed isles].[51] This is good topography.
The ghosts come first to the tower of the dead because
this revolving tower "belongs to the same general category
as perpetually slamming doors and clashing cliffs (*symple-
gades*)," [52] and is an obstacle to be passed at the entrance to
the land of the dead.

Very often in the romances the hero comes first to the
tower of the dead. In the second story from Andreas
Capellanus outlined above [53] the hero comes first to a round
palace with no apparent entrance from which emerges a
giant bearing a copper club. Afterwards the hero comes
to the square-cornered Castle of Maidens or castle of the
fées. In *Perlesvaus*,[54] *Perceval* rides through a turning
castle to reach the Isle of Elephants, where he slays the
Knight of the Dragon and frees the Queen of the Golden
Circlet. Afterwards he comes to the Grail castle. In *La
Mule sanz Frain*,[55] Gawain rides into a revolving castle, cuts
off an opponent's head, and later rescues a queen. In *Le
Bel Inconnu*,[56] the hero comes first to the castle of Lanpars,
whom he must fight, and afterwards to the Waste City.

Chrétien probably did not understand the two castles,
but, by analogy from the romances just referred to, we
can see that in *Yvain*, W, if we omit introductory incidents, the hero comes first to the tower of the dead with its

---

[51] Edition Sir John Sandys, Loeb Classical Library, *Olympian Odes*
(London, 1915), ode II, ll. 70, 74.

[52] Quoted from Kittredge, *Gawain*, p. 245.

[53] Page 346.

[54] Edition Nitze and Jenkins, I, 247 f., ll. 5700 f. (see also their note II,
316).

[55] Edition R. T. Hill (Baltimore, 1911), p. 32, vss. 454 f.

[56] Edition G. P. Williams, vss. 2490–2780.

terrible iron portcullis that cuts his horse in two, and then reaches the adjoining castle of Lunete and Laudine, which is the Castle of Maidens. In *Perceval*, Chrétien mentions no Dolorous Tower near the Grail castle, but Wolfram preserves a trace of it. When Parzival approaches the Grail castle in AB, he comes first to a tower "shaped as if turned in a lathe. Unless an enemy flew in or was borne in by the wind, it could not be stormed" [so round and smooth it was].[57] Afterwards he enters the great square hall of the Grail castle.

In the Chastel Merveilleus part of *Perceval*, AA, Gawain comes first to a Dolorous Tower. It is reached by a bridge consisting of a plank and is called a garden, but, as has been argued above, it is evidently the Castle of Orquelenes, a deformation of Orcus. Some verses in Wolfram's *Parzival* descriptive of this castle, which, although he calls it Lôgroys, must be Chrétien's Orquelenes, have been interpreted by Heinzel and with apparent independence by Singer [58] to mean that it was once a revolving tower.

Revolving towers in Irish before the time of Chrétien are the fiery revolving rampart in the thirty-second island of *Imram Maeile Dúin* [59] and Cu Roi's revolving fort in *Fled Bricrend*.[60]

[57] Edition E. Martin, I, 80, and see his note, II, 210:
> "Si stuont reht als si wære gedræt.
> Ez enflüge od hete der wint gewæt,
> Mit sturme ir niht geschadet was."
> (vss. 226, 15–226, 17)

[58] *Sitzungsberichte der Wiener Akademie der Wiss.*, phil.-hist. Klasse, CXXX (1893), 92 f. and CLXXX, iv (1916), 80 f. The verses are:
> "Nâch trendeln mâze was ir berc:
> Swâ si verre sach der tumbe,
> Er wând si liefe alumbe." (vss. 508, 2 f.)

[59] Page 275.   [60] Edition G. Henderson, *ITS*, II, 103, § 80.

Prester John had a turning castle; [61] so did Hugo in the *Pèlerinage de Charlemagne*, but there is considerable agreement that the revolving castle came into Arthurian romance from Irish.[62]

An idea that the castle of the king of the dead revolves turns up in various lands. Such a revolving house belonging to the king of the dead appears in the *Kalevala*. Lowytar, daughter of Tuoni, the king of the dead, turns round a dungeon beneath a rock at the junction of three arms of the Tuoni River.[63] In Russian folk tales the evil principle, a snake, lives in a revolving house that stands on hen's legs.[64] In a Hungarian tale a dragon who rules the land of the dead lives in a copper fortress that turns on a goose-leg.[65]

The Castle of Maidens

It has not before been noticed that the Castle of Maidens and the Grail castle are both square. First may be considered some examples of the fairy palace.

In the first example it is not said that the fairy palace is square but that the island upon which it stood is square. The passage is in the seventh-century *Imram Brain*, where a *fée* who is inviting Bran to the Isle of Women sings to

[61] F. Zarncke, *Abhandlungen d. k. Sächs. Ges. d. Wiss.*, phil.-hist. Klasse (Leipzig, 1876), VIII, 166, § 33.

[62] J. D. Bruce (*Mod. Phil.*, X [1912], 522) followed G. Huet (*Romania*, XL [1911], 235 f.), in conceding that the turning castle in the *Pèlerinage* seems less original and lacks the magic atmosphere of the Irish stories. Compare R. S. Loomis, *Romanic Review*, XXXII (1941), 21.

[63] J. M. Crawford, *Translation of the Kalevala* (New York and London, 1888), I, XXVIII; II, 657–658, rune 45.

[64] Ralston, *Russian Folk-Tales*, pp. 67, 144; R. N. Bain, *Russian Fairy-Tales* (London, 1901), pp. 44, 99, 125.

[65] W. H. Jones, *Folk-lore of the Magyars*, Folk-Lore Society (London, 1889), pp. 78–79.

him a number of stanzas of which the second is as follows:

> There is distant isle
> Round which sea-horses glisten
> A fair course against the white-swelling surge
> Four feet uphold it.[66]

The grotesqueness of Irish fancy here astonishes us, but there can be no mistake. The sixth stanza repeats the idea: "Feet of white bronze were under the island." Since the island stood upon four bronze legs, it most likely was a square island.

In *Créde Daughter of Cairbre*, L, it is definitely said that her palace is square: "A hundred feet in Créde's house from one angle till you reach another." [67]

A poem of twelve lines beginning "Measurement of Mac ind Oc's house" tells us that this most famous of fairy dwellings had four doors, and, since only one measurement is given, it was probably square. The poem exists in sixteenth-century manuscripts, but it appears to be *bona fide* Irish and shows no trace of influence from French romances. It may be translated as follows: [68]

> The measurement of Mac ind Óc's house,
> A length without harm, with hosts of treasures,

---

[66] Possibly the feet are a *Märchen* symbol for the land of the dead; they suggest the house on fowl's legs in fairy tales. (On *Imram Brain* see p. 271.)

[67] "Céd traiged i tigh Créidhi ón chuirr gu roich a chéle," *Acallam*, ed. Stokes, l. 804. Translated by O'Grady, *Silv. Gad.*, II, 120.

[68] For valuable suggestions in this translation I am indebted to Dr. Vernam Hull. The text as printed by Kuno Meyer (ZCP, VIII [1912], 108) is as follows:

> Tomus tighe mec ind Ócc,
> fót cen bine buidnib sét,

Between two walls it extended
More than seven feet, more than seven hundred.

Four doors lead into it without grief;
[People] there are drinking through long ages.
[It has] copper towers since it is fair;
Music is under the thatches of birds' feathers.

There is a vat of silver — great its content —
A throng stands above it without any silence;
There is room for one hundred and forty [people];
The caldron is large enough to contain one
    hundred and sixty wild boars.

(vss. 1–12)

In the Book of Taliesin is the oldest Welsh account of
the castle of fairyland which nobody supposes has been
influenced in any way by French romances. The *Preiddeu
Annwn* here, among eight other names, twice calls the
castle of Annwn, *pedryvan*, "four-cornered." [69] This four-

---

etir dá fraigid rosíacht,
mó secht traigid, mó secht cét.

Cethri dorais ind cen brón,
bith oc ól tria bitha sír,
turib ciprib, úair is cæm,
cóel fo tuighib d'itib én.

Dabuch deargiubair mór lucht,
slóg óss a ucht cen nach socht,
suide fichet co ba secht,
coire cert ocht fichet torc.

(vss. 1–12)

[69] Edition J. G. Evans, *The Text of the Book of Taliesin,* Old Welsh
Texts, IX (Llanbedrog, 1910), 54, l. 25; 55, l. 9. His translation is in his
Poems from the Book of Taliesin (Llanbedrog, 1915), p. 126, ll. 12, 24.
See, above, p. 305, and, on Nennius, p. 253.

cornered castle [Castle of Maidens] is beyond *Kaer Wydyr*, "glass castle," with a "silent sentinel." The latter is, doubtless, a Dolorous Tower, like that told of by Nennius.

In agreement with these descriptions of the fairy palace, Chrétien in *Perceval* calls the central tower of the Grail castle square: "Quarree fu de pierre bise" (vs. 3054). The great hall where the Grail appears is also square:

> An la salle qui fu quarree
> Et autant longue come lee.
> (vss. 3083–3084)

Moreover, the castle of Gornemant, which, as we have seen, is a mere doublet of the Grail castle, has four corners, one central and four smaller towers:

> A quatre parties del mur,
> Don li quarrel estoient dur,
> Avoit quatre basses torneles.
> (vss. 1335–1337)

In *Sone de Nausay*, the Grail castle, which is on an island called Galoche, has four towers on the outer wall. In the center is a round tower which is the palace. In the center of the palace is a hearth supported on four gilded columns.[70] All this might be in imitation of Chrétien's *Perceval*. Near Galoche, however, is another noteworthy island. It is so square that no one can tell which side is the longer:

> Et l'ille si quaree estoit
> Que nus hons savoir ne pooit,
> Au quel les il en a le plus.
> (vss. 17135–17137)

[70] Edition M. Goldschmidt, *Stuttgart Litt. Verein*, CCXVI (Tübingen, 1899), vss. 4371–4394. J. D. Bruce interprets Galoche as "Wales" (*Evolution of Arthurian Romance*, I, 350).

On it are four palaces and a causeway having a sword bridge leads toward it. It formerly belong to Bademagu and Meleagant. In *Historia Meriadoci*, a late twelfth-century Latin romance, is a square island belonging to Gundebaldus, "king of the land whence no man returns." This island is exactly as long as broad. "Ejusdem latitudinis cujus et longitudinis est." [71] It is guarded by four towers and approached by four causeways. Somewhat like these square islands is the castle of the four horns in *Perlesvaus* which, according to the Brussels manuscript, has four corners. [72]

Another form of the square castle is the four-divided island in the Irish voyage stories. In *Imram Maeile Duin* at the sixteenth island were "four fences which divided it into four parts." Kings, queens, warriors, and maidens were in the four divisions. [73] In *Imram Curraig hua Corra* [74] the voyagers come to "an island with four sets of various men." They divided the island "into four" between them.

A late Irish tale, *Eachtra Iollainn Airmdheirg*, which exists in no manuscript older than the eighteenth century, but which can be traced back to 1674, [75] describes a magic well in the island of Finnchoire that could make the old young and restore the maimed or dead. The account of Finnchoire [76] may be summarized as follows:

[71] Edition J. D. Bruce, *Hesperia*, Ergänzungsreihe (Baltimore: Johns Hopkins University Press, 1913), II, 44.

[72] Edition Nitze and Jenkins, I, 387, l. 9547.

[73] Page 273. *Rev. celt.*, IX (1888), 447 f. Compare a fourfold division of the dead in Irish visions (St. J. D. Seymour, "The Eschatology of the Early Irish Church," ZCP, XIV [1923], 195 f.).

[74] Page 276. *Rev. celt.*, XIV (1893), 42 f.

[75] R. Flower, *Catalogue of Irish Manuscripts*, II, 360. The story has certainly passed through the alembic of Irish fancy, although R. T. Christiansen (*The Vikings and the Viking Wars* [Oslo, 1931], p. 421) calls it "an international fairytale."

[76] Other references to Finnchoire are given above (p. 277).

The island is surrounded by four seas: a sea of gold, a sea of silver, a sea of white bronze, and a sea of iron. One hundred warriors guard each side, and there are besides two hundred *ban gaisceda*, "women-warriors," to be fought. After visiting this island, the hero, Iollainn comes next to *Oileán na marbh*, "island of the dead," where with a sword that he finds there, he slays a *gruagach* and carries off the *gruagach's* wife.[77]

This story belongs to the Journey to Fairyland type. Finnchoire is evidently the island of the Castle of Maidens and, as usual, adjacent to it is the island of the dead or Dolorous Tower. A recently collected Journey to Fairyland called *Giolla na Fhiuga* puts a caldron of plenty at the junction of four roads:

We saw at a distance from us a high hill, in which there were four roads which led to it *ó ceithre h-árdaib*, "from the four airts," of the great world and there was never a road of them but had a hundred full valiant warriors watching and guarding the hill. On top of the hill was the caldron and seven hundred full valiant heroes *ag gach aon cúinne dé*, "at each corner of it." [78]

Another peculiarity shared by the Irish castle of fairyland and by the Grail castle is service by four. At Créde's palace in L, four serving men wait on table:

Pleasant is the house in which she is . . . both cupbearer and doorkeeper, both tireless equerry and butler of the pantry

[77] For the above outline I am indebted to the kindness of Dr. Vernam Hull and the courtesy of the reverend Fathers at Stonyhurst College, S. J., who allowed him to examine their manuscript A. II, 20. The story has been printed from a more recent manuscript in *An Claidheam Soluis*, beginning July 9, 1904, p. 4. In this version the tale begins by the arrival of a marvelous ship having on it four knobs, made one of gold, another of silver, etc., on which sat four birds discoursing fairy music.

[78] Other references to Finnchoire are given above (p. 277).

are at her command. . . . Four posts are round every couch
. . . in each post's head is a crystal gem. . . . A vat there of
noble bronze out of which runs the juice of merry malt. An
apple tree stands over the vat . . . when Créde's horn is
filled with mead from the vat, there fall into the horn with
precision four apples at one time. The four that are numbered above, they set about serving (mead) to four that sit
there: a drink to each man and an apple.[79]

In *Perceval*, as soon as the hero passes the drawbridge of
the Grail castle, he is met by four servants: "Vaslet vienent
contre lui quatre" (vs. 3069). In the center of the room
between four columns burns a fire:

> Et fu antre quatre colomes
> Bien poïst an quatre çanz homes
> Asseoir anviron le feu.
>
> (vss. 3095–3097)

Four servants set a table for Perceval and the Fisher King:

> Dui vaslet ont aportee
> Une table lee d'ivorie. . . .
>
> (vss. 3260–3261)
> Dui autre vaslet vindrent,
> Qui aporterent deus eschaces. . . .
>
> (vss. 3266–3267)
> Sor ses eschaces fu assise la table.
>
> (vs. 3275)

[79] Edition W. Stokes, *Acallam, Ir. Texte*, IV, i, 22, ll. 776 f. (a translation by S. H. O'Grady is in *Silva Gadelica*, II, 120): "Aibinn in tech
ina tá . . . idir dháiliumh is doirseoir. Idir gilla scuir nach sceinn ocus
ronnaire re roinn. . . . Cetra huaithne um gach leabaidh . . . gem glaine
i cind gach uáitne. . . . Dabhuch ann do chruan flatha a sileann sugh
suarcbracha, abhull ós cinn na daibhche. . . . In uair líntar corn Créidhi
do mhidh na dabhcha déne, tuitit isin corn co cert, na cethra hubla a

When it is time to sleep, four serving men take up by the four corners the couch upon which the Fisher King reclines and carry him out:

> Quatre serjant delivre et fort. . . .
>
> (vs. 3344)
>
> La coute as quatre corz seisissent,
> Qui el lit estandue estoit,
> Sor coi li prodon se gisoit
> Si l'an portent la ou il durent.
>
> (vss. 3346–3349)

In these passages from *Perceval* the insistence on the number four might be missed by a casual reader. It is much plainer in the corresponding passages in Wolfram's *Parzival*:

When Parzival entered the Fisher King's hall he saw one hundred couches and one hundred cushions. Four knights sat on each couch. . . . Three four-cornered fireplaces of marble with great fires of lign-aloe wood occupied the middle of the hall. . . . A lad sprang in the door with a spear from which blood ran. He carried the spear to each of the four walls and went out. Two maidens entered bearing golden candlesticks and two more bringing trestles that they placed before the host. All four stood together and were dressed alike. Then four times two maidens entered. Four carried tall candles. Four carried a jacinth-stone that when placed upon the trestles served as a table. Then entered four more maidens with candles and two with silver knives. . . . When they wished for supper, to every four knights was a server. There were one hundred tables. At each table sat four knights. When they ate, wherever stood a table, four lads served the four who sat there. . . . Four wagons were rolled in toward the four

---

n-aeinfecht. An cethrar út do háirmhedh, éirghit isin frithdhaileam, tabrat don ceathrar anunn, deoch gach fir ocus ubull."

walls and four knights distributed gold dishes from the wagons.
. . . Finally four maidens brought to Parzival's bed sirup and
wine. (Vss. 229,28 to 243,21.)

In several places an ancient Irish fairy cup of plenty is
pictured as a square object. In the passage from *Créde
Daughter of Cairbre*, L, quoted above, four apples fall into
Créde's horn at one time, which probably implies that the
horn is square so that one apple drops into each corner. In
Togail Bruidne Da Derga,[80] the *fée*, Etáin, had a *long*,
"bowl" (literally "boat"), with four golden birds upon it.
This, I suppose, means that the bowl is square and has a
golden bird at every corner. Stokes translates the passage
as follows: "He saw at the edge of a well a woman . . .
washing in a silver basin wherein were four golden birds
and little, bright gems of purple carbuncle in the rims of
the basin." [81]

In *Dáirenn Daughter of Bodb Derg*, N,[82] the heroine gave
Finn a white silver cup filled with mead. According to the
Franciscan manuscript, she gave him "an exquisite cup of
white silver with four crystalline gems on its mouth." [83]
These four jewels on the rim of the cup probably indicate
that it is quadrangular.

In the Harleian text of *Baile in Scáil*, where the palace of
Lug with its rooftree of white bronze is described, the
maiden, who is virtually the sovereignty personified, sits in
a glass chair wearing a gold crown, and before her is "a

[80] Edition Eleanor Knott, ll. 3–6: "Con-accai in mnaí for ur in tobair
. . . oc folcud a lluing argit ocus ceithri heóin óir furri, ocus gleorgemai
beccai di charrmogul chorcrai hi forfleascuib na luingi."

[81] *Rev. celt.*, XXII (1901), 14.

[82] Page 78.

[83] "Cuach féta findairgid co cetheora ngem nglainidi ima bél." Quoted
by Stokes, *Ir. Texte*, IV, i, 315, l. 4958.

bowl of silver with four golden corners full of the red ale." [84] Most significant of all, Fothaid Canainn in describing his plenty-giving *criol* calls it "a four-cornered *criol*." [85]

These passages show that the fairy cup of plenty in ancient Irish stories was often thought of as square. It is surely identical with the "Quadrangular Cup of the Fiana" which is sometimes mentioned in recently collected Gaelic tales. *Cupa ceithirchearnach na Féinne* it is called in Mac Innes' "Finn MacCool and the Bent Gray Lad," and *cupan ceathraraich* in MacDougal's "Lad of the Skin Coverings." [86]

Of interest in this connection is the square cup preserved at Dunvegan Castle in the Island of Skye.[87] It stands on four small silver feet and is over ten inches high. It is doubtless the cup referred to by Sir Walter Scott in his "Lord of the Isles":

> "Fill me the mighty cup," he said,
> "Erst owned by royal Somerled."
>
> (Canto II, st. 4)

The square Dunvegan Castle situated on the Island of Skye, which is separated from the mainland by a channel only a quarter of a mile wide, corresponds curiously to the descriptions of fairyland in some of the Arthurian romances.[88]

---

[84] "Dabach arcait co cethraib cernaib órdaib, lán di dergflaith" (ZCP, XIII [1921], 373). (See also p. 219.)

[85] Page oo. K. Meyer, *Fianaigecht*, pp. 14 f.

[86] *Folk and Hero Tales from Argyllshire* (London, 1890–1891), Waifs and Strays, II, 40 f., and III, 30, 45, 267.

[87] For pictures of this square oaken cup, which is embossed with silver and was once studded with jewels, see J. MacDonald, *Voices from the Hills* (Glasgow, 1927), p. 112, and *Proceedings of the Society of Antiquaries of Scotland*, Fourth Ser., XI (Edinburgh, 1912–1913), 99–109.

[88] See E. Brugger, "The Hebrides in Arthurian Literature," *Arthuriana*, II (Oxford, 1929), 15.

In *Cath Maige Tured*,[89] symbolism by four is thrust upon the reader. It begins by saying that the Tuatha Dé learned wizardry from four druids in four cities and brought thence their famous four talismans. Their magic well that restored the dead is thus described: "The mortally wounded became whole through the might of the chant of the four physicians who were about the well." [90] Toward the end we are told about the Dagda's harp called *Coir cetharchoir*, "four-angled music."

The only adequate explanation for all this symbolism of four is that the castle of fairyland was a cosmic palace,[91] like the palace of the god of love in the first story by Andreas Capellanus,[92] and was built with reference to the four points of the compass.

That Paradise is square is a familiar idea in vision literature before the time of Chrétien. The *Visio Baronti* about 700 gives Paradise four gates: at the first gate were the cloister-brothers of Barontus, at the second, children and maidens, at the third, priests and martyrs, and at the fourth, a shining light. The ninth-century *Vision of Paulus* says that the celestial city is surrounded by a wall with twelve gates, and by four rivers that flow with honey, milk, oil, and wine. By the river of milk dwell the children slain by Herod, etc.[93] Genesis speaks of four rivers that water the garden,

---

[89] Page 228. Lehmacher's translation, *Anthropos*, XXVI, 435 f., 452.

[90] Bran's caldron of regeneration in *Branwen Daughter of Llyr* (*Mab.*, I, 66), which corresponds to this well of healing, "broke into four fragments." This suggests that it was a square object.

[91] See R. Eisler, *Weltmantel*, pp. 337 f., who regards the cosmic numbers as 4, 12, 100, and 360. See also Margaret Schlauch, "The Palace of Hugon de Constantinople," *Speculum*, VII (1932), 500 f.

[92] Page 346.

[93] See C. Fritzsche, "Die lateinischen Visionen des Mittelalters bis zur

and ancient Babylonian tradition made Eden square. Eden was identified with the Square of Pegasus.[94] The celestial city in Revelation, 21:15, is foursquare, "the length and the breadth and the height of it are equal." [95] The never-failing Dish of Plenty in an Irish fairy palace doubtless symbolized the unfailing fertility of the earth and perhaps on this account was made square like the castle.

The Irish were accustomed to identify fairyland with Ireland and the fairy castle with the banqueting hall at Tara. Professor Nitze has shown [96] that the internal arrangements of the Grail castle resemble those of the banqueting hall. That famous hall was oblong,[97] but faced the four winds and had beside it a round royal castle.

The ancient Irish located the land of the dead in a small island: Tech Duinn to the south, Tory Island or the Ork-

---

Mitte des 12 Jahrhundert," in K. Vollmüller's *Romanische Forschungen* (Erlangen, 1886), II, 272–273.

[94] Arthur Ungnad, *Das Wiedergefundene Paradies* (Breslau, 1923); H. Gunkel, *Hand-Commentar* (Göttingen, 1901). In Perlesvaus, the Grail castle is said to have three names: "Edem," "Chastel de joie," and "Chastel des ames." It is watered by a stream "de Paradis Terrestre" (edition Nitze and Jenkins, ll. 7200–7206).

[95] *Navigatio sancti Brendani* thus describes the island of a hermit (§ 23): "The top of the island was bare rock, longitudo et latitudo et altitudo mensure equalis erat" (C. Wahlund, *Brendans Meerfahrt* [Upsala, 1900], p. 88).

[96] *Studies in Honor of A. M. Elliott* (1911), pp. 19 f. See now R. A. S. Macalister, *Tara* (1931), pp. 64–65.

[97] The square fairy hall may possibly have been associated not merely with the four corners of the earth but with four provinces of Ireland. Partholon's sons divided the island into four parts, and this partition persisted four hundred years (Van Hamel, ZCP, X [1914], 153–156). The next ruler, Nemed, had four sons. The *Táin Bó* seems to know but four provinces.

neys to the north. Later they placed it in Norway. The Welsh put the land of the dead north of the Roman Wall in Galloway, Lothain, and Gorre. They also placed it in the Orkneys and in Norway. The scrawny death-horse and the death-wagon found their way into Journey to Fairyland stories. From the land of the dead came the two castles of fairyland: the red, iron tower of the Fomorians and the square, cosmic palace of the numerous *fées*.

The square Grail castle, with its vast, shadowy interior, illuminated by a fire and by glittering talismans and filled with people, has developed out of an Irish *síd* or underground, fairy palace and retains some features that came from the square, cosmic castle of the dead.

CHAPTER XII

Irish Names

UNLESS characters bearing similar names play similar parts in similar plot-patterns, resemblances between names in ancient Irish and names in Chrétien's romances will by a prudent observer be regarded as accidental. In this chapter a number of resemblances in name between characters, who resemble each other also in function, are pointed out. Future research may disprove one or two of these resemblances but it would seem that enough are here collected to establish the borrowing of names from Irish into Chrétien's French as a solid fact.

AINGEN

Aingen seems to be a traditional name for the king of the dead. In Irish he was a red Fomorian giant; in the French romances he became lord of a Dolorous Tower.

An old appearance of the word is in the form Aincgeis, "trouble," name of a great-grandfather of the husband of that Carmun for whom the famous triennial games were held.[1] Aincgeis' son is Dorche, "dark," his grandson, Díbad, "death," and his great-grandson is nameless, but from the story he is pretty surely Death who has seized upon Carmun (i.e. Ireland personified as a goddess, like Tailtiu, and thought of as wife alternately to a god and a giant).

[1] Gwynn, *Met. Dinn.*, III, 5. Aincgeis is *co méit ratha*, "rich in substance," and Dorche is *dírmaig*, "host-commanding," which are doubtless references to the wealth of the underworld.

Another old appearance of the word is in the form Aigine, according to Giolla Coemhain writing before 1072,[2] the name of an ancestor of the kings of Orkney. The Orkney Islands were by popular etymology connected with Orcus (Hades) and their kings were kings of the dead. This conception of the Orkneys has been observed in AA, the last part of Chrétien's *Perceval*,[3] and, it is safe to infer, was present in the materials used by Geoffrey and the French romance writers.

Aingen perhaps meant at first "ill-birth," i.e. "monster." It was confused by the early Irish with Amargen "grief-born." [4] Evidence that Aingen and Amargen were inter-changed exists in the *Auraicept na n-Éces* or "Scholars' Primer," in a passage describing Gaedel, the eponymous hero of the Gael and his "selection" of the Irish language. The passage is as follows: [5] The man who selected the language "was Gaedel, son of Angen, so that Gaedil, Gaels, is derived from him, from Gaedel son of Angen son of Whiteknee son of Whitehand son of Agnumon. Now Gaedel son of Aimergen is the same as Gaedel son of Éther, to wit, his father bore two names, Aingen and Ether." What the *Auraicept* explicitly says is that Aingen and Ether were the same; but since it calls Gaedel "son of Aimergen," and seems to know but one Gaedel, ancestor of the Irish, it implies that Aimergen, Aingen, and Ether were all three the same. All three, together with Balar and Galam, were

[2] Quoted above, p. 261.

[3] Page 143.

[4] Thurneysen, *Heldensage*, p. 315, n. 3, and p. 93.

[5] Edition G. Calder (Edinburgh, 1917), p. 78. See also "Aingen" in the index of persons. The *Auraicept* is not later than the eleventh century (p. xxxi). Ether probably stands for Ith, the name of the first Fomorian invader of Ireland.

probably names for a mythological Fomorian who was, or who became, Death personified.

That Aingen belonged to the red Fomorians with one leg, who come from the land of the dead, is shown by the *Táin Bó Regamna*. In this tenth-century tale, which is introductory to the great *Táin*, Cuchulinn is warned of impending death as follows:

Cuchulinn sees a red woman with red eyebrows and a red mantle, riding on a wagon drawn by a red horse which has but one leg. Beside the wagon strides a huge man in a red cloak with a fork on his shoulder. The woman, as we are told in *Echtra Nerai*,[6] is Bé Aingene, "wife of Aingen," so that this tall man is doubtless Aingen. Horse, wagon, woman, man, and cow vanish, but the woman reappears as a blackbird sitting on a bough [called the Badb, or in another manuscript, the Morrigu], and threatens Cuchulinn with death at the Táin Bó. The woman is given a very long name beginning *Fáebur*, "edge," which suggests that what the man carried was perhaps a scythe.[7]

This ancient vision resembles that of the *char de la mort* as described by peasants in Brittany.[8] The dreaded wagon is attended by two men: one rides and the other of gigantic stature, named Ankou, stalks along with a scythe on his shoulder. To see this vision betokens death.

In the accounts from Brittany, cow and woman are missing, but the forewarning of death and the tall man beside the wagon with a weapon on his shoulder indicate a

[6] Thurneysen, *Heldensage*, p. 315, n. 3. On *Echtra Nerai* or *Tain be Aingen*, see p. 93. The Badb was wife to Tethra, a Fomorian (see p. 41). The red woman of *Táin Bó Regamna* is clearly a Fomorian.

[7] My summary follows Windisch's text and translation, *Ir. Texte*, II, ii, 241–254.

[8] A. LeBraz, *La Légende de la Mort*, I, 111 f.

foundation for both visions in the same superstition. It is a reasonable hypothesis that Aingen, the Irish Fomorian, drew to himself the *char de la mort* superstition. When the story was told in Wales and Brittany, the name may have been assimilated to the words for death: *angheu* in Early Welsh, *ankow* in Cornish, and *ankou* in Breton.

Geoffrey, in his mention of the Castle of Maidens and the Dolorous Mountain,[9] calls the latter Mons Agned. Evidently his source knew Aingen as lord of the Tower of the Dead. Since Nennius too mentions Mons Agned (although not the Battle of Camlan) it looks as if Aingen, and not Modred, was at first the name of Arthur's great enemy.

A natural inclination was at work tending to modify Fomorian names into words of evil significance. Aingen may have been influenced by the Early Welsh words, *anghen*, "necessity," and *angheu*, "death," and have been interpreted to mean "sorrow" or "death." Aingen passed into Middle English as King Anguish,[10] an enemy of Arthur. It would be easy for a Frenchman to alter Aingen into Angrés, "hostile." A story like this seems to lie at the basis of the neglected Angrés episode in Chrétien's *Cligès*, which, in brief, is as follows:

King Arthur entrusts Britain to Count Angrés and crosses the sea to Brittany. Angrés turns traitor, steals the treasures of London and flees to his castle at Windsor, which he fortifies with triple walls. Arthur employs one of his knights, named Alexander, to crush Angrés. Alexander persuades a few of

[9] Quoted above, p. 355. Aingen appears in another guise as Anguselus, king of Albania (*Historia*, bk. ix, chap. 9, p. 444). See now Dr. Blenner-Hassett, "Geoffrey's Mons Agned," *Speculum*, XVII (1942), 250–254.

[10] Malory, *Morte Darthur*, bk. xviii, chap. 8. See Rhŷs, *Arthurian Legend*, p. 239.

his followers to disguise themselves by taking shields and lances from men of the castle whom they have slain. With this stolen armor they deceive the porter and enter the triple walls. At the door of an inner tower Alexander encounters Angrés, stuns him by a mighty blow, and sends him as prisoner to King Arthur.[11]

This is nothing but the story of Modred, with Queen Guenevere omitted. "Windsor" must not be taken literally, as everybody has taken it. Angrés' castle, which has three encircling walls (vss. 1243, 1879), iron portcullises, and a great square tower of stone (vss. 1252, 1253), with only one entrance (vs. 1971), resembles the Dolorous Tower or castle of the dead. Angrés flees to this tower (vs. 1946) just as in mythological tales Death flees to his tower.

If Chrétien were inventing this, or were following a French chivalric tale, it is incredible that he should have made his hero, Alexander, conquer by deceit. Chrétien has kept here, I believe, a traditional method of gaining entrance to a *síd* or to the land of the dead, namely by disguising oneself in the attire of an elf or of a dead man.[12] My hypothesis is that Chrétien is here using a story about a Welsh character called Angheu, "death," and has changed the name to the nearest French word that suits the meaning, namely, Angrés, "the hostile one."

Aingen, as seems established, was a traditional name for

---

[11] Edition Foerster, vss. 421–440, 1054–1260, 1859–2203.

[12] In the Irish tale, "Conn-eda or the Golden Apples of Loch Erne" (*Cambrian Journal*, II [1885], 110), the hero passes the gate of the castle of the Fir Bolg (Dolorous Tower) by disguising himself in the skin of a horse. In F, Laeg, when he enters the giants' or Fomorians' island, wears the cloak of a woman whose companion Cuchulinn has just killed. In Y, Perceval wears the armor of the Red Knight whom he has slain and who was evidently in origin a Fomorian. When Perceval enters

a red Fomorian king of the dead. It is a natural inference that it was the origin of the first part of the long name, Anguingueron, given by Chrétien in *Perceval* to the deputy of King Clamadeu. Anguingueron, which has often been suspected to be a compound name,[13] separates into Anguin and Guerrier, and means: "Aingen the warrior." In Y, Anguingueron plays the part of a Fomorian and is an enemy to the Grail folk, who play the part of the Tuatha Dé.

In AA this rôle of an enemy is played by Guiromelant. Guiromelant is deputy to the "clers sage" who built Chastel Merveilleus and who, as a leader against the Grail folk, corresponds to Clamadeu. Perhaps Guiromelant was at first "guerrier-aingen" and was altered to its present form in imitation of the name Meliant which occurs earlier in AA.

In Chrétien's *Lancelot* the name Meleagant looks as if it had been influenced by a supposed derivation from *mal* and *angheu* or Aingen. In the prose *Lancelot*, Malaquin seems to be compounded from *mal* and Anguin. Both Meleagant and Malaquin are hostile to the Grail folk and behave as if former Fomorians.

Another trace of Angheu probably appears in *Diu Crône*, where Ansgü is the name of that warrior who in *Perceval* is called "nephew of Greoreas." [14] Since Ansgü is here associated with Orgelûse, her dwarf, and the ferryman of the dreadful river, he is rather clearly a former Fomorian and a prince of the dead.

Blancheflor's castle, and when he fights the former Fomorian, Clamadeu, he is disguised in this red armor.

[13] See Brugger, ZFS, XLIX (1926–1927), 249 and 477. The late Alexander Bugge ("Tristan og Isolde," *Edda*, XVI [1921], 240), commenting on E. Löseth, *Tristan* (Paris, 1891), pp. 24 and 475, explained Anguinguerrant le Roux as "Anguin the red warrior," but be wrongly tried to connect Anguin with Hagen.

[14] *Diu Crône*, vs. 20185; *Perceval*, vs. 7302 (and see p. 188).

AMARGEN

Donn and Amargen are chief figures in the invasion of the sons of Míl. Donn died, according to *LG*, before the sons of Míl landed, so that Amargen was left the actual leader and king. In the story of the sons of Míl, as Van Hamel remarks,[15] "Amargen is the only character." He is the only hostile person mentioned in the extract from the tenth-century Cín Droma Snechta which describes his meeting with Banba.[16]

In the early history of Ireland, Amargen is an important person. Máelmura, before 887, in the poem quoted above,[17] calls him Amairgen Glungel, "white knee," a hero mighty, wide ruling among the sons of Míl. The *Ancient Laws of Ireland* declare that the *file*, Aimergin Glungel, made the first judgment in Erin; and a little farther on say that Aimergin was the first author in Erin, and was the pupil of "Cai of the fair judgment."[18] *Mesca Ulad*, a sagá as old as the beginning of the twelfth century,[19] says: "Amargin Glunmar, 'big knee,' was *ríg-fili ocus ríg-brithem*, 'king-poet and royal judge.'" He divided Erin into two halves, gave the part underground to the Tuatha Dé and the surface of the land to the sons of Míl. Besides five poems in *LG* attributed to this Amargen, another manuscript contains a "rhetoric" also ascribed to him entitled "The Caldron of Poesy," and beginning *Mo coire cóir goiriath*.[20] This rhetoric, which is obscure enough, attaches

---

[15] *ZCP*, X (1914), 179.

[16] Page 250. [17] Page 256.

[18] *Senchus Mór* (I, 18, l. 11): "Ruc cét-breth i nEre," and (p. 20, l. 2): "Cetna ugdur ceta robuidh i nE·rinn Aimeirgin Gluingeal in file, dalta Cai Cainbrethaig eiside in dala descipul lxx at scoile Feiniusa Farsaid."

[19] Edition W. M. Hennessy, *RIA*, Todd Lect. Ser., I, 2.

[20] Manuscript T. C. D., H. 3. 18. The text is in *Anecdota*, V, 22–28.

to Amargen Glungel, who composed verses for Eber Donn, the epithets *gairglas* and *greliath*. *Greliath*, "gray-haired," — compare *Donn*, "dusky," — is a suitable epithet for a prince of death, and evidently refers to the same peculiarity as the epithet *iargiunnach* which is regularly attached to the Amargen of the sagas. The title *iargiunnach*, "iron-haired" or "of the iron jaw," is proof that the Amargen of the sagas has borrowed traits from the Amargen of the invasion stories, just as the historical Queen Medb has from the fairy queen Medb.

On account of the importance of Amargen as one of three figures in the mythical battle, it is worth while to assemble here information about the Amargen of the Cuchulinn saga. In the *Táin Bó Cúailnge*, Amargen appears only in a semi-detached episode called *Oisligi Amargin*.[21] We are told that Amargen rested on his left elbow at Tailtiu and for three days and nights fought by throwing stones which his people brought to him. His antagonist, Cu Roi, who is well known to be in origin a giant monster,[22] likewise fought with stones, so that flying stones clashed together in the clouds over the armies. The title "Oisligi" is unexplained, as is also Amargen's leaning on his elbow to fight. To my mind the picture is of two giants crouched on their elbows on either side of fighting armies of smaller men who are fetching stones for the two giants to throw. This incident which is in no way attached to the main action of the *Táin Bó*, is no doubt a distorted borrowing from the mythical battle of gods and giants.

In the *Táin Bó* this episode is immediately preceded by

[21] Edition E. Windisch, ll. 4637–4683.
[22] See Thurneysen, ZCP, IX (1913), 189, 336; X (1914), 423; J. Baudiš, *Ériu*, VII (1913), 200.

another detached incident called *Mellgleo nlliach*,[23] in which Amargen's brother Iliach [24] likewise fought with stones. Iliach, with a supply of stones in his chariot, was of enormous size and entered battle naked. Evidently these two giant brothers, Amargen and Iliach, have a mythological background.

Amargen in the Cuchulinn stories is generally the son of the cleverest of smiths, Ecet or Echen Salach, "dirty," of Buas (the River Bush). He is *Iargiunnach*, an epithet appropriate for a king of the dead and probably borrowed from the mythical Amargen. His wife is Findchaem, the sister of King Conchobar.[25] He is father of Conall Cernach, and of Mes Dead or Dead-al, and he and Findchaem are Cuchulinn's foster-parents.[26] He is called *rig-file* and *ard-*

[23] "The hilarious battle of Iliach," ll. 4590–4636. *Mell* is a word of uncertain meaning.

[24] Amairgen is "mac Caiss meic Baicc (Fecc) meic Rosa Ruaid meic Rudraigi" (l. 4638), and Iliach is "mac Caiss meic Baicc meic Rosa Ruaid meic Rudraige (l. 4590, Windisch, *Táin Bó*). Amairgen mac Caiss who lived at Tailtiu (l. 4638), is the one called Iargiunnach, the father of Conall Cernach, but he seems to be confused with Amairgen mac Ecet Salach who lived at Buas (l. 4918). See Windisch, pp. 660–661, notes. Both Amairgens are poets, "filid," and it seems impossible to keep them apart. Thurneysen (*Heldensage*, p. 674) does not separate them.

[25] *Fled Bricrend*, ed. Henderson, *ITS*, II (1899), 34, § 28: "Findchæm ingen Cathbad ben Amargin Iarngiunnaig."

[26] *Compert Conculainn*, Windisch, *Ir. Texte*, I, 142. Van Hamel (*ZCP*, X [1914], 180), struck by a verbal similarity between the boasts of Sencha, Fergus, and Amargen here, when they wished to become foster-parents to Cuchulinn, and Amargen's boastful poem, "Amm góeth i muir" (O'Clery's *Leabhar Gabhála*, ed. Macalister and Mac Neill, p. 262), has argued that Amargen was introduced into *LG* from the Ulster saga. I agree that Amargen has been thrust into *LG* – not, however, from the Ulster saga, but rather from a lost mythological tale about a battle of gods and giants. Van Hamel's sole argument is that

ollam, but his actions are mostly those of a *rí*, "king," and not of a *file*, "poet." In *Cath Ruis na Ríg*,[27] two *filid*, Aithirne Ailgesach and Amargen, enter battle with twelve hundred followers apiece. Amargen lived at Dunn Imrith, county Louth, where he brought up Cuchulinn.

Amargen, according to Cormac's *Glossary*, was in childhood an unusual-appearing creature who ate strange food. One text[28] says that at seven years of age he was no bigger than a man's fist, and another text[29] lays stress on the strange food the boy ate. Both texts agree that his speech at this age was so shrewd that Aithirne, fearing lest he might be superseded as *file* by the boy, tried unsuccessfully to kill him. When the attempt became known, Aithirne was punished by being forced to adopt Amargen as a foster-son and to teach him all his art.

In *Togail Bruidne Da Derga*[30] we have a picture of Amargen as an old man who wonders at the wounds of his son Conall Cernach and praises him.

Amargen is usually associated with a hard, merciless *file* named Aithirne Ailgesach, "the urgent." This Aithirne

---

Amargen's boasts seem out of place in *LG*. They are out of place because they have, I think, been transferred from the winter giant. Even if Van Hamel were right and the poem were made up out of scraps from the Ulster saga instead of vice versa, it would not injure our present argument unless he were to disprove the existence of a mythical Amargen, something which he has no wish to do.

[27] Edition E. Hogan, *RIA*, Todd Lect. Ser., IV (1892), 38 f.

[28] *Anecdota*, IV, 57. Amargen's smallness is a close parallel to that of Taliessin who, when caught in Elphin's net, was so small a boy that Gwyddno exclaimed, "Art thou able to speak, and thou so little?" Amargen was ugly, but Taliessin was handsome, "radiant brow."

[29] Thurneysen, *Heldensage*, p. 514.

[30] Edition Stokes, *Rev. celt.*, XXII (1901), 327–329; ed. Eleanor Knott, pp. 45–46.

is more notorious for outrages on women than any other character in the sagas. Amargen's two sons, Conall Cernach and Mes Dead, were with Aithirne at Howth in his most infamous raid on women.[31] This association of Amargen and his sons with wrongs to women and with other cruel deeds is best explained as a surviving trace of his original hateful character as a Fomorian giant and a god of the underworld. Both Amargen Iargiunnach, husband of Findchaem, and Amargen Gluingeal of *LG* have borrowed so many traits from the mythical Amargen that they resemble each other a good deal.[32]

The importance of Amargen as leader of the giants or Fomorians in the mythical battle was such that his name, and to some extent his character, reappear in the Cuchulinn sagas. Irish tales do not connect Amargen with talismans or with a cup of plenty. Doubtless these pseudo-historians who invented *LG*, when they extracted from the mythological battle several successive invasions of Ireland, removed all miraculous features. They obliterated the in-

---

[31] *Cath Etair*, ed. Stokes, *Rev. celt.*, VIII (1887), 47 f.

[32] Rhŷs (*Celtic Heathendom*, p. 569) said that Amargen Gluingeal had "nothing except his name and his title of *file* in common with Amargen the pupil of Aithirne." He, however, did not know all the texts. Other Amargens are: Amergin mac Amhalghada *file* of the Dési who, according to the *Dinnschenchas*, fasted upon Finntan in order to force him to relate the "true history of Irish places." This Amargen makes but one speech (*Rev. celt.*, XV (1894), 277): "Te-Mair," quoth Amargen, "is the *múr*, 'rampart,' of Tea daughter of Lugaid the son of Ith." Since he refers to Ith, it is probable that he is in origin only a pale reflection of Amargen Gluingeal. Aimhirgin mac Cinaedh, lord of the Ui Failghe, is in the *Annals of Ireland by Four Masters* at the year 944, ed. J. O'Donovan (1848–1851). Aimirgin *Iurtunach*, "the ravager," is mentioned in *Aided Ferghusa maic Léide* (*Silva Gadelica*, I, 238, cf. II, 269). Amargenus *faber* was the father of St. Bairre of Cork, according to the life edited by Plummer (*Vitae sanct. Hib.*, I, 65–67).

cidents of a Journey to Fairyland and omitted the talismans because they could not pass them off as historical. The pseudo-historians, however, associated Amargen with Ériu and we know that she, who is virtually Ireland personified, is usually described — for example, in *Baile in Scáil* [33] — as in possession of talismans of plenty. Just as the different kings named Nuadu are copies of the god Nuadu, so the different Amargens are copies of the Fomorian giant Amargen.

CAI

It has not before been observed that Kay, Arthur's sharp-tongued seneschal, derives his name from Irish story. Cai, Amargen, and Míl are mentioned together in the following ancient Irish documents: *Auraicept na n-Éces*, *LG*, *Senchas Mór*, prose *Dinnshenchas*, *Verse Dinnshenchas*, and *Echtra Cormaic*.

Cormac's *Glossary* [34] relates that Cái Cáinbrethach, "of the fair judgment," was a pupil of Fenius, that he went to the Children of Israel to learn Hebrew, and that he was a judge among the sons of Míl on their voyage. One of the judgments of Cái is quoted in the *Glossary*.[35]

In the *Auraicept*,[36] Cae is mentioned in seven places, and in five of these places his name is associated with that of Amargen. It can scarcely be an accident that in *Erec*, the first French Arthurian romance, Keu and Amauguins are twice mentioned together.[37]

[33] Page 218.   [34] *Anecdota*, IV, 14, § 144.
[35] *Anecdota*, IV, 19, § 209.
[36] Edition G. Calder, l. 1024: according to Amairgen's *Primer*, the fourth letter was named after "Cae," and the fifth after "Amirgen son of Naende." Besides this, Cae and Amairgen are mentioned near each other in ll. 246, 1038, 2561, 3980.   [37] *Erec*, vss. 317 and 1726.

In the *Ancient Laws*,[38] Amargen was a pupil of Cai Cáinbrethach. Cai was both a *brehon* and a *file*. "From him was named Brethchath or Brathcai." "Brathcai," according to Cormac's *Glossary*, meant a *brehon* elected to administer the laws of a territory during an interregnum. According to O'Mulconry's *Glossary*,[39] however, it must have been the name of a book or primer.

In the prose *Dinnshenchas* we find much the same account, except that in the account of Loch Cé we get what seems at first an inconsistent statement that Cé was the druid of Nuadu at the battle of Moytura and was wounded while fighting against the sons of Míl. Stokes' translation is as follows: [40] "Cé the druid of Nuada Silverhand entered the battle of Magh Turedh. Having been wounded in the fight, he went to Corrshlébhe and (then) he went to Magh Airni where the lake is. And there Cé fell, and at his burial the lake burst forth. Whence is Loch Cé." [41]

According to Cormac's *Glossary* as quoted above, Cai was the *brehon* of the sons of Míl when they set out on

[38] *Senchas Mór*, I, 20, ll. 3–5: cf. p. 22, l. 1 and p. 274, l. 30.

[39] Cormac's *Glossary*, *Anecdota*, IV, 14, § 144; O'Mulconry's *Glossary* (*Archiv f. Celt. Lex.*, I [1900], 240, § 125): "Bráthchai .i. bretho Cai, ainm aicepta bélri."

[40] Edition W. Stokes, *Folk-Lore*, IV (1893), 492–493, § 75, from manuscript Egerton 1781. The text is: "Cé .i. drái Nuadhat Airgetlaim meic Eterlaim rotáet a cath Maige Turedh iarna guin isin cath co rainic Carn Coirrslébhi ocus co rainic in Magh Airni a fuil in loch, ocus docer Cáe ann sin, conid ica idhnacal ro mebaidh in loch. Unde Loch Cé." Stokes also prints a version from manuscript H. 66. B. Another version, in the Book of Lecan, was printed by W. M. Hennessey, *Annals of Loch Cé* (London, 1871), I, xxxvi. These versions add no important details.

[41] Geoffrey (*Historia*, bk. X, chap. 9, p. 488) of course connects Kay with Arthur, not Nuadu, and tells of a battle against the Romans, not of the battle of Moytura, but Geoffrey agrees with the *Dinnshenchas of Loch Cé* that Kay was wounded in battle and died later.

their voyage. As we shall see, *Echtra Cormaic* relates that he came to the Tuatha Dé. We seem forced to believe, therefore, that he forsook the sons of Míl at some time on their voyage and attached himself to the Tuatha Dé.

It is a plausible conjecture that Cé was at first an officer of the Fomorians who had been sent to Ireland to supervise the collection of their taxes or tribute at King Nuadu's court. Later the story was retold by men who had forgotten Cé's Fomorian origin. They supposed that he belonged to King Nuadu's court and called him Nuadu's druid. When Nuadu's story was transferred to King Arthur, Cé was transformed into a seneschal. His Fomorian origin was forgotten, but he kept some of his Fomorian unpopularity, and his Fomorian tendency to aid invaders. In Chrétien's *Lancelot*, for example, it is Kay who browbeats Arthur into yielding up Queen Guenevere at Meleagant's hostile demand.

In *Echtra Cormaic and the Ordeals*,[42] in an account of one of the ordeals, occurs the following statement:

Now Cai Cáinbrethach, — the pupil of Fenius Farsaid, the twelfth, or the seventy-second, disciple of the school which Fenius collected from the Greeks in order to learn the many languages throughout the countries of the world, — it was that Cai who brought this ordeal from the land of Israel when he came to the Tuatha Dé. . . . It was that same Cai, moreover, who first ordained in Erin the Law of the Four Tracks, for only two of the school came to Erin, namely, Amergin White-knee, the poet, and Cai, the judge. And Cai remained in Erin until he had outlived nine generations.

This statement in the *Echtra Cormaic* connects Cai, Amargen, and the ordeals with Tara. It would be natural

[42] Edition Stokes, *Ir. Texte*, III, i, 192–193, 211–212.

to explain these twelve ordeals as a later expansion of the
Four Jewels which were brought to Ireland by the Tuatha
Dé except for the remark above that Cai brought one of
the ordeals himself. Probably this remark is an error caused
by some confusion. Certainly the hypothesis that Cai was
at first a Fomorian tax collector who later became regarded
as Nuadu's druid will explain why he should be depicted as
in charge of Nuadu's treasures, namely, the Four Jewels.
When the Welsh took over the story of the battle between
the sons of Míl and the Tuatha Dé, they substituted, we
may suppose, Arthur for Nuadu. King Conchobar had a
chief speaker called *sencha*.[43] Cai may have been called
Nuadu's *sencha*, and this word transmitted through Welsh
may have suggested to a French writer that Cai was a
seneschal. In this way Cé, King Nuadu's druid, may have
become Kay, King Arthur's seneschal.

In Irish Cai is generally called *Cáinbrethach*, "of the fair
judgment." This epithet finds no reflection in Chrétien's
romances, but in *Kulhwch and Olwen*,[44] and in a poem from
the *Black Book of Carmarthen*,[45] Cai appears as "Cei guin."
The translators render this the "blessed Kay" or the "worthy
Kay," [46] but *guin* really means "fair" [47] and I conjecture
that this epithet is a carry-over from the Irish *Cáinbrethach*,
"fair judgment." However this may be, no reasonable
doubt need remain that Irish Cé is the origin of Arthurian
Kay. Kay's name, moreover, binds together the Irish god
Nuadu and King Arthur.

[43] *Táin Bó*, edition Windisch, p. 744.
[44] Rhŷs and Evans, *The Text of the Red Book*, I, 105.
[45] Translated by Rhŷs in his preface to Malory's *Morte Darthur*,
Everyman's Library, XLV (1906), xviii.
[46] *Mab.*, I, 177.
[47] Rhŷs, *Celtic Heathendom*, p. 527, n. 1.

GALAM

Galam son of Balar or Bile is also called Míl or Míled.[48] He was evidently a protagonist against Brión in the mythical battle and became in *LG* the leader of the Irish in their supposed invasion from Spain. The name Galam, I think, lies behind that of Esclados li Ros in *Yvain*; of Clamadeu des Isles [49] in *Perceval*; and of Galaholt in the prose *Lancelot*. Both Esclados and Clamadeu are red knights, but Chrétien probably did not know that they are both forms of Galam. Chrétien calls King Clamadeu's seneschal, Anguingueron. This, as has been pointed out,[50] separates into "Anguin the warrior."

Galam and his son and subordinate Amargen have given rise to several pairs of evil warriors or giants. In Irish, in *CMT*, they are Balar and Bres; in the *Dinnshenchas* they are Conaing and Morc who levy taxes upon the children of Nemed, and in another paragraph they are Cendtarcluais, king of the Fomorians, and his *rechtaire*, "seneschal," Marg, who exacts tribute from the Leinstermen; in Q they are Cétach Crobderg, "Hundred fighter of the red hand," and his son Aed Alaind; in T they are the "king" and Cathmann. In Welsh, in *Kulhwch and Olwen*, they are the two giants Yspaddaden and Gwrnach. In Chrétien's *Perceval* they are not only King Clamadeu and his seneschal Anguingueron but also in the Gawain section the "clers sages d'astrenomie" (vs. 7548) and his viceroy Guiromelant. In

[48] Page 244.

[49] Galam might be shortened to Clam, just as in mediaeval Welsh Caradoc was, we know, shortened to Cradoc. Change of "c" to "g" is due to Welsh mutation. Clamadeu is, therefore, not an impossible corruption of Galam.

[50] Page 376.

Yvain they are Esclados li ros and his seneschal (vs. 4413) who must be fought, and in the latter part of *Yvain* they are two "fiz de deable" (vs. 5271). In the English *Sir Perceval* they are Gollerotherame who is called "sowdan" (vs. 1651), and his brother, an unnamed giant (vs. 2043).[51] In the prose *Lancelot* a similar pair of giants make their appearance as Galaholt and his seneschal Malaquin. Galaholt is not mentioned by Chrétien, and it may be some other name that has become confused with Galam. It looks Scandinavian, not Celtic. When, however, one calls to mind that Galaholt was lord of "l'isles lointaines" and "l'estraignes isles,"[52] that he was "son of a giantess" and lived in the "chastel des pleurs" in "l'ile des géants" or "l'ile perdu,"[53] it is hard to deny that he has been confused with a Fomorian prince of the dead.

If Galaholt be a deformation of Galam, his father ought to be Balar, but, according to the romances, Galaholt's father is Brunor. Brunor, however, may be a translation of Irish Donn, "the brown or shadowy one." Donn, as Kuno Meyer has shown,[54] was a god of the dead. Perhaps, therefore, when a French romance calls Galaholt "son of Brunor," it is another way of saying "son of Balar."

The wars of Arthur and Galaholt are told in the prose

[51] One may conjecture that Gollerotherame is an Englishman's corruption of Irish *Galam rí(g) Eireann*, "Galam, king of Ireland."

[52] H. O. Sommer, *Vulgate Romances*, III, 236; III, 50. These "strange islands" are identical with the *indsi gall*, "islands of the strangers," a name transferred to the Hebrides but meaning the "islands of the dead." See E. Brugger, *Arthuriana* (Oxford, 1929–1930), II, 16. Balar came from *indsi gall*, *CMT*, § 50 (p. 230).

[53] E. Löseth, *Tristan*, p. 33, and prose *Lancelot*. Dr. K. G. T. Webster ([Harvard] *Studies and Notes*, XVI [1934], 216) believes that Galaholt was an abductor of Guenevere.

[54] Page 258.

Lancelot.[55] No doubt this narrative has been influenced by Chrétien, but it must, I think, have a basis in Irish wars between Tuatha Dé and Fomorians; that is, between Nuadu and Galam. Arthur has taken the place of Nuadu, and Galaholt the place of Galam. A contrary hypothesis — namely, that somebody invented the Galaholt section, having only Chrétien as a model — is, I think, impossible. Such an inventor who by hypothesis worked at random could not have succeeded in connecting all of Galaholt's generals and officers, as they are connected, with giants and with the land of the dead. The author of this Galaholt narrative must have had a pattern ultimately of Irish origin before him.

Galaholt's generals [56] are as follows: Malaquin, "rois des cent chevaliers"; "Rois premier conquis," called Cleolas; "Rois del Vadoan"; "Rois Clamadeus des lointaine illes"; Baldemagus de Gorre. This list is not always adhered to, but any changes made are not contradictory to the connection with giants and with the land of the dead. In this list Malaquin is, I think, *mal* + Anguin or Amargen. "Rois premier conquis" is Ither or Ith, the first Fomorian to arrive in Ireland; Vadoan is for Avalon, the Welsh land of the dead; Clamadeus is Chrétien's Clamadeu, or Galam again; Baldemagus is father of Meleagant or Melwas. All five names are Fomorian epithets and are connected with the land of the dead.

In the Welsh *Branwen*, Galam son of Balar reappears as Caswallawn son of Beli, who wears a veil of illusion so that only his sword is visible. He slays Bran's friends and takes

---

[55] Sommer, *Vulgate Romances*, from III, 201 to IV, 155.
[56] Sommer, III, 236.

from him, and from his son Caradawc, the throne of Britain.[57] He is clearly a leader of the same hostile folk who
in Irish are called Fomorians, and he corresponds therefore
to Galam. Caswallawn is made up of *cas*, "hateful," +
Galam. It is one of those epithets for the castle of the dead
and for the rulers of the dead that are compounded with
the element "evil."

Some Irish Fomorians having names that signify evil are:
Amargen, "grief-born"; Balar mac Doid mac Néit,[58] "death
son of fire son of battle"; Donn, "dark"; Garb, "rough";
Liag, "woe"; Lot, "destruction"; Morc, probably connected with *moirc*, later *mairg*, "sorrow"; Scathach, "the
shadowy"; Dun Scaith, "fort of the shadow." An Irish
picture of a Fomorian is vividly drawn in the *Pursuit after
Diarmuid and Grainne*.[59] Shearban, "surly," is a wicked
giant of the race of Cain. He has one eye and guards a
magic mountain-ash tree with its red berries. The red
woman, horse, and man in the *Táin Bó Regamna* make
another such picture. Characteristic Irish ideas are that Fomorians are wicked, one-eyed giants, clad in red or associated with red.

Some names in the romances having similar evil significa-
tion are as follows. In *Tandareis und Floribel*,[60] Malmon-
tân is a city surrounded by three rivers where Karedôz, a
companion of the devil, a giant, and other giants, one of
them named Margôn, hold people captives. It is manifestly

---

[57] *Mab.*, I, 68.

[58] See p. 232, and the *Banshenchas*, ed. M. C. Dobbs, *Rev. celt.*, XLVII
(1930), 292, 318.

[59] Edition S. H. O'Grady, Society for the Preservation of the Irish
Lang. (Dublin, 1880–1881), II, 11.

[60] Edition F. Khull (Graz, 1885), vss. 5267 f.

a *male montagne* or a land of death, and perhaps Karedôz is a corruption of Charon. In *Le Bel Inconnu*,[61] Malgiers li gris is a giant who guards l'Ille d'Or and who must be fought. In *Lanzelet*,[62] Malduc is a similar adversary, who is here called an enchanter. In the prose *Lancelot*, Malaquin, the name of Galaholt's seneschal, is plainly *mal* + aguin. *Male pucele* and Mancipicelle [63] are the same sort of compound names. Wolfram calls Orgeluse's dwarf Malcrêâtiure. Names were compounded in extraordinary ways. For example, in the English *Arthour and Merlin*,[64] Amandauorgulous, the name of a knight, seems to be made up of Amangon + *orgulous*. Romance writers went on a theory that these hostile characters were devilish and *maufé* [65] was the proper term for them. In *Amadis et Ydoine*,[66] the hero fights a *maufé* at a tomb. Significant names for evil characters are well known in later Arthurian romances, as, for example, in Spenser's *Faery Queen*. It has not heretofore been pointed out that names of this sort may be traced in some of the oldest stories.

Caswallawn in the Welsh *Branwen* must be identical with Gallan who in the Huth *Merlin* [67] rides invisible and slays a knight in Balin's safe conduct. He is in *Merlin* called "Gallans li rous" and "cel rous chevalier," so he is one of those red or black warriors [68] that come from the land of

[61] Edition G. P. Williams, vs. 2192.

[62] Edition K. A. Hahn (Frankfurt, 1845).

[63] Page 152. In the Thornton *Morte Arthure* (ed. Mary M. Banks [London, 1900], vss. 4062, 4174), the king's foe is "Sir Modrede the Malebranche."

[64] Edition E. Kölbing (Leipzig, 1890), vs. 5485.

[65] See Chrétien's *Perceval*, edition Hilka, vs. 5955 variants.

[66] Edition J. R. Reinhard (Paris, 1926).

[67] Edition G. Paris and J. Ulrich (Paris, 1886), II, 7.

[68] In Malory's *Morte Darthur* (ed. H. O. Sommer [London, 1889],

the dead. He must, I think, be Death personified. Only his blood will restore those whom he has slain. In this he is like Partinal in Manessier's continuation of *Perceval*, and like the giant Eocho Glas in F.[69]

The Gallan episode in the Huth *Merlin* is a mere fragment, retold by somebody who did not understand what he was telling. Nevertheless, that we are right in identifying Gallan in *Merlin* with Galam is proved by Manessier's story [70] of a knight who rides invisible and slays Grail folk who are enemies to King Margon. The invisible riding knight must be Galam, so once more we find Galam and Amargen, here called Margon, working together as enemies of the Grail folk.

"King of the Hundred Knights" is a title given to King Margon when he is received into Arthur's company. It is often in the romances given to Margon, Malaquin, and Aguingnier (Anguis). This makes it probable that it is in origin a general title for the king of the dead and refers to his numerous subjects. In *Le Bel Inconnu*,[71] the King of the Red City brings one hundred knights. In *Sir Orfeo*, the king of the dead, who like Conaing is nameless, has one hundred knights:

> þo com her king al so bliue
> wiþ an hundred knightes and mo.[72]

(vss. 140–141)

---

bk. II, chap. 14), he is "Garlon of the black face." In the Welsh *Bruts* (ed. A. Griscom, *Hist. reg. Brit.*, p. 453), he is Kasswallawn Lawhir, lord of Gwynedd. *Lawhir*, "long arm," may refer to the invisible sword and may be connected with the Irish epithet, Balar *birugderc*, "Balar of the piercing eye."

[69] Potvin, *Perceval*, VI, 130, vss. 44615 f. (see p. 58).
[70] Potvin, *Perceval*, III, 352, vss. 19675 f.
[71] Edition Williams, vs. 5481.
[72] French and Hale, *Middle Eng. Met. Rom.*, p. 327. On the "fairy

The same idea that made Máelmura [73] call Bregond "full of troops," Amargen "wide-ruling," that led another poet in LG [74] to call the tower of Bregond, *bruinig*, "of large companies," and another to call Tech Duinn "rich in hosts," may have caused the romance writers to invent the name "King of the Hundred Knights."

Because they take a part in the story exactly like that taken in Irish saga by the Fomorian leader, it is highly probable that Clamadeu and Esclados in Chrétien's romances bear names that are deformations of Galam.

ITH

Ith and Bile were sons of that Bregon who built a tower in Spain. According to a version of LG at least as old as 887,[75] Ith saw Ireland from the tower and voyaged thither. There he met three Irish kings, MacCuill, MacCecht, and MacGrene (who, as has been seen, were forms of Nuadu), praised their country, and was slain by them. Ith's followers carried his body back to Spain and, by showing it, aroused Bile's son, Galam, also called Míl, and the sons of Míl, to their famous invasion. Ith was the first man of the Milesians who died in Ireland.[76] No reason why he was killed is given. An explanation is supplied by a late text, *Oided Chloinne Tuirenn.*[77] This says that Fomorians were at Nuadu's court demanding tribute, as we know they customarily did. Lug, who had just come to court, grew

---

cavalcade" or fairy host, see L. C. Wimberley, *Folklore in English and Scottish Ballads* (Chicago, 1928), p. 193; and Andreas Capellanus, p. 346.

[73] Page 256.

[74] Edition R. A. S. Macalister, II, 113.

[75] The date of Máelmura's poem (see p. 255).

[76] Page 256.

[77] Page 236.

angry, slew many of them and sent the survivors back with a refusal. These stirred up the Fomorians to their invasion. I accept here the idea, which is really demanded by the context in *LG*, that Ith came to collect tribute or to assert some claim to the land, perhaps to seize upon the queen Ériu, and was slain by Lug.

The slaying of Ith I suppose to have occurred under circumstances similar to those in which the Red Knight was slain by Perceval. The queen represented the sovereignty. Both here and in *Perceval* I conjecture that the invader in an older form of the story took the queen, Ériu or Guenevere, as his wife, just as Amargen evidently seized Queen Banba in the invasion myth.[78]

Evidence for this hypothesis is as follows: In invasion 4 occurs the statement: "Topa is the same as Ith," [79] which probably means that their stories were the same. Topa, according to *LG*, seduced Partholon's queen, Elgnat, and was slain by him. It is therefore probable that in another form of the Irish story Ith carried off Nuadu's queen, Ériu, and for that abduction was slain.

It has been shown that Nuadu corresponds to Arthur, Ériu to Guenevere, and Ith to Modred. Modred in an older form of the story probably carried off Guenevere. This inference finds support in the Welsh triads. A triad in the Red Book [80] says that Medraut dragged Guenevere from her royal chair and struck her. A triad in the *Myvyrian Archaiology* [81] says that Medraut made a criminal assault on Guenevere. It will be remembered that Geoffrey wrote

[78] Pages 250 f. [79] Page 263.
[80] J. Loth, *Les Mabinogion*, II, 247, triad 19 of the Red Book.
[81] Page 406, triad 52. Geoffrey's *Historia*, bk. x, chap. 13, p. 496: "Ganhumaram . . . eidem [Modred] nefando uenere copulatam fuisse."

"Queen Guanhumara, in violation of her first marriage, had wickedly married [Modred]." The story probably was at first like that of Amargen and Banba.

Ith, I suppose, has been changed in French to Ither, which is Wolfram's name for the Red Knight, and then, perhaps by the influence of the well-known Yders li fiz Nut, to Yders. He is, I think, the Yders of the following passage from *Erec*,[82] where Arthur's knights are assembled:

> Au consoil granz partie cort
> Des mellors barons de la cort.
> Li rois Yders i est alez,
> Qui premiers i fu apelez.
> Aprés li rois Cadoalanz
> Qui mout fu sages et vaillanz.
> Keus et Girflez i sont venu,
> Et Amauguins li rois i fu,
> Et des autres barons assez
> I ot avuec aus amassez.
>
> (vss. 311–320)

This passage declares that Yders was the first one summoned to Arthur's court, which may be a distortion of the statement in the Irish *LG* that Ith was the first Milesian visitor to Nuadu's court.

Yders del Mont Dolereus, "Dolorous Mountain" (which I take to be a Dolorous Tower or a tower of the dead), who is mentioned in a longer list of knights of the Round Table which occurs some fourteen hundred lines later, must again be our Ith of Bregon's tower in Spain. The passage is as follows:

> Et Caverons de Robendic
> Et li fiz au roi Quenedic

[82] Edition W. Foerster.

Et li vaslez de Quintareus
Et Yders del Mont Dolereus,
Gaherïez et Keus d'Estraus,
Amauguins et Gales li chaus,
Grains, Gornevains et Carahés
Et Torz li fiz le roi Arés.
Girflez li fiz Do et Taulas
Qui onques d'armes ne fu las;
Et uns vaslez de grant vertu,
Loholz li fiz le roi Artu,
Et Sagremors li desreez,
Cil ne doit pas estre obliëz,
Ne Bedoiiers li conestables,
Qui mout sot d'eschas et de tables,
Ne Bravaïns ne Loz li rois,
Ne Galegantins li Galois,
Ne li fiz Keu le seneschal
Gronosis qui mout sot de mal.

(vss. 1721–1740)

It has been shown that Yders in these passages [83] is not the Yders li fiz Nut of the romance *Yder* [84] but the same person

[83] J. H. Scholte, *Neophilologus*, V (1920), 119 f. Compare Margaret F. Richey, *Mod. Lang. Rev.*, XXVI (1931), 326 f. Hartmann von Aue's *Erec* (ed. M. Haupt [Leipzig, 1871], p. 352), according to the manuscript, reads at vs. 1658 "Iher Gaheries." This is probably a better reading than Yders of the Chrétien manuscripts, which besides offer the variants, "Hisoons, hideus, Idol, jdoc" (edition Foerster [Halle, 1890], p. 64).

[84] Edition H. Gelzer, *Gesellschaft f. rom. Lit.*, vol. XXXI (Halle, 1913). The following passage from *Rigomer* (ed. W. Foerster and H. Breuer, *Gesell. f. r. L.*, vols. XIX [1908], XXXIX [1917]), which may be imitated from *Erec* or from the source of *Erec*, mentions both *Itier li fius Nu* and our *Yders*, proving that they were not regarded as the same:

"Girfles et Amangons i fu
Gauduins et Itier li fius Nu.

(vss. 7065–7066)

as Wolfram's Ither von Gaheviez. Wolfram's Ither is, I
suppose, identical with Chrétien's Red Knight who came
to Arthur's court, carried off Arthur's cup, and was slain
by Perceval. Like Ith, this Red Knight was the first enemy
that came to court.

The truth, I conjecture, is that Ith was not in origin an
ancestor of the Irish at all, but a hateful Fomorian tax collector — perhaps a prince of the dead. Ith may appear to
us too little known to have influenced French romance,
but his memory was vivid in Irish tradition.[85] A trace of
the Irish story that Ith's body was carried to Spain to stir
the sons of Míl to vengeance appears to be preserved in
Gerbert's continuation of *Perceval*,[86] where we are told
that the body of the Red Knight slain by Perceval is found
in a casket that comes in a boat.

Gaherïez [87] is not the name of Gawain's brother but a
modification of Gaheviez. Wolfram always writes Ither
von Gaheviez, the meaning of which is unknown. In *Per-*

> . . . Lor vint l'Orgïlous de la Lande
> Drius et Garradains c'on i mande,
> Idiers i vint et Elibrans
> Et Pierchevaus et Gornimans
> Et li Valés de Quinquareus
> Et Bedinous et Gonereus.
> Don i vint Carahués Briébras."
> > (vss. 7091–7097)

Itiers is mentioned again later:

> "Et aprés Kes li senescals
> Et Itiers et Wales li Caus."
> > (vss. 10481–10482)

[85] W. J. Watson (*Scottish Gaelic Studies,* I [London, 1926], 19)
prints a fifteenth-century poem that calls a hero "a sea-borne Ith."

[86] Edition Mary Williams, II, 118 f., vss. 10741 f.

[87] *Erec,* vs. 1725, p. 178.

lesvaus,[88] Clamados des Onbres is said to be the son of
Chrétien's Red Knight (= Ither). Further on another
knight, Cahot li Roux, brother to this Clamados, is evidently one of those red or black warriors who hail from
the land of the dead. Clamados of the Shadows is surely
from the land of the dead. Since this Clamados, whom
Chrétien calls Clamadeu, is probably identical with Galam,
the following parallel appears between the Irish and French.
In Irish Galam is Ith's nephew; in French Clamadeu is
Ither's son. In both cases, Galam (Clamadeu) belongs to
the next generation from Ith (Ither). In the Irish *Auraicept*[89] neither Breogan nor Ith is mentioned, but possibly
Gaedel son of Ether is the same as Galam nephew of Ith.
The coincidences between what we are told of Ith in
Irish and what we know of Ither in the romances seem
numerous enough to prove that the one is the source of
the other.

LOTH

In the continuations of *Perceval* and in other romances,
Loth is king of the Orkneys.[90] As has been said, the kings
of the Orkneys were regarded as kings of the dead. Geoffrey in his *Historia* makes Loth ruler of two countries,
Lothain and Norway,[91] both of which were confused with
the land of the dead. Lothain was the supposed deadly
region north of the Roman Wall;[92] Lochlann or Norway

[88] Edition Nitze and Jenkins, vss. 3042 f. and 3207.

[89] Edition Calder, *Auraicept na n-Éces*, l. 1107.

[90] See Hilka, *Perceval*, p. 762 (note on vs. 8135); Foerster, *Li Chevaliers
as deus espées* (Halle, 1877), p. 93, vs. 2944; "le roi Loth d'Orcanie."
See above, p. 142.

[91] Bk. viii, chap. 21, p. 428; and bk. ix, chap. 11, p. 447.

[92] Page 340.

was to the Irish a land of the Fomorians and of the dead.

It does not seem possible to keep the name *Loth* [93] apart from *Lot*, which in Irish means "destruction." In invasion 5 the Fomorians are led by Morc son of Dela.[94] In invasion 6 the Fir Bolg are the children of Dela the son of Loth.[95] In origin this Dela was doubtless the same as the Dela in invasion 5, and the Fomorians and Fir Bolg were identical. In invasion 4 the leader of the Fomorians is Cichol Grigenchos. His father was Goll, and Lot *luamnach* was his mother.[96] This Lot must be the Loth of invasion 6 turned into a woman. Her deformed appearance proves that she belongs to the ugly Fomorians.

According to Geoffrey's *Historia*,[97] Anna, Arthur's sister, was Loth's wife. This, I suppose, is another case of a Fomorian seizing upon a *fée* who is virtually the country personified. That Gawain is Loth's son is surprising, but in *CMT* the god Lug is grandson to the terrible Fomorian Balar, who may be equated with Loth.[98] In short, what we know tends to show that *Loth* or *Lot*, like *Balar*, was a traditional name for a Fomorian king of the dead.

MARG

According to the Invasion of Nemed in *LG*,[99] Conaing, king of the Fomorians, lived at Tor Conaing which is the modern Tory Island. He and his deputy, Morc son of Dela son of Lot, oppressed the children of Nemed by

[93] To the St. Gall glossator, *loth* meant "mud," or [the infernal] "fen" (*Thesaurus Paleohibernicus*, II, 149 [St. Gall, 127a]).

[94] R. A. S. Macalister, *LG*, III, 123.

[95] Macalister, *LG*, IV, 16.

[96] Macalister, *LG*, III, 10; and II, 260.

[97] Bk. viii, chap. 21, pp. 427–428.   [98] Page 229.

[99] Edition Macalister, III, 122 f. (summarized on p. 263).

collecting a tax of two-thirds of their grain, milk, and children. According to the *Dinnshenchas of Mag Léige* [100] the tribute was actually collected by Liag, "woe," who was Morc's sister. Lot, the name of Morc's grandfather, means "destruction" [101] and is probably a name for the king of the dead. Conaing, "king," is, I think, a name for Balar. Tory Island evidently, like Tech Duinn and like Móin Conaing [102] (modern Anglesey), was believed by the ancient Irish to be an island of the dead.

The *Dinnshenchas of Sliab Mairge* tells of Margg, steward of the king of the Fomorians, collecting taxes from Leinster-men. It runs as follows: "Marg, son of Giusach, son of Lodan the Grey of Luchair, was the steward of the Fo-morians' king, whose name was 'Century-ear,' that is, having one hundred ears. Now Eocho Muniste was king over the province of Leinster. The Leinstermen brought their law-ful tribute [to Marg]." [103]

The first two stanzas of the corresponding metrical *Dinnshenchas* read:

> Margg, son of Giusca, fair of form,
> Son of Lodan Liath from Luachair,
> Came, in spite of fasting from food,
> To the house of Eochu Muniste.

> The noble steward came
> From the powerful king of the hundred ears

[100] Edition Stokes, the prose *Dinnshenchas, Rev. celt.,* XVI (1895), 160.

[101] Macalister, *LG,* II, 258, and III, 192.

[102] J. Rhŷs, *Arthurian Legend,* p. 356.

[103] Edition Stokes, *Rev. celt.,* XV (1894), 426. The text is: "Marg mac Giusoigh meic Lodoin Leith Luachra, rechtaire ríg Fomoire .i. Cend-tarcluais a ainm .i. cétcluasta. Eocha dano Munisti for cóicid Gailian ann. Targlamsat Laigin a cís rechtaidhe do."

To demand tribute afar
To the house of the valiant king of the Leinstermen.[104]

Three more stanzas relate the collecting of taxes and the slaying of Margg.

The Bodleian manuscript of the prose *Dinnshenchas* in the corresponding passage reads: "Marg son of Giuscach son of Lodan the Red." [105] Lodan the Red exhibits the red color attributed to Fomorians. This Lodan the Red is evidently the same as Lodan Léith, "the Gray," of Lúachair, in Gwynn's text. The Gray of Lúachair is well-known. In *Macgnímartha Finn*,[106] he is Cumall's great enemy who wounded him and took his treasures. The Gray of Lúachair, who was finally slain by Cumall's son Finn, is in *Macgnímartha Finn* a parallel figure to the Red Knight in Chrétien's *Perceval*. In the poem "Ériu ard inis na ríg," Morc is *drech-deirg*, "red-faced." Marg was Lot's grandson, and Geoffrey [107] calls Modred Loth's son. The name Marg, I conjecture, had some connection with that of Modred, who seized Arthur's throne and queen.

Margg, steward of the king of the Fomorians, who is slain while collecting taxes from the men of Leinster, must be the same as Morc who collected taxes for the king of

[104] Gwynn, *Met. Dinn.*, III, 162. The text of the second stanza is:
"Tánic in rechtaire rán
ó ríg na cét clúas comlán,
do chungid chobaig co cían,
co tech ríg golaich Galían."
[105] Edition Stokes, *Folk-Lore*, III (1892), 502: "Marg mac Giusccaig mac Ladain Ruaidh."
[106] Edition Kuno Meyer, *Ériu*, I, 185 f. The poem "Ériu ard" is attributed to Giolla Coemhain, and was edited by B. Mac Carthy (*RIA*, Todd Lect. Ser., III [Dublin, 1892], p. 147).
[107] *Historia*, bk. ix, chap. 9, p. 444.

the Fomorians in the first story. The two stories outlined are the same story, except that in the first the king of the dead is Conaing, and in the second Cendtarcluais. The king of terrors has no proper name, only epithets, and Cendtarcluais is an epithet meaning "having one hundred ears." Why this should be appropriate for the king of the dead is not clear to me; but Death, the unconquered king to whom all the human race are subjects, has vast domains and countless followers. Hence he is sometimes called King of the Hundred Knights.[108] "One hundred ears" may have some connection with that title.

This unusual name Cendtarcluais perhaps reappears in Chrétien's *Erec* as Quintareus:

> Et li vaslez de Quintareus
> Et Yders del Mont Dolereus
> Gaherïez et Keus d'Estraus
> Amauguins et Gales li chaus.

(vss. 1723–1726)

The rechtaire, "steward," of the Fomorians' King Cendtarcluais is, I conjecture, the same as the "vaslez de Quintareus" in *Erec,* and as the "valés de Quinquareus" in *Rigomer.*[109] Both names occur in lists of enemies, corresponding to Fomorians, who have been conquered and, according to King Arthur's well-known custom, have been made members of the Round Table.

Nemed, in the invasion of Nemed, corresponds, as was shown above, to Nuadu in the invasion of the sons of Míl. Both have wives named Macha. It is clear that Balar or Conaing corresponds to Galam or Míl. All four names are

[108] Page 391.
[109] Page 396.

epithets for the king of the dead. Morc or Margg, the deputy of Conaing, corresponds to Amargen, the son or seneschal of Galam. In the Nemed story the seneschal is Margg; in the Nuadu story he is Amargen. Margg and Amargen do not appear together. Marg, Aingen, and Amargen seem to be interchangeable. All three are probably names for one personage who is the deputy of the king of the Fomorians or the king of the dead.

RION AND BALAR

The Irish regarded the land of death as an island. A usual location for it was south of Ireland at Tech Duinn, but later it was moved north to Tory Island, and then to *insi gall*, "the Hebrides," and *Orc*, "the Orkneys." The mythical giants or Fomorians of the land of the dead were confused with the hostile Lochlannach, "Norsemen," who came to Ireland by way of the Orkneys and the Hebrides. In H, Lochlann is Fomorian land and in R, Garb, "rough," a Fomorian, comes from Lochlann.[110]

Balar, a Fomorian monster with one dreadful eye that killed all who beheld it was, or became, death in person.[111] He has been regarded as a personification of the "evil eye" which in modern Irish is called *súil Balair*, "Balar's eye." [112] According to *CMT*, Balar was "king of the isles." It is probable that this was an Irish epithet for the king of the dead that passed over into the French Arthurian romances.

[110] Pages 66, 81. The Irish transferred to the Norwegians all the Fomorian epithets. For example, Sumerled, who was king of the Hebrides in the year 1164, was called "ri insi-gall," a title that was often shortened to "rí inse" (Tigernach's continuator, *Rev. celt.*, XVIII [1897], 195).   [111] Page 172.

[112] Page 233. See "Einäugigkeit" in *Handwörterbuch des deutschen Märchens*, I, 477.

In Irish mythological stories, death is almost always designated by some epithet. He is Donn, "the brown one," Míl, "the soldier," or Conaing, "the king." In the French romances death is nameless, and his abode is the "cité sans nom," the "castiel sans nom," or "l'ille perdue." [113] The ferryman in *Perceval* is terror-struck when asked the name of the lord of Chastel Merveilleus and cannot answer.[114] Chrétien never calls the terrible lord who built this castle anything except "un clers sage d'astrenomie." Wolfram calls him Clinschor, "clutcher," which has been recognized as an epithet for the king of the dead.

In Pseudo-Wauchier's continuation of *Perceval* it is said of Brangemuer:

> Rois fu des illes de la mer;
> En une des illes estoit
> Où nus mortiez hom n'abitoit.
>
> (vss. 21875–21877)

In Gerbert's continuation of *Perceval*,[115] the king of the dead, who is called Knight of the Dragon and is brother to King Maragon, has a city in "les illes de mer." In the prose *Lancelot*, Branduz des Illes is Sires de la Dolereuse Garde — that is, of the tower of the dead. In *Humbaut* [116] the "king of the isles" is certainly a king of the dead.

Near the beginning of *Perceval*, Chrétien implies that his readers know that Rion means "king of the isles," or at least know him to be "king of the isles." Without explanation Chrétien introduces Rion thus:

[113] Edition M. Friedwagner, *Meraugis*, vs. 2816; *Raguidel*, vs. 5056; Vulgate *Lancelot*, III, 125.
[114] Pages 139, 192.
[115] Edition Mary Williams, vss. 8981 f.
[116] Edition Stürzinger and Breuer, pp. 99 f.

Li rois Artus o tote s'ost
S'est au roi Rion conbatuz.
Li rois des isles fu veincuz.

(vss. 850–852)

No student of the romance seems to have noticed that
Rion is merely the Irish epithet *rí inse* made into a name.
"Ryence" is a spelling used by Malory [117] and others. The
spelling Rion may be like *pean* for *penn*, an attempt to
represent an Irish velar "n." [118]

To some it will occur at once to object that Geoffrey of
Monmouth could not have extracted his form Rithon from
Irish *rí inse*. Geoffrey [119] makes Arthur tell how he once
slew on Mount Snowdon a giant named Ritho. This giant
had fashioned for himself furs out of the beards of the
kings he had killed, and had sent word to King Arthur to
cut off his beard and send it to him. To the above objection
some forms of the name mentioned by Zimmer [120] supply
an answer. Geoffrey may have followed not a French or
English but a Breton source in which the name had become
first Rith and then Rithan. Geoffrey's Ritho is the same as
Rion and has evidently attributes belonging to the king
of the dead. The tribute of beards, as has been shown above,
is an attenuated form of Charon's fee and indicates that
Rion is a king of the dead. Arthur talks about Ritho immediately after killing at Mont Saint-Michel a very similar
giant who came from Spain. Spain, as we now know, means
the land of the dead. The two giants Arthur talks about
are alike, and they probably both came from the land of
the dead.

[117] *Morte Darthur*, bk. I, chap. 17 (ed. Sommer, I, 62).
[118] On the spelling see Max Förster, *Englische Studien*, LVI (1922),
233.   [119] *Historia*, bk. x, chap. 3, p. 473.
[120] *ZFS*, XIII (1891), 41.

Brugger has identified Rion des isles with Ris de Valen in Pseudo-Wauchier's continuation,[121] who in a tournament is leader of the party opposed to Arthur. Valen is, of course, for Avalon and is an appropriate name for a king of the dead. Brugger recognizes [122] Rion again in Roi Ris d'Outre Ombre who in Li Chevaliers as deus espées [123] sends an insolent message to Arthur demanding his beard. *Ombre*, although doubtless understood as the River Humber, probably originally stood for Onbres and meant the land of Scath or "shadow." [124] Thomas in his *Tristan* tells the same story of Riton and the beards that is in Geoffrey, but he calls the giant "l'Orguillus." [125]

Orguilleus is an old traditional name for the king of the dead. Shakespeare gives death this epithet in *Hamlet*: "Alas, proud death, what feast is toward in thy eternal cell." [126] Galaholt's chief castle is l'Orguellouse Emprise.[127] Orguilleus, the giant of Mont Dolerous in *Fergus*,[128] who has

[121] Potvin, *Perceval*, vss. 13492 f.

[122] *ZFS*, XXVII (1904), 102 f., and compare XLIV, 46. The King of the Red City is the same person.

[123] Edition Foerster, vss. 166 f. Roi Ris is besieging the Queen of Caradigan, which seems to be for Caer Agned or Edinburgh, which is the "Castle of Maidens." It is good mythology to find the king of the isles (Balar) besieging the Castle of Maidens (palace of the Tuatha Dé). Two triads make "Rhitta the Giant" one of three tyrants over the isle Britain (J. Loth, *Les Mabinogion*, II, 314). As Balar tyrannized over Ireland, his Welsh equivalent is pictured as a tyrant over Britain.

[124] In *Perlesvaus* (vs. 3042) Clamados is said to be son to the "Chevalier au Vermel Escu de la Forest des Onbres." Since this is the Red Knight whom Perceval slew, it is surely right to understand this to be the Forest of Shadows, i. e. land of death.

[125] Edition J. Bédier (Paris, 1902, 1905), I, 289, n.

[126] V, ii, 352; compare *Sir Orfeo* (ed. French and Hale, *Middle Eng. Met. Rom.*, p. 334, vs. 374); "þe proude court of paradis."

[127] Prose *Lancelot*, III, 430.

[128] Edition E. Martin (Halle, 1872), vss. 4440 f.

captive two wretched damsels, is evidently a prince of the dead. Orguilleus de la lande in the first part of Chrétien's *Perceval, Y,* and Orguilleus de la roche in the third part, *AA,* are probably in origin one and the same person, who was a prince of the dead. The title l'Orguillus is appropriate for the giant Riton.

In the Vulgate *Merlin,*[129] Rion is king of the land of giants where no man dare dwell. Arthur is told by Merlin that he must drive Rion out of Carmelide, the kingdom of Leodegan whom Rion is oppressing, and win Leodegan's daughter, Gwinevere, as queen. Arthur does this and also wins from Rion a marvellous sword, Marmidoise. In the English *Sir Launfal,*[130] "Gwennere" is daughter of King Ryon of Ireland. A Welsh triad [131] makes Gwenhwyvar daughter of Ocurvran the giant. These references are best explained by supposing that King Rion is a Fomorian giant who personifies winter and darkness, and who has absorbed many of the characteristics of the king of the dead. Leodegan is the oppressed Hospitable Host whom Arthur rescues and displaces. Guenevere is virtually the sovereignty of Britain. She was at first the giant's wife, but later, by natural development, his daughter and then daughter to the Hospitable Host. Arthur is the youthful hero who delivers her from the giant and wins with her the kingdom and a set of talismans, especially his sword Excalibur and his Round Table. Since Rion appears in the romances as a hostile giant, it is well-nigh certain that his name comes from *rí inse.*

[129] Sommer, *Vulgate Romances,* II, 92 f.

[130] Edition French and Hale, *Middle Eng. Met. Rom.,* p. 347, vs. 42.

[131] See J. Loth, *Les Mabinogion,* I, 259, n. 3. The Welsh *Brut* (translated in A. Griscom, *Historia,* p. 445) calls Guenevere "daughter of Gogvran the giant."

The resemblances in names pointed out above tend to prove that the marvelous material in Chrétien's romances, although transmitted doubtless with additions, by Welsh or Bretons, was worked up by the Irish. Already in *Erec*, his first romance, Chrétien had before him a list of names that included the Irish Cai in the form Keu; Finnabair in the form Guenievre; Ith in the form Yder; Lot in the form Loz, and Amargen in the form Amauguins. In his *Perceval* he mentions Keu and Lot, and in addition the Irish words *criol* in the form *graal*, *Calad-bolg* in the form Escalibor, *rí inse* in the form Rion, and the Irish names, Turbe as Triboet, and Galam as Clamadeu. Other names, Anfortas, Brion, and Granlande, point toward Irish sources.

CHAPTER XIII

Loch Erne

AN ECHO of the old myth which represented Ireland
as a lady fought for by a friendly god and a hostile
giant is preserved in a fragment called *Loch Erne* in the
Dinnshenchas. In this fragment the lady is called Findchaem, and the combatants are Amargen and Olc Ai. It is
believed that these three figures correspond respectively to
Ériu, Amargen, and Brión in the form of the myth outlined
in previous chapters. This version of the ruin of fairyland
by Fomorians, although incomplete, is of importance because it has not been altered, like the stories of *LG*, into an
invasion of Ireland, and it still tells of talismans belonging
to the queen of the country. The queen in this story is not
Ériu but Medb. *Loch Erne* connects Amargen with the
treasures and cups of Medb, and throws light on his character. Stokes translates it as follows:

Erne daughter of Borg the bellowing,[1] son of Manchín, son
of Machu, chieftainess of the girls of Cruachan, and keeper of
Medb of Cruachan's combs and caskets. Once upon a time
Olc Ai issued from the Cave of Cruachu to contend with
Amargen the Blackhaired when he slept with Findchoem
daughter of Magach. And then Olc Ai shook his beard and
gnashed his teeth so that Erne and her maidens because of her

---

[1] Perhaps all that this means is that Borg had the loud voice of a god.
Compare *Cóir Anmann*, §§ 78, 247, *Ir. Texte*, III, ii, 325; and Gwynn,
Met. Dinn., III, 330, l. 16; 334, l. 23.

terror went to flight, and reached Loch Erne, and there they were all drowned. Whence Loch Erne is said.[2]

Two other manuscripts, *BB* and H. 3. 3., contain the prose *Loch Erne*. In every case it is immediately followed in the manuscript by the verse *Loch Erne*.[3] A shorter prose *Loch Erne* has been edited by Stokes from manuscript XVI Kilbride. His translation is as follows:

Erne, daughter of Borg the Bellowing, son of Manchin, was the keeperess of Medb of Cruachu's comb-baskets, and leader of the maidens of the men of Connaught. Now when Olca Ai went out of the cave of Cruachu to contend against Amargen

[2] The prose *Dinnshenchas*, *Rev. celt.*, XV (1894), 483–483, § 80. Because the Rennes manuscript, which Stokes elsewhere follows, has lost a leaf containing sections Loch Rí, Loch Erne, Ess Ruaid, and Druim Cliab, he uses here manuscript Lecan (p. 498, col. a). His text is: Erni ingen Buirc Buireadaich mac Ma(n)chin maic Machon, bantaisech ingenraid(e) na Cruachnai ocus banchoimedaith do chiraib ocus do clioirib Meidbi Cruachan. Fecht ann doluid Olc Ai a huaim Chruachan do chomroc fri hAimirgin nIargi(u)ndach dia rofai la Findchaim ingin Magach, conad and rochroith Olc Ai a ulcha ocus robean a deda, co ndeachaid Erne cona hingenaib for fualang ar a imoman, co riacht Loch nErne, co robaidead and diblinaib. Unde Loch nErne dicitur.

[3] *BB* (p. 391, col. a, ll. 21–29) reads: "Eirni ingen buirg buiredaig mac Mainchin mac Macon bantoisec ingenraidi na Cruacan ocus bancoimedaig do cirib ocus do cleráib Medbi Cruacan. Fecht and doluid olccai a huaim Cruacan do comrag fri hAmirgen inurargiunnac dorofai la Findciem ingin Magac conid and forochroit olcan a ulca ocus robean a deta condeochaid Erne cona ingenraid for fualang ar a imomon co riact loc nErne robaidead and ganglan ford." According to a transcript kindly made for me by Dr. Vernam Hull, H. 3. 3. reads: "Erni .i. buirc buiredach mac mainchin mac mochon bantoisech ingenraide naCruachna ocus bancoimetaighe do chioraib ocus chriolaibh medb cruachan Fecht ann doluit olccai a hoaim cruachan do comrad fri haimircin niarghriunach dia rofaidh la Fincaim .i. maghach conid and forochroit olccai a ulchai ocus robean adettai ocus (robean adettai) condechaid erni co na .i. raid for fualang ara imomon co riest loch nerni corobaidhit and diblinaib unde Loch Eirni dicitur."

the Blackhaired, he shook his beard at them and gnashed his teeth, so that the boys and girls of the country went mad, and their tragical death was caused by dread of him. Then Erne with her maidens ran to Lough Erne, and the lough drowned them. Thence is the name Loch Erne.[4]

As will be seen, this Edinburgh manuscript omits the sentence, "Because he slept with Findchoem." The motive for this omission might be reticence. For example, B. O'Looney who printed the Lecan prose,[5] translated the words: *dia rofai la Findchaim*, as "who had espoused Findchaom."

The verse *Dinnshenchas* has been edited from seven manuscripts by Edward J. Gwynn.[6] His translation of the verses in which we are interested is as follows:

> The chaste Erne, who knew no art of wounding,
> The daughter of loud-shouting Borg Bán
> The name was an insult to the noble (?)
> The white-skinned son of Mainchin son of Mochu.

> The noble Erne, free from venom,
> Was chief among the maidens
> In Rath Cruachan, home of lightsome sports;
> Women not a few obeyed her will.

> She had in keeping to her credit
> The trinkets of Medb, famed for combats,

[4] Stokes' text (*Folk-Lore*, IV (1893), 476) reads: "Eirne ingen Buirg Buireadhaigh meic Manchin, banchoimhedaid do chir comraraib Meadbha Cruachan, ocus bantaiseach ingenraidhe fer Ollnegmacht. Intan iarumh doluidh Olca ái a huaimh Cruachan do chomrag fri Amhairghin Iarghiundach rochroith a ulcha ann doibh (ocus roben a déta) go ndeachadar for dasacht macrada ocus ingenradha in tiri, go ndernadh a n-aidhead ann ar a omhon. Da reith dano Eirne cona hingenraidh go Loch nEirne, go rosbaidh in loch. Is desin ata Loch nEirne."

[5] *RIA, Irish Manuscript Series* (Dublin, 1870), I, 186–193.

[6] *Metrical Dinnshenchas*, III, 464–465.

Her comb, her casket unsurpassed,
With her fillet of red gold.[7]

There came to thick-wooded Cruachu
Olcai with grim and dreadful fame,
And he shook his beard at the host,
The sullen and fiery savage.

The young women and maidens
Scattered throughout Cruach Cera
At the apparition of his grisly shape
And the roughness of his brawling voice.

Erne fled with a troop of women,
Under Loch Erne, that is never dull,
And over them poured its flood northward
And drowned them all together.

The verse *Loch Erne,* it will be observed, omits not only the words "because he slept with Findchoem," but also the phrase "to fight with Amorgen." The words omitted, in part in the shorter prose version and altogether in the verse, must belong to the original story because they supply the motive for Erne's flight. She and her maidens fled because violence had been done to one of their number.

Loch Erne is discussed in one stanza of a poem written by Gilla na nem O'Duind in 1166 [8] which reads as follows:

[7] Gwynn's text of this stanza reads:

"Aicci nobítis ria mess
Min-seóit Medba na mór-thress,
A cír a criol cen chlod
Cona diol do derg-ór."

[8] Edition E. Gwynn, *Ériu,* X (1926), 80 (from the Book of Uí Maine). His text reads:

"Eirni, robaidh usce a hanma
A ath(air) Buireadach Bolc:

Erne, the water that was named from her, drowned her,
Her father was Bolc the Bellowing;
Servant-maid [was] she to Medb [who was] no coward,
She lost her form before the outbreak of Olch,
When Olch came from Cruachan
She stopped from among the peoples of the boar.[9]

The statement that Erne was drowned in Loch Erne is the usual euhemerism. Erne is, of course, the lake personified. Originally she and her maidens fled to a fairy dwelling beneath Loch Erne. According to Irish popular belief this lake contains fairy dwellers.[10]

Findchaem in ninth-century sagas is Amargen's wife.[11] Everything indicates that this is because of the existence of a tradition like that recorded in *Loch Erne* and not vice versa. *Loch Erne* does not present Amargen in a sufficiently favorable light to make it possible to consider it a late invention, made after Amargen and Findchaem became important epic figures and the parents of the well-known Conall Cernach. The Amergen of *Loch Erne* is a black-haired monster who comes from the land of the dead, not the *rígfile* of the heroic sagas.

Inailt hi do Meidb na midlach
Fa cli dheilbh re hindlach n-Olch:
A h-Olch don cuinis o Cruachain
Roscuir o thuathaib na torch."

[9] This is my translation. The last line probably means that she died, but I am not certain.

[10] The Irish story, "Conn-eda or The Golden Apples of Loch Erne" (*Cambrian Journal*, II [1855], 101–115), tells of talismans belonging to a king who lives under Loch Erne. In regard to the general idea compare how LíBan lived for three hundred years under Loch Echach (O'Grady, *Silv. Gad.*, I, 234; and II, 267).

[11] "Findchæm ingen Cathbad ben Amargin Iarngiunnaig," *Fled Bricrend*, edition Henderson, *ITS*, II, 34.

Whatever hypothesis we may adopt about the relationship of the prose to the verse, it is certain that the prose of
Loch Erne is older than the time of Chrétien,[12] and probably much older. *Loch Erne*, and its companion piece
Loch Rí, which comes just before it in the manuscripts,
are fragments of ancient mythology. Doubtless both are
based upon two *tomaidmann*, "floods," *Tomaidm Loch
Echdach*, and *Tomaidm Locha Eirne*, which are mentioned
together in lists A and B of Irish sagas.[13] These *tomaidmann*
are lost, but, since they occur in both lists, they existed in
some form in the tenth century. The prose of *Loch Erne*
and *Loch Rí*, doubtless because it is founded upon these
ancient *tomaidmann*, is more complete and better than the
verse, as inspection will show. For instance, the verse of
Loch Rí[14] omits two important points, namely that the
flight discussed was an elopement and, secondly, that the
síd referred to was the famous *Brug maic in Oc*. These
points, which are given in the prose of *Loch Rí*, were in
the original story, for they are told in the verse *Dinnshenchas of Tuag Inber* and in a lake legend in *LU* called
Aided Echach maic Maireda.[15] Unless we are entirely on
the wrong track, *Loch Rí* and *Loch Erne*, because they are
stories of beginnings dealing with the formation and the
settlement of Ireland, are very old and are a part of the
ruins of ancient mythology.

Loch Erne is evidently an imperfect report of a myth
resembling the Greek tale of the rape of Persephone by

[12] Gwynn, *Met. Dinn.*, V (1935), 114.
[13] On these lists see Thurneysen, *Heldensage*, p. 23.
[14] Gwynn, *Met. Dinn.*, III (1913), 450–459.
[15] Gwynn, *Met. Dinn.*, IV (1924), 58–67; S. H. O'Grady, *Silv. Gad.*,
I, 233 f., II, 265 f.

Hades. The Greek story tells, according to an Homeric hymn,[16] that Persephone daughter of Demeter, while straying in a field of flowers in Enna in the island of Sicily, was carried off by Hades to the land of the dead. Another hymn [17] tells how Zeus saw Europa gathering flowers and carried her off. This field of flowers in an island is like the Irish "Island of Women." Europa, of course, as a country personified, is an exact parallel to Banba, who is a personification of Ireland.

Medb corresponds to Demeter or the Earth-Mother. In neither story is the mother present. The Irish incident varies from the Greek in that Medb is not anywhere said to be Findchaem's mother. Findchaem, "lovely fair," [18] represents Ireland in the glory of summer and corresponds to Persephone. Both Findchaem and Persephone have a troop of maidens. Erne, who is the lake personified, takes the place of the absent Medb and actually plays the rôle of Banba.[19]

A difference between the Greek and the Irish is that in the Irish the heroine, Findchaem, is not carried away to the land of the dead but is overpowered in her own land. Amargen in Irish is more of an assailant than an abductor, and yet the idea of permanently carrying Findchaem off is surely present, for the Irish sagas make her wife to Amargen. The Homeric Hymn goes on to relate that Demeter in her sorrow became ugly but suddenly transformed herself to

[16] *Hesiod, the Homeric Hymns, and Homerica,* Loeb Classical Library, hymn ii, p. 289.   [17] *Ibid.,* 171.

[18] Rhŷs (*Celtic Heathendom,* p. 539) conjectured that Findchaem was a "dawn goddess."

[19] Erne playing the rôle of Banba makes one think of an ancient Greek name for Ireland Ἰέρνη. For this name see J. F. Kenney, *Sources of the Early History of Ireland,* I, 130, 133.

be beautiful again; also how she by spells withheld the crops till Rhea persuaded her to release her spells. Both of these incidents find parallels in the stories of Banba. She was ugly at first and she could withhold prosperity. The symbols of Demeter [20] included a basket of fruit and a little pig. The basket was no doubt a plenty-object like the Grail, and the little pig reminds us of the name Banba, which means a "suckling pig." The symbols of Persephone include a little box. The "comb and caskets of Medb" that Erne kept correspond to this little box and to the cornucopia with which Demeter and Persephone are often pictured. These objects are the symbols and the sources of plenty.

Olc Ai corresponds to nothing in the Greek myth. He is a warrior who came to the aid of the fairy maidens. The notion that they fled from his roughness, instead of from the attack of Amargen, is surely a mistake, doubtless made by the same redactor who inserted the statement that Erne and her maidens were drowned under the lake. Our difficulty is probably that *Loch Erne* is told from the point of view of the sons of Míl; that is, of Amargen. He married Findchaem. Any bad results of his carrying her off were laid to the blame of the Tuatha Dé; that is, to Olc Ai. Olc Ai seems to be a defender of the cup and the maidens; that is, of the Grail and the Grail damsels. He must, therefore, be Brión in one of his three forms.

Olc Ai I take to be the same person as Olc Acha the smith. Both *Cath Mucríme* and *Compert Cormaic* [21] tell a story of

---

[20] Pauly-Wissowa, *Real-Encyclopädie der klassischen Alterumswissenschaft* (Stuttgart, 1901), article *Demeter.*

[21] Edition Stokes from *LL, Rev. celt.,* XIII (1892), 455 f.; edition O'Grady, *Silv. Gad.,* I, 253; II, 286 f.

how Olc Acha the smith became the grandfather of King Cormac. Cormac, as we have seen, has borrowed talismans and stories from Brión. Probably this birth-story means to tell us that Brión was really Cormac's grandfather, just as Lug was Cuchulinn's father and Nuadu was Finn's grandfather. Olc Acha is probably another name for Goibniu the smith god. It has been shown above [22] that Goibniu is sometimes one form of the triformed Brión. It is highly probable that Olc Ai in the Loch Erne episode is a name for Goibniu who, as innkeeper and smith, was certainly lord of a caldron, which is probably the prototype of the Grail. Another story about Amargen in the *Cath Mucríme* seems to indicate that Brión was Amargen's opponent in battle. Stokes' translation is as follows:

Magh Mucríme, now, pigs of magic came out of the cave of Cruachain, and that is Ireland's gate of Hell. For out of it issued the monstrous triple-headed Bird that wasted Erin till Amairgene, the father of Conall Cernach, killed it in single combat before all the men of Ulster.

Out of it came the Red Birds that withered up everything in Erin that their breaths would touch, till the Ulstermen slew them with their slings.

Out of it moreover came these swine. Round whatever thing they used to go, till the end of seven years neither corn nor grass nor leaf would grow through it. (§§ 34–36.) [23]

This story looks like a confused version of the combat of Amargen and Olc Ai. The triple-headed bird may be a form assumed by Brión. Brión, like the Tuatha Dé in general, could doubtless assume bird form. In a gloss to the

[22] Page 161.
[23] *Rev. celt.*, XIII (1892), 448 f. Compare *Silv. Gad.*, I, 310–318; II, 347–359.

poem *Forty Questions*,[24] for example, one reads that the three brothers of Cessair, namely the triformed Brión, as I conjecture, for he would be her brother or husband, "were in bird form on Benn Boirche." The three birds of Rhiannon "that wake the dead and put the living to sleep" seem to be a manifestation of Brión.[25]

This passage in *Cath Mucríme* reverses the point of view to which we have been accustomed because it represents Brión of the Tuatha Dé as hostile, and even as laying Ireland waste. The same reversal of the usual point of view has been pointed out above in *Loch Erne*. In both stories Brión is hostile. The reason for this, doubtless, is that the pseudo-historians who wrote *LG* had taught the Irish that they were descendants of the sons of Míl. Although the black-haired Amargen, as has been seen above, never became popular as an ancestor, still he was one of the sons of Míl and as such became considered a friendly hero. His son, Conall Cernach, became a great Irish hero. Both stories, that in *Cath Mucríme* and that in the gloss to the poem, *Forty Questions*, are told from the point of view of the sons of Míl. To understand these stories we must adopt the point of view of these invaders to whom Brión, established king of Ireland, and of the Tuatha Dé, naturally appeared a dangerous and hostile figure. We, the readers, must consider ourselves as descended from Míl and must picture Brión as our enemy.

Loch Erne is a fragment accidentally preserved from the myth out of which the various invasions of *LG* were made. According to *LG* the sons of Míl married women of the Tuatha Dé, and from these marriages the Irish are descended.

[24] Edition Thurneysen, ZCP, XIII (1921), 131 (see p. 248).
[25] Page 302.

So, in *Loch Erne*, Findchaem becomes Amargen's wife and, according to the sagas, Conall Cornach, the well-known Ulster hero, was their son.

Loch Erne does not say that the land lost its fertility after the withdrawal of Erne and her maidens, but this destruction is probably implied. Irish sagas relate that after the sons of Míl captured Ireland, the Tuatha Dé fled to their underground dwellings, from which they issued to destroy the crops of the sons of Míl. *De Gabáil int Sída*, a ninth-century text,[26] relates that the Tuatha Dé after the conquest of Ireland by the sons of Míl retired to underground palaces, but thereafter destroyed the wheat of the sons of Míl till the latter made friendship with the Dagda.

Mesca Ulad B, which was composed about 1100–1125, says:

> When the sons of Míled of Spain reached Ériu, their sagacity circumvented the Tuatha Dé so that Ériu was left to the partition of Amargin Glunmar son of Míled; for he was a king-poet, and a king-judge. And he divided Ériu in two parts, and gave the part of Ériu that was underground to the Tuatha Dé, and the other part to the sons of Míled, his own clan. The Tuatha Dé went into hills and fairy places, so that they spoke with sidhe underground. They left five of their number before the five provinces of Ériu to excite war, and conflict, and valour, and strife, between the sons of Míled.[27]

Tochmarc Treblainne, a somewhat later text, says: "For the nobles of the sons of Míled were accustomed to take as foster-children the sons and daughters of the neighboring

[26] See p. 71.

[27] W. M. Hennessy's translation, *RIA*, Todd Lect. Ser., I, 2. His text is from *LL*, 261, col. b. On the date see Thurneysen, *Heldensage*, p. 473.

elf-kings in order that they might not injure their corn, and milk, and flowers." [28]

Loch Erne begins by picturing a golden age when Ériu was a land of women (except Olc Ai, the inhabitants seem to be women) or fairyland. The picture resembles that which we have observed in preceding pages in the stories of Cessair, Banba, and in the *Imram Brain*.[29] Traces of a former golden age, when Ireland was a fairy forest inhabited by damsels who supplied food from inexhaustible cups, are preserved in the Finn saga. The ninth-century Cormac's *Glossary*, under the heading *orc-tréith*, also tells of such a fairy forest. I translate as follows:

A woman of the Leyney was with Finn, for in every mountain and in every forest that Finn with his warriors used to frequent there was a particular woman awaiting him always in every woodland that was nearest to him. They were women-hosts, and they were good to nourish the warriors, for (Finn's) people spread over the woodlands so that none durst do wrong to the women.[30]

That an aggressor might invade this paradise of dames is implied by the last sentence which says that Finn's men were spread throughout the woodlands "so that none durst do wrong to the women." Finn's men seem to be guardians

[28] Kuno Meyer prints this text from the Book of Fermoy in ZCP, XIII (1920), 167, ll. 18 f. Thurneysen (*Heldensage*, p. 296) thinks that the text may be of the thirteenth century. It is apparently a garbled account of the blight caused by the Tuatha Dé. The ravaging bird fought by Amargen (*Rev. celt.*, XIII [1892], 426 f.) and the injurious pigs of Drebriu (*Met. Dinn.*, III, 552) may be developments of the idea. Compare fairies in the form of destructive mice in the Welsh *Manawyddan*.

[29] Pages 245–248, 271.

[30] Compare J. O'Donovan's translation, *Cormac's Glossary* (Calcutta, 1868), p. 130. The Irish text is in *Anecdota*, IV, 86.

of the fairy damsels. Similar accounts of damsels who provide food on the Journey to Fairyland occur in other
stories.[31] Other fragments from the Finn saga indicate
that there must have been in this fairy forest a chief damsel, perhaps dwelling in a castle like that of the Fisherman
in the Grail romances. The first of these fragments is the
prose *Dinnschenchas of Cenn Cuirrig*.[32] Stokes translates
the lines in which we are interested as follows: "In the
eastern part of Femen, on the eastern bank of the Suir, in
Cathair Dúne Iascaig, 'the town of Fish Castle,' Finn had
a paramour named Badammair (from her Rath Badamm-
rach is called). 'Tis she that used to sustain Finn with food
and raiment."

This Badammair, living in Fish Castle and supplying
Finn with food, resembles the French stories about the
Grail damsels. The *Banshenchas* tells a little more about
Badammair: "Badamair daughter of Lugair the Fisherman
was Finn's wife." [33] Lugair is sometimes put for the god
Lug. The entry therefore about Cenn Cuirrig looks like
a faded survival of an old myth about the god Lug living
in a mysterious castle in a fairy forest.[34]

[31] On the journey to the Land of *Scath* (p. 49) a fair maiden entertains
Cuchulinn with drink and food. Andreas Capellanus (p. 347) describes
a fairy forest supplied with food, dishes, napkins, and exposed to aggression by a giant.

[32] Edition Stokes, *Rev. celt.*, XV (1894), 442–443.

[33] K. Meyer, *Fianaigecht, Todd Lect. Ser.*, XVI, p. xxix; the text is:
"Ba ben do Find Badhamair ingen Lugair iascaire." See now *Rev. celt.*,
XLVIII (1931), 214.

[34] Badamair may be in origin the same as Bodbmall, Finn's foster-
mother. Bodbmall is called *bendron*, "sorceress," in *Fotha Catha Cnucha*
(ed. E. Windisch, *Kurzgefasste Irische Gram.* [Leipzig, 1879], pp. 121 f.).
Badamair and Bodbmall may be differing names for the *fée* who controlled Finn's destiny (p. 53).

Erne, the eponymous heroine of this Irish lake legend, is either Queen Medb under another name or she is her companion *fée*, and is related to her somewhat as Lunete, who has charge of Laudine's talismanic rings, is related to Laudine in Chrétien's *Yvain*. Erne is the leader of a band of maidens or *fées*, and is the keeper of Queen Medb's treasures, including a *criol*, "casket," which probably is a plenty-giving object like the Grail. Black-haired Amargen carries off one of the maidens and marries her. Because of this aggression Erne and her fairies disappear from the upper world to live in a palace under the lake.

Poor short-lived mortals care little for the past except as it explains some problem of their present existence. A handsome sheet of water in Ulster stirs men of every generation to account for the name Erne. For a long time this mythological story of how a fairy lady named Erne lived beneath the lake satisfied their curiosity. Then a sceptical age changed the story to the prosaic notion of a lake's deriving its name from a lady who was drowned in it. Thus place-name curiosity has preserved to us the briefest possible skeleton of an old mythological story. The account in *Loch Erne* has been so much cut down that we could not understand it unless we had stories of fairy folk carried off by Fomorians with which to compare it. The skeleton story in *Loch Erne* supplements what we learned in Chapter IX from the successive invasions of Ireland in *LL*. It shows us the Brión-Ériu-Amargen myth pretty much in its original form, before it was worked up into invasion stories.

CHAPTER XIV

The *Elucidation*

A PROLOGUE of four hundred eighty-four verses, called the *Elucidation*, occurs prefixed to Chrétien's *Perceval* in some manuscripts.[1] The *Elucidation*, so far as I know, is the only Arthurian story that answers the question, "How did the Grail country become ruined, and the Fisher King in need of rescue?" It describes Logres, the Grail country, as formerly abounding in damsels, food, and plenty, until a ruthless aggressor put an end to the golden age. In the *Elucidation* the name of the aggressor is Amangon; in the Irish *Loch Erne* his name is Amargen. This similarity of name invites a comparison of the two stories. I translate and summarize from the *Elucidation*: [2]

The author, after referring to Blihis as his authority, tells us that the rich country of Logres had fallen to ruin:

> The land was dead and desert. . . .
> So that they lost the voices of the wells,
> And the maidens who were in them.
>
> (vss. 30–32)

---

[1] In one extant manuscript, Mons; but the French prose of 1530 (ed. A. Hilka, *Der Percevalroman*, pp. 481–614) and the German verse (ed. K. Schorbach, *Parzifal von Claus Wisse und Philipp Colin*, Elsässische Litteraturdenkmäler, V [Strassburg, 1888]), are based on inextant French manuscripts which contained it.

[2] Edition A. Hilka, *Der Percevalroman*, pp. 418 f. Compare the edition of A. W. Thompson, Institute of French Studies (New York, 1931).

At first no traveler needed to go farther than to one of these wells to secure food:

Car lués issoit, ce m'est avis,	For forthwith there issued, this is my belief,
Fors del puis une damosele;	Out of the well a maiden;
Il ne demandassent plus bele:	They could not ask a prettier;
Coupe d'or portoit en sa main	She carried in her hand a gold cup,
Avec lardés, pastés at pain.	With roasts, pasties, and bread.
Raportoit une autre pucele	Another maiden brought
Touaille blanke et escuiele	A white napkin and a dish
D'or et d'argent, en coi estoit	Of gold and silver, in which was
Li més ke cil requis avoit	The food that he had asked for
Qui pour le més estoit venus.	Who had come there for it;
Au pui[s] moult ert biel re-ceüs,	At the well he was very well received;
Et, se cil més ne li plaisoit,	And if this food did not please him,
Plusours autres li aportoit	She brought him many other [kinds]
Fais trestout a lor volenté,	Made altogether to their wish.
A grant joie et a grant plenté.	With great joy and great plenty.
Les pucieles comunaument	The maidens generally
Servoient biel et liement	Served well and gladly
Tous ceus qui les cemins erroient	All those who wandered along the roads
Et pour mangier as puis venoient.	And came for food to the well.

Rois Amangons s'enfraint pre-miers,	King Amangons broke this custom first
Que mauvais fist et que laniers;	Who was evil and wicked....
Car mains autres aprés ce fist	
Par l'example que il en prist	
Au roi ki les devoit tenser	
Et em pais tenir et garder:	
Des puceles une esforcha,	He did violence to one of the maidens
Sor son pois le despucela	Against her will he violated her
Et la coupe d'or li toli,	And took away from her the gold cup
Si l'emporta ensamble od li,	And carried it off with him,
Puis s'en fist tot adiés servir.	Then he caused himself to be served out of it.
Si l'en dut bien mesavenir;	Well ought misfortune to come to him.
K'ains pucele ne siervi puis,	Therefore never maiden served
Ne n'issi fors de celui puis	Nor issued from the well
Por nul home ki i venist	For any traveller that came there
Et a mangier i requesist;	And sought there for food....
Et trestout li autre servoient,	
D'eus por ce ne s'apercevoient.	
Li autre vassal de l'honor	The other vassals of the court
Quant ço virent de lor signor	When they saw their lord's behavior
Qu'il enforçoit les damoiseles	That he did violence to the maidens

La ou il les trovoit plus beles,	There where he found them the most pretty
Tout autresi les esforçoient	All the others did violence to them
Et les coupes d'or enportoient.	And took away the cups of gold.
Ains puis de nul des puis n'issi	Never any more from the wells did appear
Puciele nule ne siervi;	Maidens, nor did they serve any more....
Içou saciés bien vraiment.	
Signor, issi faitierement	Sir, in this manner,
Tourna li pais a declin,	The country turned to ruin
Et li rois en fist male fin	And the king of it made a bad end
Et trestout li autre aprés lui,	And all the others after him
Qui lor orent fait maint anui.	Who had done harm to them [the maidens].
Li roiaumes si agasti	The realm then turned to waste
K'ains puis n'i ot arbre fuelli;	Never did a tree have a leaf,
Li pré et les flor s essecierent	The meadows and the flowers dried up,
Et les aiges apeticierent,	And the streams shrunk away,
Ne on ne peut puis trover jor	Then no one could ever find
Le cort au rice Pescheour,	The Court of the Rich Fisher
Qui resplendissoit le pais.	Who made splendid the country.

Afterward, at the time of King Arthur, the knights of the Table Round came and wished to recover the wells,

> And to guard valiantly
> The maidens that would issue from them
> And the cups that they would bring
> And to destroy the lineage
> Of those who did them harm.

They overthrew several knights whom they found:

> The first knight whom they conquered
> Had for his name Blihos Bliheris,
> And my lord Gawain conquered him
> By the great courage of which he was full.
> He sent him to render himself to King Arthur.

At the court Blihis was not known but he

> Knew such very good stories
> That no one could grow weary
> Listening to his words.

He declared to the knights of Arthur that he and the other warriors in the forest were sons of the damsels whom King Amangons and his followers violated. He told them that they would have to search by forest and by field.

> Until that God shall grant them to find
> The court from which the joy shall come
> Of which this land shall be resplendent again.

Arthur's knights set about the quest at once:

Puis cerkeront par grant vigor	Then they will search with great vigor
Le court au rice Pesceour,	For the court of the Rich Fisher
Qui moult savoit de ningre- mance	Who knew much of necro- mancy,

Qu'il muast .C. fois sa sam- blance;	So that he would change his semblance a hundred times;
Nus ne kerroit en nule guise,	No one could recognize him
Li autres en autre devise.	When he had shifted his shape to another.
Mesire Gauwains le trova	My lord Gawain found him
En icel tans k'Artus regna	In the time that Arthur reigned
Et fu a la court par vreté.	And was at the court [of the Rich Fisher] in truth,
Ça avant vos ert bien conté.	Further on ye shall be told about it.

After this the *Elucidation* has been rather crudely altered to make it serve as an introduction to a *Perceval* poem. It unexpectedly declares that Perceval the Welshman found the Grail.

The names Amargen in the Irish *Loch Erne* and Amangon in the French *Elucidation* are almost identical. By the change of a single letter Amargen becomes Amangen, which is close to the French form Amangon. This change might occur in several ways. The Irish write what is called the "long *r*," and in Irish handwriting *r* and *n* are easily mistaken for each other. The spelling of Amangin for Amargen occurs in ancient Irish manuscripts,[3] and the spelling Amargons occurs in one French manuscript.[4]

Because of the spirant *m* which it contains, the Irish name Amargen must have been transmitted in writing to

[3] The pedigree of St. Berach is given in one place as "Beirech m. Amargin m. Nemaid," and in another place as "Beraig m. Nemaill m. Nemangin" (*LL*, p. 347, col. d; p. 373, col. a, l. 53).

[4] MS Vienna 2599, ed. M. Friedwagner, *Méraugis*, vs. 2233. Another manuscript, Turin L. IV. 33, reads "Amagonz."

the French romances. The spirant *m* was pronounced something like English *w*. If transmission had been strictly oral, Irish spirant *m* would scarcely have been written *m* in Welsh.

There is no difficulty about believing in written transmission,[5] for Latin chronicles must have made important names in Irish history familiar to Welsh and perhaps even to French writers. For example, the name of the Irish king Amhallghuidh righ Connacht, whose sons were baptised by Patrick, has a spirant *m*. By oral transmission it becomes in modern English "Awley."[6] Yet in Nennius, *Historia Britonum*, composed about 825, it is spelled Amolgith. The well-known Irish name with two spirant *m*'s, Nemid mac Agnomain, appears in Nennius[7] as "Nimeth filius Agnominis," and none of the manuscripts make any attempt to represent the sound of spirant *m*. The spelling "Nemed" seems established in Latin and English writers. Giraldus Cambrensis[8] writing about 1184 has "Nemedus Agnominii filius," and Spenser[9] writing in 1596 has "Nemed." The name Amargen is not in our text of Nennius. It is in the Irish translation of Nennius, made by Giolla Coemhain before 1072, in the form "Amergin." It seems certain that Latin historians would spell the name "Amergin." It is probable that their usage determined the spelling "Amangon" or "Mangon" in French.

[5] Thurneysen (ZCP, XX [1933], 133, n. 1) assumes that Geoffrey derived his spelling Guenhuuara from a written source.

[6] "Awley" is mentioned in J. H. Todd, *St. Patrick* (Dublin, 1864), p. 442, n. 4. The baptism of his sons is told on p. 449.

[7] Edition T. Mommsen (1894), pp. 154, 197.

[8] *Top. Hib.*, dist. iii, chap. 3.

[9] Edition Sir James Ware, *View of the Present State of Ireland* (Dublin, 1633), p. 30.

The *Elucidation* and *Loch Erne* agree in many particulars. Both tell of a well-watered land which is occupied by a troop of fairies who are all women.[10] The land is evidently *Tír na m-Ban*, "Isle of Women." In both, the happiness of the land is interrupted by the coming of a king who does violence to one of the fairy maidens, and in the *Elucidation* his example is followed by his warriors. In both, the fairy folk take refuge from the invaders. In the French the damsels retreat under the wells; in the Irish the maidens flee under Loch Erne. In the French the land is devastated, and in the Irish some injury to the land seems implied.

The number of points in which the *Elucidation* agrees with *Loch Erne*, considering the laconic style of the latter, is remarkable. *Loch Erne* is undoubtedly a variation of the Brión-Ériu-Amargen myth. If we make comparison with the myth, our parallels may be extended. In the French the country is after a time repeopled by those who sprang from the marriages between the invaders and the fairy maidens. In the Brión-Ériu-Amargen myth Ireland is repeopled by the Irish who trace their descent back to marriages between the sons of Míl and the Tuatha Dé. In the French, to restore the prosperity of the land, the court of the vanished Fisher King must be found. In the Irish, how the people found the vanished Tuatha Dé is not told, but it is said that the sons of Míl were obliged "to make peace with the Dagda" before they could enjoy the corn and milk of Ireland." [11]

In Manessier's continuation of *Perceval*, and in Gerbert's

---

[10] "Die Bewohner von Mag Mell sind vorwiegend weiblichen Geschlechts" (E. Windisch, *Abhandlungen d. k. Sächsischen Gesell. d. Wissenschaften*, phil.-hist. Klasse, XXIX [1912], 110).

[11] Page 71.

addition to *Perceval*, are two wicked brothers who wish to seize a Grail damsel. The first brother, who is nameless, is, I think, Death personified. In Manessier's part this first brother is a knight who rides invisible, and the second brother is King Margon. In Gerbert's part the first brother is a monster who fights with fire and who is called the Knight of the Dragon; the second brother is King Maragon. The names Margon and Maragon are both probably variations of Amargen, with loss of initial "a."[12] These two wicked brothers are, I think, Galam and Amargen, sons of Míl, who were regarded by the Irish as Fomorian kings of the dead. King Amangons then appears in Manessier and Gerbert as well as in the *Elucidation*. How can we explain this? Most likely King Amangons played a part in the original Grail story that Chrétien used and which was preserved, perhaps, in minstrel versions, and known to the author of the *Elucidation* as well as to Manessier and Gerbert.

Manessier introduces King Margon as wishing to compel the *Sore Pucele*, "Golden Damsel," to marry his son, Cargrilon.[13] The Golden Damsel is niece to the Fisher King and sister to Silemarc, a knight who in Wauchier's part of the *Perceval*[14] had been slain while in Gawain's company by an invisible-riding warrior. In Chrétien's part the Golden Damsel sent a sword to Perceval. This gift of a sword doubtless implied that she needed rescue. We may infer

---

[12] E. Cross (*PMLA*, XLIX (1934), 994–1009) shows that initial syllables in Old French are generally kept, but he finds initial "a" dropped in one tenth of the cases he examines. Another possibility is that these clipped names are influenced by the name *Morc*. Morc or Margg was the seneschal of Conaing, the king of the dead.

[13] Edition Ch. Potvin, *Perceval*, vs. 38219. Other spellings are Cargrilo (vs. 38186) and Agrilon (vs. 38330).

[14] Chrétien, vs. 3145; ed. Potvin, vss. 19679–20330.

that in the lost original Grail story, which Chrétien used and to which Manessier had access, both the Golden Damsel's castle and the Grail castle were besieged by King Margon. Both castles are, I think, different aspects of one fairy castle besieged by an invisible-riding warrior (Irish Galam, prince of the dead) and by his brother, King Margon (Irish Amargen). I summarize the story [15] as follows:

The Golden Damsel came to Gawain and said: "Margon *rois des marches* wished to marry me to his son Cargrilon. I refused because I had a lover. Margon thereupon laid siege to my castle, took my lover prisoner, and hanged him before my eyes. The next day my warriors captured Cargrilon and I foolishly caused him to be killed in a cruel way. Then Margon demanded that I produce a champion to fight for me or he would destroy my castle. I sent for my brother Silemarc. He set out, but, while in your safe conduct, was slain by Kay.[16] Will you be my champion against King Margon?" Gawain, after telling the Golden Damsel that Kay did not slay Silemarc, granted her request and accompanied her to her castle, which was in a town of more than thirty thousand people.

The next day King Margon appeared before the Golden Damsel's castle and called out loudly that the *pucele* must keep her promise to provide a champion or he would put her to death cruelly in revenge for Cargrilon. Gawain fought

[15] Edition Potvin, vss. 38167-39127.

[16] The reference apparently is to vss. 19639-19900 in Wauchier's part, where a knight in Gawain's safe conduct was slain by an invisible warrior. It is puzzling, however, to find so casual a reference to an incident that was told almost 20,000 verses before. The invisible knight is evidently Death. In *Huth Merlin* (ed. G. Paris and J. Ulrich, II, 7) a knight in Balan's safe conduct was slain by Gallan, who rides invisible. Gallan is, I think, Galam, brother to Amargen, one of the sons of Míl and a prince of the dead. The King Margon of our story is the Irish Amargen.

Margon and sent him vanquished to King Arthur. Arthur pardoned Margon, received him into his fellowship, and called him King of the Hundred Knights. After leaving the Golden Damsel, Gawain came to the castle of her niece, where he was treated as an enemy until the arrival of the Golden Damsel, who told what Gawain had done. The Golden Damsel said:

> J'ai à nom la Sore Pucele,
> Et mes frère ot Silemarc nom. . . .
> Sire ert del castel de la roce,
> Ses surnoms de la Roce estoit.
>
> (vss. 39128–39133)

Gawain stayed a short time with the damsels and then departed.

The above summary fails to reveal the fragmentary character of this story, which has evidently been repeatedly retold by men who were trying to adapt it to the customs of twelfth-century France. The Golden Damsel's account of her doings resembles the capricious and cruel behavior of a *fée* like Queen Medb. King Margon's brutal threats are like the things told in Irish sagas about Amargen Iarngiunach and about his friend and foster-father Aithirne, and appear to reflect Amargen's original character as a king of the dead.

In Gerbert de Montreuil's continuation of *Perceval*, King Maragon is brother to the Knight of the Dragon [17] and his story [18] is as follows:

[17] In *Perlesvaus* (ed. Nitze and Jenkins, vss. 5632 f. and 5753 f.) a "knight of the dragon" cuts off the feet and arms of those whom he kills, which is one of the traits of Charon, and Perlesvaus finds the "knight of the dragon" beyond a castle that revolves, a peculiarity of the tower of death. The knight's city is in the isles of the sea. On p. 81, above, Bé Dreccain, "woman dragon," is one of the leaders of over-sea enemies that attack the Tuatha Dé. This suggests that "knight of the dragon" is a name for a Fomorian leader and king of the dead.

[18] Edition Mary Williams, II, 64, vss. 8980–9306.

Perceval receives a shield and is told that anyone who attempts to recover the Grail and the lance must first obtain this shield. When Perceval approaches Montesclaire, he is recognized by the shield as the hero who is destined to conquer the King of the Dragon. The Knight of the Dragon has a brother, King Maragon, and both brothers are wicked tyrants. Maragon has seated the Pucele au Cercle d'Or,[19] who is daughter to King Esclador, at the Pui de Montesclaire and the brothers are besieging the Pui, which is beyond the river "Gordane," in order to force her to marry the Knight of the Dragon.[20] Perceval finally slays the Knight of the Dragon and thereby releases the Pucele au Cercel d'Or.

Galam, who may be Death in person, and his brother Amargen appear to be the original pair from which were developed the two wicked brothers of the two stories just outlined.[21]

Amargen, the Fomorian king, has entered Arthurian romances in other places. He appears first in Chrétien's *Erec* [22] in the spelling Amauguins. So long ago as 1895 Ferdinand Lot pointed out [23] that Amargon in Raoul's

[19] This Damsel of the Gold Circle is the same, I think, as Chrétien's *Sore Pucele*, "Golden Damsel."

[20] Gerbert is referring to the ugly-messenger passage in Chrétien's *Perceval*, vss. 4706 f. (see p. 134). The ugly messenger asked for a knight to rescue a damsel who was seated "au pui qui est soz Montescleire."

[21] Page 402.

[22] Vss. 318 and 1726. Amaugins is a better reading.

[23] *Romania*, XXIV (1895), 326 f. "Le roi Amargon (en *Méraugis*) me paraît bien être un des héros du plus ancien cycle épique de l'Irlande, Amorgen 'à la chevelure de fer,' père du fameux rival de Cûchulainn, Conall Cernach. Il figure dans la Naissance de Conchobar, etc. Ce n'est pas que je croie que le nom de ce personnage a passé directement de l'épopée irlandaise à Raoul de Houdenc, ou même aux récits très ignorés d'où il a tiré des matériaux pour fabriquer son roman en vers. Il me semble assez vraisemblable que le nom de ce héros a été connu des

Méraugis must be derived from Amargen, the name of Conall Cernach's father in Irish sagas.

The points that establish the identity of Amargen and Amangon, Margon, or Maragon, are as follows:

1. In Irish, Amargen is the adversary of the queen of Ireland, who is virtually the land personified, and who was undoubtedly regarded as in possession of talismans of plenty. In the continuations of *Perceval*, Margon or Maragon is the adversary of the Golden Damsel, the Grail King's niece. We read that he had killed the Grail King's nephew and wished to abduct the niece. The two Amargens play the same rôle, and both in Irish story and in French are cruel adversaries and abductors of women.

2. Both in Irish and in French this character is *roi*. In Irish, Amargen is *ríg-file*. In the French continuations of *Perceval* he is never called *conte* or *duc* but always "Rois Margon," or "Roi Maragon." Likewise, in the *Elucidation* he is invariably "Roi Amangon."

It might be thought a difficulty that of the two parts of the Irish word, *ríg*, "king," and *file*, "poet," only the first has left any trace in the French romances. No poetic activity is ascribed to Margon, Maragon, or Amangon. This difficulty vanishes upon examination of the Irish records. In Irish documents, although Amargen is always called *ríg-file*, he acts like a king at the head of an army, and little is

Gallois comme ce fut le cas de Curoi mac Daire, de Cuchullin, des dieux Math, Manannan, etc., et que c'est à eux que l'ont emprunté les chanteurs ou conteurs anglo-normands. C'est dans une composition perdue de ceux-ci que Raoul aura recueilli ce nom." This is a very brilliant anticipation made years ago by the historian Lot of an identity which the discoveries of these pages, I venture to think, establish. The proof is that the two characters play the same rôle in what are, in origin, identical plots.

said of his poetic skill. Since king-poets were unknown
to French writers, Amargen, who acted like a king in Irish,
would naturally lose his poetic activities in passing into
French.

3. Both Amargen and Amangon come from the land of
the dead. Previous to the publication of Kuno Meyer's
paper, "Der irische Totengott und die Toteninsel," [24] it
might not have been possible to prove that Amargen came
from the land of the dead. Meyer proved that Donn, the
reputed leader of the Milesian invasion of Ireland, was
really the Irish god of the dead, and of course his brother
Amargen must have come from that land. This was something forgotten by everybody, something indeed that had
left no trace in the life of today, except that a few Gaelic-
speaking peasants in Kerry talked about the little island
of Tech Duinn. The Milesian invaders did not come from
Spain, as *LG* declares, but from a much more mysterious
land.

Amargen's connection with the land of the dead has
passed over with his name from Irish into French. In the
Arthurian romance *Li Chevaliers as deus espées,* written
about 1225, Amargen is mentioned as follows: [25]

> Si uint li rois Bademagus,
> Li rices rois de Galoee
> I ra mout grant gent amenee,
> Et li rois Amangons ki tint
> La terre dont nus ne reuint.
>
> (vss. 12118–12122)

[24] *Sitzungsberichte d. Preuss. Akad. d. Wiss.,* XXXII (Berlin, 1919),
537 f. (see p. 257).

[25] Edition W. Foerster. In his note to vs. 12122, on p. 424, Foerster
wrote: "Dies gilt von Bademagus, nicht von Amangon." On p. 384 (in

Foerster was surprised to find Amangon called "king of the land from which nobody returns" because, as he says, this is true of Bademagu. E. Brugger has since pointed out that King Amangon in *Méraugis* plays the same rôle that is played by King Bademagu in *Raguidel*, and, although he proposed an alternative, Brugger has suggested that Bademagu may be the same name as Amangon.[26] This is unnecessary. Possibly Chrétien's sole reason for making Bademagu king of the dead was because he pictured him as father of Meleagant (Welsh, Melwas). Chrétien's idea, strange in French romances, of making Bademagu father to Meleagant probably comes from Welsh. In *Kulhwch and Olwen*, Maelwys is the son of Baedan,[27] and Baedan + magus, "enchanter," gives Chrétien's Bademagu. It was doubtless in imitation of Chrétien's *Lancelot* that the author of *Li Chevaliers as deus espées* made Bademagu king of the land from which nobody returns. Chrétien makes Bademagu, although he is Meleagant's father, a Hospitable Host and a friendly ruler in the land of the dead.

Near the beginning of *Chevaliers as deus espées* we learn that Amangon was king of Granlande:

> Li rois Amangons
> De Granlande, ki pere estoit
> Si con toute la cors sauoit
> Ma damoisiele Guinloie.
>
> (vss. 88–91)

---

a note on vss. 101–103: "Bademagus de cui tiere n'est revenus nus estranges ne ne revient") he wrote: "Merkwürdiger Weise wird 12121 dasselbe vom Könige Amangon gesagt." Compare also Foerster, *Karrenritter* (1899), p. 369, n. 645.

[26] *ZFS*, XXVIII² (1905), 13 and 49. Brugger's alternative suggestion is that the name is composed of Bangon and Madus (Madoc).

[27] *Mab.*, I, 180. Rhŷs and Evans, *The Text of the Red Book*, p. 106, l. 17.

This is probably not Greenland, as Foerster thought, but an attempt to translate Mag Mór, "great plain," an Irish name for the land of the dead from which Amargen came.[28]

4. In Irish story Donn and Amargen come from Tech Duinn, "a red-cornered rock in the sea." [29] Probably, therefore, Amargen, like other Irish visitors from the land of the dead, appears in red.

In the French romances, Amargen is a red knight like Mabonagrain, Esclados li ros, Clamadeu, Partinal of the Red Tower in Gerbert's *Perceval,* and other hostile warriors. In *Diu Crône,* a romance of some thirty thousand verses, which was written by Heinrich von dem Türlin about 1220, Aumagwîn is in three places called "the Red Aumagwîn." [30] He is mentioned all together sixteen times,[31] and there can be no doubt that he is the same character as the Amangon of the French romances.

5. The passage of the Irish Amargen into the French Amangon is no isolated phenomenon. In the French ro-

---

[28] D'Arbois (*Cours,* II [Paris, 1884], 85) long ago proved that the sons of Míl came from Mag Mór, which the historians altered to Spain. That Spain here means the land of the dead is affirmed by F. Lot (*Nennius* [Paris, 1934], pp. 43–44). In support of the explanation of Mag Mór, d'Arbois quoted *Tochmarc Etáine,* ed. Windisch, *Ir. Texte,* I, 132, l. 27; *Echtra Conli,* ed. Pokorny, ZCP, XVII (1927), p. 199; *CMT,* § 55. To d'Arbois' list may be added: *Echtra Cormaic, Ir. Texte,* III, i, 195; *CMT,* § 43; W. J. Gruffydd, *Math vab Mathony,* p. 177. Gruffydd in the poem of the graves (Skene, *Four Books,* II, 35, from the *Black Book*) finds that Beli "son of a giant" was buried in *y maes mawr,* "the great plain." Probably this is a way of saying that Beli (Irish Balar) became a ruler of the land of the dead.

[29] Page 168.

[30] Edition G. H. F. Scholl, Stuttgart Verein, XXVII (1852): vs. 2317, "der rôte Aumagwîn"; vs. 3290, "Er vragte den rôten Aumagwîn"; vs. 4241, "Aumagwîn der rôte."

[31] Vss. 2317, 3268, 3290, 3571, 3641, 3658, 4241, 4260, 4287, 4297, 5196 ("Aumagwîn und Gales und Keiî"), 5255, 5294, 10227, 24229, 24239.

mances the oldest lists of knights subject to Arthur contain at least three names which are also found together in
the oldest Irish documents. Ce, Ith, and Amargen came
across in some way from ancient Irish to the pages of
Chrétien's *Erec*.[32]

From the evidence assembled above it seems reasonable
to infer that the Irish king-poet Amargen has given rise
in the French romances to King Margon, King Maragon,
and King Amangons.

[32] Page 394.

CHAPTER XV

The *Criol*

THE answer to the question how fairyland became enslaved is found in the brief *Loch Erne* story. The answer to the question how the Grail kingdom became enchanted or enslaved is in the *Elucidation*. The Irish story runs parallel to the French story, and the Irish aggressor Amargen reappears in French as Amangon. Has the dissyllabic word *criol* in the *Loch Erne* story anything to do with "golden cups" and "graal" in the *Elucidation*?

In *Loch Erne* the word used for Queen Medb's casket is *criol*. In Early Welsh this word would in many positions in a sentence [1] be written and pronounced, by mutation, *griol*, and in that form it is very close to the mysterious French word *graal*. [2]

My hypothesis is that the Irish word *criol* was transmitted by written Welsh or Breton, and by French intermediaries to Chrétien. It is not necessary to suppose that *criol* ever became a Welsh or Breton word. It may always have remained an Irish word, but even so it would in Welsh or Breton, in many positions, be spelled *griol* and might pass into French as *graal*. The word almost certainly

---

[1] Early Breton or Welsh syntax would change the initial "c" of a masculine noun like *criol* to "g" in a number of the situations in which the word might occur. Many forms of the verb cause mutation in a following noun.

[2] The first appearance of the word is in *Perceval* (vss. 3220–3221): "Un graal antre ses deus mains une dameisele tenoit."

existed in mediaeval Welsh, although unrecorded, for the alternate form *clior* is an acknowledged Welsh word.[3] Since Irish possessed both forms, *criol* and *clior*, Welsh probably did also. On the metathesis by which *criol* becomes *clior*, see H. Pedersen.[4]

What do we know about the oldest instances of the Irish word *criol*? Does the word occur in any context that would suggest our deriving the word *graal* from it? The following four ancient examples of the word *criol* are to the point:

1. *Criol*, as has been seen, occurs in the verse *Loch Erne*.[5] This *criol* belongs to Queen Medb of Cruachan. She, as has been shown above, was a plenty-giving goddess and amounted to a personification of one of the provinces of Ireland. As such, she surely had talismans of plenty.

2. *Criol* occurs in Broccan's hymn, *Ní car Brigit*,[6] in the sentence: "Dobert dillat i criol Ronchinn hi charput dá rath." The editors translate this: "He put a garment in Ronchenn's basket in a chariot of two wheels." [7]

---

[3] John Davies (*Dictionary* [London, 1632], Latin-Welsh) defines the Latin word *capsa* (box or reliquary) by the Welsh words, "clior, cistan, prennol, prenfol."

[4] *Vergleichende Grammatik d. keltischen Sprachen* (Göttingen, 1909): I, 310, "criol, pl. crela, Korb"; I, 493, "Antizipierung eines L, criol [gives] clior."

[5] E. Gwynn, *Metrical Dinnshenchas*, III, 465. The prose *Dinnshenchas* in the Book of Lecan (ed. Stokes, *Rev. celt.*, XV [1894], 483-484) reads *clioirib*, but Stokes in a note suggests that this stands for *crioilib*, "caskets." *BB* reads *cleráib*, but H. 3. 3. appears to have the right reading, *criolaib*. Both *criol* and *clior* were good forms (see Pedersen, *loc. cit.*).

[6] Edition Stokes and Strachan, *Thesaurus Palaeohibernicus*, II, 347, vs. 84. Other editions are: Bernard and Atkinson, *Liber Hymnorum*, I, 125 f., and II, 45 f.; Windisch, *Ir. Texte*, I, 36 f.

[7] *Tulach dá Roth*, "Hill of Two Wheels," is a place in Mag Mell (see *Dinnshenchas of Tonn Clidna*, ed. Stokes, *Rev. celt.*, XV [1894],

Two Irish glosses on this verse in the *Liber Hymnorum*, an eleventh-century manuscript, repeat the word *criol:*

(1) "Frith iarum iarsen etach i criol roboi ic Ronchiund i charpat dá rath," "Thereafter a garment was found in the basket of Ronchenn in a chariot of two wheels."

(2) "I criol di croccund róin robói int etach," "The dress was in a basket of sealskin."

Rawlinson B 512 [8] contains what seems to be another version of the above glosses: "Condla asked Brigit for his garment. Brigit thereupon asked Ronchenn, namely a subdeacon who always had charge of the robes, whether there was a garment. 'Make a prayer,' said he, 'And there will be.' She made a prayer then and a garment was obtained from Ronchenn's criol."

Ní car Brigit, although not older as it stands than the ninth century,[9] is written in the cryptic style of the older poets and alludes in verse after verse to Brigit's miracles, which were plainly well known. For the order of these miracles it follows a Latin *Life of Brigit* by Cogitosus. Cogitosus was an Irishman who wrote about the middle of the seventh century. He does not mention the *criol* but says only: "[Brigit vestimenta] perlata sibi in curru duarum acceperat rotarum." [10] The story of the *criol* that supplied

---

437). Perhaps there is a trace here of an original reference to fairyland (see p. 87).

[8] Edition J. Fraser, P. Grosjean, S. J., and J. G. O'Keeffe, *Irish Texts*, I (London: Sheed and Ward, 1931), 17. The Irish reads: "Co ro chuindgid Connla a etgud co Brigit, coro fhiarfaig Brigit co Ronchend .i. suibdheochain ro baí oc coimet a hétaigh-si dogres dús in rabe étach agi. 'Doné-si irnaigthi,' or sé, 'Ocus biaid.' Fecit oracionem post, ocus frith etach a criol Ronchind."

[9] J. F. Kenney, *Sources for the Early History of Ireland*, I, 360.

[10] *Acta sanctorum Bollandi*, Feb. 1 (1658), pp. 135-141.

a garment when needed seems to have interested the Irish glossators. Doubtless, like most of the other miracles, it began as folklore about the heathen goddess Brigit and was transferred to the saint, her successor at Kildare.

3. *Criol* occurs in the *Reicne Fothaid Canainne*, a poem edited by Kuno Meyer [11] from a seventeenth-century manuscript, and thought by him to have been composed "about the end of the ninth or the beginning of the tenth century." This poem was spoken by Fothad Canann's dissevered head to the lady with whom he had a tryst (apparently his wife, namely the Hag of Beare, who was a form of Ériu), and to whom he now bequeathed all his treasures, namely, a crimson cloak, a white tunic, a belt of silver, a venomous five-pronged spear, a shield, a glittering cup, finger ring and bracelets that "Nia Nár brought across the sea," i.e., of fairy origin, Cailte's brooch, a draught-board with bronze and gold pieces, four candlesticks, a marvelous bag, and last, and from the space given to it evidently most important, a *criol*, "casket." The stanzas describing it are [12] translated by Meyer as follows:

35. "A four-cornered casket — it is tiny — it has been made of coils of red gold. One hundred ounces of white bronze have been put into it firmly."

36. "For it is of a coil of firm red gold, Dínoll the goldsmith brought it over the sea; even one of its clasps only has been priced at seven lay-women."

37. "Memories describe it as one of Turbe's master-works: in the time of Art — he was a luxurious king — 'tis then Turbe, lord of many herds, made it."

---

[11] *Fianaigecht, RIA, Todd Lect. Ser.*, XVI (1910), 14 f.

[12] The text of stanza 35 is:

"Criöl c(h)etharc(h)uir, is fóil,   roces de dúalaib dergóir,
Dron forfuirmedh i suide   cét uinge do fionndruine."

38. "Many a skirmish has been fought about it by the king of the Romans in Latium; after a banquet of wine — 'twas an intoxicating drink — 'tis then it was revealed to Find."

39. "Smiths never made any work to which it can be compared; earth never has hidden with a king a jewel that is so marvellous."

40. "If thou be cunning as to its price, 'tis plain to me thy children will not be miserable; if thou hoard it, a close treasure, no race of thine will be in want."

The Fothads were three brothers, Fothad Canann, Fothad Airgthech, and Fothad Cairpthech. As we have seen, they are another manifestation of Brión, Iuchar, and Iucharba. This poem then, although it uses other names, is in fact describing the talismans of Brión and of his queen, Brigit, who is a plenty-goddess.

4. *Criol* occurs in *Scéla Cano meic Gartnáin*, which has been edited by Kuno Meyer[13] and which Thurneysen thinks was originally written about the year 900. The sentence in which the word occurs is: "Rofacbad leesi in lie ocus doberthe asin chriol cach dia," "The stone was left with her [Cred] and every day it was taken out of the casket." This stone was the life-index of Cred's lover, Cano. Since the life-index is a marvelous or fairy object, probably the *criol* in which it was kept may be assumed to have had a similar character.

Thurneysen[14] has shown that *Scéla Cano* is in all likelihood the kernel of the Tristram saga. Cred, the heroine, to whom the *criol* belongs, corresponds to Iseult.

The following considerations lead me to believe that this word *criol* may be the origin of the word *graal*. In

[13] *Anecdota*, I, 10, from *YBL*, p. 131, col. a, ll. 28 f.
[14] ZRP, XLIII (1923), 385 f.

three of our four examples the *criol* belongs to a woman, and in the fourth instance it is given by Fothad Canann to a woman. This agrees with Chrétien's picture of the Grail which is carried by a woman. In two of our four examples the *criol* belongs to a set of talismans. In *Loch Erne* the *criol* goes with the comb, fillet, and other *minseóit*, "treasures," of Queen Medb. In *Reicne Fothaid Canainne* it belongs to a set of seventeen objects which includes a spear, a chessboard, and four candlesticks. In French romances the Grail also belongs to a set of objects; in Chrétien's *Perceval* they are a sword, a spear, two candlesticks, and a silver *tailleor*, "platter." [15]

That the Grail belongs to a set of talismans has further implications. As Alfred Nutt pointed out, it leads us to the oldest set of talismans known in Irish, namely, the Four Jewels of the Tuatha Dé: the *Lia Fáil*, the spear of Lug, the sword of Nuadu, and the Dagda's cauldron. The *criol* is, I think, in origin identical with the Dagda's cauldron.

The *criol* in *Reicne Fothaid Canainne* was one of Turbe's masterpieces. In the *Dinnshenchas* is the following entry [16] about him which shows that he was a mythological smith:

> Tuirbe, Trágmar, father of the Gobbán Saer, 'tis he that owned it. 'Tis from that heritage he used to hurl a cast of his

[15] Verses 3130–3240. No chessboard is mentioned, but *Perlesvaus* (vss. 2458 f.) describes a chessboard in the Grail castle. In Wauchier's continuation (edition Potvin, vss. 22395 f.) a marvelous chessboard is mentioned at a castle resembling the Grail castle.

[16] Quoted from the prose *Dinnshenchas* as translated by Stokes, *Rev. celt.*, XVI (1895), 77. See also the *BB* version in *Silva Gadelica*, II, 473 and 518, and the Edinburgh version in *Folk-Lore*, IV (1893), 488. On the Gobbán Saer see George Petrie, "Inquiry into the Origin of the Round Towers," *Transactions of the Royal Irish Academy*, XX (1845), 382–383.

axe, from *Tulach in Bela,* "the Hill of the Axe," in the face of the flood-tide, so that he forbade the sea, and it would not come over the axe. And no one knows his genealogy unless he be one of the defectives who fled from Tara before the *Sabnildanach* (i.e., Lug) and who are in the Diamrai of Bregia. Whence *Tráig Tuirbi,* "Tuirbe's Strand."

In Chrétien's *Perceval* the sword given to the hero at the Grail castle was the work of a smith called Trebuchet:

> N'alez se chiés Trebuchet non,
> Un fevre qui einsi a non;
> Que cil la fist et refera,
> Ou ja mes feite na sera
> Par home qui s'an antremete.
>
> (vss. 3679–3683)

It flashes upon the student at once on reading this that Trebuchet must be a corruption of the Irish Turbe or Tuirbe.[17] This conclusion is confirmed by the reading of one manuscript,[18] "T'boet," which Hilka expands to Triboet, but which might be expanded to Turboet. Furthermore, the prose of 1530, which is evidently based upon a lost manuscript of Chrétien, reads Tibuer.[19]

Trebuchet lived "au lac qui est sor Cotoatre." Four manuscripts read "soz Cotoatre." Probably he was a sub-

---

[17] The same Irish smith probably appears in L as Tuile who made a golden couch for the fairy queen, Créde (see p. 76). Hilka's reading, Trebuchet, in *Perceval* is most likely a corruption due to the influence of the well-known Old French word *trebuchet.*

[18] MS. Paris, 12576. See J. L. Weston, *Legend of Sir Perceval,* I, 136; and Hilka, *Perceval,* p. 166.

[19] Hilka, *Perceval,* p. 551. Manessier's continuation reads "Tribuet" (ed. Potvin, vss. 41547 f.). Wolfram says that Trebuchet made not only the sword (vs. 253,29) but Orilus' helmet (vs. 261,1) and the two silver knives that were carried in procession at the Grail castle (vs. 490,20).

lacustrine smith like Lén Línfiaclach in the *Dinnshenchas*.[20] The text already quoted associates Tuirbe with the sea, for it makes him keep back the tide.

In two out of our four examples the *criol* is a plenty-giving object. In *Ní car Brigit*, Bishop Conlaed's attire had been given by Brigit to a leper. When Conlaed, who was about to set out on a journey to Rome, needed his raiment, Brigit was in difficulty. She went, however, to Ronchenn's *criol*, which was in a two-wheeled cart, and there found raiment miraculously provided. This is evidently a plenty-giving miracle; other miracles of abundance precede and follow in the poem. In *Reicne Fothaid Canainne* the words in stanza 40, "If thou hoard (i.e., keep) it, no race of thine shall be in want," prove beyond a doubt that this *criol* had plenty-giving powers. Probably, like the Grail, it supplied food.

In three out of our four examples, the *criol* is more or less connected with Brión. (1) In *Loch Erne* the *criol* belongs to Queen Medb, who, as we have seen, is virtually Ireland personified, and the god Brión is the mythological husband of Ireland personified.

(2) In *Ní car Brigit* the garment needed for Bishop Conlaed was miraculously found in Ronchenn's *criol*. A glossator explains that Ronchenn was the name of a sub-deacon who was in charge of clothing. Ronchenn means "seal head," so another glossator endeavors to force a meaning out of the words by translating: "The garment was found in a *criol* of sealskin."

Ronchenn is doubtless, however, the name of somebody who was at first not a "sub-deacon" but an under-water

---

[20] See Hilka, *Perceval*, vs. 3675; Stokes, *Rev. celt.*, XV (1894), 451; and Gerbert's continuation of *Perceval*, ed. Mary Williams, vss. 530 f.

mythological figure. He is probably the same as Ronchu the Fisherman at whose house Cuchulinn spent a night on his journey to Forgall's *dún*, in *Tochmarc Emire*. Ronchu was the Hospitable Host and the Herdsman of that Journey to Fairyland. He "opposes the cattle of the plain of Tethra." Cuchulinn said of him: "It is he that catches the fish on his line under the sea; for the fish are the cattle of the sea, and the sea is the plain of Tethra, a king of the kings of the Fomorians." [21] Ronnchenn is probably a name for Brión, who in *OCT* "put on his water-dress and was a fortnight under sea," [22] seeking talismans. It is probable that "Seal Head's" *criol* is really Brión's *criol*.

(3) In *Reicne Fothaid Canainne*, Fothad, who owned the *criol* is probably, as has been shown above, a name for Brión. The gods have many names.

It has been recognized for some time that the Irish god Brión, called Bran by the Welsh, is the original of the French Bron, who, according to Robert de Boron, had the Grail. If the *criol*, as we have seen, belongs in Irish to Brión, little doubt can remain that it is the original of the *graal* that in French belongs to Bron. Chrétien's name for Bron, "the Fisher King," is also cleared up. Brión's great exploit was a sea-voyage, and under the sobriquet Roncu we have found him called a fisherman in Irish.

The passages quoted in this chapter establish the meaning of Old and Middle Irish *criol* as "bag," "basket," or "box."

[21] Page 47.

[22] Edition O'Curry, *Atlantis*, IV, 219 f. Todd (*St. Patrick*, p. 20) refers to a gloss at least as old as the eleventh century which declares that Conlaed, Bridget's bishop at Kildare, and Ronchenn were the same. The "creel" carried by the Hag of Beare (p. 335) is doubtless another trace of the magic *criol*, the source of the Grail. The Hag is the same mythological person as Ériu and Brigit.

My theory is that Breton or Welsh narrators transmitted this word in its mutated form to the Grail romance writers. The first four passages quoted above show that at a time long before the rise of French romances *criol* was in Irish the name of a plenty-giving object. It seems a reasonable conclusion that Irish *criol* is the source of French *graal*.[23]

[23] For further examples of the word *criol*, see Appendix.

Conclusion

THE purpose of this book is to examine the sources of the marvelous adventures in the romances of Chrétien de Troyes.

An important new idea is that wars between good fairies or Tuatha Dé and bad fairies or Fomorians, which cluster round the recurrent battle of Moytura in Irish mythology, were the basis from which grew the battles of King Arthur and his knights against outlandish foes in the romances. The Irish wars were fought between Nuadu, king of the Tuatha Dé, who has to be rescued by the youthful Lug, and Galam, leader of the Fomorians, for possession of a queen who was virtually Ériu personified, and for her magic possessions: spear, sword, stone, and *criol*, which symbolize the natural wealth of the country. The place of these wars was Ireland but Ireland of long ago, thought of as fairyland. It was believed that the Tuatha Dé had long ago retired to underground abodes where they still lived as fairies, and that the Irish were descendants of the former Tuatha Dé and Fomorians.

The Welsh adopted these Irish stories, changing the battle of Moytura to the battle of Camlan, changing King Nuadu to King Arthur, Lug to Perceval, Galam (at least in *Perceval*) to Clamadeu, and Queen Ériu to Queen of Logres. Ériu's magic belongings they kept, except the stone, which they probably did not understand and altered in various ways. They probably did not adopt the idea that the fairies were still living in underground palaces. For them the place of Arthur's wars was hazy. Probably they thought of the wars as waged in Britain of long ago, against people dwelling beyond the Roman Wall in Galloway, Lothain, and Gorre; countries that were confused with the land of the dead.

French romance writers took over these stories, and, as Chrétien indicates, when he wrote, they were already well known to all people of any social attainment. Chrétien writes as if he believed that the battles were fought in France or Britain, and as if the marvels that occur at various conquered castles were caused by sorcerers. When one thinks it out, however, it grows clear that the battles in his romances must have taken place after the battle of Camlan, and consequently after Arthur has been wounded and has withdrawn to Avalon, where he is engaged in repelling demon foes who are virtually kings of the dead. Like Finn's battles against giants and dragons in Irish sagas, Arthur's battles in Chrétien's romances are fought in an imaginary world which is either fairyland or the land of the dead.

Explanation of the Arthurian legend is made difficult by the failure of the Welsh to transfer all of Nuadu's story to King Arthur. Nuadu had three forms or aspects, and only one of these aspects, that of a king reigning at Tara, was transferred to Arthur, who is regarded not as a god but as a historical monarch ruling at Carleon or elsewhere in Britain. Nuadu had a second aspect, that of a wounded god, kept alive by fairy talismans, of which the *criol* was one, and needing to be found and rescued from giants who are virtually kings of the dead. This aspect of Nuadu the Welsh transferred to the Fisher King. It has long been observed that Arthur and the Fisher King are parallel figures. The relationship between the two was probably confused by the Welsh and even more by the French. Only the Irish stories furnish any key. A third aspect of Nuadu, that of a foster-father, is represented in *Perceval* by Gornemant.

Two other difficulties disturb the explanation of the legend. First, Christian Irish narrators occasionally forget the distinction between friendly Tuatha Dé and hostile Fomorians: in the *Serglige ConCulainn*, Manannán, who is of the Tuatha Dé, fights on the side of the Fomorians; and in *Echtra Cormaic* he plays the rôle of a Fomorian and carries off a mortal to the land of the dead. Secondly, a difficulty is caused by Arthur's absurdly generous custom of admitting to his Round Table any warrior, however dastardly, provided that when conquered he begs for mercy and promises fidelity. Lists of names in *Erec* include as members of King Arthur's fellowship many queer warriors taken from the ranks of Fomorians. It looks as if Chrétien understood very little of the sources of his stories. Despite these difficulties, a background of strife between Tuatha Dé and Fomorians can, I think, be detected in Chrétien's romances.

A second new idea is that the marvelous castles in Chrétien's romances, however numerous they may be, are different pictures of the castle of the other world. When ruled by a Fomorian the place is a Dolereuse Garde, but when Lancelot, or other Arthurian knight, conquers, it becomes straightway a Joieuse Garde. In the first marvelous adventure told by Chrétien, a dolorous garden is turned by Erec's victory into a joyous garden, and the episode is named the Joy of the Court. Two castles near each other are often in the picture: one a round tower belonging to red Fomorians, and the other a large, square castle inhabited by *fées*.

A third idea is the explanation furnished by the Irish stories for the fickleness of the heroines in Chrétien's romances. The Irish stories grew out of the mythical battle of Moytura in which the heroine, who was virtually Ireland personified, was wife alternately to a good king and then to a Fomorian. Whether a memory of this alternation was kept alive by the performance of a yearly ritual may be left in the limbo of things not known. The alternation is clearly apparent in Irish accounts of those stormy queens named Medb. Medb of Cruachan trained up Ailill as her foster-child, and then persuaded him to kill her husband Eochaid and marry her himself. Medb Lethdearg was successively wife to four kings, and at least one of them, Feidlimid, killed his predecessor.

This alternation explains the main plot of Chrétien's *Yvain*, where Laudine is at first the wife of Esclados (Fomorian) and then wife of Yvain who slew Esclados. It explains why Arthur's Queen Guenevere in *Lancelot* was carried off by Meleagant (Fomorian) and yet Arthur is evidently eager to take her back. In the Grail story this alternation is, of course, blurred over, but it is easy to discover it. Clamadeu, Blancheflor's unwelcome suitor is, I think, the Fomorian Galam. Perceval conquers him and marries Blancheflor. The alternation is apparent in the Chastel Merveilleuse story, where Orguelleuse's paramours are, successively, an unnamed knight whom Guiromelant slew, Guiromelant, Orguelleus de la Roche, and Gawain. More of it is preserved in Wolfram's *Parzival*, where Orgelûse's lovers are, successively, Cidegast, Gramoflanz (Fomorian), Anfortas the Fisher King, Clinschor (Fomorian), and Gawain.

The Irish story that Medb of Cruachan brought up Ailill to kill her husband and marry her explains a plot like that of *Le Bel Inconnu*, where the hero is brought up by a *fée*, Blancemal, and marries a *fée*, Blances Mains. Blancemal and Blances Mains were, I suppose, at first the same. At the basis was, no doubt, the Irish myth of Danu or Ériu, and her son Brión who later married her.

Chrétien's marvelous material was not all of Irish invention, and additions were made by Welsh and French who transmitted it; nevertheless, the discovery of names of Irish origin in Chrétien's romances tends to prove that the Grail legend and the allied marvelous adventures were worked up by the Irish. This is an important fact in the history of civilization. The marvelous adventures were not invented by any one artist, however cunning, at any one particular time or place. Their roots are in the mythology, the religion – and the Irish are always a religious folk – of a whole people. Men of literary skill have from time to time retouched and renewed the Grail story, but its source is far back in ages gone by. It is a brook of clear water proceeding out of the impenetrable forest of the past.

Irish imagination and Irish storytelling influenced French literature at one of its greatest and most important periods. In this way Irish fancy had an effect on the whole civilized world. The incredible activity of Irish teachers who in the eighth and ninth centuries spread Christianity and learning in many parts of western Europe is well-known. The present argument, it is believed, shows that the same Irish, operating through Welsh or Breton intermediaries, gave rise to a new school of storytelling in France in the twelfth century, which had a great vogue in all of western Europe, and which, in the form of the Arthurian legends, preserves its vitality even in our own day.

The argument of this book is based upon resemblances of incident and character. Resemblances of proper names are noticed, but they are of minor importance unless they agree with evidence from incident and character. They may all, or nearly all, be disproved without shaking the main argument for the origin of Arthur's battles in wars between two races of Irish fairies, the good and the bad.

That the mythology of the Irish gave rise to the Arthurian legend and that wars of the ancient Irish gods, who survive today as fairies, are the basis of Arthur's battles and, especially, of the Grail legend is the argument of this book. Whatever in this theory can be disproved, must and ought to be disproved. That the argument will be rigorously examined is what the author hopes. Some will no doubt test the theory by applying it to romances later than Chrétien. A way is opened for more study of the beginnings of the great imaginative legend of the western world, the legend of the Grail.

APPENDIX

APPENDIX

HEREWITH are all other examples of the word *criol* in older Irish that are known to me. They show that the word meant some kind of a box or basket that might form part of a woman's household equipment. First I put two passages in which the reading *criol* admits of doubt.

1. In the "Dinnshenchas of the Brug" (Gwynn, *Metrical Dinnshenchas*, II, 22) occurs the phrase *a cír a currel na mná*, "the comb, the coral of the woman." Gwynn (II, 96, note) prefers to translate *currel* in this way and refers to *curel*, "coral," in the Irish version of Marco Polo (ZCP, I [1897], 384). The prose *Dinnshenchas* in the Rennes manuscript (ed. Stokes, *Rev. celt.*, XV [1894], 292) reads: *Cir ocus cuirreill mna in Daghda .i. da cnoc*, which Stokes translates, "The comb and casket of the Dagda's wife, i. e., two hills." Stokes presumably connects *cuirreill* with *criol*, and his translation is more likely to be correct, I think, than Gwynn's. If it is right, then the *Dinnshenchas* identifies this *criol* with the Dagda's caldron. Unless we are entirely on the wrong track, the Grail ought to be identified with this caldron. An additional bit of evidence for this identification appears in a copy of the prose *Dinnshenchas* in *BB*, p. 354, col. b, l. 31, where the text reads: "A cir a cui na mna," and another hand has written over *cui* the word *coiri*, "caldron." This *currel* or *cuirreill* belongs to Boand, the Dagda's wife.

2. In *Togail Bruidne Da Derga* (ed. W. Stokes, *Rev. celt.*, XXII [1901], 13) is a difficult passage: "Conaccai in mnai for ur in tobair, ocus cír chuirréil argit . . . ," which Stokes translates: "He saw at the edge of the well a woman with a bright comb of silver adorned with gold washing in a silver basin." Eleanor Knott in her edition (Dublin, 1936), lines 2–3, has

the same text and translation. The words *cír chuirréil*, which
Stokes translates "bright comb," are very obscure. There is a
chance that O'Curry was right (*On the Manners and Customs*,
London, 1873, III, 189–190) in deriving *cuirréil* from *criol*
and translating "with a comb and a casket of silver." This
cuirréil belongs to the *fée* Etáin.

In the following passages the presence of the word *criol* is
undisputed.

3. *Longes mac n-Usnig* (ed. Windisch, *Ir. Texte*, I, 68)
reads: "Cid fom chriol brond becestar" (*LL*); or "Fod críol
brunn béccustar" (Egerton, 1782). "Though from the re-
ceptacle of my womb it screams." This is the mother's remark
when her unborn baby (Deirdre) screams. Cathbad repeats
the word *criol* in the next line. *Criol* is here used figuratively
of a cavity (the womb or belly). It is used the same way in
the following example.

4. A Hymn to the Virgin (printed by J. Strachan from MS.
23 N 10, RIA, p. 18, *Ériu*, I [1904], 122) reads:

"A Muire min maithingen tapair furtacht dún.
A criol chuirp chomdeta!"

My translation of this is:

"O Mary, gentle, good maiden give help to us.
O casket of the divine body!"

5. In *Cáin Adamnáin* or "Law of Adamnan" (ed. Kuno
Meyer [1905], p. 2, § 2, from two manuscripts, Brussels 2234,
76a, and Rawlinson 512, 45a) is the passage: "Ní uíth cuit
don m(n)ái sin i mbulg nach a criol" (Rawlinson 512 reads
"nach a clior," etc.). "The woman had no share in bag nor
in basket; nor in the company of the house-master; but she
dwelt outside." Meyer showed that both of the manuscripts
which he used were copied from an older original, and the
language of *Cáin Adamnáin* would indicate it to be a compila-
tion of the ninth century. *Criol*, which Meyer translates

"basket," is evidently here a familiar household article of some sort to which a woman might naturally have claim.

6. In *Stair ar Aed baclámh* or "The Life of Aedh Baclamh" (ed. O'Grady, *Silva Gadelica*, I, 71, l. 29) is the sentence: "Dobeir léinid as in criol ocus brat ocus nosgeibh uime." O'Grady translates (II, 75, l. 5) "Out of the bag that she had she drew a shirt and a mantle which he puts on." *Criol*, which O'Grady translates "bag," is evidently a woman's article which holds a man's raiment. It will be remembered that above, in *Ní car Brigit*, a *criol* likewise contained raiment for a man.

7. In *The Ancient Laws of Ireland*, the word *criol* occurs several times as follows:

Vol. I, p. 150, l. 9: "Im iadag cona ecortaig, im criol." "For the wallet with its contents, for the basket."

Vol. I, p. 152, l. 26 (a gloss on the above passage): "Im criol .i. im croiall, cro fuaigther d'i allaib no cro a ssdiallaib." "For the basket, i. e. crioll, i. e. 'cro-iall,' i. e. a 'cro' which is sewed with thongs (allaib) or a 'cro' of slips (ssdiallaib)."

Vol. I, p. 148, l. 4 (a gloss on a law of distress): ".I. im caem orba uais a mathar .i. cairig ocus crela .i. orba feirtsi .i. orba craib no sliasta a mathar." "Respecting the fair noble property of her mother, i. e., sheep and utensils; i. e., the property of the spindle; i. e., the marriage gift or the portion of her mother." *Crela*, which the editor, Atkinson, translates "utensils," is the plural of *criol*. It evidently refers to women's implements of some kind.

Vol. III, p. 404, l. 3 (Book of Aicill): "No comad cairig ocus cliora." "It may be the sheep and the bag she is to get." *Cliora* is here translated "bag" and is an object which a daughter inherits even when the other property goes to the sons.

8. In *Airec Menman Uraird Maic Coisse* (ed. Mary E. Byrne, *Anecdota*, II, 55, 17, from manuscripts: *RIA*, 23. N. 10; Rawlinson B. 512; Harleian 5280) occurs the expression *Criol mac Croeslintaid*, "Chest son of Mouth-Filler." *Criol* is here a comic epithet for a man.

For the sake of completeness, a Welsh word "crul" found in the dictionaries may be mentioned, but it is most likely of late origin and without bearing on our problem. "Crul" occurs in W. O. Pughe, *Dictionary of the Welsh Language*, first edition, 1803, and second edition, 1832, as follows: "crùl, s.m.pl. iau (cru)" defined "a belly or paunch." "Crul" is not in the *Red Book of Hergest* and was introduced, I think, into Llywarch Hen's poem *Y Gorwynion*, *Myvyrian Archaiology* (1870), p. 97, l. 29, by an eighteenth-century emendation. It seems therefore that a link-word in Welsh or Breton to connect Irish *criol* and French *graal* has not been found. Perhaps this lost link-word was spelled *criol* and was always regarded in Breton and Welsh as a borrowed Irish word. The initial "c" would, even in a borrowed word, often mutate to "g."

INDEX

INDEX